FEMINIST CRITICISM
—— AND ——
SOCIAL CHANGE

SEX, CLASS AND RACE
IN LITERATURE AND CULTURE

Edited by Judith Newton
and Deborah Rosenfelt

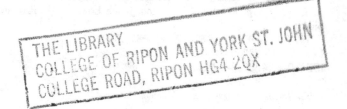
METHUEN
New York and London

First published in 1985 by
Methuen, Inc.
29 West 35th Street, New York, NY 10001

Published in Great Britain by
Methuen & Co. Ltd
11 New Fetter Lane, London EC4P 4EE

Printed in the USA

Library of Congress Cataloging in Publication Data
Feminist criticism and social change.

Bibliography: p.
Includes index.
1. American literature—History and criticism—Addresses, essays, lectures. 2.
Feminist literary criticism—Addresses, essays, lectures. 3. Marxist criticism—
Addresses, essays, lectures. 4. English literature—History and criticism—
Addresses, essays, lectures. 5. Social history in literature—Addresses, essays,
lectures. 6. Sex role in literature—Addresses, essays, lectures. 7. Social classes
in literature—Addresses, essays, lectures. 8. Race relations in literature—
Addresses, essays, lectures. I. Newton, Judith Lowder. II. Rosenfelt, Deborah
Silverton.
PS152.F46   1985   810′.9   85–15209
ISBN 0–416–38700–4
ISBN 0–416–38710–1 (pbk.)

British Library Cataloguing in Publication Data
Feminist criticism and social change: sex, class and race in literature and culture.
1. Sex differences (Psychology) in literature
I. Newton, Judith L. II. Rosenfelt, Deborah S.
809′.93353   PN56.S52
ISBN 0–416–38700–4
ISBN 0–416–38710–1 Pbk

For Anna — JUDITH NEWTON

For Florence Howe and Tillie Olsen,
who will not approve of everything here
but whose passion for both literature and social change
has nurtured and challenged my own — DEBORAH ROSENFELT

CONTENTS

CONTRIBUTORS

MICHELE BARRETT teaches sociology at the City University, London, and is a member of the *Feminist Review* editorial collective. She is the author of *Women's Oppression Today: Problems in Marxist feminist analysis* (1982) and, with Mary McIntosh, of *The Anti-Social Family* (1982).

CATHERINE BELSEY lectures in English at University College, Cardiff. She is the author of *Critical Practice* (1980) and *The Subject of Tragedy* (1985).

BARBARA CHRISTIAN is Associate Professor of Afro-American Studies at the University of California, Berkeley, and a member of the Women's Studies Board there. She is the author of *Black Women Novelists: The development of a tradition, 1892–1976* (1980) and *Black Feminist Criticism* (1985). She also lectures in Berkeley's public schools for the project, Poetry in the Schools.

ANN ROSALIND JONES joined the women's movement in New York City in 1969. An Associate Professor in Comparative Literature at Smith College, she teaches courses on contemporary literary theory and women writers and does research in feminist literary theory and women writers of the Renaissance and the twentieth century.

CORA KAPLAN teaches literature and women's studies at the University of Sussex, Brighton, and is a member of the *Feminist Review* collective. Her publications include *Salt and Bitter and Good: Three centuries of English and American women poets* (1975) and an edition of *Aurora Leigh and Other Poems* by Elizabeth Barrett Browning (1978). She is working now on a book on class, gender, sexuality and literature in the nineteenth century.

ANNETTE KUHN is the co-editor of *Feminism and Materialism* (1978) and the author of *Women's Pictures: Feminism and cinema* (1982) and *The Power of the Image* (1985). She lives in London, where she writes and lectures on media studies and is a script writer for British television.

PAUL LAUTER has published numerous books and articles on American literature and American studies and has edited several reprints of works by American women writers, as well as such pedagogical and curricular volumes as *The Politics of Literature: Dissenting essays in the teaching of English* (with Louis Kampf, 1973) and *Reconstructing American Literature: Courses, syllabi, issues* (1983). A co-founder of the Feminist Press and for many years a member of its Board and Reprints Committee, he is now helping to organize a series of reprints of working-class fiction for Monthly Review Press. He is an editor of the *Radical Teacher* and a member of the Board of *Resist*. He is currently working on a comparative theory for viewing the distinctive literatures of the United States.

JUDITH NEWTON is Associate Professor of English at La Salle University in Philadelphia, where she teaches women's studies and nineteenth-century British literature. She is the author of *Women, Power, and Subversion: Social strategies in women's fiction, 1780–1860* (1982) and a co-editor of *Sex and Class in Women's History* (1983). An editor of *Feminist Studies*, she is now working on a study of gender and social vision in Britain in the 1840s.

LESLIE W. RABINE teaches French and women's studies at the University of California, Irvine. She is the author of *Reading the Romantic Heroine: Text, history, ideology* (1985) and articles on feminist criticism and theory. For several years she has been involved with community organizing in the low-income city of Santa Ana, California, currently on the issue of reproductive freedom.

DEBORAH ROSENFELT is Professor of Women Studies and Coordinator of the Women Studies Program at San Francisco State University. She has written several articles on women and literature and the theory of women's studies and has edited five volumes of curricular and pedagogical materials in women's studies and ethnic studies. She is a contributing editor of the *Women's Studies Quarterly* and an editor of *Feminist Studies*. She is continuing her study of women writers on the left in the United States.

SONJA RUEHL is a lecturer in economics at the Open University, Milton Keynes, Bedfordshire. After having taught a course in women's studies, she has returned to her original discipline and is now working on changes in corporate financing in Japan as a result of deregulation of Japanese financial markets.

BARBARA SMITH is a founding member of the Combahee River Collective, a black feminist organization that did work in Boston from 1974 to 1980. She is also a co-founder of Kitchen Table: Women of Color Press and a newly appointed board member of the National Coalition for Black Gays. With Gloria T. Hull and Patricia Bell Scott she co-edited *All the Women Are White, All the Blacks Are Men, but Some of Us Are Brave: Black women's studies* (1982). Her two most recent books are *Home Girls: A black feminist anthology* (1983) and *Yours in Struggle: Three feminist perspectives on anti-semitism and racism* (with Elly Bulkin and Minnie Bruce Pratt, 1984).

—— ACKNOWLEDGEMENTS ——

The editors and publisher would like to thank the following for permission to reproduce copyright material:

The editors of *Conditions* for chapter 1, Barbara Smith, 'Toward a black feminist criticism', reprinted from *Conditions Two* (1970), pp. 25–44; Paul Lauter for chapter 2, 'Race and gender in the shaping of the American literary canon: a case study from the twenties', from *Feminist Studies* 9 (1983), pp. 435–63; Verso and New Left Books for chapter 4, Michèle Barrett, 'Ideology and the cultural production of gender', from Michèle Barrett, *Women's Oppression Today: Problems in Marxist Feminist Analysis*, chapter 3, London: Verso Editions, 1980; Feminist Studies, Inc., c/o Women's Studies Program, University of Maryland, College Park, Md 20742, for three chapters: chapter 5, Ann Rosalind Jones, 'Writing the body: toward an understanding of *l'écriture féminine*', reprinted from *Feminist Studies* Volume 7, no. 2 (1981): 247–63; chapter 10, Deborah Rosenfelt, 'From the thirties: Tillie Olsen and the radical tradition', from *Feminist Studies* Volume 7, no. 3 (1981): 371–406; and chapter 11, Leslie W. Rabine, 'Romance in the age of electronics: Harlequin Enterprises', revised from *Feminist Studies* Volume 11, no. 1 (1985): 39–60; Georgia University Press, for chapter 6, Judith Newton, '*Villette*', from Judith Lowder Newton, *Women, Power and Subversion: Social Strategies in British Fiction 1778–1860*, chapter 3, Atlanta, University of Georgia Press, 1981; The Women's Press Ltd. for chapter 7, Cora Kaplan, '*Aurora Leigh*', Introduction to *Aurora Leigh and Other Poems* by Elizabeth Barrett Browning, London, The Women's Press, 1977; Laurence & Wishart for chapter 8, Sonja Ruehl, 'Inverts and experts: Radclyffe Hall and the lesbian identity', from R. Brunt and C. Rowan (eds), *Feminism, Culture and Politics*, London, Laurence & Wishart, 1982; Greenwood Press for chapter 9, Barbara Christian, 'Shadows uplifted', from Barbara Christian, *Black Women Novelists: The Development of a Tradition, 1892–1976*, Westport, Ct, Greenwood Press, 1980, pp. 3–34, 253–7; and Routledge & Kegan Paul for chapter 12, Annette Kuhn, 'Real women', from Annette Kuhn, *Women's Pictures: Feminism and Cinema*, London, Routledge & Kegan Paul, 1982, 131–55. Chapter 3, Catherine Belsey, 'Constructing the subject: deconstructing the text', is revised from Catherine Belsey, *Critical Practice*, London, Methuen, 1980, pp. 103–25.

PREFACE

The essays in this collection represent an attempt to theorize about and to practice a materialist-feminist criticism of literature and culture. The criticism in this volume is 'materialist' in its commitment to the view that the social and economic circumstances in which women and men live – the material conditions of their lives – are central to an understanding of culture and society. It is materialist in its view that literature and literary criticism are both products of and interventions in particular moments of history. It is materialist too in its assumption that many, perhaps most, aspects of human identity are socially constructed. It is 'feminist' in its emphasis on the social construction of gender and its exploration of the intersections of gender with other social categories like class, race and sexual identity. It is feminist in its emphasis on relations of power between women and men, though it insists on examining them in the context of other relations of power and it assumes that such relations of power and the ways in which they are inscribed in texts change with changing social and economic conditions. Finally, this criticism is ideological – concerned with the relation of ideology, especially though not exclusively ideologies of gender, to cultural practice and to social change.

The volume is divided into two sections: theoretical essays and applied criticism, both exemplifying typical concerns of materialist-feminist criticism. The first group of selections examines race, ideology, feminist criticism and the literary canon from a materialist-feminist perspective, and explores the ways in which other current critical discourses such as those of deconstruction, psychoanalysis and French feminism might be useful to a feminist and materialist criticism. The second group of essays represents examples of feminist-materialist criticism in practice.

Although most of the contributors to this volume are, inevitably, white middle-class women, we have attempted to present a spectrum of approaches by drawing together authors who are British and American, white and of color, lesbian and heterosexual. Most of their essays have been published before in journals and as chapters in books, but they acquire new dimensions of meaning when presented as part of a collective critical endeavor.

We begin with Barbara Smith's classic essay 'Toward a black feminist criticism', which argues for the recognition in feminist criticism of black women's literary traditions and for the inclusion of a lesbian feminist perspective in our readings of texts. Smith asks all of us to consider how our 'thoughts connect to the reality of black women's writing and lives'.

Paul Lauter's 'Race and gender in the shaping of the American literary canon: a case study from the twenties' applies a materialist-feminist perspective to the formation of the literary canon. Lauter argues that the canon of American literature is itself a historical construct, the product of specific forces, events and institutional formations in American history rather than a natural emergence of the 'greatest' of literary works. In revealing the historicity of aesthetic judgments and the resultant suppression of work by women and people of color, Lauter lays the basis for proposing new categories of American literary history, categories that will be inclusive and pluralist rather than exclusive and monolithically male, white and middle class.

From the contours of literary history and the role of ideology and the critic in producing it, Michèle Barrett's 'Ideology and the cultural production of gender' and Catherine Belsey's 'Constructing the subject: deconstructing the text' (revised from Belsey's *Critical Practice*) move us to the terrain of current debate about the meaning and political implications of ideology. For many of us a first encounter with a criticism that explicitly and demandingly asserted its engagement in the struggle for progressive social change was with Lillian S. Robinson's now classic essay, 'Dwelling in decencies: radical criticism and the feminist perspective' (originally published in *College English* 32 (1971)). Robinson persuaded many of us of the inadequacy of less politically informed approaches. Belsey and Barrett consider, in a more elaborate and nuanced way than Robinson's pioneering polemic, the relationship between changing social institutions and dismantling repressive ideologies of gender. Just as Lauter suggests new categories for writing literary history, Belsey and Barrett pose a set of critical foci through which one might elaborate a materialist-feminist analysis of culture and literature.

Where Belsey considers the intersection of materialist-feminist approaches with deconstruction and psychoanalysis, Ann Rosalind Jones in 'Writing the body: toward an understanding of *l'écriture féminine*' examines the intersection of a materialist-feminist approach with French feminism (the latter itself a mixture of several discourses). What both essays suggest is the range and flexibility of materialist-feminist criticism in its capacity at once to critique and to use other current critical discourses while infusing them with a more historically grounded understanding of culture and gender.

The section of applied criticism focuses on English and American work of the nineteenth and twentieth centuries. Both Judith Newton's study of *Villette* and Cora Kaplan's essay on *Aurora Leigh* locate these exemplars of the female 'great tradition' in relation to the class structure and sex/gender systems peculiar to the Victorian England and Italy of Brontë and Browning. Newton explores the implications of Brontë's contradictory relation to the ideology of woman's sphere for the structure and language of *Villette*. Kaplan views *Aurora Leigh* as a textual terrain on which issues of gender difference, class warfare and the relation of art to politics intersect to produce 'the fullest and most violent exposition of "the woman question" in mid-Victorian literature'. These two detailed readings suggest the compatibility of a materialist-feminist approach with the deepest understanding of literary form and language; they suggest, that is, the ways in which an understanding of history and an understanding of literature can interpenetrate to illuminate one another.

Sonja Ruehl's 'Inverts and experts: Radclyffe Hall and the lesbian identity' applies Foucault's concepts of discourse and reverse discourse in an analysis of Radclyffe Hall's popular lesbian classic *The Well of Loneliness*. Ruehl shows how Hall, speaking from within the historical category of 'invert' developed by Havelock Ellis, was able to initiate the transformation of that category. The essay makes a crucial contribution to our understanding of the social construction of sexuality and sexual identity – as distinct from, though intersecting with, the social construction of gender and class.

Our essays on American literature look at black and working-class writers and at mass culture. 'Shadows uplifted', the first chapter of Barbara Christian's *Black Women Novelists: The development of a tradition 1892–1976*, explores the intersections of economic relations in the antebellum South, ideologies of race and gender, and portrayals of black women in literature. Deborah Rosenfelt's study of Tillie Olsen's *Yonnondio*, 'From the thirties: Tillie Olsen and the radical tradition', suggests that contemporary feminists, who justifiably value Olsen as a shaping voice of contemporary literary feminism, have not sufficiently understood the roots of her vision and her work in the radical social movements of the 1930s; her essay analyzes the relationship between Olsen's class background, her work as a writer and her commitment as an activist. Leslie W. Rabine's essay on Harlequin Romances discusses the ways in which this popular genre adapts ancient narrative patterns to the tensions specific to a particular moment in history. Rabine locates in Harlequin Romances a power hierarchy between male boss and female workers, a hierarchy in which class structure and the sex/gender system reinforce one another. Within this hierarchy, modern working women's conflicts between desire for love and desire for work, between an impulse toward submission and the assertion of autonomy, play themselves out to an enforced reconciliation. Finally, Annette Kuhn in her essay on 'Real women' decodes the cinematic language of both Hollywood films and documentary to reveal the intersections of gender, ideology and film form. She suggests one mode of feminist intervention in mass media: appropriating the documentary form to feminist concerns and visions.

We hope these essays, diverse as they are, suggest together the efficacy of a criticism committed to an understanding of the complex relations among history and literature; consciousness and ideology; gender, culture and power; art and social change. The criticism here differs in appreciable ways from that produced by feminists with a more cultural or traditionally literary orientation. It is a criticism distinct also from that produced by traditional Marxists, for whom gender is not a major category of analysis. In our introduction we want to explore more fully the qualities and vision that characterize this kind of criticism and to situate it in the world of criticism and the broader world of political engagement and practice.

Judith Newton
Deborah Rosenfelt
March 1985

INTRODUCTION
Toward a materialist-feminist criticism

JUDITH NEWTON AND
DEBORAH ROSENFELT

Lillian Robinson once said that the most important question we can ask ourselves as feminist critics is 'So what?' Implied in that question is a view most of us share – that the point of our work is to change the world. But to begin with the question 'So what?' is to take on the task of asking other questions as well – like what is the relation of literature and therefore of literary criticism to the social and economic conditions of our lives? Most feminist critics still work within a central insight of the women's movement – that gender is socially constructed and that its construction has enforced unequal relations of power. From that insight it is a relatively short step to the assumption that products of consciousness, like literature and literary criticism, are also socially constructed, and that they too are political. Like women's studies generally, in fact, feminist criticism began with the assumption that we make our own knowledge and are constantly remaking it in the terms which history provides – and that in making knowledge we act upon the power relations of our lives.[1]

As feminist critics, for example, we speak of making our knowledge of history, choosing to see in it not a tale of individual and inevitable suffering, but a story of struggle and relations of power. We speak of making our notion of literary texts, choosing to read them not as meditations upon themselves but as gestures toward history and gestures with political effect. Finally, we speak of making our model of literary criticism, choosing to see in it not an ostensibly objective reading of a text but an act of political intervention, a mode of shaping the cultural use to which men's and women's writing will be put.[2]

This reconstruction of our knowledge, however, has been a form of struggle, a political action carried out upon our culture and ourselves, for to assert that literature and culture are political is radically to challenge modes of thinking that are dominant in our world. For those of us trained as literary critics, moreover, these modes of thinking are apt after a long apprenticeship to seem like deeply ingrained aspects of ourselves, and our struggle with our culture, in particular, to seem like a struggle with ourselves.[3] For literary studies, more than most other disciplines, has divorced the study of ideas and language from the study of social conditions and has fostered a view of intellectual activity as a solitary individual enterprise rather than as a project with social origins and political consequence.[4] As feminist critics, therefore, many of us have implicitly committed ourselves to resist an extended history of training in our craft. We have committed ourselves to resist a view of literature – formalism – that sees literature and literary critics as divorced from history, a view still perpetrated – despite their air of currency and French fashionableness – by much of the post-structuralist criticism now dominant in Britain and the United States.[5] We have also committed ourselves to resist a view of history still beloved by humanities departments, the view that history, especially modern history, is the essentially tragic story of individual suffering, a suffering often universalized and guaranteed permanency as part of the human condition. This is a view, of course, which permits us to 'see' literature and history in relation but which nullifies what is potentially radical in such a vision by denying the possibility of meaningful social change.

But given that knowledge is constructed and that remaking knowledge is a form of struggle against our culture and ourselves, and given our training as critics in particular, it is not surprising that we should still be immersed in critical practices which it is against our interest to maintain, that our primary assumptions and our theory, our theory and our practice, have not always developed hand in hand.[6] Thus, despite our assumption that ideas, literature and culture are socially constructed, that mental oppression is rooted in the material conditions of our lives, much of our literary theory implies a version of the world in which women are oppressed, for the most part, by literary constructs or in which female counter-myths are more powerful than (or as powerful as) economics.[7] Rather than elucidating the complex web of relations – social, economic, linguistic – of which literature is a part, we disassociate ideas from material realities. This disassociation replicates and enforces a habit of mind already dominant in the culture at large and blunts the radical edge of feminist critical intervention. As Lillian Robinson observed in 1970, there is 'a kind of idealism to which we become susceptible when we explore the question of feminine consciousness. For we, too, have a tendency to ignore its material basis.'[8]

This looseness of our hold upon the material is also reflected in the fact that applied feminist criticism frequently offers little explicit history at all while its implicit history tends unwittingly to recapitulate the politics of the English departments and the culture in which we were trained. Much feminist criticism, that is, although it assumes the existence of unequal gender-based relations of power, implicitly constructs those relations in such a way as to render them tragic – unchanging, universal, monolithic. Many feminists still identify an emphasis upon the universal and unchanging with 'patriarchy'. In so far, however, as our own constructions of history obscure historical change, cultural complexity and women's agency, they themselves replicate the habits of thought they intend to challenge. They produce, in fact, a feminist version of 'the' human condition.[9] This tendency to tragic essentialism in regard to male domination is the obverse of an inclination to comedic essentialism on the other side of the equation. This essentialism, for example, subsumes women into the sisterly category of 'woman' despite real differences of race, class and historical condition, or posits women's nurturing and relational qualities as in themselves a counter to male domination.[10]

These inclinations in feminist criticism, of course, are part of larger currents in feminist theory and politics as a whole. Polarization of the masculine and the feminine, or of male and female; denigration of the masculine or the male as violent and possibly irretrievable; valorization of male power into a 'monolithic and unchanging out there'; the construction of women as at once totally dominated and essentially good; and the celebration of a unifying woman's nature have in varying ways characterized the discourse of cultural/ radical feminists in England and the United States, some women in sectors of the peace and antipornography movements and many French feminists.[11] These theoretical tendencies, of course, have been expressed in a variety of political actions, including 'Take Back the Night' marches, ritual theater at military bases and campaigns for more stringent laws against pornography. Such actions, whether one agrees with them or not, have been visible, dramatic and sometimes effective.[12] But more than ever – in a context of backlash and cutbacks, the absence of a unified progressive movement, the rise in the United States of the New Right and Moral Majority, and economic hard times – the theoretical constructions of history on which they rest seem too simplistic adequately to analyze the possibilities and priorities for long-term political struggle.

In the United States, where feminist poets have powerfully influenced feminist politics, this tendency has sometimes expressed itself in poetic language imbued with a kind of wishful thinking. In an article about the role of feminist poets as theoreticians and political spokeswomen, for example, poet and critic Jan Clausen writes of three poems by Judy Grahn, June Jordan and Susan Sherman that while their optimistic conclusions about women's power are strong and moving, 'their impact seems to rest more on our *desire* to believe their closing assertions than on the intrinsic credibility these assertions possess based on what we know of the world'. Clausen then warns feminist poets and leaders to avoid 'the rote chanting of slogans we are unable to make real, the temptation to dish up to the audience what it wants or has learned to expect in the way of exhortation and uplift'.[13] It is of course the nature of poetry to work better as rhetoric than as analysis, and we need poetry to inspire as much as we need analysis to guide us. Still, Clausen advises us not to confuse inspiration with understanding.

There have been, of course, important counters to this polarization of male domination and female powerlessness and to this utopian celebration of female virtue, with the essentialism or universalism which so much of it implies. A dialectic of criticism and self-criticism has continued to characterize feminist debate over pornography, peace, the gender gap, French feminism and sexuality, and new work by feminist scholars continually reworks our history and theory. Theories of gender construction advanced by feminist theorists like Gayle Rubin, Nancy Chodorow, Dorothy Dinnerstein and Jane Flax, for example, have re-emphasized the idea that gender identity and ideologies of gender, as one part of a sex/gender system, are socially constructed rather than innate and that they are created by women as well as men, despite women's lesser access to cultural power.[14] Feminist history by historians like Mary Ryan and Judith Walkowitz has, in addition to its other contributions, countered the ahistorical quality of much feminist psychoanalytic theory by illuminating the ways in which constructions of gender and sexuality have changed with changing historical situations.[15] And an extensive literature by feminist anthropologists has corrected the ethnocentric bias of many white western theories about the subordination of women, women's culture and women's nature in the present.[16]

In feminist literary criticism, similar tendencies have invited us to tighten our hold upon the material and have challenged us to interrogate the tragic conceptions of history we have inherited. These currents appear most consistently and consciously in the work of feminists who are also socialists, but we refer to work in which such currents dominate as 'materialist-feminist' rather than 'socialist-feminist'. We do so because the former term is more inclusive and because it reminds us that materialist analysis appears, however unevenly, in the work of many feminist critics who do not consider themselves socialists (especially in the United States where Marxism and socialism are so marginalized and negatively viewed by the culture as a whole).[17] The boundaries, that is, between materialist-feminist criticism and other feminist criticisms are fluid.[18] What this means is that analysis and critique will inevitably be self-analysis and self-critique. What it also means, since all of us are situated in history and since we and our work change with changing circumstances, is that analysis and critique must address themselves not to individuals but to their work. Still, even given this fluidity of boundaries, we can make distinctions that help to define a materialist-feminist critical practice.

We have said that most feminist criticism shares a materialist assumption: that gender is socially constructed and that its construction enforces unequal power relations. But materialist-feminist criticism is for the most part doubly committed to materialist analysis. It is committed out of its concern with gender relations and it is committed out of its concern with the economic.

Many materialist-feminist critics, in fact, have a triple or quadruple commitment by virtue of being racial and/or lesbian liberationists as well. Barbara Smith's essay in this volume represents this quadruple commitment. Understanding the intersections of multiple oppressions, however, as June Howard reminds us, is not 'a simple choice of perspective but a long labor'.[19] And to most materialist-feminist critics the labor of constructing and using a theoretical position entails a double work shift: work on the power relations implied by gender and simultaneously on those implied by class, race and sexual identification; an analysis of literature and an analysis of history and society; an analysis of the circumstances of cultural production and an analysis of the complexities with which at a given moment in history they are inscribed in the text.

Like other feminists, materialist feminists are also concerned with the importance of ideas, language and culture to women's oppression. This emphasis on culture, indeed, is one of the central contributions of the women's movement – along with the black liberation movement that preceded it – to political thought.[20] What a materialist-feminist criticism tends to mean, therefore, aside from more work than one is used to, is more focus on material realities than in most feminist criticism and more power granted to ideas, language and culture than in much traditional Marxist criticism – that is, in much Marxist criticism written before the 1970s.

For the materialist-feminist critic this analysis of ideas, language and culture frequently takes the form of discussing ideology. The term 'ideology,' a staple of critics working within a Marxist tradition, or at least of critics familiar with that discourse, has been defined in various ways. Terry Eagleton, for example, in *Marxism and Literary Criticism*, provides a familiar working definition: ideology is 'that complex structure of social perception which ensures that the situation in which one social class has power over the others is either seen by most members of the society as "natural", or not seen at all'.[21] Ideology, however, is not simply determined by the economic and the political but may be thought of as having a relative power and life of its own. What this means, in the words of Annette Kuhn, is that 'ideology is not necessarily a direct expression of ruling-class [or gender] interests at all moments in history and that at certain conjunctures it may even move into contradiction with those interests'.[22] Ideology, then, is not a set of deliberate distortions imposed on us from above, but a complex and contradictory system of representations (discourse, images, myths) through which we experience ourselves in relation to each other and to the social structures in which we live. Ideology is a system of representations through which we experience *ourselves* as well, for the work of ideology is also to construct coherent subjects: 'the individual thus lives his [or her] subject-ion to social structures as a consistent subject-ivity, an imaginary wholeness.'[23]

In materialist-feminist and in much current Marxist work, as the preceding paragraph suggests, ideology is granted 'relative autonomy' from economic conditions.[24] This tendency to view ideology as functioning somewhat independently parallels and has been shaped by the tendency of feminist criticism as a whole to examine the power of images, myths, cultural ideals and linguistic categories over our thinking and therefore over our lives. But where a materialist-feminist criticism still insists upon the intersection of ideas and language with the social and historical, reminding us that 'we can't look to culture alone to liberate us',[25] much feminist criticism implies the *primacy* of the psyche as the essential terrain on which political struggle is waged, viewing texts, discourses, categories of language and symbolic modes as the *major* armaments in that struggle. Gilbert and Gubar's *Madwoman in the Attic,* for example, a rich and perceptive work, focuses almost entirely on the entrapment of women in male literary constructs and women's literary resistance, and in so doing emphasizes the power of ideas alone which a materialist-feminist criticism would seek to qualify.[26] Nina Auerbach's impressive *Woman and the Demon* takes a similar tack when it suggests that freedom from Victorian constructions of womanhood, which, she argues, granted women an almost mythic power, produced more loss than gain for women of the 1880s and 1890s despite the fact that middle-class women of this period had greater access than before to work, higher education and the vote.[27]

In a sense Rachel Brownstein's *Becoming a Heroine: Reading about women in novels* takes this propensity in feminist critics and in other book-loving females as its study. But while Brownstein points out some of the dangers for feminists of giving power to literary texts, of seeking to become the 'integral self' which literary heroines represent, she does not see inattention to social and economic realities as one of the problems.[28] Finally, Annette Kolodny's brilliant reading of American pastoral literature in *The Lay of the Land* does examine economic and social relations, but the book's analysis is determined by an explicitly articulated belief that 'what we label as historical and economic processes are, at least in part, the external projections of internal patterns – be they called psychology or myth'.[29] Thus the book concludes: 'If this study has suggested anything, it must be that what we need is a radically new symbolic mode for relating to "the fairest, frutefullest, and pleasuntest [land] of all the worlde"' (p. 148). The book reflects an awareness, of course, that a new symbolic mode is not *all* we need, but its analysis privileges the 'male psyche' to such an extent that the real struggle begins to seem a contest of symbolic modes.[30]

Jan Clausen has questioned this tendency to valorize the transformation of the symbolic, of language, as in itself a sufficient political transformation. Citing examples from criticism by Adrienne Rich and Judith McDaniel, she writes that 'it is hard to come away from a reading of the works in which the passages I have quoted appear without feeling that for these writers the politics of language actually take precedence over other politics'. Clausen feels that the blurring of distinctions in the United States between literary prominence and political leadership has meant that 'sometimes feminist theory and practice have been skewed in the direction of too much stress on the transformation of language, too little emphasis on other sorts of transformations which a political movement that hopes to succeed in the material world must undertake'. Or perhaps (she goes on) the causal relationship goes the other way;

> perhaps it is in part precisely because of what a Marxist would call an 'idealist' bent in our movement, a weakness for mind-over-matter approaches, that poets have emerged as leaders. This would help to account for the popularity of such feminist thinkers as Mary Daly, who has focused almost exclusively on language as a vehicle for feminist transformation.[31]

Those in the left community who have emphasized the relative autonomy of ideology have done so for different reasons from those of feminist poets and critics like Rich and Daly who have emphasized the primacy of language. For Rich and Daly, the transformation of language seems virtually synonymous with social change. The better Marxist critics, in contrast, have emphasized the autonomy of ideology in an effort to avoid the pitfalls of a narrow economic determinism, but they have remained within a left materialist tradition that critics like Rich have explicitly attacked. Michèle Barrett, however, feels that elements of the left community in England who have privileged discourse almost to the exclusion of anything else have also gone too far. Her criticism of these elements for overprivileging discourse echoes Clausen's criticism of cultural feminism in the United States: 'Are we really to see the Peterloo massacre, the storming of the winter palace in Petrograd, the long march, the Brunswick picket as the struggle of discourses?' (p. 72 below).

Materialist-feminist criticism, then, while acknowledging the importance of language as a site of political activity, is skeptical of the isolation of language and ideas from other realms of struggle. While suspicious of analysis for its own sake, however, materialist-feminist criticism is itself committed to analysis, to the difficult task of exploring the changing relationships among ideas, language, and social conditions and relations. Michèle Barrett's essay in this collection, for example, suggests a methodology for doing so consistently.[32] One need not, however, use the terms and categories of a specifically Marxist discourse, as Barrett does, to undertake a materialist-feminist reading of history and of texts. The excerpt here from Barbara Christian's *Black Women Novelists* is a nuanced discussion of the connections among the 'public dream' of the plantation as happy family, the real relations among whites and blacks, male and female, in the antebellum South, and the portrayals of black women in the literature of the era. Christian's 'public dream' is essentially synonymous with what we mean by 'ideology' — a structure of perception that helps maintain a particular set of social and economic relations at a particular juncture in history, and that affects the way all of us (for Christian, antebellum southerners – black and white, male and female) construct our own subjectivity.

This sustained attention to the complex ways in which ideas and material conditions intersect, and this concern with the process of historical change, mean that materialist-feminist work also aspires to be 'dialectical'. One of the key aspects of both dialectical art and dialectical film criticism, as defined by materialist-feminist film critic, Julia Lesage, is that they elucidate 'the relation of human consciousness to historical and social process and change'. Thinking dialectically has as its end 'elucidating its object, the concrete world, in terms of that world's all-sidedness, contradictions, determinations and necessities. Dialectics explains process and change.' This way of thinking, as Lesage asserts in her analysis of the Cuban film *One Way or Another*, locates movement, transformation, process in the incompatible development of two necessarily related entities (e.g. labor and capital) or in the contradictory aspects of a single phenomenon – such as the contradictory implications of women's work in the domestic sphere. Lesage acknowledges that feminist art and criticism cannot directly change power relations, cannot alone effect the transformation of relations between public and private spheres that she sees as the goal of feminism. But she argues that the greater self-awareness and imaginative capacity fostered by such art, when linked with a social movement, is an essential component of revolutionary change.[33]

This kind of dialectical, as opposed to static and linear, mode of analysis distinguishes feminist-materialist criticism from many other feminist criticisms. It is a way of seeing that prompts us to locate in the same situation the forces of oppression and the seeds of resistance; to construct women in a given moment in history simultaneously as victims and as agents. One might compare, for example, Sonja Ruehl's analysis of Radclyffe Hall's *The Well of Loneliness*, reprinted here, with Catherine R. Stimpson's discussion of the same novel in 'Zero degree deviancy: the lesbian novel in English'.[34] Both Stimpson and Ruehl locate their analysis historically, analyzing the origins of 'lesbian' as a social category and tracing the emergence of homophobia as a historical phenomenon. But whereas Stimpson finds in the novel a tale of damnation that helped, along with the controversy surrounding its publication, to 'submerge, screen, and render secondary' a more progressive consciousness about the possibilities of lesbian experience (p. 372), Ruehl argues that the novel is the start of a 'reverse discourse', a process by which the

> category of lesbianism derived from a medical discourse is firstly adopted and then eventually transformed by those defined by it. ... Hall's intervention can be seen as a contribution to the formation of ... political self-consciousness; later generations of lesbians were to follow her model of public identification even if they repudiated her particular views (p. 170).

Thus the novel, in accepting and propagating the rigid segregation of lesbians, of 'congenital inverts', as a separate group, lays the basis for 'a later political solidarity'. The moment of extreme categorical rigidity which is codified in the text becomes a moment of birth and change as well.

Most of the essays in this volume demonstrate this capacity to embrace contradiction. They interpret history not as an assortment of facts in a linear arrangement, not as a static tale of the unrelieved oppression of women or of their unalleviated triumphs, but as a process of transformation. They read the act or artifact of cultural production as an intervention in that process – usually with contradictory implications of its own. This dialectical approach enables us to view ideological struggle and social change as possible, for through it we may examine and understand the tensions and contradictions within both ideology and society.

Literature and culture, of course, as sites at which ideology is produced and reproduced, are also sites on which the outlines and contradictions of ideology may be made visible. Materialist-feminist critics do not assume that literature and cultural production 'reflect' history in a simple mimetic moment. Since we live within myths and narratives about history, there can in fact *be* no reflections of it. Literature, rather, draws upon various ideological productions of history or discourses about history to make its own production. What a literary text does not say, therefore, becomes as interesting as what it does say. The discourse suppressed tells us as much as the discourse expressed, for omission throws the margins of a text's production into relief, allowing us to see the limits and the boundaries of what it posits as the real.[35] In Catherine Belsey's essay here, for example, the scientific rationality of the Sherlock Holmes stories is revealed as ideological precisely because the stories mystify and thereby marginalize what they cannot at this moment in history subject to a positivist approach: the sexuality of women. 'The presentation of so many women in the Sherlock Holmes stories as shadowy, mysterious and magical figures,' Belsey argues, 'precisely contradicts the project of explicitness ... and in doing so throws into relief the poverty of the contemporary concept of science' (p. 62 below). Since positivism is linked with classic realism as a literary mode, and since the haunted treatment of women in the Holmes stories defies a positivist approach, they ultimately undermine the very mode in which they are cast as well as the very assumptions they ostensibly endorse.

Materialist-feminist work also frequently emphasizes the way in which a text is reproduced by its readers, and reproduced differently in changing historical situations. There is an articulation here between currents in materialist criticism and the body of work known as reader theory or reader-response criticism. Not all reader-response criticism is materialist or feminist, but this approach does accommodate a materialist and feminist perspective more easily than many other tendencies in contemporary criticism. What is inherent in the text is not a fixed verbal structure but, in Belsey's words, 'a range of possibilities of meaning'.[36] Specific interpretive communities, to use Stanley Fish's helpful phrase, will share common readings of the same text but different interpretive communities, with different experiences and different understandings of aesthetic and cultural codes, will produce widely different meanings.[37] Janice Radway, for example, in 'Women read the romance', argues that feminist critics who have written about the romance and its supposed effect on readers come from interpretive communities utterly different from those of romance readers themselves. Thus they have produced different meanings from those produced by readers whose behavior they are trying to explain. 'They have severed the form from the women who actually construct its meaning from within a particular context. ... This assumption has resulted ... in an incomplete account of the particular ideological power of this literary form.' Radway herself uses ethnographic methods to investigate how a specific community of women readers interprets the texts of romance novels.[38] Since readers in different historical situations will produce different versions of the text, each with its own political effect, the political function of a text will change along with the goals and strategies of a reader in different historical situations.[39]

Although most feminist criticisms regard literary canons as socially constructed, materialist-feminist criticism is more likely to insist on the social and historical relativity of aesthetic standards.[40] It also analyzes the interests which those standards serve, considering race and class as well as gender. Paul Lauter, for example, examines in the essay here the historical process by which white female and also black writers were eliminated from the American literary canon in the 1920s. He shows how our very conceptions of literary history are derived from the experience of élite white men, at the expense of both women and people of color. Our traditional focus on Puritanism, for example, has 'led to the study of the ideology by which a narrow group of male divines construed and confirmed their dominant roles in New England society', distorting among other things our understanding of 'colonial family and sex life, and the systematic extermination of "Indians"' (pp. 34–5 below).

In materialist-feminist criticism, moreover, a more sustained focus on the process of social construction means that the category of literature itself is more consistently regarded as historical construction and that literature is apt to be seen in relation to, rather than in isolation from, other forms of discourse such as advertising or film. From this perspective cultural production and discourse at large are opened up to a radical revision in which ideas on every level are seen in relation to systems of power and in which literary – now cultural – studies become a mode of intervening politically in a much wider field.[41] In this volume, for example, Leslie Rabine's analysis of Harlequin Romances and Annette Kuhn's analysis of feminist documentary both focus on popular and mass culture as crucial realms of investigation and struggle.

This emphasis on cultural studies as opposed to purely literary ones has characterized much contemporary Marxist and post-Marxist criticism. Yet the commitment of materialist-feminist criticism to articulating the relation between ideas and material conditions in terms of gender as well as of class enforces a somewhat different view of literature and culture from that maintained by traditional Marxist criticism and by other feminist criticisms as well. Materialist-feminist criticism differs from most Marxist criticism in emphasizing difference between women and men and in foregrounding the extent to which cultural discourse is gender-specific.[42] It gives emphasis, say, to the way in which middle-class women are constructed differently from middle-class men, refusing to see them as just one more bourgeois subject. Criticism which is solely within a Marxist or socialist perspective fails to account for the specific oppression of women within gender relations and gender ideology. Thus, it is likely to register the desire for autonomy or achievement in a middle-class woman's text as one more example of bourgeois individualism. This is true, for example, of Terry Eagleton's *Myths of Power*, which despite its theoretical recognition of women's oppression is, in its readings, a pre-feminist book. Failing to grasp the radical thrust in Brontë's *Villette* of Lucy Snowe's desire for self-fulfillment, the book dismisses her desire as 'an overriding need to celebrate bourgeois security'.[43] A materialist-feminist reading, in contrast, registers the socially transforming potential of a desire for autonomy and achievement even in a woman of the middle class. Thus Cora Kaplan in the essay on *Aurora Leigh* included here cautions that we should remember that 'the description of Aurora as an independent author living and working in London is possibly the most "revolutionary" assertion in the poem, the item most likely to corrupt the daughters of the gentry' (p. 158 below).

But if materialist-feminist criticism differs from traditional Marxist criticism in its emphasis on gender relations and on the transforming potential of white middle-class female desire, it also differs from other feminist criticisms in its refusal to valorize that desire almost to the exclusion of other values. The work of a materialist feminist, indeed, reminds us how inadequate that desire is as a single response to a social formation fractured by inequities not only of gender but of race and class. Many feminist readings of *Villette*, for example, tend to focus exclusively on and to give unmediated value to Lucy's desire for self-development or to the text's fantasies of power. Materialist-feminist readings like that of Mary Jacobus, in contrast, qualify the value we can give to such individualist longings: 'the drive to female emancipation, while fueled by revolutionary energy, has an ultimate conservative aim in successful integration into the existing social structure.'[44] Similarly, Cora Kaplan reminds us that 'the strains in *Aurora Leigh* which prefigure modern radical feminism are not only those which appear in the heroine's relation to art, but those which surface in Barrett Browning's manipulation of her working-class figure, Marian Erle' (p. 140 below).

Materialist-feminist criticism, moreover, differs from other feminist criticisms in its assumption that men as well as women are ideologically inscribed. It is likely, therefore, to examine the similarities between men and women of the same class or racial group as well as their differences. And where much feminist criticism refers to men and male domination as if men really were the free agents proposed by bourgeois and patriarchal ideology, materialist-feminist criticism stresses men's relative imprisonment in ideology. In so doing it works against the notion that men are a monolithic, totally different and controlling out-there. Thus where feminist books like *Madwoman in the Attic* or *Lay of the Land* tend to use terms which suggest deliberate, almost conscious male power – 'man's society', 'the roles that men assign women', 'male pride that seeks to control', 'the patterns of the male psyche had seized the power and determined the course of history' – materialist-feminist criticism tends to use terms such as 'gender ideology' or 'sexual caste system'.[45] That is, it tends to use terms which suggest the relative autonomy of gender ideology even from those who most benefit from its restrictions. Or it refers to ideologies in which gender is only one level of concern.[46]

While materialist-feminist criticism, like other feminist criticisms, examines men's imagined superiority, real dominance and undeniable exploitation of women, it views men not in terms of gender ideology and relations alone but also in terms of class and race ideologies, class and race relations. Thus the relative powerlessness of working-class men and men of color, and men's divisions from one another along the lines of race, class or sexual identification, become part of the critical perspective.[47] Since women, too, are seen in terms of class and race ideologies and relations, they appear in situations of relative power to others. Since their ideological investment in these relations is generally explored, women are not viewed as an unalloyed force for good or as a unified sisterhood or nature. Women, like men, appear divided from each other, enmeshed not in a simple polarity with males but in a complex and contradictory web of relationships and loyalties.

Materialist-feminist criticism by women of color is perhaps most likely to be conscious of the racial and class differences among women, although obviously not all criticism by women of color is explicitly materialist. Some of it, for example, posits a universalized 'the Black Woman' or *'La Chicana'* – concepts which reflect an inclination toward cultural nationalism that runs parallel as a tendency to cultural feminism.[48] Some of this work explores – often quite usefully – the textual integration of myth, folklore and oral tradition, but it tends not to interpret the political implications of this contemporary recuperation of traditional materials or to consider in any depth the changes in social fabric which demarcate the time of origin from the moment of adaptation.[49] In contrast, work by critics like Barbara Smith, Barbara Christian (in this volume, for example), Gloria Hull, Mary Helen Washington, Gloria Wade Gayles, Sherley Williams and Elaine Kim offers rich interpretations of the dynamic of oppression and liberation as lived by women of color and as mediated in literature.[50] But even white middle-class readings of a white middle-class text like *Villette* differ in their assessment of women's relationships to each other. Where a feminist criticism such as Rachel Brownstein's reading of the novel might see Lucy Snowe's distance from Paulina purely in terms of their relative approximations to the feminine ideal – 'other women are composed within their bodies; for Lucy enclosure is torment'[51] – a materialist-feminist reading such as Judith Newton's in this volume is more likely to maintain that Lucy is distant from Paulina not only because she is traditionally feminine, that is 'subordinate and half-existant', but because she flouts the privilege of her class.

A materialist-feminist criticism, in short, a criticism combining feminist, socialist and anti-racist perspectives, is likely to assume that women are not universally the same, that their relations are also determined by race, class and sexual identification; that social change cannot be conceived of in terms only of women who are white and privileged; that integration into existing social structures is not likely to liberate even white middle-class women; and that unequal relations of power in general must be reconstructed, not only for women but for all the oppressed.[52] It is because of assumptions such as these that a materialist-feminist criticism is more likely than a simply feminist one to analyze working-class and other non-traditional literatures[53] or, like Deborah Rosenfelt's analysis in this volume of Tillie Olsen's relation to feminism and the left, to consider women writers as agents in social transformations not limited to those determined by gender alone.

This emphasis on transforming power relations which extend beyond those of gender accounts for the fact that materialist-feminist criticism is more likely to think of working not just in opposition to but in relation to men. The transformation of all power relations cannot be achieved without such collaboration – however difficult this alliance has often proved for individual women in their political and personal lives, however awkward and painful the contradictions. A materialist-feminist critic, therefore, is less opposed to using male-authored theories for her own purposes than many cultural feminists. She is likely to perceive such labor less as a form of 'ladies' auxiliary' than as 'fruitful alliance' or revolutionary activity – though she is likely as well to wince at the persistence in such theories of assumptions about gender that she has long ago learned to question.[54]

For these reasons too a single focus on women and on women's culture may be of less interest as a critical imperative to materialist-feminist than to other feminist work, although other feminist criticisms have begun to express restiveness with prolonged residence in communities of women.[55] To a materialist-feminist, writing about men may well seem essential both to an understanding of women and of women's culture and to an understanding and transformation of our gender systems. A focus on women's culture, moreover, might well seem to work against an exploration of the real class and race divisions among women, divisions which must be encountered before any real sisterhood, that is, any sisterhood which extends beyond women who are white and middle-class, can be established.[56] Perhaps a more compelling critical imperative should be to explore communi*ties* of women, to compare the experience and visions of women writers of color and white working-class writers with the experience and visions of women who are white and middle-class.[57]

Like other feminists, materialist-feminists have long understood that the ideas and structures we wish to transform are not just 'out there' but also within our movement and within ourselves. It is the desire to account both for the *persistence* of oppressive structures and ideologies *and* the possibilities of change that has led some materialist-feminist critics to explore psychoanalytic theories of the way in which gender is constructed on the most basic levels of consciousness. In Britain and France particularly, the theories of Jacques Lacan – despite criticism of their lingering phallocentrism – have seemed helpful.[58] According to Lacan it is in language that we come to consciousness, that a sense of identity is imposed upon us, for language offers us a series of subject positions, a range of discourses in which we are constructed. In the language of bourgeois society, in particular (according to a materialist-feminist application of Lacan), we are constructed as fixed, autonomous and coherent. In reality, however, the ego is 'necessarily *not* coherent', for language cannot fully formulate unconscious desire. Because there is no continuity of psychic life, according to Jacqueline Rose, 'there is no stability of sexual identity, no position for women (or for men) which is ever simply achieved'. This indeed is at the bottom of what Rose sees as an affinity between feminism and psychoanalysis, the 'recognition that there is a resistance to identity which lies at the very heart of psychic life'.[59]

In addition, the range of positions from which we are liable to grasp ourselves as subjects may be incompatible. Women, according to Belsey in her essay here, 'participate both in the liberal–humanist discourse of freedom, self determination and rationality and at the same time in the specifically feminine discourse offered by society of submission, relative inadequacy and irrational intuition'. This in turn creates intolerable pressures and may lead to a number of responses from falling sick to seeking 'a resolution of the contradiction in the discourses of feminism' (p. 50 below).

As Jacqueline Rose suggests, however, this construction of women's identity is in some ways a difficult one to maintain for women whose goal as feminists is to establish a strong sense of ego and identity. It is equally difficult for women trying to forge a political movement to feel at home with a relentless focus on the social construction of knowledge, on the necessary partialness of all truth.[60] For if we accept the logic of a materialist position, how can we privilege materialist-feminist readings of culture and history over readings which are not? Do we not end up with a world which is

ultimately arbitrary and inscrutable, and in which one discourse (and therefore one mode of action) is as good as any other?' How do we extricate
ourselves from an intellectual and political pluralism which validates no higher
value than that of the right to choose, an ideology that in our present society,
to quote Terry Eagleton, means 'the right to make profit while throwing men
and women out of work' or 'the right to buy one's child expensive education
while other children are deprived of their school meals'?[61]

Changing the world requires a set of values and perceptions that we can
commit ourselves to, a set of values, moreover, that is compelling to others. If
as feminists together we are to transform our readings of culture and the
ideological and material structures of our social life, can we afford to designate
ourselves as one more critical approach in the market place of ideas? On the
other hand, how do we confront the necessary partialness of knowledge and
the reality of diversity within the women's movement (for it is these realities
too that Kolodny's notion of 'playful pluralism'[62] was meant to address)?

One answer perhaps is that absolute knowledge is not necessary for political
action, since absolute knowledge is impossible and yet political transformation
has taken place.[63] A second is that seeing knowledge as a form of historical
practice does not mean we cannot lay claim to degrees of its relative coherency
and completeness while maintaining all the while a vision of its inescapable
provisionality, its ongoing process of being transformed.[64] This is a view of
knowledge that befits a women's movement which is changing and diverse and
which has consistently imposed challenges to what has seemed to be 'natural'.
It is a view of knowledge that leaves rooms for unity and diversity as well.
Unity, at any rate, cannot finally be achieved through appeals to some final
knowledge, for the provisionality of our vision assaults us at every corner. Nor
can we expect to rally women against a monolithic male out there. Our lived
experience of men and even of male domination is too complex. Nor finally
can unity be achieved through idealist proclamations about woman's nature
and her unmediated capacity for good. For as Ann Jones asks, in her analysis
in this volume of French feminism, 'if we concentrate our energies on
opposing a counterview of Woman to the view held by men in the past and
present, what happens to our ability to support the multiplicity of women and
the various life possibilities they are fighting for in the future?' (p. 94 below).

A materialist-feminist analysis offers a more complex and in the end less
tragic view of history than one polarizing male and female, masculine and
feminist; constructing gender relations as a simple and unified patriarchy;
and constructing women as universally powerless and universally good. A
materialist-feminist analysis actively encourages us to hold in our minds the
both-ands of experience: that women at different moments in history have
been both oppressed and oppressive, submissive and subversive, victim and
agent, allies and enemies both of men and one another. Such an analysis
prompts us to grasp at once the power of ideas, language and literature; their

importance as a focus of ideological struggle; and their simultaneous embed-
dedness in and difference from the material conditions of our lives. Such an
analysis, of course, does not offer us simple answers. Indeed, the uncompromising complexity of its vision may sometimes discourage those who long
for certainty and simplicity. None the less, in its insistent inclusiveness, in its
willingness to embrace contradictions, materialist-feminist analysis seems to
us the most compelling and potentially transformative critical approach to
culture and society, offering us theory for our practice as we work toward a
more egalitarian world.

NOTES

We are deeply indebted to Elizabeth Abel, Jane Caplan, Darlaine Gardetto, Cora
Kaplan, Paul Lauter, Caryn Musil, Leslie Rabine and Judith Stacey for their thorough
and incisive readings of this introduction. Although we have not always followed their
suggestions, we have been consistently challenged and educated by them.

1. See, for example, the essays of Florence Howe on both interdisciplinary women's
   studies and feminist literary criticism, now collected in *Myths of Coeducation:
   Selected essays, 1964–1983* (Bloomington: Indiana University Press, 1984); the
   essays in *Female Studies VI: Closer to the Ground: Women's classes, criticism, pro-
   grams*, ed. Nancy Hoffman, Cynthia Secor and Adrian Tinsley (Old Westbury,
   NY: Feminist Press, 1972); or the essays in the first anthology of feminist literary
   criticism, *Images of Women in Fiction: Feminist perspectives*, ed. Susan Koppelman
   Cornillon (Bowling Green, Ohio: Bowling Green University Popular Press, 1972).
   One might argue that this assumption also informs the first major work of feminist
   literary criticism in the twentieth century, Virginia Woolf's *A Room of One's Own.*
2. For work which reflects these assumptions to varying degrees see, for example,
   Mary Ellmann, *Thinking About Women* (New York: Harcourt, Brace, 1968); Kate
   Millett, *Sexual Politics* (New York: Doubleday, 1968); Florence Howe, 'Feminism
   and literature', in *Images of Women in Fiction*, ed. Susan Koppelman Cornillon;
   Judith Fetterley, *The Resisting Reader: A feminist approach to American fiction*
   (Bloomington: Indiana University Press, 1978); Lillian Robinson, *Sex, Class, and
   Culture* (Bloomington: Indiana University Press, 1978); Catherine Belsey, *Critical
   Practice* (London: Methuen, 1979); Adrienne Rich, *On Lies, Secrets, and Silence:
   Selected prose 1966–1978* (New York: W. W. Norton, 1979); Barbara Christian,
   Black Women Novelists: The development of a tradition (Westport, Conn.: Greenwood
   Press, 1980); Annette Kolodny, 'Dancing through the minefield: some observa-
   tions on the theory, practice, and politics of a feminist literary criticism', *Feminist
   Studies* 6 (Spring 1980), pp. 1–25; Dale Spender, 'Introduction', in *Men's Studies
   Modified: The impact of feminism in the academic disciplines*, ed. Dale Spender
   (Oxford: Pergamon Press, 1981), pp. 1–9; Gloria T. Hull and Barbara Smith,
   'The politics of black women's studies', in *All the Women Are White. All the Blacks
   Are Men. But Some of Us Are Brave: Black women's studies*, ed. Gloria T. Hull,
   Patricia Bell Scott and Barbara Smith (Old Westbury, New York: Feminist Press,
   1982), pp. xvii–xxxi.
3. For three accounts of the changing (and unchanging) relation between develop-
   ments in literary criticism and dominant modes of thought in England and

America, see Belsey, *Critical Practice*; Terry Eagleton, *Literary Theory: An Introduction* (Minneapolis: University of Minnesota Press, 1983); and Frank Lentricchia, *After the New Criticism* (Chicago: University of Chicago Press, 1980). See Kolodny, 'Dancing through the minefield', p. 11, for an interesting account of the way in which critical training socializes us to dominant notions of literary value.

4. This generalization is not of course universally applicable, nor is this critique new. See, for example, the essays in *The Politics of Literature: Dissenting essays on the teaching of English*, ed. Louis Kampf and Paul Lauter (New York: Random House, 1972). According to Eagleton, *Literary Theory*, 'it is the *extremism* of literary theory, its obstinate, perverse, endlessly resourceful refusal to countenance social and historical realities, which most strikes a student of its documents, even though "extremism" is a term more commonly used of those who would seek to call attention to literature's role in actual life'. Eagleton sees this reduction of literary criticism to a private contemplative act as an equivalent in the literary sphere 'to what has been called possessive individualism in the social realm', *Literary Theory*, pp. 196–7.

5. For early feminist critical attacks on formalism, see the essays in *Images of Women in Fiction*, especially Fraya Katz Stoker, 'The other criticism: feminism vs. formalism', pp. 315–27; and in *Feminist Literary Criticism: Explorations in theory*, ed. Josephine Donovan (Lexington: University Press of Kentucky, 1975), especially Donovan's Afterword. For the critique of much post-structuralism as a new variety of formalism, see Lentricchia, *After the New Criticism*; Michael Ryan, *Marxism and Deconstruction: A critical articulation* (Baltimore: Johns Hopkins University Press, 1982); and Paul Lauter, 'Society and the profession, 1958–83', *PMLA* 99 (May 1984), pp. 414–26.

6. Kolodny, for example, writes of 'our reticence at taking full responsibility for the truly radicalizing premises that lie at the theoretical core of all we have so far accomplished' ('Dancing through the minefield', p. 7). June Howard, 'Informal notes toward "Marxist-feminist" cultural analysis', *Minnesota Review* 20 (Spring 1983), pp. 77–92, continues this feminist self-critique by citing Kolodny's work as one example of the way in which feminist criticism has not always lived up to its own potential. Writing of black feminist criticism in particular, Gloria T. Hull and Barbara Smith, 'The politics of Black women's studies', in *Black Women's Studies*, p. xxi, note that 'much of the current teaching, research, and writing about Black women is not feminist, is not radical, and unfortunately is not always even analytical'.

7. Archetypal feminist criticism, for example, posits counter-myths of female heroes and female quests that oppose the 'life-denying myths of female inferiority, virginity, romantic love, and maternal self-sacrifice' without as a rule concerning itself with the social conditions that generate or impede the imagining and experiencing of 'heroism' in daily life. Such work includes Carol Christ, *Diving Deep and Surfacing: Women's spiritual quest* (Boston: Beacon, 1980); Carol Pearson and Katherine Pope, *The Female Hero in American and British Literature* (New York: R. R. Bowker, 1981; quotation here, p. 48); and Annis Pratt, *Archetypal Patterns in Women's Fiction* (Bloomington, Indiana: University of Indiana Press, 1981). Even feminist criticism focused on a particular historical era often tends toward a history of ideas, even when the *conflicts* among ideas are foregrounded. Brilliant as their

readings are, these are the implied histories of much of Sandra Gilbert and Susan Gubar's *The Madwoman in the Attic: The woman writer and the nineteenth century literary imagination* (New Haven: Yale University Press, 1979) and of Nina Auerbach's counter-interpretation of nineteenth-century writing, *Woman and the Demon: The life of a Victorian myth* (Cambridge, Mass.: Harvard University Press, 1982), as well as of such fine and often politically impassioned readings as Annette Kolodny's *The Lay of the Land: Metaphor as experience and history in American life and letters* (Chapel Hill: University of North Carolina Press, 1975) and Judith Fetterley's *The Resisting Reader*.

8. 'Dwelling in decencies: radical criticism and the feminist perspective', *College English* 32 (1970).

9. Both Simone de Beauvoir and Kate Millett have influenced this tendency, although the works of each have materialist dimensions. In *The Second Sex* de Beauvoir offers something close to an essentialist vision of women's nature; Millett in *Sexual Politics*, a universalist vision of patriarchal power, both of which lock women forever in our places. Adrienne Rich, who has contributed significantly to our critical understanding of the importance of material circumstances, including race and class, in women's lives has tended increasingly to posit an omnipresent and ahistorical patriarchy whose 'creative energy', she insists, is 'running out' (revised version of 'When we dead awaken: writing as re-vision', in *On Lies, Secrets, and Silence*, p. 49). Nina Auerbach, in 'Why communities of women aren't enough' (unpublished paper), observes of feminist criticism in the mid-1970s that 'to free ourselves from patriarchal ideologies, we had paradoxically invested men with a mythic, dehumanizing power; in their looming forms we saw woman's entire history of oppression'.

10. See Ann Rosalind Jones in this volume on the way in which *fémininité* as defined by French feminists like Irigaray and Cixous implies these assumptions. Among the most eloquent American writers who express these assumptions are Rich in *On Lies, Secrets, and Silence* and Susan Griffin in *Women and Nature: The roaring inside her* (New York: Harper, 1978).

11. Kate Ellis sees this trend in regard to the construction of the masculine or of men in the discourse of the antipornography movement. This discourse, she argues, surrounds us 'with a monolithic world "out there", a patriarchal system of which all the parts are equally developed and fit perfectly together'. Such discourse, she continues, despairs of the process of 'finding fissures and weak points in the armor of patriarchy' ('I'm black and blue from the Rolling Stones and I'm not sure how I feel about it: pornography and the feminist imagination', *Socialist Review* 75–6 (May–August 1984), p. 115). The same trend is apparent in some sectors of the peace movement. See, for example, Donna Warnock's 'Patriarchy is a killer: what people concerned about peace and justice should know', in *Reweaving the Web of Life: Feminism and nonviolence*, ed. Pam McAllister (Philadelphia: New Society Publishers, 1982), pp. 20–9. See Alice Echols, 'The new feminism of Yin and Yang', in *Powers of Desire: The politics of sexuality*, ed. Ann Snitow, Christine Stansell and Sharon Thompson (New York: Monthly Review Press, 1983), p. 442, on the tendency to simplify and celebrate women's nature in the discourse of the antipornography movement and of cultural feminism generally: 'if the source of the world's many problems can be traced to the dominance of the male principle,

its solution can be found in the reassertion of the female principle'. See Karen Rosenberg, 'Peaceniks and soldier girls', *The Nation*, 14 April 1984, p. 453, on this same tendency among sectors of the peace movement: 'the [gender] gap has been taken as evidence that women are inherently more benevolent and caring than men, and even as heralding the long-awaited appearance of a force large enough to form a major peace movement'. See Ann Jones, finally, 'Writing the Body', on both tendencies in French feminism.

12. Although socialist feminists view some of the actions springing from cultural/ radical feminist analysis as wrong-headed, it would be erroneous to argue that the cultural or radical feminist tendency has led to withdrawal from the political sphere. Indeed, in a recent forum among four women associated with socialist feminism – Barbara Haber, Judy McClean, Barbara Epstein and Deirdre English – all the participants except English expressed the belief that radical and liberal feminists had been more engaged and successful as activists than left feminists and that the connection of radical feminists with the peace movement suggests a displacement of socialist feminists to the periphery of political struggle. According to Epstein, 'socialist feminism has become part of academia and has been killed by it' (*Socialist Review* 79 (January–February 1985), pp. 93–110; quotation p. 107). Yet socialist feminists (including these four) have been active in the peace movement, in anti-imperialist work, in reproductive rights, and so on. The question here is, what kind of *theory* can best guide us in the long run?

13. Jan Clausen, *A Movement of Poets: Thoughts on poetry and feminism* (Brooklyn, NY: Long Haul Press, 1982), p. 26.

14. Gayle Rubin, 'The traffic in women: notes on the "political economy" of sex', in *Toward an Anthropology of Women*, ed. Rayna R. Reiter (New York: Monthly Review Press, 1975). Dorothy Dinnerstein, *The Mermaid and the Minotaur: Sexual arrangements and human malaise* (New York: Harper & Row, 1976); Nancy Chodorow, *The Reproduction of Mothering: Psychoanalysis and the sociology of gender* (Berkeley: University of California Press, 1978); Jane Flax, 'The conflict between nurturance and autonomy in mother–daughter relationships and within feminism', *Feminist Studies* 4 (June 1978), pp. 171–91.

15. Mary Ryan, *Cradle of the Middle Class: The family in Oneida County, New York, 1790–1865* (Cambridge: Cambridge University Press, 1981); Judith R. Walkowitz, *Prostitution and Victorian Society: Women, class, and the state* (Cambridge: Cambridge University Press, 1980); see also Jeffrey Weeks, *Sex, Politics and Society: The regulation of sexuality since 1800* (London: Longman, 1981). For a critique of the ahistorical tendencies of Chodorow and Dinnerstein, see Judy Housman, 'Mothering, the unconscious, and feminism', *Radical America* 16 (November–December 1982), pp. 47–62.

16. Michelle Z. Rosaldo, 'The use and abuse of anthropology: reflections on feminism and cross-cultural understanding', *Signs* 5:3 (1980), pp. 389–417, is especially important in this regard. For critical reviews of the literature on these and other issues, see Rayna Rapp, 'Review essay: Anthropology', *Signs* 4:3 (Spring 1979), pp. 497–513, and Jane Monnig Atkinson, 'Review essay: Anthropology', *Signs* 8:2 (Winter 1982), pp. 236–58.

17. The assumptions of much feminist criticism about literature and culture are quite parallel to the assumptions of the new Marxist cultural theory, an observation

which can be documented by comparing the work cited in note 1 above with the following new Marxist theory: Tony Bennett, *Formalism and Marxism* (London: Methuen, 1979); Fredric Jameson, *The Political Unconscious: Narrative as a socially symbolic act* (Ithaca, NY: Cornell University Press, 1981); Michael Ryan, *Marxism and Deconstruction*; Terry Eagleton, *Literary Theory*. Among the critics who have begun to articulate this connection are Kolodny, 'Not so gentle persuasion: a theoretical imperative of feminist literary criticism', *Feminist Literary Criticism*, Working Paper no. 3, National Humanities Center, 1981: 'Despite all the garbs of radicalism or innovation to which almost every critical community or clan lays claim, only the feminists – with the possible exception of the Marxists and some Afro-American literary critics – actually attempt the true meaning of the paradigm: that is, a revolution in consciousness so thoroughgoing as to truly dislodge, not simply alter or reform, reigning belief systems', p. 7. Eagleton makes similar connections in *Literary Theory*, pp. 209, 215.

18. Judith Kegan Gardiner's 'Response' to Kolodny's 'Dancing through the mine-field' employs the political categories of liberal, radical and socialist feminist. It is both helpful and sisterly but its assignation of critical strategies to each position somewhat suppresses the fluidity of boundaries characteristic of feminist and materialist-feminist work. Gardiner recognizes this herself, of course, since she points out that at different moments Kolodny's essay is radical, socialist and liberal feminist.

19. Howard, 'Informal notes', p. 1.

20. On this contribution of feminism, see Annette Kuhn, *Women's Pictures: Feminism and cinema* (London: Routledge & Kegan Paul, 1982), p. 4: 'one of the major theoretical contributions of the women's movement has been its insistence on the significance of cultural factors, in particular in the form of socially dominant representations of women and the ideological character of such representations, both in constituting the category "woman" and in delimiting and defining what has been called the "sex/gender system"'. See also June Howard: 'long before Marxists began citing Gramsci on hegemony and construction of consent, feminists recognized the political importance of cultural analysis' ('Informal notes', p. 5). In fact, the black liberation movement preceded the women's movement in this regard. The motive behind the simple and effective slogan, 'Black is beautiful', was to change the way black people are *seen* by the dominant culture and consequently the way they *see*, that is construct, themselves.

21. Eagleton, *Marxism and Literary Criticism* (Berkeley: University of California Press, 1976), pp. 5–7.

22. 'Structures of patriarchy and capital in the family', in *Feminism and Materialism: Women and modes of production*, ed. Annette Kuhn and AnnMarie Wolpe (London: Routledge & Kegan Paul, 1978), p. 63.

23. Rosalind Coward and John Ellis, *Language and Materialism: Developments in Semiology and the Theory of the Subject* (London: Routledge & Kegan Paul, 1977), p. 71.

24. Most of this draws on the work of Louis Althusser. See especially 'Marxism and humanism' (1965) and 'Ideological state apparatuses' (1969), both in *Lenin and Philosophy, and Other Essays* (London: New Left Books, 1971). See also Barrett, 'Ideology and the cultural production of gender', pp. 65–85 below; Howard, 'Informal notes', pp. 11–12, 17–18; Kuhn, *Women's Pictures*, p. 4.

25. Barrett, 'Ideology and the cultural production of gender'.
26. Gilbert and Gubar, *Madwoman in the Attic*, pp. xxi, xxii, 16.
27. *Woman and the Demon: The life of a Victorian myth* (Cambridge, Mass.: Harvard University Press, 1982), p. 222.
28. Rachel Brownstein, *Becoming a Heroine: Reading about women in novels* (Harmondsworth: Penguin, 1982), especially p. 295.
29. *The Lay of the Land: Metaphor as experience and history in American life and letters* (Chapel Hill: University of North Carolina Press, 1975), p. 36.
30. See Kolodny, however, for a materialist analysis of the way in which (middle-class white academic) men's material and ideological situations in the world interfere with their reading of (white middle-class) women writers: 'Dancing through the minefield', pp. 12–13.
31. *A Movement of Poets*, pp. 24, 25.
32. Other examples include the scholarship of those who have contributed to the Feminist Press's reprint series and its Women Working Series, including Mary J. Buhle, Florence Howe, Nancy Jo Hoffman, Elaine Hedges and Tillie Olsen.
33. 'One Way or Another: Dialectical, Revolutionary, Feminist', *Jump Cut* 20 (May 1979), pp. 1, 2, 5, 8.
34. *Critical Inquiry* 8 (Winter 1981), pp. 363–80.
35. See Belsey, 'Constructing the subject', pp. 45–64 below; Barrett, 'Ideology and the cultural production of gender', pp. 65–85 below. Both draw from the work of Pierre Macherey, *A Theory of Literary Production* (London: Routledge & Kegan Paul, 1978) (see especially 'Lenin, critic of Tolstoy', pp. 105–35); and from the work of Terry Eagleton, *Criticism and Ideology: A study in Marxist literary theory* (London: Verso, 1978) (see especially 'Categories for a materialist criticism', pp. 44–63). For a helpful summary of both see Bennett, *Formalism and Marxism*, pp. 106–12.
36. Belsey, *Critical Practice*, p. 20.
37. *Is There a Text in This Class?: The authority of interpretive communities* (Cambridge, Mass.: Harvard University Press, 1980).
38. Radway, 'Women read the romance: the interaction of text and context', *Feminist Studies* 9 (Spring 1983), pp. 53–78; quotation, p. 55.
39. See also Bennett, *Formalism and Marxism*, pp. 136–7; Eagleton, *Literary Theory*, pp. 211–14; and the essays in *Reader-Response Criticism: From formalism to post-structuralism*, ed. Jane P. Tompkins (Baltimore: Johns Hopkins University Press, 1980).
40. The question which Kolodny poses is the same question posed by materialist-feminist and by Marxist criticism: 'what ends do those judgments serve, the feminist asks; and what conceptions of the world or ideological stances do they (even if unwittingly) help to perpetuate?' Kolodny also suggests, however, that feminist criticism has dealt only piecemeal 'with the difficulties inherent in challenging the authority of established canons and then justifying the excellence of women's traditions, sometimes in accord with standards to which they have no intrinsic relation' ('Dancing through the minefield', pp. 15, 7).
    Materialist-feminist positions on the canon are perhaps more uncompromising in their insistence on the relativity of aesthetic standards. See, for example, Barrett, 'Ideology and the cultural production of gender', p. 78 below, who

suggests that the preoccupation with aesthetic value has been detrimental to feminist criticism in that it has reproduced 'the assumption that aesthetic judgment is independent of social and historical context'. Martha Vicinus in *The Industrial Muse* (New York: Barnes & Noble, 1974) argues that 'our definitions of literature and our canons of taste are class bound; we currently exclude street literature, songs, hymns, dialect, and oral storytelling, but they were the most regular forms used by the working class' (p. 1).

41. See Howard, 'Informal notes', p. 25: 'it is, in its mild way, a political undertaking just to advocate viewing works of high culture as part of a wider field of signifying practices, rather than as unique creative achievements'. See also Eagleton, *Literary Theory*, pp. 204–8. Michael Ryan, 'Literary criticism and cultural science: transformations in the dominant paradigm of literary study', *North Dakota Quarterly* 51 (Winter 1983), pp. 100–12, is a particularly thoroughgoing discussion of this issue, although not particularly feminist.

42. See Marxist-Feminist Literary Collective, 'Women's writing: *Jane Eyre, Shirley, Villette, Aurora Leigh*', *Ideology and Consciousness* 3 (1978), pp. 27–48. 'Marxist critics must confront the proposition that all subjects are gendered and that all literary discourse is gender specific' (p. 47).

43. *Myths of Power: A Marxist study of the Brontës* (New York: Barnes & Noble, 1975), p. 71. Eagleton's work, of course, has become increasingly feminist. See, for example, *The Rape of Clarissa: Writing, sexuality and class struggle in Samuel Richardson* (Minneapolis: University of Minnesota Press, 1982).

44. This focus on and valorization of self-development characterizes the readings of *Villette* in *Madwoman in the Attic, Becoming a Heroine* and Helene Moglen's *Charlotte Brontë: The self conceived* (New York: W. W. Norton, 1976). Nina Auerbach's reading in *Communities of Women: An idea in fiction* (Cambridge, Mass.: Harvard University Press, 1978), focuses less on individual development than on fantasies of women's collective power. Mary Jacobus, 'The buried letter: feminism and romanticism in *Villette*', in *Women Writing and Writing about Women*, ed. Mary Jacobus (London: Croom Helm, 1979), p. 57.

45. *Madwoman in the Attic*, pp. 388, 420. *Lay of the Land*, p. 73. Carol Ohmann, 'Historical reality and divine appointment in Charlotte Brontë's fiction', *Signs* 2 (Spring 1977), p. 778. Judith Lowder Newton, *Women, Power, and Subversion: Social strategies in women's fiction 1780–1860* (Athens, Georgia: University of Georgia Press, 1981).

46. See Jacobus, 'The buried letter', p. 54. As noted earlier, Christian's *Black Women Novelists* also uses terms such as 'public dream' or 'world view', in which gender ideology is only one level of concern (pp. 10, 15).

47. Tillie Olsen, *Silences* (New York: Delacorte, 1978), is an excellent example of an analysis that treats the 'circumstances' of men's as well as women's lives historically and sympathetically.

48. The essays in *The Black Aesthetic*, ed. Addison Gayle, Jr (New York: Doubleday, 1971) provide the clearest articulation of black cultural nationalism in criticism. The influence of this tendency survives in some of the essays and interviews in Roseann P. Bell, Bettye J. Parker and Beverly Guy-Sheftall's anthology, *Sturdy Black Bridges: Visions of black women in literature* (Garden City, NY: Anchor Books, 1979). The conclusion of Darryl C. Dance's 'Black Eve or Madonna? A study of

the antithetical views of the mother in black American literature' exemplifies this
universalizing tendency of cultural nationalism:

> As we look back over the history of the Black American mother, we see that she
> emerges as a strong Black bridge that we all crossed over on, a figure of courage,
> strength, and endurance unmatched in the annals of world history. She is
> unquestionably a Madonna, both in the context of being a savior and in terms of
> giving birth and sustenance to positive growth and advancement among her
> people. It is she who has given birth to a new race; it is she who has played a
> major role in bringing a race from slavery and submission to manhood and
> assertiveness. (p. 131)

49. For example, Paula Gunn Allen's classic article, 'The sacred hoop: a contemporary
    Indian perspective on American Indian literature' in *Literature of the American
    Indians*, ed. Abraham Chapman (New York: New American Library, 1975), offers
    an important interpretation of American Indian values and myths, one related to
    Allen's perspective as a cultural feminist, without suggesting any essential differ-
    ences between pre-Columbian tribal life and contemporary Native American
    experiences; Elizabeth Ordoñez's 'Narrative texts by ethnic women: rereading the
    past, reshaping the future', *Melus* 9:3 (Winter 1982), pp. 19–28, suggests that texts
    by Toni Morrison, Estela Portillo, Maxine Hong Kingston and E. M. Broner
    explore 'a particular female and ethnic socio-historical identity' but focuses exclu-
    sively on 'the text itself' as 'both the means and embodiment of modifying and
    reshaping female history, myths, and ultimately personal and collective identity'
    (p. 19).
50. Barbara Smith's widely anthologized essay, 'Toward a black feminist criticism',
    originally published in *Conditions Two* (1977), pp. 25–44, and reprinted here,
    provided the basis for much subsequent critical work on the intersections of race,
    gender and sexual identity in literature. In a sense, Alice Walker's *The Color Purple*
    is a response in fiction to the plea at the end of this essay for 'One book based in
    black feminist and black lesbian experience . . . one work to reflect the reality that I
    and the black women whom I love are trying to create'. See also Barbara
    Christian, *Black Women Novelists: The development of a tradition, 1892–1976*; the
    essays in Hull, Scott and Smith, *All the Women Are White*, on black women's
    literature; Mary Helen Washington's introductions to *Black-Eyed Susans: Classic
    stories by and about black women* (Garden City, NY: Anchor Books, 1975), *Midnight
    Birds: Stories of contemporary black women writers* (Garden City, NY: Anchor Books,
    1980), and *I Love Myself When I Am Laughing: A Zora Neale Hurston reader* (Old
    Westbury, NY: Feminist Press, 1979); Gloria Wade-Gayles, *No Crystal Stair:
    Visions of race and sex in black women's fiction* (New York: Pilgrim Press, 1984);
    Sherley Anne Williams, 'Papa Dick and sister–woman: reflections on women in
    the fiction of Richard Wright', in *American Novelists Revisited: Essays in feminist
    criticism*, ed. Fritz Fleischmann (Boston: G. K. Hall, 1982); and Elaine H. Kim,
    Asian American Literature: An introduction to the writings and their social context
    (Philadelphia: Temple University Press, 1982).
51. *Becoming a Heroine*, p. 171.
52. In a talk delivered at a women's conference, for example, Barbara Smith
    remarked, 'the question has been raised here whether this should be an

activist association or an academic one. In many ways, this is an immoral question, an immoral and false dichotomy. The answer lies in the emphasis and the kinds of work that will lift oppression off of not only women, but all oppressed people – poor and working-class people, people of color in this country, and in the colonized Third World. If lifting this oppression is not a priority to you, then it's problematic whether you are a part of the actual feminist movement' (Hull and Smith, 'The politics of black women's studies'), p. xxi.

53. See, for example, Vicinus, *The Industrial Muse*; Paul Lauter, 'Working-class women's literature – an introduction to study', *The Radical Teacher* 15 (March 1980), pp. 16–26; and the essays on letters and diaries in *Teaching Women's Literature from a Regional Perspective*, ed. Leonore Hoffman and Deborah Rosenfelt (New York: Modern Language Association, 1982).

54. Elaine Showalter, 'Feminist criticism in the wilderness', in *Writing and Sexual Difference*, ed. Elizabeth Able (Chicago: University of Chicago Press, 1982), p. 69, characterizes feminist critics who make a practice of using male-authored theories as 'a sort of ladies' auxiliary of the male critical community, constantly revising and remaking literary theory in order to suit its own purposes'. But her own citation of male theorists, Edward Ardener and, in another version of this essay, Clifford Geertz, suggests the difficulty, and perhaps the ahistorical nature, of insisting that we spin purely female-authored webs. See Barrett, 'Ideology and the cultural production of gender', below.

55. See, for example, Auerbach's 'Why communities of women are not enough', which asserts that writing about men rather than reinforcing the patriarchy at the expense of a female literary power base seems rather 'my way of claiming power over it; its magic is dispelled by being understood, it loses its frightening otherness as it takes on the shape of my consciousness and my language', p. 6. See also Gilbert and Gubar's new, insightful (and much more materialist) work on male and female modernists. One example is Gilbert's 'Soldier's heart: literary men, literary women, and the Great War', *Signs* 8 (Spring 1983), pp. 422–50.

56. Carolyn J. Allen, 'Feminist(s) reading: A response to Elaine Showalter', in *Writing and Sexual Difference*, p. 300, makes this criticism of Showalter's call for a focus on women's culture. See Bonnie Thornton Dill's critique of the term 'sisterhood' in 'Race, class, and gender: prospects for an all-inclusive sisterhood', *Feminist Studies* 9 (Spring 1983), p. 146:

> I would argue for the abandonment of the concept of sisterhood as a global construct based on unexamined assumptions about our similarities, and I would substitute a more pluralistic approach that recognizes and accepts the objective differences between women. Such an approach requires that we concentrate our political energies on building coalitions around particular issues of shared interest. Through joint work on specific issues, we may come to a better understanding of one another's needs and perceptions and begin to overcome some of the suspicions and mistrust that continue to haunt us.

57. Barbara Christian speaks of the need to recognize variations among black communities and to avoid 'a homogenized picture of black culture', *Black Women Novelists*, p. 240.

58. See, for example, Juliet Mitchell and Jacqueline Rose, 'Introduction I and II', in

Introductions to Feminine Sexuality: Jacques Lacan and the école freudienne, ed. Juliet Mitchell and Jacqueline Rose (New York: W. W. Norton, 1982), pp. 1–58. For a more sustained critique of Lacan's 'sexism' see Ryan, *Marxism and Deconstruction*, pp. 104–11. See also Marxist-Feminist Literature Collective, 'Women's writing': 'the problem with Lacanian psychoanalysis is that the concept of the symbolic order consolidates as it theorizes patriarchal structures' (p. 47).

59. 'Femininity and its discontents', *Feminist Review* 14 (Summer 1983), pp. 11, 9.
60. ibid., pp. 5–21.
61. Eagleton, *Literary Theory*, p. 200.
62. Kolodny, 'Dancing through the minefield', p. 19.
63. Ryan, *Marxism and Deconstruction*, p. 213.
64. ibid., p. 214.

PART ONE
THEORY

ONE
Toward a black feminist criticism

BARBARA SMITH

For all my sisters, especially Beverly and Demita

I do not know where to begin. Long before I tried to write this I realized that I was attempting something unprecedented, something dangerous merely by writing about black women writers from a feminist perspective and about black lesbian writers from any perspective at all. These things have not been done. Not by white male critics, expectedly. Not by black male critics. Not by white women critics who think of themselves as feminists. And most crucially not by black women critics who, although they pay the most attention to black women writers as a group, seldom use a consistent feminist analysis or write about black lesbian literature. All segments of the literary world – whether establishment, progressive, black, female, or lesbian – do not know, or at least act as if they do not know, that black women writers and black lesbian writers exist.

For whites, this specialized lack of knowledge is inextricably connected to their not knowing in any concrete or politically transforming way that black women of any description dwell in this place. Black women's existence, experience and culture, and the brutally complex systems of oppression which shape these, are in the 'real world' of white and/or male consciousness beneath consideration, invisible, unknown.

This invisibility, which goes beyond anything that either black men or white women experience and tell about in their writing, is one reason it is so difficult for me to know where to start. It seems overwhelming to break such a massive silence. Even more numbing, however, is the realization that so many of the women who will read this have not yet noticed us missing either from their reading matter, their politics or their lives. It is galling that ostensible feminists and acknowledged lesbians have been so blinded to the implications of any womanhood that is not white womanhood and that they have yet to struggle with the deep racism in themselves that is at the source of this blindness.

I think of the thousands and thousands of books, magazines and articles which have been devoted, by this time, to the subject of women's writing and I am filled with rage at the fraction of those pages that mention black and other Third World women. I finally do not know how to begin because in 1977 I want to be writing this for a black feminist publication, for black women who know and love these writers as I do and who, if they do not yet know their names, have at least profoundly felt the pain of their absence.

The conditions that coalesce into the impossibilities of this essay have as much to do with politics as with the practice of literature. Any discussion of Afro-American writers can rightfully begin with the fact that for most of the time we have been in this country we have been categorically denied not only literacy, but the most minimal possibility of a decent human life. In her landmark essay 'In search of our mothers' gardens', Alice Walker discloses how the political, economic and social restrictions of slavery and racism have historically stunted the creative lives of black women.[1]

At the present time I feel that the politics of feminism have a direct relationship to the state of black women's literature. A viable, autonomous black feminist movement in this country would open up the space needed for the exploration of black women's lives and the creation of consciously black woman-identified art. At the same time a redefinition of the goals and strategies of the white feminist movement would lead to much needed change in the focus and content of what is now generally accepted as women's culture.

I want to make in this essay some connections between the politics of black women's lives, what we write about and our situation as artists. In order to do this I will look at how black women have been viewed critically by outsiders, demonstrate the necessity for black feminist criticism, and try to understand what the existence or nonexistence of black lesbian writing reveals about the state of black women's culture and the intensity of *all* black women's oppression.

The role that criticism plays in making a body of literature recognizable and real hardly needs to be explained here. The necessity for non-hostile and perceptive analysis of works written by persons outside the mainstream of white/male cultural rule has been proven by the black cultural resurgence of the 1960s and 1970s and by the even more recent growth of feminist literary scholarship. For books to be real and remembered they have to be talked about. For books to be understood they must be examined in such a way that the basic intentions of the writers are at least considered. Because of racism, black literature has usually been viewed as a discrete subcategory of American literature and there have been black critics of black literature who did much to keep it alive long before it caught the attention of whites. Before the advent of specifically feminist criticism in this decade, books by white women, on the other hand, were not clearly perceived as the cultural manifestation of an oppressed people. It took the surfacing of the second wave of the North American feminist movement to expose the fact that these works contain a stunningly accurate record of the impact of patriarchal values and practice upon the lives of women and more significantly that literature by women provides essential insights into female experience.

In speaking about the current situation of black women writers, it is important to remember that the existence of a feminist movement was an essential precondition to the growth of feminist literature, criticism and women's studies, which focused at the beginning almost entirely upon investigations of literature. The fact that a parallel black feminist movement has been much slower in evolving cannot help but have impact upon the situation of black women writers and artists and explains in part why during this very same period we have been so ignored.

There is no political movement to give power or support to those who want to examine black women's experience through studying our history, literature and culture. There is no political presence that demands a minimal level of consciousness and respect from those who write or talk about our lives. Finally, there is not a developed body of black feminist political theory whose assumptions could be used in the study of black women's art. When black women's books are dealt with at all, it is usually in the context of black literature which largely ignores the implications of sexual politics. When white women look at black women's works they are of course ill-equipped to deal with the subtleties of racial politics. A black feminist approach to literature that embodies the realization that the politics of sex as well as the politics of race and class are crucially interlocking factors in the works of black women writers is an absolute necessity. Until a black feminist criticism exists we will not even know what these writers mean. The citations from a variety of critics which follow prove that without a black feminist critical perspective not only are books by black women misunderstood, they are destroyed in the process.

Jerry H. Bryant, the *Nation*'s white male reviewer of Alice Walker's *In Love and Trouble: Stories of black women*, wrote in 1973: 'The subtitle of the collection, "Stories of Black Women," is probably an attempt by the publisher to exploit not only black subjects but feminine ones. There is nothing feminist about these stories, however.'[2] Blackness and feminism are to his mind mutually exclusive and peripheral to the act of writing fiction. Bryant of course does not consider that Walker might have titled the work herself, nor did he apparently read the book which unequivocally reveals the author's feminist consciousness.

In *The Negro Novel in America*, a book that black critics recognize as one of the worst examples of white racist pseudoscholarship, Robert Bone cavalierly dismisses Ann Petry's classic, *The Street*. He perceives it to be 'a superficial social analysis' of how slums victimize their black inhabitants.[3] He further objects that:

It is an attempt to interpret slum life in terms of *Negro* experience, when a larger frame of reference is required. As Alain Locke has observed, '*Knock on Any Door* is superior to *The Street* because it designates class and environment, rather than mere race and environment, as its antagonist.'[4]

Neither Robert Bone nor Alain Locke, the black male critic he cites, can recognize that *The Street* is one of the best delineations in literature of how sex, race *and* class interact to oppress black women.

In her review of Toni Morrison's *Sula* for *The New York Times Book Review* in 1973, putative feminist Sara Blackburn makes similarly racist comments. She writes:

> Toni Morrison is far too talented to remain only a marvelous recorder of the black side of provincial American life. If she is to maintain the large and serious audience she deserves, she is going to have to address a riskier contemporary reality than this beautiful but nevertheless distanced novel. *And if she does this, it seems to me that she might easily transcend that early and unintentionally limiting classification 'black woman writer' and take her place among the most serious, important and talented American novelists now working.*[5] [Italics mine]

Recognizing Morrison's exquisite gift, Blackburn unashamedly asserts that Morrison is 'too talented' to deal with mere black folk, particularly those double nonentities, black women. In order to be accepted as 'serious', 'important', 'talented' and 'American', she must obviously focus her efforts upon chronicling the doings of white men.

The mishandling of black women writers by whites is paralleled more often by their not being handled at all, particularly in feminist criticism. Although Elaine Showalter in her review essay on literary criticism for *Signs* states that: 'The best work being produced today [in feminist criticism] is exacting and cosmopolitan', her essay is neither.[6] If it were, she would not have failed to mention a single black or Third World woman writer, whether 'major' or 'minor', to cite her questionable categories. That she also does not even hint that lesbian writers of any color exist renders her purported overview virtually meaningless. Showalter obviously thinks that the identities of being black and female are mutually exclusive, as this statement illustrates: 'Furthermore, there are other literary subcultures (black American novelists, for example) whose history offers a precedent for feminist scholarship to use.'[7] The idea of critics like Showalter *using* black literature is chilling, a case of barely disguised cultural imperialism. The final insult is that she footnotes the preceding remark by pointing readers to works on black literature by white males Robert Bone and Roger Rosenblatt.

Two recent works by white women, Ellen Moers's *Literary Women: The great writers* and Patricia Meyer Spacks's *The Female Imagination*, evidence the same racist flaw.[8] Moers includes the names of four black and one Puertorriqueña writer in her seventy pages of bibliographical notes and does not deal at all with Third World women in the body of her book. Spacks refers to a comparison between Negroes (sic) and women in Mary Ellmann's *Thinking About Women* under the index entry, 'blacks, women and'. '*Black Boy* (Wright)' is the preceding entry. Nothing follows. Again there is absolutely no recognition that black and female identity ever coexist, specifically in a group of black women writers. Perhaps one can assume that these women do not know who black women writers are, that they have little opportunity like most Americans to learn about them. Perhaps. Their ignorance seems suspiciously selective, however, particularly in the light of the dozens of truly obscure white women writers they are able to unearth. Spacks was herself employed at Wellesley College at the same time that Alice Walker was there teaching one of the first courses on black women writers in the country.

I am not trying to encourage racist criticism of black women writers like that of Sara Blackburn, to cite only one example. As a beginning I would at least like to see in print white women's acknowledgment of the contradictions of who and what are being left out of their research and writing.[9]

Black male critics can also act as if they do not know that black women writers exist and are, of course, hampered by an inability to comprehend black women's experience in sexual as well as racial terms. Unfortunately there are also those who are as virulently sexist in their treatment of black women writers as their white male counterparts. Darwin Turner's discussion of Zora Neale Hurston in his *In a Minor Chord: Three Afro-American writers and their search for identity* is a frightening example of the near assassination of a great black woman writer.[10] His descriptions of her and her work as 'artful', 'coy', 'irrational', 'superficial' and 'shallow' bear no relationship to the actual quality of her achievements. Turner is completely insensitive to the sexual political dynamics of Hurston's life and writing.

In a recent interview, the notoriously misogynist writer, Ishmael Reed, comments in this way upon the low sales of his newest novel:

> but the book only sold 8000 copies. I don't mind giving out the figure: 8000. Maybe if I was one of those young *female* Afro-American writers that are so hot now, I'd sell more. You know, fill my books with ghetto women who can *do no wrong*. … But come on, I think I could have sold 8000 copies by myself.[11]

The politics of the situation of black women are glaringly illuminated by this statement. Neither Reed nor his white male interviewer has the slightest compunction about attacking black women in print. They need not fear widespread public denunciation since Reed's statement is in perfect agreement with the values of a society that hates black people, women and black women. Finally the two of them feel free to base their actions on the premise that black women are powerless to alter either their political or their cultural oppression.

In her introduction to 'A bibliography of works written by American black women' Ora Williams quotes some of the reactions of her colleagues toward her efforts to do research on black women. She writes:

> Others have reacted negatively with such statements as, 'I really don't think you are going to find very much written.' 'Have "they" written anything that is any good?' and 'I wouldn't go overboard with this woman's lib thing.' When discussions touched on the possibility of teaching a course in which emphasis would be on the literature by black women, one response was, 'Ha, ha. That will certainly be the most nothing course ever offered!'[12]

A remark by Alice Walker capsulizes what all the preceding examples indicate about the position of black women writers and the reasons for the damaging criticism about them. In response to her interviewer's question 'Why do you think that the black woman writer has been so ignored in America? Does she have even more difficulty than the black male writer, who perhaps has just begun to gain recognition?' Walker replies:

> There are two reasons why the black woman writer is not taken as seriously as the black male writer. One is that she's a woman. Critics seem unusually ill-equipped to intelligently discuss and analyze the works of black women. Generally, they do not even make the attempt; they prefer, rather, to talk about the lives of black women writers, not about what they write. And, since black women writers are not – it would seem – very likable – until recently they were the least willing worshippers of male supremacy – comments about them tend to be cruel.[13]

A convincing case for black feminist criticism can obviously be built solely upon the basis of the negativity of what already exists. It is far more gratifying, however, to demonstrate its necessity by showing how it can serve to reveal for the first time the profound subtleties of this particular body of literature.

Before suggesting how a black feminist approach might be used to examine a specific work I will outline some of the principles that I think a black feminist critic could use. Beginning with a primary commitment to exploring how both sexual and racial politics and black and female identity are inextricable elements in black women's writings, she would also work from the assumption that black women writers constitute an identifiable literary tradition. The breadth of her familiarity with these writers would have shown her that not only is theirs a verifiable historical tradition that parallels in time the tradition of black men and white women writing in this country, but that thematically, stylistically, aesthetically and conceptually black women writers manifest common approaches to the act of creating literature as a direct result of the specific political, social and economic experience they have been obliged to share. The way, for example, that Zora Neale Hurston, Margaret Walker, Toni Morrison and Alice Walker incorporate the traditional black female activities of rootworking, herbal medicine, conjure and midwifery into the fabric of their stories is not mere coincidence, nor is their use of specifically black female language to express their own and their characters' thoughts accidental. The use of black women's language and cultural experience in books *by* black women *about* black women results in a miraculously rich coalescing of form and content and also takes their writing far beyond the confines of white/male literary structures. The black feminist critic would find innumerable commonalities in works by black women.

Another principle which grows out of the concept of a tradition and which would also help to strengthen this tradition would be for the critic to look first for precedents and insights in interpretation within the works of other black women. In other words she would think and write out of her own identity and not try to graft the ideas or methodology of white/male literary thought upon the precious materials of black women's art. Black feminist criticism would by definition be highly innovative, embodying the daring spirit of the works themselves. The black feminist critic would be constantly aware of the political implications of her work and would assert the connections between it and the political situation of all black women. Logically developed, black feminist criticism would owe its existence to a black feminist movement while at the same time contributing ideas that women in the movement could use.

Black feminist criticism applied to a particular work can overturn previous assumptions about it and expose for the first time its actual dimensions. At the 'Lesbians and literature' discussion at the 1976 Modern Language Association convention Bertha Harris suggested that if in a woman writer's work a sentence refuses to do what it is supposed to do, if there are strong images of women and if there is a refusal to be linear, the result is innately lesbian literature. As usual, I wanted to see if these ideas might be applied to the black women writers that I know and quickly realized that many of their works were, in Harris's sense, lesbian. Not because women are lovers, but because they are the central figures, are positively portrayed and have pivotal relationships with one another. The form and language of these works are also nothing like what white patriarchal culture requires or expects.

I was particularly struck by the way in which Toni Morrison's novels *The Bluest Eye* and *Sula* could be explored from this new perspective.[14] In both works the relationships between girls and women are essential, yet at the same time physical sexuality is overtly expressed only between men and women. Despite the apparent heterosexuality of the female characters, I discovered in re-reading *Sula* that it works as a lesbian novel not only because of the passionate friendship between Sula and Nel, but because of Morrison's consistently critical stance toward the heterosexual institutions of male/female relationships, marriage and the family. Consciously or not, Morrison's work poses both lesbian and feminist questions about black women's autonomy and their impact upon each other's lives.

Sula and Nel find each other in 1922 when each of them is 12, on the brink of puberty and the discovery of boys. Even as awakening sexuality 'clotted their dreams,' each girl desires 'a someone' obviously female with whom to share her feelings. Morrison writes:

> for it was in dreams that the two girls had met. Long before Edna Finch's Mellow House opened, even before they marched through the chocolate halls of Garfield Primary School ... they had already made each other's acquaintance in the delirium of their noon dreams. They were solitary little girls whose loneliness was so profound it intoxicated them and sent them stumbling into Technicolored visions that always included a presence, a someone who, quite like the dreamer, shared the delight of the dream. When Nel, an only child, sat on the steps of her back porch surrounded by the high silence of her mother's incredibly orderly house, feeling the neatness pointing at her back, she studied the poplars and fell easily into a picture of herself lying on a flower bed, tangled in her own hair, waiting for some fiery prince. He approached but never quite arrived. But always, watching the dream along with her, were some smiling sympathetic eyes. Someone as interested as she herself in the flow of her imagined hair, the thickness of the mattress of flowers, the voile sleeves that closed below her elbows in gold-threaded cuffs.
>
> Similarly, Sula, also an only child, but wedged into a household of throbbing disorder constantly awry with things, people, voices and the slamming of doors, spent hours in the attic behind a roll of linoleum galloping through her own mind on a gray-and-white horse tasting sugar and smelling roses in full view of someone who shared both the taste and the speed.
>
> So when they met, first in those chocolate halls and next through the ropes of the swing, they felt the ease and comfort of old friends. Because each had discovered years before that they were neither white nor male, and that all freedom and triumph was forbidden to them, they had set about creating something else to be. Their meeting was fortunate, for it let them use each other to grow on. Daughters of distant mothers and incomprehensible fathers (Sula's because he was dead; Nel's because he wasn't), they found in each other's eyes the intimacy they were looking for. (*Sula*, pp. 51–2)

As this beautiful passage shows, their relationship, from the very beginning, is suffused with an erotic romanticism. The dreams in which they are initially drawn to each other are actually complementary aspects of the same sensuous fairytale. Nel imagines a 'fiery prince' who never quite arrives while Sula gallops like a prince 'on a gray-and-white horse'.[15] The 'real world' of patriarchy requires, however, that they channel this energy away from each other to the opposite sex. Lorraine Bethel explains this dynamic in her essay

'Conversations with ourselves: black female relationships in Toni Cade Bambara's *Gorilla, My Love* and Toni Morrison's *Sula*'. She writes:

> I am not suggesting that Sula and Nel are being consciously sexual, or that their relationship has an overt lesbian nature. I am suggesting, however, that there is a certain sensuality in their interactions that is reinforced by the mirror-like nature of their relationship. Sexual exploration and coming of age is a natural part of adolescence. Sula and Nel discover men together, and though their flirtations with males are an important part of their sexual exploration, the sensuality that they experience in each other's company is equally important.[16]

Sula and Nel must also struggle with the constrictions of racism upon their lives. The knowledge that 'they were neither white nor male' is the inherent explanation of their need for each other. Morrison depicts in literature the necessary bonding that has always taken place between black women for the sake of barest survival. Together the two girls can find the courage to create themselves.

Their relationship is severed only when Nel marries Jude, an unexceptional young man who thinks of her as 'the hem – the tuck and fold that hid his raveling edges' (p. 83). Sula's inventive wildness cannot overcome social pressure or the influence of Nel's parents who 'had succeeded in rubbing down to a dull glow any sparkle or splutter she had' (p. 83). Nel falls prey to convention while Sula escapes it. Yet at the wedding which ends the first phase of their relationship, Nel's final action is to look past her husband toward Sula:

> a slim figure in blue, gliding, with just a hint of a strut, down the path towards the road. ... Even from the rear Nel could tell that it was Sula and that she was smiling; that something deep down in that litheness was amused. (p. 85)

When Sula returns ten years later, her rebelliousness full-blown, a major source of the town's suspicions stems from the fact that although she is almost thirty, she is still unmarried. Sula's grandmother, Eva, does not hesitate to bring up the matter as soon as she arrives. She asks 'When you gone to get married? You need to have some babies. It'll settle you. ... Ain't no woman got no business floatin' around without no man' (p. 92). Sula replies: 'I don't want to make somebody else. I want to make myself' (p. 92). Self-definition is a dangerous activity for any women to engage in, especially a black one, and it expectedly earns Sula pariah status in Medallion.

Morrison clearly points out that it is the fact that Sula has not been tamed or broken by the exigencies of heterosexual family life which most galls the others. She writes:

> Among the weighty evidence piling up was the fact that Sula did not look her age. She was near thirty and, unlike them, had lost no teeth, suffered no

bruises, developed no ring of fat at the waist or pocket at the back of her neck. (p. 115)

In other words she is not a domestic serf, a woman run down by obligatory childbearing or a victim of battering. Sula also sleeps with the husbands of the town once and then discards them, needing them even less than her own mother did, for sexual gratification and affection. The town reacts to her disavowal of patriarchal values by becoming fanatically serious about their own family obligations, as if in this way they might counteract Sula's radical criticism of their lives.

Sula's presence in her community functions much like the presence of lesbians everywhere to expose the contradictions of supposedly normal life. The opening paragraph of the essay 'Woman identified woman' has amazing relevance as an explanation of Sula's position and character in the novel. It asks:

> What is a lesbian? A lesbian is the rage of all women condensed to the point of explosion. She is the woman who, often beginning at an extremely early age, acts in accordance with her inner compulsion to be a more complete and freer human being than her society – perhaps then, but certainly later – cares to allow her. These needs and actions, over a period of years, bring her into painful conflict with people, situations, the accepted ways of thinking, feeling and behaving, until she is in a state of continual war with everything around her, and usually with herself. She may not be fully conscious of the political implications of what for her began as personal necessity, but on some level she has not been able to accept the limitations and oppression laid on her by the most basic role of her society – the female role.[17]

The limitations of the *black* female role are even greater in a racist and sexist society as is the amount of courage it takes to challenge them. It is no wonder that the townspeople see Sula's independence as imminently dangerous.

Morrison is also careful to show the reader that despite their years of separation and their opposing paths, Nel and Sula's relationship retains its primacy for each of them. Nel feels transformed when Sula returns and thinks:

> It was like getting the use of an eye back, having a cataract removed. Her old friend had come home. Sula. Who made her laugh, who made her see old things with new eyes, in whose presence she felt clever, gentle and a little raunchy. (p. 95)

Laughing together in the familiar 'rib-scraping' way. Nel feels 'new, soft and new' (p. 98). Morrison uses here the visual imagery which symbolizes the women's closeness throughout the novel.

Sula fractures this closeness, however, by sleeping with Nel's husband, an act of little import according to her system of values. Nel, of course, cannot understand. Sula thinks ruefully:

> Nel was the one person who had wanted nothing from her, who had accepted all aspects of her. Now she wanted everything, and all because of *that*. Nel was the first person who had been real to her, whose name she knew, who had seen as she had the slant of life that made it possible to stretch it to its limits. Now Nel was one of *them*. (pp. 119–20)

Sula also thinks at the realization of losing Nel about how unsatisfactory her relationships with men have been and admits: 'She had been looking all along for a friend, and it took her a while to discover that a lover was not a comrade and could never be – for a woman' (p. 121). The nearest that Sula comes to actually loving a man is in a brief affair with Ajax and what she values most about him is the intellectual companionship he provides, the brilliance he 'allows' her to show.

Sula's feelings about sex with men are also consistent with a lesbian interpretation of the novel. Morrison writes:

> She went to bed with men as frequently as she could. It was the only place where she could find what she was looking for: *misery and the ability to feel deep sorrow*. ... During the lovemaking she found and needed to find the cutting edge. When she left off cooperating with her body and began to assert herself in the act, particles of strength gathered in her like steel shavings drawn to a spacious magnetic center, forming a tight cluster that nothing, it seemed, could break. *And there was utmost irony and outrage in lying under someone, in a position of surrender, feeling her own abiding strength and limitless power*. ... When her partner disengaged himself, she looked up at him in wonder trying to recall his name ... waiting impatiently for him to turn away ... *leaving her to the postcoital privateness in which she met herself, welcomed herself and joined herself in matchless harmony*. (pp. 122–3) [Italics mine]

Sula uses men for sex which results not in communion with them, but in her further delving into self.

Ultimately the deepest communion and communication in the novel occurs between two women who love each other. After their last painful meeting, which does not bring reconciliation, Sula thinks as Nel leaves her:

> 'So she will walk on down that road, her back so straight in that old green coat ... thinking how much I have cost her and never remember the days when we were two throats and one eye and we had no price.' (p. 147)

It is difficult to imagine a more evocative metaphor for what women can be to each other, the 'pricelessness' they achieve in refusing to sell themselves for male approval, the total worth that they can only find in each other's eyes.

Decades later the novel concludes with Nel's final comprehension of the source of the grief that has plagued her from the time her husband walked out. Morrison writes:

> 'All that time, all that time, I thought I was missing Jude.' And the loss pressed down on her chest and came up into her throat. 'We was girls together,' she said as though explaining something. 'O Lord, Sula,' she cried, 'girl, girl, girlgirlgirl.'
>
>   It was a fine cry – loud and long – but it had no bottom and it had no top, just circles and circles of sorrow. (p. 174)

Again Morrison exquisitely conveys what women, black women, mean to each other. This final passage verifies the depth of Sula and Nel's relationship and its centrality to an accurate interpretation of the work.

Sula is an exceedingly lesbian novel in the emotions expressed, in the definition of female character, and in the way that the politics of heterosexuality are portrayed. The very meaning of lesbianism is being expanded in literature, just as it is being redefined through politics. The confusion that many readers have felt about *Sula* may well have a lesbian explanation. If one sees Sula's inexplicable 'evil' and nonconformity as the evil of not being male-identified, many elements in the novel become clear. The work might be clearer still if Morrison had approached her subject with the consciousness that a lesbian relationship was at least a possibility for her characters. Obviously Morrison did not *intend* the reader to perceive Sula and Nel's relationship as inherently lesbian. However, this lack of intention only shows the way in which heterosexist assumptions can veil what may logically be expected to occur in a work. What I have tried to do here is not to prove that Morrison wrote something that she did not, but to point out how a black feminist critical perspective at least allows consideration of this level of the novel's meaning.

In her interview in *Conditions:One* Adrienne Rich talks about unconsummated relationships and the need to re-evaluate the meaning of intense yet supposedly non-erotic connections between women. She asserts: 'We need a lot more documentation about what actually happened: I think we can also imagine it, because we know it happened – we know it out of our own lives.'[18] Black women are still in the position of having to 'imagine', discover and verify black lesbian literature because so little has been written from an avowedly lesbian perspective. The near non-existence of black lesbian literature which other black lesbians and I so deeply feel has everything to do with the politics of our lives, the total suppression of identity that all black women, lesbian or not, must face. This literary silence is again intensified by the unavailability of an autonomous black feminist movement through which we could fight our oppression and also begin to name ourselves.

In a speech, 'The autonomy of Black lesbian women,' Wilmette Brown comments upon the connection between our political reality and the literature we must invent:

> Because the isolation of Black lesbian women, given that we are super-freaks, given that our lesbianism defies both the sexual identity that capital gives us and the racial identity that capital gives us, the isolation of Black lesbian women from heterosexual Black women is very profound. Very profound. I have searched throughout Black history, Black literature, whatever, looking for some women that I could see were somehow lesbian. Now I know that in a certain sense they were all lesbian. But that was a very painful search.[19]

Heterosexual privilege is usually the only privilege that black women have. None of us have racial or sexual privilege, almost none of us have class privilege, maintaining 'straightness' is our last resort. Being out, particularly out in print, is the final renunciation of any claim to the crumbs of tolerance that nonthreatening ladylike black women are sometimes fed. I am convinced that it is our lack of privilege and power in every other sphere that allows so few black women to make the leap that many white women, particularly writers, have been able to make in this decade, not merely because they are white or have economic leverage, but because they have had the strength and support of a movement behind them.

As black lesbians we must be out not only in white society, but in the black community as well, which is at least as homophobic. That the sanctions against black lesbians are extremely high is well illustrated in this comment by black male writer Ishmael Reed. Speaking about the inroads that whites make into black culture, he asserts:

> In Manhattan you find people actively trying to impede intellectual debate among Afro-Americans. The powerful 'liberal/radical/existentialist' influences of the Manhattan literary and drama establishment speak through tokens, like for example that ancient notion of the *one* black ideologue (who's usually a Communist), the *one* black poetess (who's usually a feminist lesbian).[20]

To Reed, 'feminist' and 'lesbian' are the most pejorative terms he can hurl at a black woman and totally invalidate anything she might say, regardless of her actual politics or sexual identity. Such accusations are quite effective for keeping black women writers who are writing with integrity and strength from any conceivable perspective in line, but especially ones who are actually feminist and lesbian. Unfortunately Reed's reactionary attitude is all too typical. A community which has not confronted sexism, because a widespread black feminist movement has not required it to, has likewise not been challenged to examine its heterosexism. Even at this moment I am not convinced that one can write explicitly as a black lesbian and live to tell about it.

Yet there are a handful of black women who have risked everything for truth. Audre Lorde, Pat Parker and Ann Allen Shockley have at least broken ground in the vast wilderness of works that do not exist.[21] Black feminist criticism will again have an essential role not only in creating a climate in which black lesbian writers can survive, but in undertaking the total reassessment of black literature and literary history needed to reveal the black woman-identified women that Wilmette Brown and so many of us are looking for.

Although I have concentrated here upon what does not exist and what needs to be done, a few black feminist critics have already begun this work. Gloria T. Hull at the University of Delaware has discovered in her research on black women poets of the Harlem Renaissance that many of the women who are considered minor writers of the period were in constant contact with each other and provided both intellectual stimulation and psychological support for each other's work. At least one of these writers, Angelina Weld Grimké, wrote many unpublished love poems to women. Lorraine Bethel, a recent graduate of Yale College, has done substantial work on black women writers, particularly in her senior essay, 'This infinity of conscious pain: Blues lyricism and Hurston's black female folk aesthetic and cultural sensibility in *Their Eyes Were Watching God*,' in which she brilliantly defines and uses the principles of black feminist criticism. Elaine Scott at the State University of New York at Old Westbury is also involved in highly creative and politically resonant research on Hurston and other writers.

The fact that these critics are young and, except for Hull, unpublished merely indicates the impediments we face. Undoubtedly there are other women working and writing whom I do not even know, simply because there is no place to read them. As Michele Wallace states in her article 'A Black feminist's search for sisterhood':

> We exist as women who are Black who are feminists, each stranded for the moment, working independently because there is not yet an environment in this society remotely congenial to our struggle – [or our thoughts].[22]

I only hope that this essay is one way of breaking our silence and our isolation, of helping us to know each other.

Just as I did not know where to start I am not sure how to end. I feel that I have tried to say too much and at the same time have left too much unsaid. What I want this essay to do is lead everyone who reads it to examine *everything* that they have ever thought and believed about feminist culture and to ask themselves how their thoughts connect to the reality of black women's writing and lives. I want to encourage in white women, as a first step, a sane accountability to all the women who write and live on this soil. I want most of all for black women and black lesbians somehow not to be so alone. This last will require the most expansive of revolutions as well as many new words to tell us how to make this revolution real. I finally want to express how much easier both my waking and my sleeping hours would be if there were one book in existence that would tell me something specific about my life. One book based in black feminist and black lesbian experience, fiction or nonfiction. Just one work to reflect the reality that I and the black women whom I love are trying to create. When such a book exists then each of us will not only know better how to live, but how to dream.

NOTES

1. Alice Walker, 'In search of our mothers' gardens', *Ms.*, May 1974, and *Southern Exposure 4:4, Generations: Women in the South*, Winter 1977, pp. 60–4.
2. Jerry H. Bryant, 'The outskirts of a new city', *Nation* 12 (November 1973), p. 502.
3. Robert Bone, *The Negro Novel in America* (New Haven: Yale University Press, 1958), p. 180.
4. ibid. (*Knock on Any Door* is a novel by black writer Willard Motley.)
5. Sara Blackburn, 'You still can't go home again', *The New York Times Book Review*, 30 December 1973, p. 3.
6. Elaine Showalter, 'Review essay: literary criticism', *Signs* 2 (Winter 1975), p. 460.
7. ibid., p. 445.
8. Ellen Moers, *Literary Women: The great writers* (Garden City, NY: Anchor Books, 1977); Patricia Meyer Spacks, *The Female Imagination* (New York: Avon Books, 1976).
9. An article by Nancy Hoffman, 'White women, black women: inventing an adequate pedagogy', *Women's Studies Newsletter* 5:1 and 2 (Spring 1977), pp. 21–4, gives valuable insights into how white women can approach the writing of black women.
10. Darwin T. Turner, *In a Minor Chord: Three Afro-American writers and their search for identity* (Carbondale and Edwardsville: Southern Illinois University Press, 1971).
11. John Domini, 'Roots and racism: an interview with Ishmael Reed', *Boston Phoenix*, 5 April 1977, p. 20.
12. Ora Williams, 'A bibliography of works written by American black women', *College Language Association Journal* 15:3 (March 1972), p. 355. There is an expanded book-length version of this bibliography: *American Black Women in the Arts and Social Sciences: A bibliographic survey* (Metuchen, NJ: Scarecrow Press, 1973; rev. and expanded edn, 1978).
13. John O'Brien, ed., *Interviews with Black Writers* (New York: Liveright, 1973), p. 201.
14. Toni Morrison, *The Bluest Eye* (New York: Pocket Books, 1972, 1976, originally published 1970) and *Sula* (New York: Alfred A. Knopf, 1974). All subsequent references to this work will be designated in the text.
15. My sister, Beverly Smith, pointed out this connection to me.
16. Lorraine Bethel, 'Conversations with ourselves: black female relationships in Toni Cade Bambara's *Gorilla, My Love* and Toni Morrison's *Sula*', unpublished paper written at Yale, 1976, 47 pp. (Bethel has worked from a premise similar to mine in a much more developed treatment of the novel.)

17. New York Radicalesbians, 'Woman identified woman', in *Lesbians Speak Out* (Oakland: Women's Press Collective, 1974), p. 87.
18. Elly Bulkin, 'An interview with Adrienne Rich: Part I', *Conditions: One* (April 1977), p. 62.
19. Wilmette Brown, 'The autonomy of Black lesbian women', MS of speech delivered 24 July 1976, Toronto, Canada, p. 7.
20. Domini, 'Roots and racism', p. 18.
21. Audre Lorde, *New York Head Shop and Museum* (Detroit: Broadside, 1974); *Coal* (New York: W. W. Norton, 1976); *Between Our Selves* (Point Reyes, Calif.: Eidolon Editions, 1976); *The Black Unicorn* (New York: W. W. Norton, 1978).

    Pat Parker, *Child of Myself* (Oakland: Women's Press Collective, 1972 and 1974); *Pit Stop* (Oakland: Women's Press Collective, 1973); *Womanslaughter* (Oakland: Diana Press, 1978); *Movement in Black* (Oakland: Diana Press, 1978).

    Ann Allen Shockley, *Loving Her* (Indianapolis: Bobbs-Merrill, 1974).

    There is at least one Black lesbian writers' collective, Jemima, in New York. They do public readings and have available a collection of their poems. They can be contacted c/o Boyce, 41–11 Parsons Blvd., Flushing, NY 11355.
22. Michele Wallace, 'A Black feminist's search for sisterhood', *Village Voice*, 28 July 1975, p. 7.

TWO

Race and gender in the shaping
of the American literary canon:
a case study from the twenties

PAUL LAUTER

The map of American literature which most of us have used was drawn fifty years ago. Its mountains, bumps and flats were charted; its deserts certified unfit for cultural habitation. Only during the past decade, in response to the movements for change of people of color and of women, have we begun to face the task – not systematically undertaken since the 1920s – of resurveying the territory.

That task, the revision of the literary canon, has been necessary because in the 1920s processes were set in motion that virtually eliminated black, white female and all working-class writers from the canon. Institutional as well as theoretical and historiographic factors were involved in that exclusion, and I shall describe some of these shortly. But why is the literary canon of importance and what precisely was the history of its development in the 1920s?

I mean by the 'American literary canon' that set of authors and works generally included in basic American literature college courses and textbooks, and those ordinarily discussed in standard volumes of literary history, bibliography or criticism. Many such books are also available in widely marketed paperback series of 'classics'. Obviously, no conclave of cultural cardinals establishes a literary canon, but for all that it exercises substantial influence. For it encodes a set of social norms and values; and these, by virtue of its cultural standing, it helps endow with force and continuity. Thus, although we cannot ascribe to a literary canon the decline in attention to the concerns of women in the 1920s, the progressive exclusion of literary works by women from the canon suggested that such concerns were of lesser value than those inscribed in canonical books and authors. The literary canon is, in short, a means by which culture validates social power.

A study of the origins of the American literary canon, then, is not simply an antiquarian exercise. Changing the canon has over the past decade become a major objective of literary practitioners of women's studies, black studies and other 'ethnic' studies – the academic wings of the social movements of the 1960s and 1970s. Fundamental alteration of the canon to include significant numbers of minority and white female writers will both reflect and help spur a widening revaluation of the significance of the experiences with which such writers are often concerned. But the American literary canon will be changed only by conscious literary and organizing efforts. This study is, therefore, part of the groundwork for that effort, an attempt to understand the processes which created the literary canon as most of us know it even today.

What was the history of the canon in the 1920s? In his 1916 preface to *The Chief American Prose Writers*, Norman Foerster wrote that 'the nine writers represented in this volume have become, by general consent, the American prose classics.'[1] Over forty years later, with – I must believe – a certain sense of irony, Foerster wrote in the preface to *Eight American Writers*: 'In the consensus of our time eight writers – Poe, Emerson, Thoreau, Hawthorne, Melville, Whitman, Mark Twain and Henry James – constitute our American Classics.'[2] Only Poe, Emerson and Hawthorne were common to both lists. We are relatively familiar with the changes of taste that, largely in the decade following World War I, devalued Benjamin Franklin, Washington Irving, James Fenimore Cooper, William Cullen Bryant, James Russell Lowell, Henry Wadsworth Longfellow, Oliver Wendell Holmes, as well as John Greenleaf Whittier, Sidney Lanier, William Dean Howells, to name but a few. Those changes of taste also rescued Melville from obscurity, elevated Twain and James, as well as Thoreau – particularly certain of their works – and eventually focused serious attention on Emily Dickinson. Less familiar is the literary or canonical history of white women and black and working-class writers of both sexes.[3]

The 1920s witnessed, as we know, a flourishing of literary work by black as well as by white writers. African Americans, as is often forgotten, had previously produced a substantial body of literary art, in the form of songs, tales and slave narratives, as well as in more 'formal' styles.[4] Newly crowded into urban ghettos, pushed back from the activism of a decade of struggle for civil and political rights, subjected to white curiosity about their supposed 'exotic' qualities, black authors and singers generated a significant literary renaissance in the 1920s. Substantial collections of black writings were issued in that decade and during the 1930s,[5] and at least some black writers managed to make a living from their trade. These facts were in no way reflected in the teaching of American literature, in general anthologies or in most critical discussions by whites of the literature of the United States.

It would have been no great revolution to include black writers; even Edmund Clarence Stedman had printed five spirituals and six poems by Paul

Lawrence Dunbar in his *American Anthology, 1787–1900* (Boston: Houghton Mifflin, 1900). Nevertheless, of twenty-one major classroom anthologies (and their numerous revised editions) produced between 1917 and 1950, nine contained no works by black artists; three included only a few spirituals; four contained one black writer each (Dunbar; Phyllis Wheatley, twice; Richard Wright); two printed some spirituals and one black writer (W. E. B. Dubois; Countee Cullen – who is dropped in a revised edition). Only three somewhat unusual anthologies included the work of more than one black writer – never more than three – as well as a few spirituals or work songs.[6] General and classroom poetry anthologies reveal a similar pattern. Conrad Aiken's Modern Library volumes, *Twentieth-Century American Poetry* (1927, 1944) and *A Comprehensive Anthology of American Poetry* (1929, 1944), included no black poets, although the latter was advertised as 'a newly edited anthology that includes every American poet of note from the seventeenth century to the present day.' Oscar Williams's 'Little Treasuries' (Scribner's) of *Modern Poetry* and of *American Poetry* (1946, 1952) similarly omitted black poets, although the latter did include a section devoted to 'American Indian Poetry'. F. O. Matthiessen's 1950 version of the *Oxford Book of American Verse* eliminated the one black poet, Dunbar, who had been included in Bliss Carman's 1927 version.

The most notable exceptions to this pattern are Alfred Kreymborg's 1930 *Lyric America* (Tudor Publishing; also called *An Anthology of American Poetry*), which included the work of seven black men, and Louis Untermeyer's *Modern American Poetry* (Harcourt, Brace). Untermeyer's editing exemplifies the rise and fall of interest in black writers. His first two editions (1919 and 1921) contained poems by Dunbar, joined in the 1925 version by Countee Cullen, James Weldon Johnson, Claude McKay and Alex Rogers, and then later by Langston Hughes and Jean Toomer. By the 1942 sixth edition, however, only Dunbar, Johnson, Cullen and Hughes remained; the seventh edition witnessed the elimination of Dunbar. The general and poetry anthologies uniformly omitted all black women with the solitary and rare exception of Phyllis Wheatley.

Similarly, Jay Hubbell's 987-page history, *The South in American Literature: 1607–1900*, consciously excludes black writers as 'northern' and outside the book's chronology, although it includes other distinctly northern and twentieth-century writers. The index conveys the operative view of African-American writing: apart from a few miscellaneous entries, the index is limited to 'See also Abolitionists, folk songs, folklore, and slavery'.[7] More recent anthologies and critical works do, of course, include some black writers, but fundamental organizing principles have seldom been altered to accommodate the fact that the significant literary work of African Americans cannot be understood as an expression of 'European culture' in an 'American environment' – to use Norman Foerster's formulation.[8]

The position of white women writers in the formation of the canon is rather more complex: some perspective is gained by examining the work of one of the earliest professors of American literature, Fred Lewis Pattee. Pattee's anthology, *Century Readings for a Course in American Literature*, first published in 1919, reflects his appreciation of women writers; it includes work by Harriet Beecher Stowe, Mary Wilkins Freeman, Sarah Orne Jewett, Helen Hunt Jackson, Rose Terry Cooke, Constance Fenimore Woolson and even Emma Lazarus, among many other women writers. In *The New American Literature* (1930), Pattee praised Willa Cather, Edith Wharton, Ellen Glasgow and Zona Gale, in particular.

> The work of these women marks the highest reaches to which the novel of characterization and manners has attained in America during our period. Perhaps no literary phenomenon in our history has been more noteworthy than this feminine assumption of leadership. The creation of fiction in most of its areas has proved to be an art adapted peculiarly for the powers of women. Feminine success has, however, come also from another peculiar fact: woman has surpassed her male competitors in workmanship, in artistry, in the quality of work toiled over and finished – she has been compelled to do this because of an age-old conception or prejudice. Her success has raised fiction-writing during the period to the rank of a new regular profession for women.[9]

A few years later, another member of the older generation of professors, Arthur Hobson Quinn, in his 1936 *American Fiction*, devoted chapters to Gale, Mary Austin, Dorothy Canfield and Susan Glaspell, as well as substantial sections to Cooke, Stowe, Elizabeth Stoddard, Rebecca Harding Davis and Elizabeth Stuart Phelps.[10]

Nevertheless, the first edition of Howard Mumford Jones and Ernest E. Leisy's *Major American Writers*, which was issued in 1935, contains no work by women whatsoever, although it includes such luminaries as William Byrd, Philip Freneau, Bret Harte and Sidney Lanier, as well as all the traditional schoolroom poets of New England. In later editions, Jones and Leisy admitted Dickinson to their canon, joined in solitude by Glasgow.[11] By 1948, when the National Council of Teachers of English (NCTE) reviewed American literature in the college curriculum, only three women appeared in the ninety syllabi of survey courses studied. Dickinson appeared in twenty-four of these courses; that placed her seventeenth on the list, tied with Holmes and Cooper, but behind Whittier, Lowell, Bryant, Longfellow and others. The other women were the last two writers listed; Wharton (number thirty-six) appeared in five courses of the ninety surveyed; Cather (number thirty-seven) appeared four times. Before both of them came Frank Norris, Hamlin Garland, Theodore Dreiser, Mather (presumably Cotton), William Bird, Abraham Lincoln, Bret Harte and Jonathan Edwards.[12] Ben W. Fuson's 1952 study of twenty-seven American literature anthologies shows significant representation of only six women among seventy authors whose works are substantially covered. In all, women represent no more than 13.7 per cent and as little as 3.2 per cent of the writers in these anthologies, on average about 8 per cent. The proportion of women is often related to the proportion of what Fuson calls 'borderline' or non-*belles lettres* items.[13] One 1950 collection, edited by Lyon Norman Richardson, G. H. Orians, and H. R. Brown, recognized that a need already existed for giving 'special attention to a reconsideration of the works of our women authors'.[14]

These academic opinions and statistics reflect a cultural reality which had developed perhaps a decade before. Interest in many of the novelists praised by Pattee and Quinn had begun to decline some time before the critics of the 1920s wrote about them. After all, to cite a reversed instance of the lag between social change, cultural consciousness and academic revision, it took fifteen years after *Brown v. Board of Education* and a decade after the sit-ins began to achieve even token representation of black writers in contemporary anthologies.[15] The essentially nineteenth-century tastes of Pattee and Quinn and their concerns for gentility did not survive the 1920s.[16] Since women were seen as the preservers of gentility and women writers as its promoters, the change in literary taste helped ensure their exclusion from the canon.

Thus, as the NCTE survey accurately shows, by the end of the 1950s, one could study American literature and read no work by a black writer, few works by women except Dickinson and perhaps Marianne Moore or Katherine Anne Porter, and no work about the lives or experiences of working-class people.

How can we account for such a development? Three important factors may be responsible: the professionalization of the teaching of literature, the development of an aesthetic theory that privileged certain texts and the historiographic organization of the body of literature into conventional 'periods' and 'themes'.

The proliferation of American literary anthologies that began in the 1920s was a product of the expansion of higher education generally. More particularly the anthologies reflected that American literature had become a legitimate subject for academic study only after World War I. Courses in American literature had seldom been taught in schools and colleges before the last decade of the nineteenth century; classroom anthologies and American literature texts began to appear only after the turn of the century. The dominant view of the cultivated was that American letters were a branch – a shaky one at that – of the British stock.[17] In the decade prior to 1915, there were four articles on American literature out of perhaps 250 in *The Publications of the Modern Language Association (PMLA)*. The American Literature Group, now one of the Modern Language Association's largest, began in 1921 with a meeting attended by only a handful of professors. By 1928, however, that group had been responsible for publishing the influential *Reinterpretation of American Literature*; and by 1929, for starting the magazine *American Literature*. Although the subject remained something of an academic stepchild, it was a major topic of concern for literati from H. L. Mencken to Virginia Woolf.

The survey courses, the anthologies, the professional specialization all contributed to the academic institutionalization of reading choices. What had been the function of individuals, of families, or of literary clubs and certain magazines – choosing books to be remembered and read, building culture and taste – became the purview of the classroom. Even on college campuses prior to 1920, and certainly in communities, a good deal of literary study, particularly of contemporary authors, was carried on within literary societies, mainly female. (The campus men's societies were concerned primarily with debating and oratory; off-campus men's clubs, whatever else they were, were *not* literary.) My own research indicates that on campus in the 1920s reading choices were increasingly 'suggested' by professors; indeed, formal courses began to absorb what had earlier been talked about 'in society'. By the 1930s, if they still existed, campus literary societies met to play bridge and to get up theatre parties. Community literary societies continued, much diminished, but the taste of participants was likely to have already been formed in college. Thus, in significant measure, influence over reading shifted before the 1930s from women who were not academic professionals to academics, the great majority of whom were white and male. And reading choices moved significantly away from the range of female writers – Mary Austin to Sigrid Undset – who had been a staple of most women's literary clubs.[18]

Demographic factors were also at work, as historian Laurence Veysey has pointed out. The proportion 'of the mature working-age population in America' who were college and university professors and librarians was rising 'spectacularly' in the decades leading to 1920 – especially in relation to older, static learned professionals, like doctors, lawyers and the clergy. Although they constituted only a tiny portion of people at work, professors had enormously larger impact 'as the universities increasingly took over training for a wide variety of prestigious occupations'. In fact, Veysey writes that

> the social effect of intellectual specialization [occurring in universities among other areas of American life] was to transfer authority, most critically over the printed word and what was taught in colleges to sons and daughters of the elite, away from the cultivated professions considered as an entirety and toward a far smaller, specially trained segment within them, those who now earned Ph.D. degrees. ... Concretely, this meant vesting such authority in a group that, as of 1900, numbered only a few hundred persons spread across the humanistic fields. The immediate effect was thus the intensification of elitism as it was transferred onto a new academic basis. A double requirement was now imposed – intellectual merit, at least of a

certain kind, defined far more rigorously, as well as a continuing expectation of social acceptability.[19]

In short, the professoriat exercised increasing control of the definition of a 'literate' reader, including those who were to become the next generation's writers.[20]

The social base of that professoriat was small. The professors, educators, critics, the arbiters of taste of the 1920s, were, for the most part, college-educated white men of Anglo-Saxon or northern European origins. They came, that is, from that tiny, élite portion of the population of the United States which, around the turn of the century, could go to college. Through the first two decades of the new century, this dominant élite had faced a quickening demand for some power and control over their lives from Slavic, Jewish, Mediterranean and Catholic immigrants from Europe, as well as from black immigrants from the rural South. Even women had renewed their demand for the vote, jobs, control over their bodies. The old élite and their allies moved on a variety of fronts, especially during and just after World War I, to set the terms on which these demands would be accommodated. They repressed, in actions like the Prohibition Amendment and the Palmer raids, the political and social, as well as the cultural, institutions of immigrants and of radicals. They reorganized schools and professionalized elementary and secondary school curriculum development, in significant measure as a way to impose middle-class American 'likemindedness' on a heterogeneous, urban, working-class population.[21] Similarly, calling it 'professionalization', they reorganized literary scholarship and teaching in ways that not only asserted a male-centered culture and values for the college-educated leadership, but also enhanced their own authority and status as well.[22]

The Modern Language Association, for example, underwent a major reorganization just after World War I, the effect of which was to concentrate professional influence in the hands of groups of specialists, most of whom met at the annual convention. The convention thus took on much greater significance, practically and symbolically in terms of defining professional leadership. As professionalism replaced gentility, the old all-male 'smoker' at the convention was discontinued. With it also disappeared a female and, on occasion, modestly feminist institution: the ladies' dinner. We do not fully know how, or even in this instance whether, such institutions provided significant support for women scholars, nor do we know what was lost with their disappearance in the 1920s.[23] Clearly, women were left without any significant organizational base within the newly important convention. For when, in 1921, specialized groups were established for MLA conventions, women's roles in them were disproportionately small, minor and largely confined.[24] If the men gave up the social institution that had helped sustain their control, they replaced it with professional authority in the new groups. Not only were women virtually excluded from leadership positions in them and given few opportunities to read papers, but they also appear to have been pushed toward – as men were certainly pushed away from – subject areas considered 'peripheral' to the profession. For example, folk materials and works *by* women became particularly the province *of* women – as papers, dissertation topics and published articles illustrate.[25]

As white women were excluded from the emerging scholarly power structures, and blacks – female or male – were kept almost entirely ghettoized in black colleges, 'their subjects', women and blacks, remained undeveloped in a rapidly developing profession. For example, in the first ten years of its existence, *American Literature* published twenty-four full articles (as distinct from Notes and Queries or Reviews) by women scholars out of a total of 208. Nine of these appeared in the first two volumes, and a number of women published more than once. An article on Dickinson appeared in volume 1, and others in volumes 4 and 6. These apart, the *only* article on a woman writer until volume 10 was one on American comments, mostly by men, on George Sand. In volume 10 one finds a piece, by a male scholar, on Cather, as well as another trying to show that Ann Cotton derived her material from husband John. It is not, I should add, that the journal confined itself to 'major' writers or to authors from the early or mid-nineteenth century. Quite the contrary, it ran pieces on stalwarts like John Pendleton Kennedy, not to speak of *Godey's Ladies' Book*, as well as articles dealing with a number of twentieth-century male authors.

While professionalization was thus erecting institutional barriers against women, their status was being attacked in other ways. Joan Doran Hedrick has shown how the ideology of domesticity and the bogey of 'race suicide', which re-emerged around the turn of the century, was used during the next thirty years to attack women teachers, both the proverbial spinster schoolmarm and the female college professor.[26] The extent to which such attacks arose from the pressure of job competition, general political conservatism, antisuffrage backlash or other factors is not yet clear. It was true, however, that women had not only been competing more and more effectively for positions in the humanities, but also that the predominance of women students in undergraduate literature courses had long worried the male professoriat. In 1909, for example, the chairman of the MLA's Central Division had devoted his address to the problem of 'Coeducation and literature'. He wondered whether the predominance of women taking literary courses 'may not contribute to shape the opinion that literature is preeminently a study for girls, and tend to discourage some men. ... This is not yet saying,' he continued, 'that the preference of women turns away that of men. There are many factors to the problem. But it looks that way.' How, he asked, can we deal with the problem that the 'masculine ideal of culture' has largely rejected what the modern languages, and we as its professors, have to offer? 'What may we teachers do more or better than we have done to gain for the humanities as represented by literature a larger place in the notion of masculine culture?'[27]

Something of an answer is provided in an unusually frank way in the *Annual Reports* of Oberlin College for 1919–20. In the section on the faculty, Professor Jelliffe, on behalf of Bibliography, Language, Literature and Art, urged the hiring of an additional teacher of composition. He writes:

> In my opinion the new instructor, when appointed, should be a man. Of sixteen sections in Composition only three are at present being taught by men instructors. This is to discredit, in the opinion of our students, the importance of the subject, for despite the excellent teaching being done by the women of the English faculty, the students are quick to infer that the work is considered by the faculty itself of less importance than that to which the men devote their time.[28]

Such ideas, the institutional processes I have described, and other historical forces outside the scope of the paper, gradually eroded the gains women had made in higher education in the decades immediately following the turn of the century. By the early 1920s, women were earning 16 per cent of all doctorates; that proportion gradually declined (except for the war years) to under 10 per cent in the 1950s. Similarly, the proportion of women in the occupational category of college presidents, professors and instructors rose from 6.4 per cent in 1900 to 32.5 per cent around 1930, but subsequently declined to below 22 per cent by 1960.[29] The proportion of women earning advanced degrees in the modern languages and teaching these subjects in colleges was, of course, always somewhat higher, but the decline affected those fields in a similar way. Because more women were educated in these fields, they were particularly vulnerable in the 1930s to cutbacks ostensibly instituted to preserve jobs for male 'breadwinners' or to nepotism regulations newly coined to spread available positions among the men. Not surprisingly, by the 1950s only 19 per cent of the doctorates being earned in the modern languages were awarded to women,[30] a proportion higher than in fields like sociology, history or biology, but significantly lower than it had been thirty years earlier. As a result, the likelihood of one's encountering a female professor even in literature – and especially at élite male or coeducational institutions – was perhaps even slighter than the chances of encountering a female writer.

Blacks, female or male, faced a color line that professionalization did nothing to dispel. Black professors of literature were, for the most part, separated into their own professional organization, the College Language Association, and into positions at segregated black colleges. The color line persisted in *American Literature* so far as articles on black writers were concerned, until 1971, when the magazine printed its first piece, on James Weldon Johnson. The outlook apparently shared by *American Literature*'s editors comes clearest in a brief review (vol. 10 (1938), pp. 112–13) by Vernon

Loggins, then at Columbia, of Benjamin Brawley's collection of *Early Negro American Writers*.

> The volume ... gives a hint of American Negro literature before Dunbar, but scarcely more than a hint. Yet it should be of practical value in American literature courses *in Negro colleges*. Professor Brawley obviously had such an aim in mind in making the compilation. [Italics mine]

Over the years a few articles appeared on images of blacks in the writings of white authors, but in general, as such reviews and notes on scholarly articles make clear, those interested in black writers were effectively referred to the *Journal of Negro History* or to the *College Language Association Journal*.[31]

Although the existence of such black professional organizations and periodicals reflected the pervasiveness of institutional racism in American life, such black-defined groups and magazines like the *Crisis* had at least the advantage of providing black writers and scholars with outlets for and encouragement of their work. Women, especially white professional writers, faced rather a different problem in this period: one can observe a significant shift in cultural authority from female-defined to male-defined institutions – in symbolic terms, one might say, from women's literary societies to *Esquire* magazine. The analogy may, at first, seem far-fetched, but it is probably more accurate than the cartoon view of women's clubs with which we have lived since the 1920s. In fact, the taste of the older generation of genteel professors and magazine editors largely accorded with that of the female literary clubs; the outlook of the new professoriat and *Esquire*, the *Playboy* of its day, largely coincided, at least with respect to the subjects and writers of fiction, as well as to certain conceptions of male camaraderie and culture.[32] To understand why, we must now turn to the aesthetic theories which helped to shape the canon.

Two aesthetic systems, ultimately in conflict, came to dominate literary thought in the 1920s and 1930s. One set of critics viewed literature – or at least some books – as important to reconstructing a 'usable past' consonant with the new role of the United States as a dominating world power. To one degree or another, all the scholars who developed American literature as a field of study were devoted to this objective. Another critical school emphasized the 'aesthetic' or formal qualities of literature – literature as *belles lettres* – above whatever historical interest it might have, or even the values presumably conveyed by it. Indeed, later formalist critics came to disparage the very idea that art – or even criticism – 'conveyed' anything at all. Both nationalist and formalist aesthetics, however disparate, produced a narrowing of the canon.

The American literature professors of the 1920s were, I have suggested, a serious group that asserted national responsibilities. And they presented the tasks of American literature in broad moral terms. In his introduction to *The*

Reinterpretation of American Literature, Norman Foerster posed the work of literary professionals in the context of the international role of the United States. 'The power of America renders it perilous to remain in the dark as to what she really is.' Literature would reveal our culture, for, as Harry Hayden Clark added, 'in the life of the past, as mirrored in literature, there exists a reasonable and dependable guide for a troubled present.'[33] For such aspirations, a focus on domesticity and family, on education and marriage, even on 'love and money', to use Jane Austen's formula, would not do, they felt. The tension for the 'new woman' between work life and family life would also not suffice as a topic of high national seriousness. Women were liberated, it was said, by the vote, a relaxed style of dress, labor-saving devices, a new sexual openness. They could enter most male professions – it was up to them. So the concerns of 'feminist fiction' were no longer relevant.

Besides, a central problem with American literature, or so some seemed to feel, was its 'feminization'. Joseph Hergesheimer, a then-popular if rapidly dated novelist, had attacked 'The feminine nuisance in American literature' in a *Yale Review* article of 1921. Literature in the United States, he claimed (pp. 719–20), 'is being strangled with a petticoat', written primarily for women, without a 'grain of masculine sand'. Hergesheimer's definition of the truly masculine hero provides, in its crude exaggerations, a useful reflection of a developing literary ideal.

I must return to the word vitality, for that alone explains my meaning: such men have perceptibly about them the air, almost the shock, of their force. It is a quality, at bottom, indescribable, without definition, subconscious; and we can do no more than recognize its presence. Such men are attended by a species of magic; they go in direct lines through the impotent turnings of sheep-like human tracks; and as their stay, they have principally that unshakable self-confidence which is condemned as conceit by lesser spirits. It is, therefore, unavoidable that the man I am describing should be, from the absolute standard of normality, abnormal; any wide imagination, any magical brain, is abnormal, with necessities, pressures, powers, altogether beyond the comprehension of the congenital clerk. ... Does anyone think that, laying an arm across the shoulders of his devoted wife, he would explain how he had repudiated the dishonest offer of the Mikado of Japan? Can you see him playing auction bridge in a room twittering like an aviary?[34]

The Bookman, more than any other periodical responsive to the interests of women readers and literary clubs, quickly ran a response from 'the feminist nuisance'.[35] Frances Noyes Hart chided Hergesheimer as ungrateful, in view of his large female readership, and pointed out that she knew of

no group of masculine authors who deal less in manufactured sunshine or specious sweetness and light than the large group of women who are now at the head of their profession in England and America – Ethel Sidgwick, Willa Sibert Cather, Rebecca West, May Sinclair, Edith Wharton, Katharine Fullerton Gerould, Dorothy Richardson, Anne Douglas Sedgwick, Sheila Kaye-Smith, Clemence Dane – I take the names at random; there are at least a score more. They face life in varied ways – some nervewracked and tense, some grateful and ironic, some lusty and ruthless, some shadowed and mysterious, some bitter and defiant – but unquestionably they all face it, with scant truckling to any public thirsting for spurious joy and the conventional happy ending.

By the end of the decade, however, even *The Bookman* had joined the antifemale parade, featuring in its March 1929 (vol. 69) issue a piece by another forgotten novelist, Robert Herrick, somewhat more subtly called 'A feline world'. Herrick begins with what he conceives to be a discovery: that younger women novelists have come to 'disregard the tradition that this is primarily a man's world and have taken to describing boldly their own primary interests, among themselves, for themselves'. He does not, he claims, 'deplore' the tendency; rather, he misses 'the stir of the old-time, standard fiction' of men, 'above all, the talk about politics and bawdy and religion and the reorganizing of our bad, old world ... mature talk even when the characters were very young' (p. 2). George Meredith, Herrick argues, did not confine his fiction 'to the tea table or boudoir or night club', and Hardy was not solely preoccupied 'with emotional subtleties, subjective illusions. Certainly never with purely social reactions and complications.' With Arnold Bennett, Herrick continues, 'we have moved farther along toward feminization ... even the males are feminized; they act and usually talk like women and their chief preoccupations are the petty daily affairs belonging in general to the home' (p. 3).

Herrick's final argument, in a magazine read mainly by women, takes an ugly turn. Women novelists are, he claims, particularly occupied with sex, not bluntly, like their brothers, but with more erotic effect.

> Women know the neurotic sides of sex, which do not eventuate in either marriage or maternity, as well as what once was called (with a hush) the perverted side, the wooing of one's own sex. A disturbing number of recent stories by women deal with this taboo and are not overly vague in the handling of it. We must assume that it interests many of their readers.

Thus the interest of women in women novelists becomes primarily a manifestation of lesbianism. It is only a short step from there to using the label 'feline' to cover everything that manly intellectuals and activists must deplore; the female, feline world becomes identified with intellectual and social reaction, with a rejection of idealism and experimentation, and even with militarism. To be sure, the absurdities of Hergesheimer and Herrick can be dismissed along with Hawthorne's competitive jealousy of that 'damned mob of scribbling women'. Yet they express a widely held set of attitudes, both about women generally and about art. They reflect the other side of the professoriat's concern that a truly American art be attractive to, embody the values of, masculine culture. For, as professors and male novelists seemed to perceive it, the problems of the United States were not to be encountered over the cup of proverbial tea, in reading novelists at once genteel and sensual, or in fretting over village life in Maine or Louisiana. America needed the grand encounters with nature of Melville or even Thoreau, the magical abnormalities of Ahab, the deeper possibilities for corruption Twain and even James in their different ways established. I do not want to overdraw the picture. But as Hergesheimer and Herrick illustrate, I am afraid that I could not. The strenuous nationalism of even the most professional scholars, the masculinist attitudes of otherwise refined novelists, defined the issues for the art of the time as fundamentally distinct from the concerns of the domestic sphere which, it was insisted, were to occupy most women, including most female writers.

These attacks on 'gentility' and 'domesticity' centered, for the most part, on the subject matter of an earlier generation and sought to substitute a more 'masculine' content for art. Still, academic scholars continued to view art as a guide to conduct, although the conduct and values being extolled were quite changed. On the other hand, the generation of literary critics who, following T. S. Eliot, began to come to prominence in the 1920s, were doubtful – if not altogether suspicious – of the power of art to shape behavior at all. Indeed, these writers, led by the American New Critics, felt that civilized values were well on the way to being overwhelmed by mass society, and that the functions of the artists and the man of letters in the modern world were much more defensive than shaping, protective of the remnants of culture rapidly being ground under. What could be defended, if anything, was the value of art itself, and what needed emphasis was not the behavior a work of art promoted, or its subject matter as such, but its language and form, which represented and sustained the best achievements of human creativity.

On the face of it there appears to be no reason why such a formalist aesthetic should narrow the canon in the ways I have indicated. But there are a number of reasons why that was in fact the result. There is, first, the basis on which the 'best' achievements of human creativity are defined. Allen Tate, for example, argues that the presence of tension – 'the full organized body of all the extension and intension that we can find in it' – accounts for the quality of great poetry.[36] Such a definition sets at a discount art which strives for simplicity, transparency and unity in its effects.[37] Obviously, it leads to the preference of 'A valediction: forbidding mourning' over 'Roll, Jordan'. No doubt the spiritual lacks the complex language and ambiguity of John Donne's poem; but then 'A valediction' has never inspired many thousands to survive tyranny. Formalist criteria of excellence developed in the 1920s by critics like

John Crowe Ransom, Cleanth Brooks, R. P. Blackmur and Tate, have emphasized complexity, ambiguity, tension, irony and similar phenomena; such standards are by no means casual. They place a premium on the skills of the literary interpreter: *he* shall unpack the ambiguities and tensions to the uninitiated students, the products of a degraded 'mass education'. Such criteria are thus directly related to the status of the literary critic. To say it another way: what the American scholar may have lost with the decline of the ability of the educated classes to establish standards of conduct shall be rescued by reinvesting 'the man of letters in the modern world' with authority at least over standards of language.

> His critical responsibility is thus ... the recreation and the application of literary standards. ... His task is to preserve the integrity, the purity, and the reality of language wherever and for whatever purpose it may be used. ... The true province of the man of letters is nothing less (as it is nothing more) than culture itself. ... It is the duty of the man of letters to supervise the culture of language, to which the rest of culture is subordinate, and to warn us when our language is ceasing to forward the ends proper to man. The end of social man is communion in time through love, which is beyond time.[38]

Such critical 'authority' over culture has, to be sure, proved illusory, but with respect to the canon it did play a significantly narrowing role.

A second and closely related factor leading to a narrowed canon derives from the critical emphasis upon 'masterpieces', rather than 'tendencies', to use Van Wyck Brooks's 1918 formulation. Focusing on the formal qualities of discrete works of art gradually eroded the earlier scholars' concern for tendencies, for the social and cultural context within which all art is born.[39] In the late 1930s, anthologies like Jones and Leisy's *Major American Writers* began to reflect the narrowing focus to fewer 'major' works by fewer 'major' writers. Successive editions of the highly successful anthology edited by Norman Foerster also show the influence of this trend: between the second and third editions such writers as Stowe, Richard Henry Dana, William Gilmore Simms, Mary Noailles Murfree, Wharton and Dorothy Canfield Fisher were eliminated, as were most of the 'cultural' pieces, including excerpts from the Bay Psalm Book and the New England Primer. Obviously, critics did not propose as a dictum that only white men could be 'major' writers, but it was pre-eminently the works of white males like themselves that they selected.[40] Further, the tide towards certain 'masterpieces', once it set in, could hardly be reversed except through the intervention of forces from outside the literary profession. For two generations or more, literary professionals, brought up under the influence of formalist criticism, knew little or nothing of the work of writers outside the hardening canon and thus had few alternative models – or

standards – for determining noncanonical masterpieces, much less for understanding tendencies.

Both critics and scholars of the period would no doubt have joined in
rejecting such an argument on the grounds that literary masterpieces have the
ability to create their own audiences, to break through existing limits of taste
and perception and to open readers to new experience. In some measure they
would be correct in this rather Romantic conception of the power of art. Yet
people survive, in part, by excluding from awareness much of what presses on
their senses. They selectively screen out these most recent victims of starvation, that student's persistent difficulties, this critic's passion for Gwendolyn
Brooks, that writer's evocation of plantation or domestic experience. It is
natural to do so – one cannot physically or psychologically respond to all
stimuli. But *what* one screens away is by no means natural or inevitable.
Rather, it is a product of particularities of nationality and time, of class and
race and gender, as well as of elements of private life.

The arbiters of taste, scholars and critics alike, were as I have pointed out,
drawn from a narrow stratum of American society. Their experience seldom
included the lives and work about which black writers, for example, wrote.
Indeed, upper-class white Americans in the 1920s acknowledged the lives of
black people, and the work of black writers, only in 'their place' – as 'exotic',
like a taste for Pernod or jazz, a quaint expression of the 'folk'. It was very well
to visit Harlem, but decidedly inappropriate to include blacks in the anthology
or the classroom, much less in the Modern Language Association. As we have
come to learn with the overthrow of the doctrine of 'separate, but equal', if
people need not be dealt with physically, socially, seriously, their experiences
are not likely to be seen as providing a basis for significant art.[41] The literary
canon does not, after all, spring from the brow of the master critic; rather, it is
a social construct. As our understanding of what is trivial or important alters in
response to developments in the society, so our conception of the canon will
change. But that perception has itself been forced on us only by the movements for social change of the 1960s and 1970s. Fifty years ago, the dominant
scholars and critics were able to dismiss lives and art beyond their experience,
concentrating instead on scrutinizing with considerable ingenuity a narrow
range of work. But part of the price was a constricted canon.

The third factor on which I shall touch is historiographic: the conventional
definitions of periods in American literature, which were, in the 1920s,
formulated by men such as Foerster, Brooks and Clark. Many generations of
their students were trained in a sequence involving the 'Puritan Mind',
'Romanticism', the 'Frontier spirit', the 'Rise of realism' – categories which
provide the basis for *The Reinterpretation of American Literature*. Such phrases
have been widely, if loosely, used, both as historical frameworks and as

cultural classifications, and while their popularity diminished in some respects with the rise of formalist criticism and the decline of literary history after the 1930s, they have remained surprisingly influential. They shape significantly the ways in which we think about culture, emphasizing works that fit given frameworks, obscuring those which do not.

In the 1920s, literary historians acknowledged that their work was perhaps a decade behind that of American historians; they used the historians' structures to frame the study of literature and thus the canon. A similar situation exists today: feminist and Third World historians have demonstrated that historical epochs are experienced differently by women and men, by whites and by people of color. To quote Gerda Lerner, for example:

> neither during or after the American revolution nor in the age of Jackson did women share in the broadening out of opportunities and in the political democratization experienced by men. On the contrary, women in both periods experienced status loss and a restriction of their choices as to education or vocation, and had new restraints imposed upon their sexuality, at least by prescription.[42]

The usual divisions of history according to wars or political events turn out to be more relevant to the lives of men than of women; moreover, such divisions are often used less to understand the dynamics of history than as convenient pigeonholes in which to place works in syllabi or anthologies. To review the canon, we must create a usable past, as Brooks advised in 1918. Simply eliminating historical frameworks, as some anthologists and scholars have done in response to the inadequacies of traditional categories, leaves us viewing discrete works in a historical void. New categories can bring into focus, rather than obscure, the experience and culture of people of color and of white women. They allow us to illuminate the interrelationships of culture and other historical forces. And from a practical standpoint, they help us construct new courses and anthologies – like that being developed by the Feminist Press project on Reconstructing American Literature, designed to present and to validate the full range of the literatures of America. Finally, alternative categories provide useful perspectives on the limitations of the traditional formulations by suggesting how different a canon posed in their terms would be. But in a way, we have little choice about proposing different literary categories, for the seams of the old ones simply cannot contain the multitude of previously ignored literary works.

As a historical category, 'Puritanism' has been used to exaggerate the significance of New England, and particularly the male, theocratic portion of it, within the complex tableau of American colonial experience. Focusing on Puritanism, a socioreligious construct, seems largely to have led to the study of the ideology by which a narrow group of male divines construed and confirmed their dominant roles in New England society. Implicitly, the category did not readily lend itself to exploration of the broader contexts of New England family, political and business life, much less to comparisons with cultural development in other English as well as non-English settlements. Emphasizing Puritanism as religious ideology distorted understanding of the witchcraft trials, Anne Hutchinson, colonial family and sex life, and the systematic extermination of 'Indians'. Imposing the label 'Puritanism' on the culture of early New England also obscures the important dynamic of colonization and decolonization, possibly a more helpful tool for framing colonial American history, as V. F. Calverton pointed out fifty years ago.[43]

The colonies embodied many now familiar aspects of settler societies. These included exploitative, if not altogether genocidal, attitudes towards the indigenous population, provincial exaggerations of imported social patterns, and increasingly ambivalent relationships to the parent society. These aspects were reflected in colonial culture, from the myths about the native Americans and the captivity narratives, to the terrors of Charles Brockden Brown, and the late-coming calls for literary decolonization contained in works like Emerson's 'The American scholar' and Margaret Fuller's 'American literature'.[44] I do not pose colonization and decolonization as the only 'correct' historical frameworks for analyzing seventeenth- and eighteenth-century white culture. The terms do seem to me, though, a useful way to understand the general development of culture in the young United States, as well as to illuminate the social origins and functions of Puritan intellectual writings generally examined only in relation to one another. And the concept of colonization and decolonization contains, I think, some inherent intellectual safeguards against the abuses to which the concept of Puritanism seems to have been open.

As an ahistorical cultural category, Puritanism also came in the 1920s to represent a legacy of repression embodied in grim Salem shades and proper Cambridge ladies. Critics like Ludwig Lewisohn celebrated Freudianism as a liberating ideology, enabling a natural sexuality to flourish in life as in literature. The counterposition of Puritanism to Freudianism not only distorted history – for the Puritans were hardly celibate – but often emphasizes a finally puerile issue of libido: 'Does she or doesn't she?' That may give prominence to Henry Miller or some of the sillier parts of Hemingway; but it obscures books like Kate Chopin's *The Awakening*, Edith Summers Kelley's *Weeds*, Agnes Smedley's *Daughter of Earth*[45] more broadly concerned with the contexts for and consequences of sexuality, with the implications of contraception and abortion, the problems of childbearing, the tension between sexuality and work.

Both as a category of history and of culture, then, Puritanism helped produce a distorted canon. A similar problem exists with respect to the category of the 'Frontier Spirit'. The phrase came to be defined in terms exalting male individualism, physical courage, and the honor code of the lone cowhand heroically confronting and triumphing over savagery. Although literary historians achieved some distance on this image of the frontier, they continued to focus on books that described human relationships with nature in terms of confrontation, conquest and exploitation; that omitted what was left back east, where most people still lived; and that produced distorted images of native American 'savages' and white female bearers of 'civilization'. They canonized works that obscured the historical reality of the 'trail of tears', of Indian starvation, of women's loneliness and self-sufficiency. Although recent feminist and native American scholarship has quite altered understanding of the history of the frontier, it is not at all clear that a category like the Frontier Spirit could, even now, be freed of its chauvinist cultural baggage and be used to validate a significantly different canon.

By contrast, 'urbanization' provides a still-relevant historical focus. The major period of urbanization in the United States stretched over the 80 to 100 years during which European and Asian immigrants came to this country, contributing, along with native-born emigrants from the South and other rural areas, to the swelling population of its cities. That process continues today, as Puerto Rican, Haitian, Dominican, Vietnamese, other Hispanic and Asian immigrants come to the United States. The life styles, values and family structures of rural peoples have been and continue to be challenged and changed as they attempt to assimilate to more homogeneous, sophisticated urban styles and to survive economically in an urban industrial environment. That clash of values, that struggle for survival is a central aspect of some of this country's best (yet noncanonical) books: Upton Sinclair's *The Jungle*, William Attaway's *Blood on the Forge*, Harriette Arnow's *The Dollmaker* and Tillie Olsen's *Yonnondio*.[46] Further, although an emphasis on the frontier helps submerge the lives and roles of women (one escapes them to 'light out' for the 'territory'), urbanization is a lens that brings into clear focus the doubly changing roles of women in the family and in work. It provides a fuller vision than the 1920s' emphasis on the frontier, which may have served the purpose of distinguishing the United States from Europe but which also obscured the experience of women, as well as of urbanized immigrant and minority men.

I have suggested two different categories of historical and cultural coherence – colonization/decolonization and urbanization. I wish to add a third cultural category that has characterized all of American history; it is embodied in W. E. B. DuBois's comment that 'the problem of the twentieth century is the problem of the color line'. To focus on the color line is to recognize, in the first place, that among the earliest indigenous literary forms in the United States were those produced by people not of European but of African origins; namely, slave narratives, work and 'sorrow' songs, dialect and other oral tales. These literary works were based in particular historic contexts – slavery, reconstruction, northern migration. That they continue to live is not only a measure of their artistic vitality, but also an indication that the struggles brought alive in Frederick Douglass's *Narrative* of his life, in Charles

Chesnutt's stories and in Gwendolyn Brooks's *Bronzeville*, continue. The art of the color line also produces an especially rich and recurrent image – invisibility. The central metaphor of Ralph Ellison's *Invisible Man*, it is also the theme of Chesnutt's 'The passing of Grandison', and important to Nella Larsen's fiction.

The canon that might have developed from categories like colonization and decolonization, urbanization and the color line differs substantially from the one that did, in fact, emerge from the categories of the 1920s. Although a few of the books and authors I mention as illustrations, like *The Awakening*, have been incorporated into the canon – or at least into anthologies – most have not; some works are even out of print. But the major issue is not assimilating some long-forgotten works or authors into the existing categories; rather, it is reconstructing historical understanding to make it inclusive and explanatory instead of narrowing and arbitrary.

To the extent that the categories I have criticized are historically valid, they raise another issue; the very conception of periodicity. Dividing experience chronologically tends to accentuate the discontinuities rather than the continuities of life. It is something like imagining the world as it is presented in a tabloid newspaper, with its emphasis on the exceptional rather than the commonplace, the ongoing. In some measure, women's lives in patriarchal society have been more fully identified with continuities – birthing, rearing, civilizing children; maintaining family and cultural stability. Indeed, there is some evidence to suggest that the rituals of female experience – regular, periodic, sustained – are culturally distinguishable from those of males. In this regard, emphasizing distinct chronological or literary periods may be one-dimensional, obscuring what is ongoing, continued. The color line persists, although its conventions and the forms of its literary expression are different in colonial and in modern, urbanized society. Urbanization is surprisingly similar over time. The point is simply that social and cultural continuities need to be understood as clearly as the periodic categories that seem to remain useful if the canon is not to be distorted in yet another way.

I have tried to outline a number of the factors that shaped the American literary canon into the rather exclusive form it had even as late as the 1960s. Certain other significant forces – for example, publishing decisions and changes in the publishing industry or the shorter-term impact of popular critics – remain to be examined in detail. But I have found nothing thus far that conflicts with the patterns I have sketched. Indeed, the one dissertation that has examined processes shaping the canon viewed literary scholars in their roles as teachers and anthologists as far more influential than publishers or critics.[47]

It is also important to understand that processes of institutionalization such as I have discussed, development of heavily capitalized anthologies and national marketing of texts – not to speak of academic tradition and inertia – all contribute to the difficulty of changing a canon once it has been formed. For well over a decade now feminist scholars and scholars of color, participants in broad social movements for human rights, have tried to reconstitute the canon. From one point of view, certain progress has been made: the Norton anthology, for example, now includes part of Frederick Douglass's *Narrative* and Kate Chopin's *The Awakening*, among other previously buried works. But it is not so clear that the institutional, aesthetic and historiographic factors which had once served to exclude such works have yet been sufficiently scrutinized, much less fundamentally altered. Thus, what is here presented must be seen as part of a work in progress toward not only a more representative and accurate literary canon, but also toward basic changes in the institutional and intellectual arrangements that shape and perpetuate it.

NOTES

1. Norman Foerster, ed., preface to *The Chief American Prose Writers* (Cambridge, Mass.: Riverside Press, 1916), p. iii.
2. Norman Foerster and Robert P. Falk, eds, preface to *Eight American Writers* (New York: W. W. Norton, 1963), p. xv.
3. I will not, primarily for reasons of space, deal with working-class literature in this article. Some of the earlier anthologies contained sections of popular songs and ballads of the Revolution and the Civil War, an occasional work song and perhaps a selection from Jack London or Upton Sinclair. But little or nothing of working-class or socialist culture of the nineteenth and early twentieth centuries was taken seriously as art. Not until the 1930s, with the resurgence of left-wing cultural institutions in the United States and the development of theories of 'proletarian literature', were the real experiences of working people validated as a basis for literature. And even then, much of what working-class writers themselves produced, in the way of songs and other occasional writings, for example, remained marginal even to progressive literary theorists. Questions concerning the basic characteristics, value and functions of working-class literature remain vexed today. They are discussed in Raymond Williams, *Culture and Society, 1780–1950* (New York: Harper, 1960); Martha Vicinus, *The Industrial Muse* (New York: Barnes & Noble, 1974); Paul Lauter, 'Working-class women's literature: an introduction to study', *Women in Print* 1, ed. Joan Hartman and Ellen Messer-Davidow (New York: Modern Language Association, 1982), pp. 109–34; and Dan Tannacito, 'Poetry of the Colorado miners, 1903–1905', *Radical Teacher* 15 (1980).
4. See, for example, the useful but not exhaustive 'Select chronology of Afro-American prose and poetry, 1760–1970' in *Afro-American Writing*, ed. Richard A. Long and Eugenia W. Collier (New York: New York University Press, 1972), 1, pp. xix–xlii; Dorothy B. Porter, *North American Negro Poets: A bibliographical checklist of their writing (1760–1944)* (1945; reprinted New York: Burt Franklin, 1963); and Ora Williams, *American Black Women in the Arts and Social Sciences: A bibliographical survey*, rev. and enl. edn (Metuchen, NJ: Scarecrow Press, 1978).

5. For example, Robert T. Kerlin, *Contemporary Poetry of the Negro* (1921; reprinted Freeport, NY: Books for Libraries Press, 1971); James Weldon Johnson, ed., *The Book of American Negro Poetry* (New York: Harcourt, Brace, 1922); Robert T. Kerlin, *Negro Poets and Their Poems* (Washington, DC: Associated Publishers, 1923); Newman Ivey White and Walter Clinton Jackson, eds, *An Anthology of Verse by American Negroes* (Durham, NC: Trinity College Press, 1924); Countee Cullen, ed., *Caroling Dusk* (New York: Harper & Row, 1927); Alain Locke, ed., *Four Negro Poets* (New York: Simon & Schuster, 1927); V. F. Calverton, ed., *An Anthology of American Negro Literature* (New York: Modern Library, 1929); Otelia Cromwell, Lorenzo Dow Turner and Eva B. Dykes, eds, *Readings from Negro Authors* (New York: Harcourt, Brace, 1931).

6. The anthologies consulted are the following: W. R. Benet and N. H. Pearson, eds, *The Oxford Anthology of American Literature* (New York: Oxford University Press, 1938); Walter Blair, Theodore Hornberger and Randall Stewart, eds, *The Literature of the United States* (Glenview, Ill.: Scott, Foresman, 1946); Percy H. Boynton, ed., *Milestones in American Literature* (Boston and New York: Ginn, 1923); Oscar Cargill, Robert E. Spiller, Tremaine McDowell, Louis Wann and John Herbert Nelson, eds, *American Literature: A period anthology*, 5 vols (New York: Macmillan, 1933); Joe Lee Davis, John T. Frederich and Frank L. Mott, eds, *American Literature* (New York: Charles Scribner's Sons, 1948); Milton Ellis, Louise Pound and George Weida Spohn, eds, *A College Book of American Literature* (New York: American Book Co., 1939); Norman Foerster, ed., *American Poetry and Prose* (Boston: Houghton Mifflin, 1923, 1934, 1947, 1962); James D. Hart and Clarence Gohdes, eds, *American Literature* (New York: Dryden Press, 1955); Jay B. Hubbell, ed., *American Life in Literature* (New York: Harper, 1936, 1949); Howard Mumford Jones and E. E. Leisy, eds, *Major American Writers* (New York: Harcourt, Brace, 1939, 1945); Ludwig Lewisohn, ed., *Creative America* (New York: Harper, 1933); Alfred E. Newcomer, Alice E. Andrews and Howard Judson Hall, eds, *Three Centuries of American Poetry and Prose* (Chicago: Scott, Foresman, 1917); Fred Lewis Pattee, ed., *Century Readings for a Course in American Literature* (New York: Century, 1919, 1922, 1926, 1931); L. W. Payne, Jr, ed., *Selections from Later American Writers* (Chicago: Rand McNally, 1926); Henry A. Pochmann and Gay Wilson Allen, eds, *Masters of American Literature* (New York: Macmillan, 1949); Arthur Hobson Quinn, Albert Baugh and W. D. Howe, eds, *The Literature of America* (New York: Odyssey, 1926); Franklyn B. Snyder and Edward D. Snyder, eds, *A Book of American Literature* (New York: Macmillan, 1927, 1935); William Thorp, Merle Curti and Carlos Baker, eds, *The Library Record*, vol. 2 of *American Issues* (New York: Lippincott, 1941); Harry R. Warfel, Ralph Henry Gabriel and Stanley T. Williams, eds, *The American Mind* (New York: American Book Co., 1937); W. Tasker Witham, ed., *Masterpieces of American Literature*, vol. 2 of *Living American Literature* (New York: Stephen Daye Press, 1947).

   By contrast, Bernard Smith's *The Democratic Spirit* (New York: Knopf, 1941) includes work by Frederick Douglass, W. E. B. DuBois, James Weldon Johnson, Claude McKay, Countee Cullen, Langston Hughes and Richard Wright. Smith, who was active on the Left, saw 'democratic writers' as constituting the central literary tradition of the United States.

7. Jay Hubbell also devotes ten pages to that eminent 'southerner', Ralph Waldo

Emerson, as well as chapters to Stowe and the white dialect 'humorists'. *The South in American Literature, 1607–1900* (Durham, NC: Duke University Press, 1934). The seventeen-volume *Library of Southern Literature*, ed. Edwin A. Alderman, Joel Chandler Harris and Charles W. Kent (Atlanta: Martin & Hoat, 1907–23), contains many 'dialect stories' by white writers like Harris, Thomas Dixon and Thomas Nelson Page, but no work by a black person. Frederick Douglass is included in the 'Biographical dictionary of authors', but not in the bibliography of works or in the Historical Chart. The index contains references to 'Negro Dialect, Life, Character, and Problems (see also Slavery)' and 'Negro Song (verse)', which turns out to be a single poem, but no other reference to a black author.

8. Norman Foerster, 'American Literature', *Saturday Review of Literature* 2 (3 April 1926): p. 678.

9. Fred Lewis Pattee, *The New American Literature* (New York: Century, 1930), p. 268.

10. Arthur Hobson Quinn, *American Fiction* (New York: D. Appleton-Century, 1936). Quinn had been working on this book for many years; it thus reflects a taste formed some decades earlier.

11. Howard Mumford Jones and Ernest E. Leisy, eds, *Major American Writers*, rev. and enl. edn (New York: Harcourt, Brace, 1945). It was suggested privately to me by a person who knew the editors that the choice of Glasgow was influenced by an editor's friendship with her.

12. Committee on the College Study of American Literature and Culture, William G. Crane, chairperson, *American Literature in the College Curriculum* (Chicago: National Council of Teachers of English, 1948), p. 27.

13. Ben W. Fuson, *Which Text Shall I choose for American Literature? A descriptive and statistical comparison of currently available survey anthologies and reprint series in American literature* (Parkville, Mo.: Park College Press; distributed in co-operation with the College English Association, 1952).

14. Lyon Norman Richardson, G. H. Orians, and H. R. Brown, eds, *The Heritage of American Literature* (Boston: Ginn, 1951).

15. The lag in secondary schools, where bureaucratic forms and political control were established early and elaborately, is far greater, as was attested by the three or even four generations of American schoolchildren for whom 'the modern novel' was represented by *Silas Marner, The Rise of Silas Lapham* and *Ethan Frome*.

16. In reviewing Carl van Doren's *American Literature: An introduction* (Los Angeles: US Library Association, 1933), for example, Pattee writes:

> It seems to be the fashion now to exclude from the roll of American authors of major importance all who were not ... shockers of *hoi polloi* readers who are old-fashioned in taste and morals. Van Doren's little volume excludes Bryant, Longfellow, Whittier, Holmes, Lowell, Stowe, Harte and the like, and fills one fourth of his space with Emily Dickinson, Henry Adams, Mencken, Cabell, Dreiser, Lewis, Paine, Poe, Melville, Thoreau, Whitman, Mark Twain and Emerson. (*American Literature* 5 (January 1934), pp. 379–80)

17. American letters, wrote Henry S. Pancoast (in *An Introduction to American Literature* (New York, 1898), p. 2), are only 'the continuation of English literature within the limits of what has become the United States, by people English in their speech,

English to a considerable extent by inheritance, and English in the original character of their civilization'. Pancoast quoted in Howard Mumford Jones, *The Theory of American Literature*, rev. edn (Ithaca: Cornell University Press, 1965), p. 98. Even Virginia Woolf pointed out that Emerson, Lowell and Hawthorne 'drew their culture from our books'. See Woolf, 'American fiction', *Saturday Review of Literature* 2 (1 August 1925). On the early development of courses in American literature, and the resistance to them, see, for example, Fred Lewis Pattee, *Tradition and Jazz* (New York: Century, 1925), pp. 209–19.

18. These generalizations are based upon research I have been conducting for a book on the origins of the American literary canon. At this writing, I have examined the papers of over a dozen such literary societies as well as materials from and for such clubs provided by periodicals such as *Bookman*.

19. Laurence Veysey, 'The humanities, 1860–1920', typescript of paper for volume on the professions, c. 1974, pp. 21, 24.

20. Pattee remarks that 'American literature today is in the hands of college-educated men and women. The professor has molded the producers of it'. See Pattee, *Tradition and Jazz*, p. 237.

21. Barry M. Franklin, 'American curriculum theory and the problem of social control, 1918–1938' (paper presented at the Annual Meeting of the American Educational Research Association, Chicago, 15–19 April 1974), ERIC, ED 092 419. Franklin quotes Edward A. Ross, *Principles of Sociology* (New York: Century, 1920): 'Thoroughly to nationalize a multitudinous people calls for institutions to disseminate certain ideas and ideals. The Tsars relied on the blue-domed Orthodox church in every peasant village to Russify their heterogeneous subjects, while we Americans rely for unity on the "little red school house".'

22. Whatever its ostensible objectives, in practice, professionalization almost invariably worked to the detriment of female practitioners – and often female 'clients' as well. The details of this argument have been most fully worked out for medicine; see, for example, Barbara Ehrenreich and Deirdre English, *Complaints and Disorders: The sexual politics of sickness* (Old Westbury, NY: Feminist Press, 1973), and *For Her Own Good: One hundred and fifty years of the experts' advice to women* (New York: Pantheon, 1979). See also Janice Law Trecker, 'Sex, science and education', *American Quarterly* 26 (October 1974): pp. 352–66; and Margaret W. Rossiter, *Women Scientists in America: Struggles and strategies to 1940* (Baltimore: Johns Hopkins University Press, 1982), especially the chapters titled 'A manly profession', pp. 73–99, which includes a wonderful discussion of the professionally exclusionary function of the male 'smoker', and 'Academic employment: protest and prestige', pp. 160–217.

23. The ladies' dinner had disappeared by 1925. A good deal of work on female cultures of support has recently been published, beginning with Carroll Smith-Rosenberg, 'The female world of love and ritual: relations between women in nineteenth-century America', *Signs* 1 (Autumn 1975), pp. 1–27. In another professional field, history, women apparently felt so excluded from the mainstream and in need of mutual support that in 1929 they formed the Berkshire Conference of Women Historians, an institution extended in the 1970s to include sponsorship of a large conference on women's history. In most academic fields, however, while the proportion of *individual* women obtaining doctorates might have increased or

been stable during the 1920s, female-defined *organizations* seem virtually to have disappeared – and with them, I suspect, centers for women's influence.

24. From 1923 on, the MLA gathered in what was called a 'union' meeting, rather than in separate conventions of the Eastern, Central and Pacific divisions – another indication of the new importance of the convention. That year 467 registered as attending the session. Fifty-nine women attended the ladies' dinner; some of the women were probably wives and other women members probably did not attend. About 24 per cent of the MLA members were female; very likely a smaller proportion attended the convention. Among the divisions and sections there were 37 male chairpersons, and 1 female, Louise Pound, who chaired the Popular Culture section. There were 29 male secretaries, and 1 woman, Helen Sandison, served as secretary for two sections. Of the 108 papers, 6 were delivered by women.

    In 1924, 978 persons registered, and 121 women went to the ladies' dinner. There continued to be 1 female chairperson, Louise Pound, and now 43 men. The female secretarial corps had increased to 5, Helen Sandison still serving twice, and 'Mrs Carleton Brown' now serving as secretary for the Phonetics section. Of the 128 papers, 7 were by women.

    In *PMLA*, the proportion of women remained, relatively, much higher. In 1924, women were 7 of 47 authors; in 1925, 9 of 47; and in 1926, 11 of 55.

25. For example, of those seven papers delivered by women in the 1924 MLA meeting, two were in Popular Literature, two on Phonetics – where, perhaps not incidentally, women were officers – one in American Literature. Similarly, the entry for American Literature prepared by Norman Foerster for the 1922 American Bibliography (*PMLA*, 1923) contains one paragraph devoted to works about Indian verse, black writers and popular ballads. Four of the scholars cited in this paragraph are women, 5 are men. Otherwise, 58 men and 9 women scholars are cited in the article. Of the 9 women, 2 wrote on women authors, 2 are cobibliographers and 1 wrote on Whittier's love affair.

26. Joan Doran Hedrick, 'Sex, class, and ideology: the declining birthrate in America, 1870–1917', unpublished MS, c. 1974. Hedrick demonstrates that many of the sociologists and educators who developed the idea of utilizing curriculum for social control were involved with the supposed problem of 'race suicide' and active in efforts to restrict immigration as well as to return women to the home.

27. A. G. Canfield, 'Coeducation and literature', *PMLA* 25 (1910), pp. lxxix–lxxx, lxxxiii.

28. *Annual Reports of the President and the Treasurer of Oberlin College for 1919–20* (Oberlin, Ohio: Oberlin College, 10 December 1920), pp. 231–2.

29. Rudolph C. Blitz, 'Women in the professions, 1870–1970', *Monthly Labor Review* 97 (5 May 1974): pp. 37–8. See also Pamela Roby, 'Institutional barriers to women students in higher education', in *Academic Women on the Move*, ed. Alice S Rossi and Ann Calderwood (New York: Russell Sage Foundation, 1973), pp. 37–40; and Michael J. Carter and Susan Boslego Carter, 'Women's recent progress in the professions, or, Women get a ticket to ride after the gravy train has left the station', *Feminist Studies* 7 (Fall 1981), pp. 477–504.

30. Laura Morlock, 'Discipline variation in the status of academic women', in *Academic Women on the Move*, pp. 255–309.

31. In 1951, the Committee on Trends in Research of the American Literature Group

circulated a report on research and publications about American authors during 1940–50, together with some notes on publications during the previous decade. For the 1885–1950 period, the report (basing itself on categories established by the *Literary History of the United States*) provided information on ninety-five 'major authors'. Of these, four were black: Charles Chesnutt, Paul Laurence Dunbar, Langston Hughes, Richard Wright – in context a surprisingly 'large' number. Chesnutt is one of the few of the ninety-five about whom no articles are listed for either period; for Dunbar, one three-page article is listed and a 'popular' book; for Hughes, there are four articles, two by Hughes himself. Only Wright had been the subject of a significant number of essays. Among 'minor authors', as defined by *LHUS*, Countee Cullen had two articles, totaling five pages, written about him; W. E. B. DuBois nothing; and James Weldon Johnson, Claude McKay and Jean Toomer, among others, were not even listed. Available in Modern Language Association, American Literature Group Files, University of Wisconsin Memorial Library Archives, Madison, Wisconsin.

32. One suggestive illustration.

> I was pleased to get your letter and hear about the hunting. I don't know whether you realize how fortunate you people are to live where the game is still more plentiful than the hunters. It is no fun up here where hunting frequently resembles a shooting duel.
>
> I am vastly amused by the report of the situation of the good and important woman who thought we should have more women on our committees in the American Literature Group. ... Beyond ... [Louise Pound and Constance Rourke] I cannot think of another woman in the country who has contributed sufficiently to be placed on a par with the men on our Board and committees. If you can think of anyone, for heaven's sake jog up my memory. We must by all means keep in the good graces of the unfair sex.

Sculley Bradley to Henry A. Pochmann, 12 January 1938, Modern Language Association, American Literature Group Files, University of Wisconsin Memorial Library Archives, Madison, Wisconsin.

33. Norman Foerster, ed., introduction to *The Reinterpretation of American Literature* (New York: Harcourt, Brace, 1928), p. vii; Henry Hayden Clark, 'American literary history and American literature', in *The Reinterpretation of American Literature*, p. 213.

34. Joseph Hergesheimer, *Yale Review*, ns, 10 (July 1921), pp. 716–25.

35. Frances Noyes Hart, 'The feminine nuisance replies', *The Bookman* 54 (September 1921), pp. 31–4.

36. Allen Tate 'Tension in poetry', *The Man of Letters in the Modern World* (New York: Meridian Books, 1955), p. 71.

37. Susan Snaider Lanser and Evelyn Beck make the same point in '[Why] are there no great women critics?' in *The Prism of Sex: Essays in the Sociology of Knowledge*, ed. Julia A. Sherman and Evelyn T. Beck (Madison: University of Wisconsin Press, 1979). Deborah Rosenfelt adds: 'Because the New Criticism valued works that could be analyzed as autonomous, self-contained structures without reference to the artist or to the historical era, certain genres (like poetry and fiction) became more highly regarded than others (like autobiography or essay).' See Rosenfelt, 'The politics of bibliography', *Women in Print* 1, p. 21.

38. Allen Tate, 'The man of letters in the modern world', in *The Man of Letters in the Modern World*, pp. 20–2.
39. Frank Lentricchia develops a similar analysis in *After the New Criticism* (Chicago: University of Chicago Press, 1980), especially p. 202:

> Whether it comes from Harold Bloom or traditional historians of American poetry like Hyatt Waggoner and Roy Harvey Pearce, the isolation of Emerson and an Academic 'tradition' ... running through Whitman, Stevens, Roethke, and Ginsberg produces a repetitious continuity which celebrates the individual authorial will ('tradition and the individual talent') and which dissolves, in the process, the myriad, changing forces, poetic and otherwise, that shaped the identities of figures as culturally separated as Emerson and Roethke.

40. Compare Rosenfelt's analysis of Perry Miller's introduction to his 1962 anthology in 'The politics of bibliography', pp. 19–23.
41. A similar problem existed with respect to art that focused on the lives of working-class people. See Alice Kessler-Harris and Paul Lauter's introduction to the books in the Feminist Press series of 1930s' women writers. And Joseph Freeman's introduction to *Proletarian Literature in the United States* (New York: International Publishers, 1935), pp. 9–19.
42. Gerda Lerner, 'Placing women in history: a 1975 perspective', in *Liberating Women's History*, ed. Berenice A. Carroll (Urbana: University of Illinois Press, 1976), p. 363.
43. V. F. Calverton, *The Liberation of American Literature* (New York: Octagon Books, 1973), pp. 1–6. The original edition was published in 1932.
44. Two key sentences catch the essence of Emerson's and Fuller's outlooks in this respect. Emerson: 'We have listened too long to the courtly muses of Europe.' Fuller: 'Books which imitate or represent the thoughts and life of Europe do not constitute an American literature.'
45. Kate Chopin, *The Awakening* (Chicago and New York: H. S. Stone, 1899); the revived edition was edited by Kenneth Eble (New York: Capricorn Books, 1964). Edith Summers Kelley, *Weeds* (New York: Harcourt, Brace, 1923); a revived edition was first edited by Matthew J. Bruccoli in 1972; it has been re-edited, with a previously omitted scene of childbirth, by Charlotte Goodman (Old Westbury, NY: Feminist Press, 1982). Agnes Smedley, *Daughter of Earth* (New York: Coward-McCann, 1929); revived edition edited by Paul Lauter (Old Westbury, NY: Feminist Press, 1973). Chopin's book was out of print from about 1906, Kelley's from about 1924, and Smedley's from about 1937.
46. Upton Sinclair, *The Jungle* (New York: Vanguard, 1905), has been available in popular editions since publication. William Attaway, *Blood on the Forge* (Garden City: Doubleday, Doran, 1941), is available new only from The Chatham Bookseller, Chatham, New Jersey. Harriette Arnow, *The Dollmaker* (New York: Macmillan, 1954). Tillie Olsen, *Yonnondio: From the Thirties* (New York: Dell 1974).
47. The only detailed study of the formation of the canon I have come across concludes that scholars, because they are the teachers of the tradition, are the prime influences on the shaping of the canon. See Joseph Darryl McCall, 'Factors affecting the literary canon' (Ph.D. dissertation, University of Florida, 1958).

THREE

Constructing the subject: deconstructing the text

CATHERINE BELSEY

THE SUBJECT IN IDEOLOGY

One of the central issues for feminism is the cultural construction of subjectivity. It seems imperative to many feminists to find ways of explaining why women have not simply united to overthrow patriarchy. Why, since all women experience the effects of patriarchal practices, are not all women feminists? And why do those of us who think of ourselves as feminists find ourselves inadvertently colluding, at least from time to time, with the patriarchal values and assumptions prevalent in our society? Since the late seventeenth century feminists have seen subjectivity as itself subject to convention, education, culture in its broadest sense. Now feminist criticism has allowed that fiction too plays a part in the process of constructing subjectivity. But how?

In his influential essay, 'Ideology and ideological state apparatuses', Louis Althusser includes literature among the ideological apparatuses which contribute to the process of *reproducing* the *relations of production*, the social relationships which are the necessary condition for the existence and perpetuation of the capitalist mode of production. He does not here develop the argument concerning literature, but in the context both of his concept of ideology and also of the work of Roland Barthes on literature and Jacques Lacan on psychoanalysis it is possible to construct an account of some of the implications for feminist critical theory and practice of Althusser's position. The argument is not only that literature represents the myths and imaginary versions of real social relationships which constitute ideology, but also that classic realist fiction, the dominant literary form of the nineteenth century and arguably of the twentieth, 'interpellates' the reader, addresses itself to him or her directly, offering the reader as the position from which the text is most 'obviously' intelligible, the position of the *subject in (and of) ideology*.

According to Althusser's reading (re-reading) of Marx, ideology is not simply a set of illusions, as *The German Ideology* seems to argue, but a system of representations (discourses, images, myths) concerning the real relations in which people live. But what is represented in ideology is 'not the system of the real relations which govern the existence of individuals, but the imaginary relation of those individuals to the real relations in which they live' (Althusser 1971, p. 155). In other words, ideology is both a real and an imaginary relation to the world – real in that it is the way in which people really live their relationship to the social relations which govern their conditions of existence, but imaginary in that it discourages a full understanding of these conditions of existence and the ways in which people are socially constituted within them. It is not, therefore, to be thought of as a system of ideas in people's heads, nor as the expression at a higher level of real material relationships, but as the necessary condition of action within the social formation. Althusser talks of ideology as a 'material practice' in this sense: it exists in the behaviour of people acting according to their beliefs (ibid., pp. 155–9).

As the necessary condition of action, ideology exists in commonplaces and truisms as well as in philosophical and religious systems. It is apparent in all that is 'obvious' to us, in 'obviousnesses which we cannot *fail to recognise* and before which we have the inevitable and natural reaction of crying out (aloud or in the "still, small voice of conscience"): "That's obvious! That's right! That's true!"' (ibid., p. 161). If it is true, however, it is not the whole truth. Ideology obscures the real conditions of existence by presenting partial truths. It is a set of omissions, gaps rather than lies, smoothing over contradictions, appearing to provide answers to questions which in reality it evades, and masquerading as coherence in the interests of the social relations generated by and necessary to the reproduction of the existing mode of production.

It is important to stress, of course, that ideology is in no sense a set of deliberate distortions foisted upon a helpless working class by a corrupt and cynical bourgeoisie (or upon victimized women by violent and power hungry men). If there are groups of sinister men in shirt-sleeves purveying illusions to the public these are not the real makers of ideology. Ideology has no creators in that sense, since it exists necessarily. But according to Althusser ideological practices are supported and reproduced in the institutions of our society which he calls Ideological State Apparatuses (ISAs). The phrase distinguishes from the Repressive State Apparatus which works by force (the police, the penal system, the army) those institutions whose existence helps to guarantee consent to the existing mode of production. The central ISA in contemporary capitalism is the educational system, which prepares children to act consistently with the values of society by inculcating in them the dominant versions of appropriate behaviour as well as history, social studies and, of course, literature. Among the allies of the educational ISA are the family, the law, the media and the arts, all helping to represent and reproduce the myths and beliefs necessary to enable people to work within the existing social formation.

The destination of all ideology is the subject (the individual in society) and it is the role of ideology to *construct people as subjects*:

> I say: the category of the subject is constitutive of all ideology, but at the same time and immediately I add that *the category of the subject is only constitutive of all ideology in so far as all ideology has the function (which defines it) of 'constituting' concrete individuals as subjects.* (ibid., p. 160)

Within the existing ideology it appears 'obvious' that people are autonomous individuals, possessed of subjectivity or consciousness which is the source of their beliefs and actions. That people are unique, distinguishable, irreplaceable identities is 'the elementary ideological effect' (ibid., p. 161).

The obviousness of subjectivity has been challenged by the linguistic theory which has developed on the basis of the work of Saussure. As Emile Benveniste argues, it is language which provides the possibility of subjectivity because it is language which enables the speaker to posit himself or herself as 'I', as the subject of a sentence. It is in language that people constitute themselves as subjects. Consciousness of self is possible only through contrast, differentiation: 'I' cannot be conceived without the conception 'non-I', 'you', and dialogue, the fundamental condition of language, implies a reversible polarity between 'I' and 'you'. 'Language is possible only because each speaker sets himself up as a *subject* by referring to himself as *I* in his discourse' (Benveniste 1971, p. 225). But if language is a system of differences with no positive terms, 'I' designates only the subject of a specific utterance. 'And so it is literally true that the basis of subjectivity is in the exercise of language. If one really thinks about it, one will see that there is no other objective testimony to the identity of the subject except that which he himself thus gives about himself' (ibid., p. 226).

Within ideology, of course, it seems 'obvious' that the individual speaker is the origin of the meaning of his or her utterance. Post-Saussurean linguistics, however, implies a more complex relationship between the individual and meaning, since it is language itself which, by differentiating between concepts, offers the possibility of meaning. In reality, it is only by adopting the position of the subject within language that the individual is able to produce meaning. As Derrida puts it,

> what was it that Saussure in particular reminded us of? That 'language [which consists only of differences] is not a function of the speaking subject'. This implies that the subject (self-identical or even conscious of self-identity, self-conscious) is inscribed in the language, that he is a 'function' of the language. He becomes a *speaking* subject only by conforming his speech ... to the system of linguistic prescriptions taken as the system of differences. (Derrida 1973, pp. 145–6)

Derrida goes on to raise the question whether, even if we accept that it is only the signifying system which makes possible the speaking subject, the signifying subject, we cannot none the less conceive of a non-speaking, non-signifying subjectivity, 'a silent and intuitive consciousness' (ibid., p. 146). The problem here, he concludes, is to define consciousness-in-itself as distinct from consciousness of something, and ultimately as distinct from consciousness of self. If consciousness is finally consciousness of self, this in turn implies that consciousness depends on differentiation, and specifically on Benveniste's differentiation between 'I' and 'you', a process made possible by language.

The implications of this concept of the primacy of language over subjectivity have been developed by Jacques Lacan's reading of Freud. Lacan's theory of the subject as constructed in language confirms the *decentring* of the individual consciousness so that it can no longer be seen as the origin of meaning, knowledge and action. Instead, Lacan proposes that the infant is initially an 'hommelette' – 'a little man and also like a broken egg spreading without hindrance in all directions' (Coward and Ellis 1977, p. 101). The child has no sense of identity, no way of conceiving of itself as a unity, distinct from what is 'other', exterior to it. During the 'mirror-phase' of its development, however, it 'recognizes' itself in the mirror as a unit distinct from the outside world. This 'recognition' is an identification with an 'imaginary' (because imaged) unitary and autonomous self. But it is only with its entry into language that the child becomes a full subject. If it is to participate in the society into which it is born, to be able to act deliberately within the social formation, the child must enter into the symbolic order, the set of signifying systems of culture of which the supreme example is language. The child who refuses to learn the language is 'sick', unable to become a full member of the family and of society.

In order to speak the child is compelled to differentiate; to speak of itself it has to distinguish 'I' from 'you'. In order to formulate its needs the child learns to identify with the first person singular pronoun, and this identification constitutes the basis of subjectivity. Subsequently it learns to recognize itself in a series of subject-positions ('he' or 'she', 'boy' or 'girl', and so on) which are the positions from which discourse is intelligible to itself and others. 'Identity', subjectivity, is thus a matrix of subject-positions, which may be inconsistent or even in contradiction with one another.

Subjectivity, then, is linguistically and discursively constructed and displaced across the range of discourses in which the concrete individual participates. It follows from Saussure's theory of language as a system of differences that the world is intelligible only in discourse: there is no unmediated experience, no access to the raw reality of self and others. Thus:

> As well as being a system of signs related among themselves, language incarnates meaning in the form of the series of positions it offers for the

subject from which to grasp itself and its relations with the real. (Nowell-Smith 1976, p. 26)

The subject is constructed in language and in discourse and, since the symbolic order in its discursive use is closely related to ideology, in ideology. It is in this sense that ideology has the effect, as Althusser argues, of constituting individuals as subjects, and it is also in this sense that their subjectivity appears 'obvious'. Ideology suppresses the role of language in the construction of the subject. As a result, people 'recognize' (misrecognize) themselves in the ways in which ideology 'interpellates' them, or in other words, addresses them as subjects, calls them by their names and in turn 'recognizes' their autonomy. As a result, they 'work by themselves' (Althusser 1971, p. 169), they 'willingly' adopt the subject-positions necessary to their participation in the social form-ation. In capitalism they 'freely' exchange their labour-power for wages, and they 'voluntarily' purchase the commodities produced. In patriarchal society women 'choose' to do the housework, to make sacrifices for their children, not to become engineers. And it is here that we see the full force of Althusser's use of the term 'subject', originally borrowed, as he says, from law. The subject is not only a grammatical subject, 'a centre of initiatives, author of and responsible for its actions', but also a *subjected being* who submits to the authority of the social formation represented in ideology as the Absolute Subject (God, the king, the boss, Man, conscience): 'the individual *is interpel-lated as a (free) subject in order that he shall submit freely to the commandments of the Subject, i.e. in order that he shall (freely) accept his subjection'* (ibid., p. 169).

Ideology interpellates concrete individuals as subjects, and bourgeois ide-ology in particular emphasizes the fixed identity of the individual. 'I'm just *like* that' – cowardly, perhaps, or aggressive, generous or impulsive. Astrology is only an extreme form of the determinism which attributes to us given essences which cannot change. Popular psychology and popular sociology make indi-vidual behaviour a product of these essences. And underlying them all, ultimately unalterable, is 'human nature'. In these circumstances, how is it possible to suppose that, even if we could break in theoretical terms with the concepts of the ruling ideology, we are ourselves capable of change, and therefore capable both of acting to change the social formation and of trans-forming ourselves to constitute a new kind of society? A possible answer can be found in Lacan's theory of the precariousness of conscious subjectivity, which in turn depends on the Lacanian conception of the unconscious.

In Lacan's theory the individual is not in reality the harmonious and coherent totality of ideological misrecognition. The mirror-phase, in which the infant perceives itself as other, an image, exterior to is own perceiving self, necessitates a splitting between the *I* which is perceived and the *I* which does the perceiving. The entry into language necessitates a secondary division which reinforces the first, a split between the *I* of discourse, the subject of the utterance, and the *I* who speaks, the subject of the enunciation. There is thus a contradiction between the conscious self, the self which appears in its own discourse, and the self which is only partly represented there, the self which speaks. The unconscious comes into being in the gap which is formed by this division. The unconscious is constructed in the moment of entry into the symbolic order, simultaneously with the construction of the subject. The repository of repressed and pre-linguistic signifiers, the unconscious is a constant source of potential disruption of the symbolic order. To summarize very briefly what in Lacan is a complex and elusive theory, entry into the symbolic order liberates the child into the possibility of social relationship; it also reduces its helplessness to the extent that it is now able to articulate its needs in the form of demands. But at the same time a division within the self is constructed. In offering the child the possibility of formulating its desires the symbolic order also betrays them, since it cannot by definition formulate those elements of desire which remain unconscious. Demand is always only a metonymy of desire (Lemaire 1977, p. 64). The subject is thus the site of contradiction, and is consequently perpetually in the process of construction, thrown into crisis by alterations in language and in the social formation, capable of change. And in the fact that the subject is a *process* lies the possibility of transformation.

In addition, the displacement of subjectivity across a range of discourses implies a range of positions from which the subject grasps itself and its relations with the real, and these positions may be incompatible or contradictory. It is these incompatibilities and contradictions within what is taken for granted which exert a pressure on concrete individuals to seek new, non-contradictory subject-positions. Women as a group in our society are both produced and inhibited by contradictory discourses. Very broadly, we participate both in the liberal–humanist discourse of freedom, self-determination and rationality and at the same time in the specifically feminine discourse offered by society of submission, relative inadequacy and irrational intuition. The attempt to locate a single and coherent subject-position within these contradictory discourses, and in consequence to find a non-contradictory pattern of behaviour, can create intolerable pressures. One way of responding to this situation is to retreat from the contradictions and from discourse itself, to become 'sick' – more women than men are treated for mental illness. Another is to seek a resolution of the contradictions in the discourses of feminism. That the position of women in society has changed so slowly, in spite of such a radical instability in it, may be partly explained in terms of the relative exclusion of women from the discourse of liberal humanism. This relative exclusion, supported in the predominantly masculine institutions of our society, is implicit, for example, in the use of masculine terms as generic ('rational man', etc.).

Women are not an isolated case. The class structure also produces contradictory subject-positions which precipitate changes in social relations not only between whole classes but between concrete individuals within those classes. Even at the conscious level, although this fact may itself be unconscious, the individual subject is not a unity, and in this lies the possibility of deliberate change.

This does not imply the reinstatement of individual subjects as the agents of change and changing knowledge. On the contrary, it insists on the concept of a dialectical relationship between concrete individuals and the language in which their subjectivity is constructed. In consequence, it also supports the concept of subjectivity as in process.

It is because subjectivity is perpetually in process that literary texts can have an important function. No one, I think, would suggest that literature alone could precipitate a crisis in the social formation. None the less, if we accept Lacan's analysis of the importance of language in the construction of the subject it becomes apparent that literature as one of the most persuasive uses of language may have an important influence on the ways in which people grasp themselves and their relation to the real relations in which they live. The interpellation of the reader in the literary text could be argued to have a role in reinforcing the concepts of the world and of subjectivity which ensure that people 'work by themselves' in the social formation. On the other hand, certain critical modes could be seen to challenge these concepts, and to call in question the particular complex of imaginary relations between individuals and the real conditions of their existence which helps to reproduce the present relations of class, race and gender.

THE SUBJECT AND THE TEXT

Althusser analyses the interpellation of the subject in the context of ideology in general; Benveniste in discussing the relationship between language and subjectivity is concerned with language in general. None the less, it readily becomes apparent that capitalism in particular needs subjects who work by themselves, who freely exchange their labour-power for wages. It is in the epoch of capitalism that ideology emphasizes the value of individual freedom, freedom of conscience and, of course, consumer choice in all the multiplicity of its forms. The ideology of liberal humanism assumes a world of non-contradictory (and therefore fundamentally unalterable) individuals whose unfettered consciousness is the origin of meaning, knowledge and action. It is in the interest of this ideology above all to suppress the role of language in the construction of the subject, and its own role in the interpellation of the subject, and to present the individual as a free, unified, autonomous subjectivity. Classic realism, still the dominant popular mode in literature, film and television drama, roughly coincides chronologically with the epoch of industrial capitalism. It performs, I wish to suggest, the work of ideology, not only in its representation of a world of consistent subjects who are the origin of meaning, knowledge and action, but also in offering the reader, as the position from which the text is most readily intelligible, the position of subject as the origin both of understanding and of action in accordance with that understanding.

It is readily apparent that Romantic and post-Romantic poetry, from Wordsworth through the Victorian period at least to Eliot and Yeats, takes subjectivity as its central theme. The developing self of the poet, his consciousness of himself as poet, his struggle against the constraints of an outer reality, constitute the preoccupations of *The Prelude, In Memoriam* or *Meditations in Time of Civil War*. The 'I' of these poems is a kind of super-subject, experiencing life at a higher level of intensity than ordinary people and absorbed in a world of selfhood which the phenomenal world, perceived as external and antithetical, either nourishes or constrains. This transcendence of the subject in poetry is not presented as unproblematic, but it is entirely overt in the poetry of this period. The 'I' of the poem directly addresses an individual reader who is invited to respond equally directly to this interpellation.

Fiction, however, in this same period, frequently appears to deal rather in social relationships, the interaction between the individual and society, to the increasing exclusion of the subjectivity of the author. Direct intrusion by the author comes to seem an impropriety; impersonal narration, 'showing' (the truth) rather than 'telling' it, is a requirement of prose fiction by the end of the nineteenth century. In drama too the author is apparently absent from the self-contained fictional world on the stage. Even the text effaces its own existence as text: unlike poetry, which clearly announces itself as formal, if only in terms of the shape of the text on the page, the novel seems merely to transcribe a series of events, to report on a palpable world, however fictional. Classic realist drama displays transparently and from the outside how people speak and behave.

Nevertheless, as we know while we read or watch, the author is present as a shadowy authority and as source of the fiction, and the author's presence is substantiated by the name on the cover or the programme: 'a novel by Thomas Hardy', 'a new play by Ibsen'. And at the same time, as I shall suggest in this section, the *form* of the classic realist text acts in conjunction with the expressive theory and with ideology by interpellating the reader as subject. The reader is invited to perceive and judge the 'truth' of the text, the coherent, non-contradictory interpretation of the world as it is perceived by an author whose autonomy is the source and evidence of the truth of the interpretation. This model of intersubjective communication, of shared understanding of a text which re-presents the world, is the guarantee not only of the truth of the text but of the reader's existence as an autonomous and knowing subject in a world of knowing subjects. In this way classic realism constitutes an ideological practice in addressing itself to readers as subjects, interpellating them in order that they freely accept their subjectivity and their subjection.

It is important to reiterate, of course, that this process is not inevitable, in the sense that texts do not determine like fate the ways in which they *must* be read. I am concerned at this stage primarily with ways in which they are conventionally read: conventionally, since language is conventional, and since modes of writing as well as ways of reading are conventional, but conventionally also in that new conventions of reading are available. In this sense meaning is never a fixed essence inherent in the text but is always constructed by the reader, the result of a 'circulation' between social formation, reader and text (Heath 1977–8, p. 74). In the same way, 'inscribed subject positions are never hermetically sealed into a text, but are always positions in ideologies' (Willemen 1978, p. 63). To argue that classic realism interpellates subjects in certain ways is not to propose that this process is ineluctable; on the contrary it is a matter of choice. But the choice is ideological: certain ranges of meaning (there is always room for debate) are 'obvious' within the currently dominant ideology, and certain subject-positions are equally 'obviously' the positions from which these meanings are apparent.

Classic realism is characterized by 'illusionism', narrative which leads to 'closure', and a 'hierarchy of discourses' which establishes the 'truth' of the story. 'Illusionism' is, I hope, self-explanatory. The other two defining characteristics of classic realism need some discussion. Narrative tends to follow certain recurrent patterns. Classic realist narrative, as Barthes demonstrates in *S/Z*, turns on the creation of enigma through the precipitation of disorder which throws into disarray the conventional cultural and signifying systems. Among the commonest sources of disorder at the level of plot in classic realism are murder, war, a journey or love. But the story moves inevitably towards closure which is also disclosure, the dissolution of enigma through the re-establishment of order, recognizable as a reinstatement or a development of the order which is understood to have preceded the events of the story itself.

The moment of closure is the point at which the events of the story become fully intelligible to the reader. The most obvious instance is the detective story where, in the final pages, the murderer is revealed and the motive made plain. But a high degree of intelligibility is sustained throughout the narrative as a result of the hierarchy of discourses in the text. The hierarchy works above all by means of a privileged discourse which places as subordinate all the discourses that are literally or figuratively between inverted commas.

By these means classic realism offers the reader a position of knowingness which is also a position of identification with the narrative voice. To the extent that the story first constructs, and then depends for its intelligibility, on a set of assumptions shared between narrator and reader, it confirms both the transcendent knowingness of the reader-as-subject and the 'obviousness' of the shared truths in question.

DECONSTRUCTING THE TEXT

Ideology, masquerading as coherence and plenitude, is in reality inconsistent, limited, contradictory, and the realist text as a crystallization of ideology participates in this incompleteness even while it diverts attention from the fact in the apparent plenitude of narrative closure. The object of deconstructing the text is to examine the *process of its production* – not the private experience of the individual author, but the mode of production, the materials and their arrangement in the work. The aim is to locate the point of contradiction within the text, the point at which it transgresses the limits within which it is constructed, breaks free of the constraints imposed by its own realist form. Composed of contradictions, the text is no longer restricted to a single, harmonious and authoritative reading. Instead it becomes *plural*, open to re-reading, no longer an object for passive consumption but an object of work by the reader to produce meaning.

It is the work of Derrida which has been most influential in promoting deconstruction as a critical strategy. Refusing to identify meaning with authorial intention or with the theme of the work, deconstruction tends to locate meaning in areas which traditional criticism has seen as marginal – in the metaphors, the set of oppositions or the hierarchies of terms which provide the framework of the text. The procedure, very broadly, is to identify in the text the contrary meanings which are the inevitable condition of its existence as a signifying practice, locating the trace of otherness which undermines the overt project.

Derrida, however, says little specifically about literary criticism or about the question of meaning in fiction. Nor is his work directly political. In order to produce a politics of reading we need to draw in addition on the work of Roland Barthes and Pierre Macherey. In *S/Z*, first published in 1970 (English translation 1975), Barthes deconstructs (without using the word) a short story by Balzac. *Sarrasine* is a classic realist text concerning a castrato singer and a fortune. The narrative turns on a series of enigmas (What is the source of the fortune? Who is the little old man? Who is La Zambinella? What is the connection between all three?). Even in summarizing the story in this way it is necessary to 'lie': there are not 'three' but two, since the little old 'man' is 'La' Zambinella. Barthes breaks the text into fragments of varying lengths for analysis, and adds a number of 'divagations', pieces of more generalized commentary and exploration, to show *Sarrasine* as a 'limit-text', a text which uses the modes of classic realism in ways which constitute a series of 'transgressions' of classic realism itself. The sense of plenitude, of a full understanding of a coherent text which is the normal result of reading the realist narrative, cannot here be achieved. It is not only that castration cannot be named in a text of this period. The text is compelled to transgress the conventional antithesis between the genders whenever it uses a pronoun to speak of the castrato. The story concerns the scandal of castration and the death of desire which follows its revelation; it concerns the scandalous origin of wealth; and it demonstrates the collapse of language, of antithesis (difference) as a source of meaning, which is involved in the disclosure of these scandals.

Each of these elements of the text provides a point of entry into it, none privileged, and these approaches constitute the degree of polyphony, the 'parsimonious plural' of the readable (*lisible*) text. The classic realist text moves inevitably and irreversibly to an end, to the conclusion of an ordered series of events, to the disclosure of what has been concealed. But even in the realist text certain modes of signification within the discourse – the symbolic, the codes of reference and the *semes* – evade the constraints of the narrative sequence. To the extent that these are 'reversible', free-floating and of indeterminate authority, the text is plural. In the writable (*scriptible*), wholly plural text all statements are of indeterminate origin, no single discourse is privileged, and no consistent and coherent plot constrains the free play of the discourses. The totally writable, plural text does not exist. At the opposite extreme, the readable text is barely plural. The readable text is merchandize to be consumed, while the plural text requires the production of meanings through the identification of its polyphony. Deconstruction in order to reconstruct the text as a newly intelligible, plural object is the work of criticism.

Barthes's own mode of writing demonstrates his contempt for the readable: *S/Z* is itself a polyphonic critical text. It is impossible to summarize adequately, to reduce to systematic accessibility, and it is noticeable that the book contains no summarizing conclusion. Like *Sarrasine*, *S/Z* offers a number of points of entry, critical discourses which generate trains of thought in the reader, but it would be contrary to Barthes's own (anarchist) argument to order all these into a single, coherent methodology, to constitute a new unitary way of reading, however comprehensive, and so to become the (authoritative) author of a new critical orthodoxy. As a result, the experience of reading *S/Z* is at once frustrating and exhilarating. Though it offers a model in one sense – it implies a new kind of critical practice – it would almost certainly not be possible (or useful) to attempt a wholesale imitation of its critical method(s).

It seems clear that one of the most influential precursors of *S/Z*, though Barthes does not allude to it, was Pierre Macherey's (Marxist) *A Theory of Literary Production*, first published in 1966 (English translation 1978). Despite real and important differences between them, there are similarities worth noting. For instance, Macherey anticipates Barthes in demonstrating that contradiction is a condition of narrative. The classic realist text is constructed on the basis of enigma. Information is initially withheld on condition of a 'promise' to the reader that it will finally be revealed. The disclosure of this 'truth' brings the story to an end. The movement of narrative is thus both towards disclosure – the end of the story – and towards concealment – prolonging itself by delaying the end of the story through a series of 'reticences', as Barthes calls them, snares for the reader, partial answers to the questions raised, equivocations (Macherey 1978, pp. 28–9; Barthes 1975, pp. 75–6). Further, narrative involves the reader in an experience of the inevitable in the form of the unforeseen (Macherey 1978, p. 43). The hero encounters an obstacle: will he attempt to overcome it or abandon the quest? The answer is already determined, though the reader, who has only to turn the page to discover it, experiences the moment as one of choice for the hero. In fact, of course, if the narrative is to continue the hero must go on (Barthes 1975, p. 135). Thus the author's autonomy is to some degree illusory. In one sense the author determines the nature of the story: he or she decides what happens. In another sense, however, this decision is itself determined by the constraints of the narrative (Macherey 1978, p. 48), or by what Barthes calls the 'interest' (in both the psychological and the economic senses) of the story (Barthes 1975, p. 135).

The formal constraints imposed by literary form on the project of the work in the process of literary production constitute the structural principle of Macherey's analysis. It is a mistake to reduce the text to the product of a single cause, authorial determination *or* the mechanics of the narrative. On the contrary, the literary work 'is composed from a real diversity of elements which give it substance' (Macherey 1978, p. 49). There may be a direct contradiction between the project and the formal constraints, and in the transgression thus created it is possible to locate an important object of the critical quest.

Fiction for Macherey (he deals mainly with classic realist narrative) is intimately related to ideology, but the two are not identical. Literature is a specific and irreducible form of discourse, but the language which constitutes the raw material of the text is the language of ideology. It is thus an inadequate language, incomplete, partial, incapable of concealing the real contradictions it is its purpose to efface. This language, normally in flux, is arrested, 'congealed' by the literary text.

The realist text is a determinate representation, an intelligible structure which claims to convey intelligible relationships between its elements. In its attempt to create a coherent and internally consistent fictive world the text, in spite of itself, exposes incoherences, omissions, absences and transgressions which in turn reveal the inability of the language of ideology to create coherence. This becomes apparent because the contradiction between the diverse elements drawn from different discourses, the ideological project and the literary form, creates an absence at the centre of the work. The text is divided, split as the Lacanian subject is split, and Macherey compares the 'lack' in the consciousness of the work, its silence, what it cannot say, with the unconscious which Freud explored (ibid., p. 85).

The unconscious of the work (*not*, it must be insisted, of the author) is constructed in the moment of its entry into literary form, in the gap between the ideological project and the specifically literary form. Thus the text is no more a transcendent unity than the human subject. The texts of Jules Verne, for instance, whose work Macherey analyses in some detail, indicate that 'if Jules Verne chose to be the spokesman of a certain ideological condition, he could not choose to be what he in fact became' (ibid., p. 94). What Macherey reveals in Verne's *The Secret of the Island* is an unpredicted and contradictory element, disrupting the colonialist ideology which informs the conscious project of the work. Within the narrative, which concerns the willing surrender of nature to improvement by a team of civilized and civilizing colonizers, there *insists* an older and contrary myth which the consciousness of the text rejects. Unexplained events imply another mysterious presence on what is apparently a desert island. Captain Nemo's secret presence, and his influence on the fate of the castaways from a subterranean cave, is the source of the series of enigmas and the final disclosure which constitute the narrative. But his existence in the text has no part in the overt ideological project. On the contrary, it represents the return of the repressed in the form of a re-enacting of the myth of Robinson Crusoe. This myth evokes both a literary ancestor – Defoe's story – on which all subsequent castaway stories are to some degree conditional, and an ancestral relationship to nature – the creation of an economy by Crusoe's solitary struggle to appropriate and transform the island – on which subsequent bourgeois society is also conditional. The Robinson Crusoe story, the antithesis of the conscious project of the narrative, is also the condition of its existence. It returns, as the repressed experience returns to the consciousness of the patient in dreams and slips of the tongue and in doing so it unconsciously draws attention to an origin and a history from which both desert island stories and triumphant bourgeois ideology are unable to cut themselves off, and with which they must settle their account. *The Secret of the Island* thus reveals, through the discord within it between the conscious project and the insistence of the disruptive unconscious, the *limits* of the coherence of nineteenth-century ideology.

The object of the critic, then, is to seek not the unity of the work, but the multiplicity and diversity of its possible meanings, its incompleteness, the omissions which it displays but cannot describe, and above all its contradictions. In its absences, and in the collisions between its divergent meanings, the text implicitly criticizes its own ideology; it contains within itself the critique of its own values, in the sense that it is available for a new process of production of meaning by the reader, and in this process it can provide a knowledge of the limits of ideological representation.

Macherey's way of reading is precisely contrary to traditional Anglo-American critical practice, where the quest is for the unity of the work, its coherence, a way of repairing any deficiencies in consistency by reference to the author's philosophy or the contemporary world picture. In thus smoothing out contradiction, closing the text, criticism becomes the accomplice of ideology. Having created a canon of acceptable texts, criticism then provides them with acceptable interpretations, thus effectively censoring any elements in them which come into collision with the dominant ideology. To deconstruct the text, on the other hand, is to open it, to release the possible positions of its intelligibility, including those which reveal the partiality (in both senses) of the ideology inscribed in the text.

THE CASE OF SHERLOCK HOLMES

In locating the transitions and uncertainties of the text it is important to remember, Macherey insists, sustaining the parallel with psychoanalysis, that the problem of the work is not the same as its *consciousness* of a problem (Macherey 1978, p. 93). In 'Charles Augustus Milverton', one of the short stories from *The Return of Sherlock Holmes*, Conan Doyle presents the reader with an ethical problem. Milverton is a blackmailer; blackmail is a crime not easily brought to justice since the victims are inevitably unwilling to make the matter public; the text therefore proposes for the reader's consideration that in such a case illegal action may be ethical. Holmes plans to burgle Milverton's house to recover the letters which are at stake, and both Watson and the text appear to conclude, after due consideration, that the action is morally justifiable. The structure of the narrative is symmetrical: one victim initiates the plot, another concludes it. While Holmes and Watson hide in Milverton's study a woman shoots him, protesting that he has ruined her life. Inspector Lestrade asks Holmes to help catch the murderer. Holmes replies that certain crimes justify private revenge, that his sympathies are with the criminal and that he will not handle the case. The reader is left to ponder the ethical implications of his position.

Meanwhile, on the fringes of the text, another narrative is sketched. It too contains problems but these are not foregrounded. Holmes's client is the Lady Eva Blackwell, a beautiful debutante who is to be married to the Earl of Dovercourt. Milverton has secured letters she has written 'to an impecunious young squire in the country'. Lady Eva does not appear in the narrative in person. The content of the letters is not specified, but they are 'imprudent, Watson, nothing worse'. Milverton describes them as 'sprightly'. Holmes's sympathies, and ours, are with the Lady Eva. None the less we, and Holmes, accept without question on the one hand that the marriage with the Earl of Dovercourt is a desirable one and on the other that were he to see the letters he would certainly break off the match. The text's elusiveness on the content of the letters, and the absence of the Lady Eva herself, deflects the reader's attention from the potentially contradictory ideology of marriage which the narrative takes for granted.

This second narrative is also symmetrical. The murderer too is a woman with a past. She is not identified. Milverton has sent her letters to her husband who in consequence 'broke his gallant heart and died'. Again the text is unable to be precise about the content of the letters since to do so would be to risk losing the sympathy of the reader for either the woman or her husband.

In the mean time Holmes has become engaged. By offering to marry Milverton's housemaid he has secured information about the layout of the house he is to burgle. Watson remonstrates about the subsequent fate of the girl, but Holmes replies:

> 'You can't help it, my dear Watson. You must play your cards as best you can when such a stake is on the table. However, I rejoice to say that I have a hated rival who will certainly cut me out the instant that my back is turned. What a splendid night it is.'

The housemaid is not further discussed in the story.

The sexuality of these three shadowy women motivates the narrative and yet is barely present in it. The disclosure which ends the story is thus scarcely a disclosure at all. Symbolically Holmes has burnt the letters, records of women's sexuality. Watson's opening paragraph constitutes an apology for the 'reticence' of the narrative: 'with *due suppression* the story may be told'; 'The reader will excuse me if I conceal the date *or any other fact*' (my italics).

The project of the Sherlock Holmes stories is to dispel magic and mystery, to make everything explicit, accountable, subject to scientific analysis. The phrase most familiar to all readers – 'Elementary, my dear Watson' – is in fact a misquotation, but its familiarity is no accident since it precisely captures the central concern of the stories. Holmes and Watson are both men of science. Holmes, the 'genius', is a scientific conjuror who insists on disclosing how the trick is done. The stories begin in enigma, mystery, the impossible, and conclude with an explanation which makes it clear that logical deduction and scientific method render all mysteries accountable to reason:

> I am afraid that my explanation may disillusionize you, but it has always been my habit to hide none of my methods, either from my friend Watson or from anyone who might take an intelligent interest in them. ('The Reigate Squires', *The Memoirs of Sherlock Holmes*)

The stories are a plea for science not only in the spheres conventionally associated with detection (footprints, traces of hair or cloth, cigarette ends), where they have been deservedly influential on forensic practice, but in all areas. They reflect the widespread optimism characteristic of their period concerning the comprehensive power of positivist science. Holmes's ability to deduce Watson's train of thought, for instance, is repeatedly displayed, and it owes nothing to the supernatural. Once explained, the reasoning process always appears 'absurdly simple', open to the commonest of common sense.

The project of the stories themselves, enigma followed by disclosure, echoes precisely the structure of the classic realist text. The narrator himself draws attention to the parallel between them:

'Excellent!' I cried.

'Elementary,' said he. 'It is one of those instances where the reasoner can produce an effect which seems remarkable to his neighbour because the latter has missed the one little point which is the basis of the deduction. The same may be said, my dear fellow, for the effect of some of these little sketches of yours, which is entirely meretricious, depending as it does upon your retaining in your own hands some factors in the problem which are never imparted to the reader. Now, at present I am in the position of these same readers, for I hold in this hand several threads of one of the strangest cases which ever perplexed a man's brain, and yet I lack the one or two which are needful to complete my theory. But I'll have them, Watson, I'll have them!' ('The crooked man', *Memoirs*)

(The passage is quoted by Macherey (1978, p. 35) in his discussion of the characteristic structure of narrative.)

The project also requires the maximum degree of 'realism' – verisimilitude, plausibility. In the interest of science no hint of the fantastic or the implausible is permitted to remain once the disclosure is complete. This is why even their own existence as writing is so frequently discussed within the texts. The stories are alluded to as Watson's 'little sketches', his 'memoirs'. They resemble fictions because of Watson's unscientific weakness for story-telling:

'I must admit, Watson, that you have some power of selection which atones for much which I deplore in your narratives. Your fatal habit of looking at everything from the point of view of a story instead of as a scientific exercise has ruined what might have been an instructive and even classical series of demonstrations.' ('The Abbey Grange', *The Return of Sherlock Holmes*)

In other words, the fiction itself accounts even for its own fictionality, and the text thus appears wholly transparent. The success with which the Sherlock Holmes stories achieve an illusion of reality is repeatedly demonstrated. In their Foreword to *The Sherlock Holmes Companion* (1962) Michael and Mollie Hardwick comment on their own recurrent illusion 'that we were dealing with a figure of real life rather than of fiction. How vital Holmes appears, compared with many people of one's own acquaintance.'

De Waal's bibliography of Sherlock Holmes lists twenty-five 'Sherlockian' periodicals apparently largely devoted to conjectures, based on the 'evidence' of the stories, concerning matters only hinted at in the texts – Holmes's education, his income and his romantic and sexual adventures. According to *The Times* in December 1967, letters to Sherlock Holmes were then still commonly addressed to 221B Baker Street, many of them asking for the detective's help.

None the less these stories, whose overt project is total explicitness, total verisimilitude in the interests of a plea for scientificity, are haunted by shadowy, mysterious and often silent women. Their silence repeatedly conceals their sexuality, investing it with a dark and magical quality which is beyond the reach of scientific knowledge. In 'The Greek interpreter' (*Memoirs*) Sophie Kratides has run away with a man. Though she is the pivot of the plot she appears only briefly: 'I could not see her clearly enough to know more than that she was tall and graceful, with black hair, and clad in some sort of loose white gown.' Connotatively the white gown marks her as still virginal and her flight as the result of romance rather than desire. At the same time the dim light surrounds her with shadow, the unknown. 'The crooked man' concerns Mrs Barclay, whose husband is found dead on the day of her meeting with her lover of many years before. Mrs Barclay is now insensible, 'temporarily insane' since the night of the murder and therefore unable to speak. In 'The dancing men' (*Return*) Mrs Elsie Cubitt, once engaged to a criminal, longs to speak but cannot bring herself to break her silence. By the time Holmes arrives she is unconscious, and she remains so for the rest of the story. Ironically the narrative concerns the breaking of the code which enables her former lover to communicate with her. Elsie's only contribution to the correspondence is the word, 'Never'. The precise nature of their relationship is left mysterious, constructed of contrary suggestions. Holmes says she feared and hated him; the lover claims, 'She had been engaged to me, and she would have married me, I believe, if I had taken over another profession.' When her husband moves to shoot the man whose coded messages are the source of a 'terror' which is 'wearing her away', Elsie restrains him with compulsive strength. On the question of her motives the text is characteristically elusive. Her husband recounts the story:

> 'I was angry with my wife that night for having held me back when I might have caught the skulking rascal. She said that she feared that I might come to harm. For an instant it had crossed my mind that what she really feared was that *he* might come to harm, for I could not doubt that she knew who this man was and what he meant by those strange signals. But there is a tone in my wife's voice, Mr Holmes, and a look in her eyes which forbid doubt, and I am sure that it was indeed my own safety that was in her mind.'

After her husband's death Elsie remains a widow, faithful to his memory and devoting her life to the care of the poor, apparently expiating something unspecified, perhaps an act or a state of feeling, remote or recent.

'The dancing men' is 'about' Holmes's method of breaking the cipher. Its project is to dispel any magic from the deciphering process. Elsie's silence is in the interest of the story since she knows the code. But she also 'knows' her feelings towards her former lover. Contained in the completed and fully disclosed story of the decipherment is another uncompleted and undisclosed narrative which is more than merely peripheral to the text as a whole. Elsie's past is central and causal. As a result, the text with its project of dispelling mystery is haunted by the mysterious state of mind of a woman who is unable to speak.

The classic realist text had not yet developed a way of signifying women's sexuality except in a metaphoric or symbolic mode whose presence disrupts the realist surface. Joyce and Lawrence were beginning to experiment at this time with modes of sexual signification but in order to do so they largely abandoned the codes of realism. So much is readily apparent. What is more significant, however, is that the presentation of so many women in the Sherlock Holmes stories as shadowy, mysterious and magical figures precisely contradicts the project of explicitness, transgresses the values of the texts, and in doing so throws into relief the poverty of the contemporary concept of science. These stories, pleas for a total explicitness about the world, are unable to explain an area which none the less they cannot ignore. The version of science which the texts present would constitute a clear challenge to ideology: the interpretation of all areas of life, physical, social and psychological, is to be subject to rational scrutiny and the requirements of coherent theorization. Confronted, however, by an area in which ideology itself is uncertain, the Sherlock Holmes stories display the limits of their own project and are compelled to manifest the inadequacy of a bourgeois scientificity which, working within the constraints of ideology, is thus unable to challenge it.

Perhaps the most interesting case, since it introduces an additional area of shadow, is 'The second stain' (*Return*), which concerns two letters. Lady Hilda Trelawney Hope does speak. She has written before her marriage 'an indiscreet letter ... a foolish letter, a letter of an impulsive, loving girl'. Had her husband read the letter his confidence in her would have been for ever destroyed. Her husband is none the less presented as entirely sympathetic, and here again we encounter the familiar contradiction between a husband's supposed reaction, accepted as just, and the reaction offered to the reader by the text. In return for her original letter Lady Hilda gives her blackmailer a letter from 'a certain foreign potentate' stolen from the dispatch box of her husband, the European Secretary of State. This political letter is symbolically parallel to the first sexual one. Its contents are equally elusive but it too is 'indiscreet', 'hot-headed'; certain phrases in it are 'provocative'. Its publication would produce 'a most dangerous state of feeling' in the nation. Lady Hilda's innocent folly is the cause of the theft: she knows nothing of politics and was not in a position to understand the consequences of her action. Holmes ensures the restoration of the political letter and both secrets are preserved.

Here the text is symmetrically elusive concerning both sexuality and politics. Watson, as is so often the case where these areas are concerned, begins the story by apologizing for his own reticence and vagueness. In the political instance what becomes clear as a result of the uncertainty of the text is the contradictory nature of the requirements of verisimilitude in fiction. The potentate's identity and the nature of his indiscretion cannot be named without involving on the part of the reader either disbelief (the introduction of a patently fictional country would be dangerous to the project of verisimilitude) or belief (dangerous to the text's status as fiction, entertainment; also quite possibly politically dangerous). The scientific project of the texts require that they deal in 'facts', but their nature as fiction forbids the introduction of facts.

The classic realist text instills itself in the space between fact and illusion through the presentation of a simulated reality which is plausible but *not real.* In this lies its power as myth. It is because fiction does not normally deal with 'politics' directly, except in the form of history or satire, that it is ostensibly innocent and therefore ideologically effective. But in its evasion of the real also lies its weakness as 'realism'. Through their transgression of their own values of explicitness and verisimilitude, the Sherlock Holmes stories contain within themselves an implicit critique of their limited nature as characteristic examples of classic realism. They thus offer the reader through the process of deconstruction a form of knowledge, not about 'life' or 'the world', but about the nature of fiction itself.

Thus, in adopting the form of classic realism, the only appropriate literary mode, positivism is compelled to display its own limitations. Offered as science, it reveals itself to a deconstructive reading as ideology at the very moment that classic realism, offered as verisimilitude, reveals itself as fiction. In claiming to make explicit and *understandable* what appears mysterious, these texts offer evidence of the tendency of positivism to push to the margins of experience whatever it cannot explain or understand. In the Sherlock Holmes stories classic realism ironically tells a truth, though not the truth about the world which is the project of classic realism. The truth the stories tell is the truth about ideology, the truth which ideology represses, its own existence as ideology itself.

REFERENCES

Althusser, Louis (1971) *Lenin and Philosophy and Other Essays*, tr. Ben Brewster (London: New Left Books).

Barthes, Roland (1975) *S/Z*, tr. Richard Miller (London: Cape).

Benveniste, Emile (1971) *Problems in General Linguistics* (Miami: University of Miami Press).

Conan Doyle, Arthur (1950) *The Memoirs of Sherlock Holmes* (Harmondsworth: Penguin).

Conan Doyle, Arthur (1976) *The Return of Sherlock Holmes* (London: Pan).

Coward, Rosalind and John Ellis (1977) *Language and Materialism* (London: Routledge & Kegan Paul).

Derrida, Jacques (1973) *Speech and Phenomena*, tr. David B. Allison (Evanston: Northwestern University Press).

De Waal, Ronald (1972) *The World Bibliography of Sherlock Holmes* (Greenwich, Conn.: New York Graphic Society).

Hardwick, Michael and Mollie (1962) *The Sherlock Holmes Companion* (London: John Murray).

Heath, Stephen (1977–8) 'Notes on Suture', *Screen* 18:4, pp. 48–76.

Lemaire, Anika (1977) *Jacques Lacan*, tr. David Macey (London: Routledge & Kegan Paul).

Macherey, Pierre (1978) *A Theory of Literary Production*, tr. Geoffrey Wall (London: Routledge & Kegan Paul).

Nowell-Smith, Geoffrey (1976) 'A note on history discourse', *Edinburgh 76 Magazine* 1, pp. 26–32.

Saussure, Ferdinand de (1974) *Course in General Linguistics*, tr. Wade Baskin (London: Fontana).

Willemen, Paul (1978) 'Notes on subjectivity – on reading "Subjectivity Under Siege"', *Screen* 19: 1, pp. 41–69.

FOUR

Ideology and the cultural production of gender

MICHÈLE BARRETT

The concept of ideology is an intractable one for Marxist feminism, not least because it remains inadequately theorized in both Marxist and feminist theory.[1] Although feminists have frequently posed ideology as central to women's oppression this very centrality is presented as self-evident rather than argued for. This can be seen in an obvious way by considering one of the major fields of women's studies – the analysis of literature. Much excellent work has been done on many aspects of this subject by feminists, and I shall be considering some of it later, but among it all I can find no sustained argument as to *why* feminists should be so interested in literature or what theoretical or political ends such a study might serve. Nor is it easy to find systematic accounts of any relationship between analysis of women's oppression in, say, literature and in, say, the family. Many women's studies courses are explicitly interdisciplinary in perspective and yet the traditional disciplinary divisions between the arts and the social sciences have been difficult to transcend, other than by the juxtaposition of their respective subject-matters.

Related to this is the inadequacy of feminist attempts to explore the ways in which material conditions have historically structured the mental aspects of oppression. Some earlier feminist writers, Simone de Beauvoir and Virginia Woolf, for example, paid more attention to this question than it has received in recent years. Approaches taken by contemporary feminism seem in comparison notably unsatisfactory. One solution has been to ground the ideology of oppression irrevocably in biology, to take procreation and its different consequences for men and women as the root cause. Another has been to present it as completely self-sustaining and in need of no further explanation; Cora Kaplan has suggested that this view of ideology – the 'energy source' of patriarchal domination – underlies Kate Millett's work.[2] Yet another solution has been found in the application of a particular Marxist perspective that sees ideology (in this case sexist ideology) as the reflection of material conditions of male power and dominance. Hence the ideology of women's inferiority is seen as a manipulation of reality that serves men's interests, and women's own collusion in oppression is explained as a variety of false consciousness. These solutions are all unsatisfactory, and the latter is particularly so in that it simply transposes an already inadequate theory of ideology on to different ground. For if a theory that sees ideology as the unproblematic reflection of class relations is inadequate, the difficulties are compounded if it is merely trans-ferred to the question of gender.

Feminism has, however, played an important part in challenging the validity of the mechanical conception that sees ideology as the playing out of economic contradictions at the mental level. As I have already suggested, there has been a fruitful alignment of interests between those who seek to raise the question of gender and its place in Marxist theory, and those who seek to challenge economism in Marxism, insisting on the importance of ideological processes. It is clear that a conception of capitalism in which all forms of ideology are perceived as a reflection of the exploitation of labour by capital, in which gender plays no part, can be of little use to feminist analysis. It should be noted, perhaps, that the strong form of economism indicated above has never gained the hold on western European Marxism that it has elsewhere. Indeed Perry Anderson has argued that the political context of the twentieth-century development of western Marxism has encouraged an exploration of culture and ideology at the expense of an insistence on the primacy of economic or political considerations.[3]

It is in this context that we should consider the argument that post-Althusserian developments in the theory of ideology offer an opportunity for feminist analysis which earlier versions of Marxism have denied. This claim can be identified with a particular tendency in recent British feminist work, the appropriation of the theory developed by Barry Hindess and Paul Hirst, and is found most systematically in articles published by the journal *m/f*. It is not relevant here to enter into a sustained engagement with the ideas of Hindess and Hirst, which I will discuss only in so far as is necessary for an assessment of the claims made by feminists who have taken them over.[4]

As a basis for discussion I want to quote a passage of argument from an article by Parveen Adams which expresses clearly the logic and assumptions of this theoretical position.

My argument is that as long as feminist theories of ideology work with a theory of representation within which representation is always a representa-tion of reality, however attenuated a relation that may be, the analysis of sexual difference cannot be advanced because reality is always already apparently structured by sexual division, by an already antagonistic relation between two social groups. And thus the complicated and contradictory ways in which sexual difference is generated in various discursive and social practices is always reduced to an effect of that always existent sexual division. In terms of sexual division what has to be explained is how reality functions to effect the continuation of *its* already given divisions. (The different ways in which sexual differences are produced is actually denied as a political fact in this position.) In terms of sexual *differences*, on the other hand, what has to be grasped is, precisely, the *production* of differences through systems of representation; the work of representation produces differences that cannot be known in advance.[5]

I will come back later to the political implications of this argument. For the moment, consider the rather startling statement that sexual differences 'cannot be known in advance'. Let us not sink to the vulgarity of pointing out that biological differences can be known in advance, since we know that this level of reality is uncongenial to exponents of this approach. More seriously, this analysis of 'social and discursive practices' appears also to deny that *gender* differences, as a set of historically constructed and systematic categories, can be predicted with any confidence within a given historical conjuncture. Underlying this argument are a series of principles which need to be examined. These can be identified (rather negatively perhaps) as (1) a rejection of theories of ideology; (2) a denial that there is any knowable relationship between representation and that which is represented; (3) an insistence that functionalist formulations are always and necessarily incorrect.

IDEOLOGY

It is clear that a position resting on a rejection of epistemological theories must inevitably reject any elements of determination in its approach to ideology. Paul Hirst, in a critique of Althusser, points to the 'fragile' character of the thesis that ideology is 'relatively autonomous' of its supposed economic determinants. He argues that the notion of relative autonomy 'attempts to overcome economism without facing the theoretical consequences of doing so'. On the face of it, such a criticism might point to an espousal of the view that ideology is 'absolutely' autonomous. But this turns out to be a naive or wilful misreading of the text. 'Autonomy from what?' asks Hirst rhetorically, insisting that even to pose questions of causality is to assume a social totality in which particular instances are governed by their place in the whole.[6] This enlightenment induces distaste for the concept of ideology itself, and a preference for that of 'discursive practices'. As the editors of *m/f* emphasize: 'it is indeed *theories of ideology* that present the categories of men and women as exclusive and exhaustive'.[7] This is certainly a stylish way of dealing with the problem. But I think we have to ask whether in following it we really have shaken the mundane dust of ideology off our feet. We have, after all, been led through a series of increasingly radical breaks with the Marxism of Marx and Althusser, and the final transcendence of the epistemological problematic of 'ideology' is built on the earlier advances made within this framework. In particular, the way in which the concept of discursive practice is deployed owes much to previous attempts to demonstrate the autonomy and materiality of ideology. To put this another way: they have shifted the discourse of ideology onto the terrain of the discourse of discourse and while in their terms this may be as real an advance as any other, to the critic of discursive imperialism it may seem a nominal rather than a conceptual gain. For this reason I want to take issue with a tenet which (although an epistemological one and therefore rejected by discourse theory) has provided for many people the stepping stone to support for the more radical position: the 'materiality of ideology'.

This tenet is now so much *de rigeur* in the British Marxist avant-garde that to be caught artlessly counterposing 'material conditions' and 'ideology' is an embarrassing error – 'but surely ideology *is* material' will be the inevitable reproof. Yet this assumption will not withstand closer investigation. The insistence that ideology *is material* arises, I suspect, from an unsuccessful attempt to resolve a classic paradox in Marxism: that being may determine consciousness but revolutionary transformation of the conditions of being will depend upon raising the level of class-consciousness. Virginia Woolf once said 'a republic might be brought into being by a poem' and indeed it is possible, if unlikely, that a powerfully wrought poem could goad an exploited proletariat into successful seizure of the means of production. Yet however colossal the material *effects* of this poem, they would have no bearing on the question of whether the poem itself had a material existence.

To reject the view that ideology is material does not imply a retreat to the view that the economic and the ideological are related in a one-way system of determination of the latter by the former. On the contrary, it is important to stress a degree of reciprocity here. It is impossible to understand the division of labour, for instance, with its differential definitions of 'skill', without taking into account the material effects of gender ideology. The belief that a (white) man has a 'right' to work over and above any rights of married women or immigrants has had significant effects in the organization of the labour force. Such a belief has therefore to be taken into account when analysing the division of labour, but its location in material practices does not render it material in the same way.

The argument turns on what might be seen as an extension of Althusser's approach to ideology. For while Althusser argues, in my view correctly, that ideology exists *in* (material) apparatuses, such as schools or the media, and their practices, it requires a considerable leap of faith to translate this meaning that ideology *is* material. Stuart Hall and Richard Johnson have made this point very clearly: Johnson suggests that a 'genuine insight' here becomes 'reckless hyperbole' and Hall argues that the *'slide'* from one meaning to the other enables 'the magical qualifier, "materialist"' to serve as an undeserved emblem of legitimation.[8]

The notion of the materiality of ideology has been influential and has reinforced the claim that ideology should be regarded as absolutely autonomous. For why, if ideology is as material as the economic relations we used to think of as 'material conditions', should it not be assigned an equal place in our analysis? The crucial questions concerning the relationship of ideological processes to historical conditions of the production and reproduction of material life are left unexamined in this attempt to colonize the world for a newly privileged concept of ideology in which everything is material. Yet in drawing the net of ideology so wide we are left with no means, no tools, for distinguishing anything. As Terry Eagleton trenchantly remarks,

> there is no possible sense in which meanings and values can be said to be 'material', other than in the most sloppily metaphorical use of the term. ..
> If meanings *are* material, then the term 'materialism' naturally ceases to be intelligible. Since there is nothing which the concept excludes, it ceases to have value.[9]

REPRESENTATION

Parveen Adams argues that 'the classical theory of representation' must be rejected. What would such a rejection entail? This classical theory, central to Marxist aesthetics, poses representation (usually seen as ideological, and often explored through the analysis of cultural products) as to some degree a reflection of specific historical conditions. Debate has raged over whether literary texts, for instance, can be understood as direct reflections, or even distortions, of reality or should be seen as mediated in complex ways. Such texts are held, however, always to bear *some* relation to the social relations in which they were produced. It is this relationship that is being challenged here. Paul Hirst, in the critique of Althusser already mentioned, has argued that representation must necessarily entail *means of* representation and that once these are allowed it must follow that they 'determine' that which is represented. It is but a step from this to arguing that *nothing other* than the means of representation determine what is represented – that 'the real' can never exist prior to its representation. This short step, however, constitutes an important break in the argument. For while it is true, as Hirst argues, that the signified does not exist (in semiotic theory) prior to its signification, this does not rule out the existence of a material referent of the sign as a whole. So Hirst's preference for the conceptual framework of signification over that of representation, and his claim that the former facilitates a break with the constraints of the classic theory of ideology, remain unjustified.

Certainly it is true that the means of representation are important. In the area of cultural production, for example, it is easy to see how forms of representation are governed by genres, conventions, the presence of established modes of communication and so on. Yet these are not determining in the absolute sense being argued for here. They do not in themselves account for what is represented. We can approach this problem by way of an example, by looking at the imagery of gender. Suppose I am an enterprising motor-car manufacturer, and it occurs to me that I can tap a market of independent salaried women for my product. I advertise my car with a seductive, scantily clad male model draped over its bonnet and an admiring, yet slightly servile, snappily dressed man politely opening the car door for my putative client. Will my efforts be crowned with success? It is unlikely – and the reason why it is unlikely is, precisely, that representation *does* bear a relation to something which we can know previously existed.

This point is explored in two interesting articles on the imagery, and cultural stereotyping, of gender. Griselda Pollock argues that we should not be content to view the cultural representation of gender as 'images of women'. She rejects this approach because it cannot explain why it should be that the inversion or reversal of accepted imagery simply does not succeed.[10] This is so not only because the representation of women is linked to a broader chain, or system, of signification. It also occurs because representation is linked to historically constituted real relations. To put the matter simply, we can understand why female models may be more persuasive to male customers than *vice versa* only if we take account of a prior commoditization of women's bodies. Why this should have been so, and how, are clearly questions for historical analysis, but the fact remains that a connection has been established in which not only have women's bodies become commodities themselves (for instance in prostitution) but the association between them and consumerism has more generally taken hold. A related case is made by T. E. Perkins in a discussion of stereotyping.[11] Perkins argues that however irrational or erroneous a particular stereotype may be thought, we do not have the option of eradicating it by the voluntary substitution of a different one. Stereotypes are tied to historical social relations, and indeed, Perkins argues, the chances of success in challenging a stereotype will depend upon the social location of the group in question.

To argue in this way does not imply any pre-given, or ahistorical, content of representation. Parveen Adams appears to be arguing that *either* we talk of 'sexual division' as 'an always already antagonistic relation between two social groups who are frozen into a mutually exclusive and jointly exhaustive division',[12] *or* we talk of 'sexual differences' as the apparently spontaneous production of something that we cannot know in advance. These, however, do not constitute our only options. We do not need to talk of sexual division as 'always already' there; we can explore the historical construction of the categories of masculinity and femininity without being obliged to deny that, historically specific as they are, they nevertheless exist today in systematic and even predictable terms. Without denying that representation plays an important constitutive role in this process we can still insist that at any given time we can have a knowledge of these categories prior to any particular representation in which they may be reproduced or subverted.

FUNCTIONALISM

It is clearly true that the problem of functionalism has been a serious one for Marxist feminism. Both feminist and Marxist accounts of women's oppression have tended to slide uncritically into a mode of explanation which is undeniably functionalist; many feminist accounts explain various forms of oppression in terms of their supposedly self-evident functions of perpetuating patriarchal dominance, and many Marxist accounts centre on the supposed benefits, or functions, for capital of women's subordinate position. These forms of functionalism, and arguments derived from functionalist sociology, have undoubtedly been influential in many Marxist feminist explanations too.[13] Clearly any account of women's oppression that is organized around its importance for the smooth reproduction of capitalist social relations must run the risk of overemphasizing this supposedly functional relationship at the expense of a proper consideration of contradiction, conflict and political struggle.

Dissatisfaction with these accounts must lie behind the appeal of the alternative approach now being discussed. Criticism of the notion of function is a central point of their attack. Adams castigates the uncritical use of the term 'sexual division' for enabling merely a description of pre-given functions.[14] Rosalind Coward suggests that the entire debate as to the profitability or otherwise of the family for capitalism can be 'cleared away' by posing the problem in terms of particular conjunctures in which specific conditions of existence of the relations of production are secured.[15] This approach draws on the rejection (by Hindess and Hirst) of general entities such as 'the capitalist mode of production' and the equally firm rejection of any 'necessary correspondence' between economic and ideological relations. It relies, in fact, on the assumption of a 'non-correspondence' – on the pre-given impossibility of establishing such relations or correspondences. This case is not however proven, even in its own terms, for if the notion of 'necessary correspondence' is invalid so also must any notion of 'necessary non-correspondence' lapse into dogmatism. The notion of 'difference' merely assumes the role of that which is 'always already' there, and is equally unjustified.

More importantly, the argument is predicated upon a caricature of the position it seeks to reject. Analyses couched in terms of modes of production, even in terms of proposed functional relations within these modes, need not *necessarily* fail to grasp the centrality of contradiction and struggle. Richard Johnson has argued that we may usefully return to Gramsci's conception of capitalist reproduction: 'a hard and constantly resisted labour, a political and ideological work for capital and for the dominant classes, on very obstinate materials indeed'.[16] Such a view is not only analytically sounder than the one I have been discussing, it is grounded in a more fruitful political context. Here it may be useful to consider briefly the political implications of the feminist application of discourse theory. This is particularly important since although these writers do spell out quite openly the political consequences of their position, the language in which the debate is cast is so impenetrable that relatively few critics have so far engaged with it.

First, in so far as a knowledge of real social relations is denied, it must follow that discourse itself must be the site of struggle. We do not even seek a cultural revolution; we seek a revolution in discourse. I do not want to deny either the importance of ideological struggle or the role of discourse within it (indeed it would be hard to see why I was writing this essay if I did). However, there is a world of difference between assigning some weight to ideological struggle and concluding that no other struggle is relevant or important. The relief with which the intellectual left has seized upon these ideas as a justification and political legitimation of any form of academic work is in itself suspicious and alarming. For although I would not dispute the political significance of such activity, a distinction must be retained between this form of struggle and the more terrestrial kind. Are we really to see the Peterloo massacre, the storming of the Winter Palace in Petrograd, the Long March, the Grunwick picket – as the struggle of discourses?

The exclusive emphasis placed on discursive practice has led to a critical consideration of the discourse of feminism itself. In some respects this is both proper and valuable, since the language in which feminist demands are expressed must be constructed with care and integrity. Political slogans, for instance, inevitably aim at popular mobilization and may do so at a cost of oversimplification or compromise. Yet the critique of feminist slogans elaborated in successive articles in *m/f* is surely politically inappropriate to the point of being destructive. One by one the campaigning slogans of women's liberation – 'The personal is political', 'A woman's right to choose', 'Control of our bodies' – are found to rest on errors of epistemology. They rely on humanism, essentialism, inadequate theories of the subject and so on.[17] This critical exercise is in my view misplaced, in that it rests on a failure to appreciate the grounding of such slogans in particular historical struggles. More importantly, perhaps, it leads us to ask what alternative political strategy is being offered if we take seriously the post-Althusserian critique of traditional ways of perceiving women's oppression.

I find the political purchase of this approach particularly negative here. Fundamentally, it is unclear that the project to deconstruct the category of woman could ever provide a basis for a feminist politics. If there are no 'women' to be oppressed then on what criteria do we struggle, and against what? The difficulty here is to see the connection between the theoretical project and its stated designation as 'feminist'.[18] The feminism enters as an act of ethical goodwill rather than a political practice tied to an analysis of the world; it remains a 'self-evident' and unexplained goal which in fact the theoretical consequences of discourse theory must systematically undermine.

I have discussed these arguments at some length, since they are proposed as a solution to the crucial question faced by Marxist feminist analysis – what is the relationship between women's oppression and the general features of a mode of production? I am unconvinced that the post-Althusserian development of discourse theory has rendered this question obsolete. These writers have, however, usefully alerted us once again to the underdeveloped nature of the theory of ideology, and in the following section I will attempt to sketch out a more useful way of deploying this concept.

I want to suggest first that for a concept of ideology to have any analytic use it must be bounded. We must retrench from a position where ideology is claimed to be as determining, as material, as the relations of production. The concept of 'relative autonomy' must, whatever its apparent fragility, be further explored and defined. This need not necessarily involve intellectual acrobatics of the kind which would be required to prove that ideology is at one and the same time autonomous and not. To perceive this problem in terms of abstract logic is to misunderstand it. What it does involve is the specification, for a given social historical context, of the limits to the autonomous operation of ideology. Hence we should be able to specify what range of possibilities exist for the ideological processes of a particular social formation, without necessarily being able to predict the specific form they may take.

Second, I want to restrict the term to phenomena which are mental rather than material. Hence the concept of ideology refers to those processes which have to do with consciousness, motive, emotionality; it can best be located in the category of *meaning*. Ideology is a generic term for the processes by which meaning is produced, challenged, reproduced, transformed. Since meaning is negotiated primarily through means of communication and signification, it is possible to suggest that cultural production provides an important site for the construction of ideological processes. Thus, it is not inappropriate to claim, as Eagleton and others have, that literature (for instance) can usefully be analysed as a paradigm case of ideology in particular social formations.[19] Ideology is embedded historically in material practice but it does not follow *either* that ideology is theoretically indistinguishable from material practices *or* that it bears any direct relationship to them. We may learn much, from an analysis of novels, about the ways in which meaning was constructed in a particular historical period, but our knowledge will not add up to a general knowledge of that social formation. For if literature does constitute a primary site of ideological negotiation, none the less it cannot provide the historian with an adequate knowledge of other, equally important aspects of a social formation. The mediation of social reality operating in any fictional work will ensure that the historian will face many dangers in pillaging literature for its 'social content'. One reason why this should be so is that literary texts operate, as Pierre Macherey has argued, through their absences as well as through what is present in them.[20] Following Althusser's method of 'symptomatic reading', in which the analyst can supposedly detect the gaps and weaknesses of the author's original problematic, Macherey suggests that we should concentrate not on what the text overtly presents to us, but on what is *not said* in it. There are clearly problems with this model, which I shall come back to later, but Macherey points to an important danger here.

Third, lest it should be thought this represents a return to an economistic base/superstructure model of society, I should emphasize the integral connection between ideology and the relations of production. This is particularly important and easily demonstrated, in the case of the ideology of gender. As I shall argue later, this ideology has played an important part in the historical construction of the capitalist division of labour and in the reproduction of labour power. A sexual division of labour, and accompanying ideologies of the appropriate meaning of labour for men and women, have been embedded in the capitalist division of labour from its beginnings. It is impossible to over-emphasize here the importance of an historical analysis. I make no claim for the inevitability of this particular ideology as a functional requisite for capitalist production – it is one of several possible options. Nevertheless there are grounds to accept a point made by Colin Sumner in his fascinating and controversial book: that once such an ideology *is* historically embedded it may *become* essential for the maintenance of the system.[21]

In stressing the role of ideology in the relations of production it is perhaps necessary, to avoid misunderstanding, to stress the fact that the term 'relations of production' does not refer simply to class relations. It must comprise the divisions of gender, of race, definitions of different forms of labour (mental, manual and so on), of who should work and at what. Relations of production reflect and embody the outcome of struggles: over the division of labour, the length of the working day, the costs of reproduction. Marx's allusion to the 'historical and moral element' in the value of labour-power requires further exploration and elaboration. It is, perhaps, useful here to distinguish between the 'relations of production', in which the ideology of gender plays a very important part, and the means and forces of production. For while it is true that the ideology of gender plays a very significant role in the *relations* of production, it is far more difficult to argue that it plays a crucial part in the essential reproduction of raw materials, installations and machinery; and although domestic labour is vital to the present form in which labour power is reproduced, this need not necessarily be the case. Indeed it can plausibly be argued that the wage-labour relation and the contradiction between labour and capital – the defining characteristics of the capitalist mode of production – are 'sex-blind' and operate quite independently of gender.

I want now to discuss the ways in which the ideology of gender is produced and reproduced in cultural practice. Much of the discussion will relate to the question of literature, since this is a practice which has generated considerable work in this area, and is the practice most familiar to me, but parallels with other forms will be drawn where possible. I shall look first of all at the question of what we need to consider if we want to arrive at a systematic analysis of gender ideology. This is important, since much of the work so far undertaken has concentrated disproportionately on describing *how* gender is presented – 'what images of women are portrayed?' is the commonest question – and has not sought to locate this in a broader theoretical framework. So it will only be after considering the *context* of this imagery that I shall attempt to draw out the dominant themes of gender imagery in contemporary cultural practice. Finally, I shall consider the political potential of cultural production, returning to the question of whether a revolution at the level of culture is possible or adequate.

The first point to make in considering the necessary elements of an analysis of gender ideology in cultural production cannot be stressed too strongly: we must avoid making the text itself our only basis for analysis. In rejecting this approach, we should be clear that we are not only rejecting the tradition of literary criticism which has constantly insisted that the text 'speaks for itself': we are also rejecting the apparently more sophisticated 'structuralist' analyses that have tended to replace conventional literary and other criticisms. To restrict our analysis solely to the text itself is to turn the *object* of analysis into its own means of explanation; by definition this cannot provide an adequate account. To reduce the problem solely to the text is a form of reductionism as unprofitable as reducing it to the mechanical expression of economic relations. As I and others have argued elsewhere, this reduction to the text 'simply privileges the artefact itself, divorced from its conditions of production and existence, and claims that it alone provides the means of its own analysis'.[22]

To avoid this form of reduction we have to move away from a dependence upon our 'reading' of the text. This is far more difficult than it might appear. The history of both bourgeois and materialist criticism is rooted in the struggle for a 'correct' reading. In bourgeois criticism this takes the form of posing moral and aesthetic questions to which the critic, depending on his or her own sensitivity, will produce more or less satisfactory answers. The text has sometimes here been seen as potentially providing answers not only about its own construction (characterization, narrative and so on) but to larger questions about 'human nature' or 'beauty'. This approach is criticized by

Marxist and feminist critics. They tend to ask instead, 'what does my reading of this text tell me about' class consciousness, or responses to industrialization, or sexism, or whatever. But the argument is still posed in terms of a subjective reading: *you* may read this text as 'about' human nature, *I* read it as 'about' capitalism or patriarchy. Nor is this debate really resolved by trying to look for what the text does not say, as a means for reading what it is 'about'. As Colin Sumner has argued, this (neo-structuralist) technique relies heavily on introspection.[23]

If we are to get beyond basing our analysis on a reading of the text we need to construct a theoretical framework in which these broader questions are built into the method. This project is at a very early stage as yet, and perhaps the most systematic attempt to develop the constituent elements of such an approach is that provided by Terry Eagleton's 'categories for a materialist criticism'. [24] Eagleton suggests that the text should be understood as the product of the 'complex historical articulations' of various structures, and proposes the following schema:

1. General mode of production.
2. Literary mode of production.
3. General ideology.
4. Authorial ideology.
5. Aesthetic ideology.
6. Text.

These categories, although somewhat unwieldy, are a major advance on the unformulated methods of materialist criticism that Eagleton has attempted to synthesize. They constitute a useful set of related structures which can profitably be used as a general framework in which to develop specific analyses. I do not want to discuss them in detail here, but will comment briefly on only one of these categories: the 'literary mode of production'.

I am not convinced that it is necessary or profitable to elevate the forces and relations of literary production to the status of a 'mode of production'. None the less, in adopting this term Eagleton creates an opportunity to explore in very fruitful ways the specifically literary constraints in which a text is historically produced. Although Eagleton does not totally displace the centrality of the text, his account does by definition constitute an attack on the idealist view that 'art' can transcend its conditions of production. Eagleton's literary mode of production is constituted by forces and relations of production, distribution, exchange and consumption. Any given period may have residual features of earlier literary modes of production, or may contain forms prefiguring later modes, but will be characterized by a dominant mode which exerts specific determinations on the text to be produced. Analysis of these processes would take into account the stage of the development of the forces of literary production (an obvious example being the effects of the invention of printing) and the relations in which work was produced (different forms of patronage and so on). In addition to this Eagleton argues that such an analysis would be essential to grasp the meaning of the text. The material conditions of its production are internalized: 'every literary text intimates by its very conventions the way it is to be consumed, encodes within itself its own ideology of how, by whom and for whom it was produced'.[25] We can conclude from this that if women are situated differently from men in respect of the forces and relations of literary production, we might expect to see this internalized in texts – and we do.

In arguing for a more systematic approach to the ideology of gender, we can isolate three specific elements in the process. These I shall refer to by the shorthand terms of production, consumption and representation, and I shall deal first with the question of *production*.

It is immediately clear that the conditions under which men and women produce literature are materially different. This important question has been curiously neglected by recent feminist work, and the most systematic exploration of this issue is still, fifty years after its publication, Virginia Woolf's *A Room of One's Own*.[26] Naive as this essay undoubtedly is in some respects, it none the less provides us with a very useful starting-point. Woolf bases her arguments in this book and in related essays on materialist propositions.[27] Writing, she argues, is not 'spun in mid-air by incorporeal creatures': it is based on material things (health, money, the houses we live in). These material conditions must govern the writer's 'angle of vision', his or her perception of society. They must influence the art-form chosen, the genre chosen within the form, the style, the tone, the implied reader, the representation of character.

Woolf argues that a crucial difference between men and women has lain historically in the restricted access of the latter to the means of literary production. Their education was frequently sacrificed to that of their brothers; they lacked access to publishers and the distribution of their work; they could not earn a living by writing, as men did, since (before the Married Women's Property Acts) they could not even retain their earnings if they were married. Relative poverty and lack of access to an artistic training meant that the bourgeois woman encountered specific constraints on her creative work: Woolf suggests that one reason why women have been so prolific in literary production and almost absent from forms such as musical composition and visual art is that the latter require greater financial resources than 'the scratching of a pen' ('For ten and sixpence one can buy paper enough to write all the plays of Shakespeare'). Less plausibly and more controversially, she argues that even the choice of literary form was affected by women's social position: they opted for the new form of the novel rather than for poetry or drama, since it required less concentration and was therefore more compatible with the inevitable interruptions of household obligations.

A strength of Woolf's analysis is that her discussion of representation is located in an analysis of both the historical production and distribution of literature and its social consumption and reception. She argues that accepted social and literary-critical attitudes that denigrated women's writing played an important part in influencing the production of literature by women. They did this not only by forcing women writers to adopt male pseudonyms in order to get their work published and neutrally assessed, but by engendering an overaggressive or overdefensive tone in women's writing. She refers here to what the Marxist-Feminist Literature Collective now call 'gender criticism': the approach that 'subsumes the text into the sexually-defined personality of its author, and thereby obliterates its literarity'.[28]

Although Woolf's account is more systematic than most, we still await a substantial account of *consumption* and reception of texts from the point of view of the ideology of gender (or from any other point of view, one could add). There has been a failure to develop a theory of reading. This is largely, I suspect, because any such analysis would have to confront directly one of the most difficult problems of a materialist aesthetics: the problem of value. Virginia Woolf, it might be noted, simply ignored this problem. Although challenging much of what constituted the canon of great literature of her period, she slides quite unremorsefully into the worst kind of aesthetic league-tabling in much of her criticism. Preoccupation with the question of value ('quality', 'standards') has been detrimental for feminist criticism and appears to have been posed as a choice between two limited options. On the one hand, we have the view exemplified by Virginia Woolf: that women have not reached the achievements of male writers, but that this is to be attributed to the constraints historically inherent in the conditions in which their work was produced and consumed. On the other hand, there is the view that women *have* achieved equally in respect of aesthetic value and we only think otherwise because of the warped and prejudiced response of a predominantly male, and sexist, critical and academic establishment.

This debate is fruitless (although admittedly seductive) in that it reproduces the assumption that aesthetic judgement is independent of social and historical context. Simply to pose the question at this level is to deny what we do already know: that not only are refined details of aesthetic ranking highly culturally specific, but that there is not even any consensus across classes, let alone across cultures, as to which cultural products can legitimately be subjected to such judgements. I am not contending that these observations obviate the problem of aesthetic value, since I believe it to be an urgent task of feminist criticism to take it on in the context of the female literary tradition, but merely that it should not be posed in simplistic terms.

In respect of literary production and distribution, consumption and reception, we should attend to the different ways in which men and women have historically been situated as authors. I am not so sure that this difference is equally relevant to the *representation* of gender in cultural products. For, while I do not wish to exculpate any particular male author from responsibility for irredeemably sexist work, it remains true that the imagery of gender affects both men and women profoundly, if differently. Problems arise when we try to distinguish, at the level of our reading of novels, between the images presented by male authors and those presented by female. The question of representation is beset by the problem of interpretation, and this is why I have been arguing that we cannot rely on subjective readings. If, for instance, a novel is published by a feminist publishing house and it carries on its jacket a blurb telling us it is 'a telling indictment of patriarchy' we are likely to read the contents (the story of a woman's humiliation at the hands of her brutal male lover) as precisely that. If, as is conceivable, a similar story is published by another firm with a blurb referring to 'sex and violence' and a cover picture of a supine woman wearing only a torn negligée, we shall read it rather differently (if we read it at all). Yet these readings will be determined not by any differences in the text itself but by the inferences about it we have drawn from its presentation.

This simple example illustrates two problems. The first is that we cannot assume that a particular meaning is intrinsic to the text, since it must depend on how it is read. Put another way: ideology is not 'transparent', and this, as I shall emphasize later, has implications for overtly politicized art. Second, it raises the question of authorial intention, which leads down many disastrous alleyways. There has been a general tendency for feminist criticism to approach male and female authors very differently. Female authors are 'credited' with trying to pose the question of gender, or women's oppression, in their work, and male authors are 'discredited' by means of an assumption that any sexism they portray is necessarily their own. It seems extraordinary that these tendencies, both of which in their rampant moralism deny precisely the fictional, the *literary*, structure of the texts, should have taken such hold in the field of 'women and literature'. The attempt to present women writers as 'trying to solve' problems of gender is particularly fraught with problems. For although women writers frequently do, quite understandably, structure their work around the issues which their experience has provided them with, we ignore the *fictional* nature of their work at our peril. To construe a novelist as a sociologist manqué is to lead to the position adopted by Rachel Harrison, who makes the singularly misplaced comment that 'in *Shirley*, Charlotte Brontë is working with a necessarily descriptive account of the changing forces and relations of production' and then goes on to specify the 'later theoretical developments' that might have improved her analysis.[29]

If this identification of text and female author is unsatisfactory, so too is the parallel treatment of male authors. Cora Kaplan, in her very interesting assessment of *Sexual Politics*, suggests that Millett's refusal to see the ambivalence in her authors' work, her intransigent criticism of their sexism, is based on 'the unproblematic identification of author, protagonist and point of view, and the unspoken assumption that literature is always a conscious rendering of authorial ideology'.[30]

It is neither plausible nor profitable to study literature for the purpose of berating morally reprehensible authors. Nor is it possible to take literary texts, or any other cultural products, as necessary reflections of the social reality of any particular period. They cannot even provide us with a reliable knowledge of directly inferrable ideology. What they can offer, I suggest, is an indication of the bounds within which particular meanings are constructed and negotiated in a given social formation: but this would depend upon considering a fairly wide range of such products. Imagery is a notoriously misleading indicator: think of the impression created by studying, for example, the iconography of royalty in contemporary Britain. The proverbial Martian might be forgiven for concluding, from all those pictures of the Queen reviewing regiments, opening Parliament, enthroning archbishops and so on, that she controlled all the repressive and ideological state apparatuses. It would take a more systematic study to dispel this illusion.

In spite of all these reservations we can usefully isolate some of the processes by which the work of reproducing gender ideology is done. In a rough and preliminary way we can identify processes of stereotyping, compensation, collusion and recuperation, across a range of cultural practices.

The notion of a 'stereotype' has become so overused that it may be thought to lack sufficient clarity, but it is I think of use in looking at the way gender difference is rigidly represented in, for instance, the mass media. Recent work has shown the pervasive operation of gender stereotypes in advertising and in children's books. Trevor Millum has described the extremely limited images of women presented in a sample of advertisements: they relate almost exclusively to women's role in the home, oscillating between the glamorous and efficient hostess and the dutiful, caring mother.[31] With regard to children's books, Nightingale and others have commented on the extent to which they represent a sexual division of labour far more rigid than even the sharp differentiation we know to exist.[32] Many children whose mothers are in regular employment must be surprised to find that the mothers in their early school reading books are invariably and exclusively engaged in housework. This process of stereotyping is probably the one best documented in feminist studies, and the existence of such rigid formulations in many different cultural practices clearly indicates a degree of hard work being put into their maintenance. We could, perhaps, be forgiven for regarding this imagery as the 'wish-fulfilment of patriarchy'.

The category of 'compensation' refers to the presentation of imagery and ideas that tend to elevate the 'moral value' of femininity. One could take examples from the plethora of practices which, in the context of systematic denial of opportunities for women, attempt to 'compensate' for this by a corresponding ideology of moral worth. The dichotomous view of woman embodied in the ideology of the Catholic Church, Rosemary Ruether argues, does precisely this: juxtaposing madonna and whore, mariolatry and an oppressive and contemptuous attitude to its female members.[33] An important element of such compensatory work is the romanticism of woman that it generates. This romanticism may well be genuinely felt by both men and women and I do not use the term compensation to imply that these processes are necessarily conscious or intentional. An interesting example of this process is given in a study by Hilary Graham of the literature handed out to pregnant women.[34] Graham's analysis of the romantic photography of this genre (softly focused shots of idyllic mother-and-child scenes) compares rather ill with the patronizing and curt clinical treatment they get when they leave the waiting room and enter the examination cubicle. Finally we should note the importance of an historical account of this process. As Catherine Hall's and Leonore Davidoff's work in different ways demonstrates,[35] the 'ideology of domesticity', with its intense moral and sentimental elevation of the family home was developed in the stultifying ethos of Victorian restrictions on female activity.

The notion of 'collusion' may be taken to refer to two processes that it is useful to distinguish. On the one hand, we can note the attempts made to manipulate and parade women's consent to their subordination and objectification. The classic example here is provided in John Berger's discussion of the female-nude painting tradition. Having stressed the blatant voyeurism of much of this genre he comments on the practice of portraying a female nude surveying herself in a mirror:

> you painted a naked woman because you enjoyed looking at her, you put a mirror in her hand and you called the painting *Vanity*, thus morally condemning the woman whose nakedness you had depicted for your own pleasure. The real function of the mirror was otherwise. It was to make the woman connive in treating herself as, first and foremost, a sight.[36]

This connivance, or collusion, does not always take the form Berger outlines. The second process to which the notion of collusion refers is crucially important: that of women's willing consent and their internalization of oppression. This point has already been touched on in connection with the question of sexuality, and indeed one reason why psychoanalytic theory has acquired its present credence among feminists is precisely that it does offer an explanation of consent and collusion. An analysis of gender ideology in which women are always innocent, always passive victims of patriarchal power, is patently not satisfactory. Simone de Beauvoir's solution to the problem was to suggest a general inclination towards 'bad faith': if women are offered the chance of relinquishing the existential burden of subjective responsibility, men may expect them to show 'complicity'.[37]

Acceptance of the importance of collusion need not necessarily lead either to a crude formulation of women's consciousness as simply false consciousness or to a denial of objective conditions of oppression. It is important to remember the extent to which our consciousness is formed in conditions of subordination and oppression. We cannot, by the simple act of will, wish away politically 'incorrect' elements of our consciousness or 'reactionary' sources of pleasure. I am not suggesting that collusion should be regarded wth complacency, for clearly it should be contested, but we need to develop further our understanding of the means by which it is constructed and of what the conditions of its amelioration would be.

Finally I want to mention the process of 'recuperation'. I refer here to the ideological effort that goes into negating and defusing challenges to the historically dominant meaning of gender in particular periods. Anyone disputing the work involved in ideological reproduction could profitably consider the hard labour that has been put into accommodating women's liberation in the media. It is, of course, particularly apparent in advertising. Although I cited Trevor Millum's account of stereotyping in advertisements, this picture should be modified by looking at the ways in which the advertising media have sought to recapture lost ground on the question of women's independence. Although clearly some advertisements that play with the notion of an independent woman are aimed at a market of female purchasers (such as the ambiguous 'Every Woman Needs Her Daily Mail'), many others are explicitly addressed to redressing the effects of women's liberation. An obvious example of this might be the advertisement of tights 'for women who don't want to wear the trousers'.

The question of recuperation is perhaps one of the most interesting in the study of ideology. Elizabeth Cowie's detailed interpretation of the film *Coma* provides a suggestive discussion of this phenomenon.[38] The film, although ostensibly constructed around a female character who plays an intelligent and courageous role of detection, takes away with one hand what it has given with the other: our heroine cracks the riddle but finally has to be saved by her boyfriend. This type of scenario is not solely a response to the activity of the present women's liberation movement, although clearly we may look forward to more of it as the movement gains ground. It is a response, to changes in the position of women, which may be generated at other times. Helen Roberts, for example, has outlined parallel processes.[39] Taking both popular fiction and the work of novelists such as Winifred Holtby and Dorothy Sayers, Roberts describes the presentation of women whose independence is initially convincingly depicted (particularly by Sayers), but eventually denied by the action of the narrative.

What implications does the approach outlined in this essay have for 'cultural revolution' and for political art? I want to recapitulate two significant points: the first, that ideology – as the work of constructing meaning – cannot be divorced from its material conditions in a given historical period. Hence we cannot look to culture alone to liberate us – it cannot plausibly be assigned such transcendental powers. Second, since there is no one-to-one relationship between an author's intentions and the way in which a text will be received, the feminist artist cannot predict or control in any ultimate sense the effects of her work. These two points constitute an important limitation for the practice of politicized art, and in addition we have to consider the material resources (of production and distribution) which limit, often cruelly, the effectiveness of such work.

None the less the struggle over the *meaning* of gender is crucial. It is vital for our purposes to establish its meaning in contemporary capitalism as *not* simply 'difference', but as division, oppression, inequality, internalized inferiority for women. Cultural practice is an essential site of this struggle. It can play an incalculable role in the raising of consciousness and the transformation of our subjectivity.

NOTES

1. The book of which this excerpt forms a part, *Women's Oppression Today*, was published in 1980 and clearly there have been further debates about the theory of ideology since that time. The early part of my discussion focuses mainly on the impact of discourse theory on certain types of feminist theory and provides a critique of the political inferences that have been drawn from this work in Britain. Since that was written, the significance of Foucault's work, and analyses of 'post-modernism', have grown and with them there has been a repetition of the challenge to theories that see the social world as a coherent totality rather than a fragmented and deconstructed history. The strongest versions of that view would be those that claim to speak for 'post-feminism' and the 'post-political' condition. From their point of view the concept of ideology is one that is too implicated in a 'realist' philosophical position (one that sees concepts and reality as separable) to be acceptable. My arguments were formulated to defend a 'realist' position as one that was both desirable and essential and I would advance them again in this context were I to be writing the book now. Discussion of the strengths and weaknesses of Foucault's methodology in general and its relationship to feminist theory in particular is still at a relatively early stage. Nevertheless it is quite clear that the appropriation of Foucault's perspective has tended to reinforce the critique of ideology as a general concept. However, I believe that it is essential to defend the value of the concept of ideology from this attack as well as from the attacks more traditionally made from a reductionist or economistic point of view. Hence the position argued in this essay, that ideology is an extremely important site of the construction of gender but that it should be understood as part of a social totality rather than as an autonomous practice or discourse, is one that I would still subscribe to.

On the question of feminist cultural intervention, the treatment here could be complemented by my later essay, 'Feminism and the definition of cultural politics', in *Feminism, Culture and Politics*, ed. Rosalind Brunt and Caroline Rowan (London: Lawrence & Wishart, 1982).

2. Cora Kaplan, 'Radical feminism and literature: rethinking Millett's *Sexual Politics*', *Red Letters* (1979), p. 7.
3. Perry Anderson, *Considerations on Western Marxism* (London: New Left Books, 1976).
4. The individual and collaborative works of Barry Hindess and Paul Q. Hirst, and their collective work with Anthony Cutler and Athar Hussain, are known colloquially as 'Hindess and Hirst', 'post-Althusserianism' and 'discourse theory'. There now exist several general critical responses to their arguments, such as Andrew Collier, 'In defence of epistemology', in vol. 3 of *Issues in Marxist Philosophy*, ed. John Mepham and David Hillel Ruben (Brighton: Harvester Press, 1979); Laurence Harris, 'The science of the economy', *Economy and Society* 7: 3 (1978) (and see the subsequent debate in 8: 3, 1979); Philip Corrigan and Derek Sayer, 'Hindess and Hirst: a critical review', *The Socialist Register*, 1978.
5. Parveen Adams, 'A note on the distinction between sexual division and sexual differences', *m/f* 3 (1979), p. 52.
6. See Paul Q. Hirst, 'Althusser and the theory of ideology', *Economy and Society* 5:4, p. 395; *On Law and Ideology* (London: Macmillan, 1979), p. 18.
7. *m/f* 4 (1980), p. 23.
8. Richard Johnson, 'Histories of culture/theories of ideology', in *Ideology and Cultural Production*, ed. Michèle Barrett, Philip Corrigan, Annette Kuhn and Janet Wolff (London: Croom Helm, 1979), p. 59; Stuart Hall, 'Some problems with the ideology /subject couplet', *Ideology and Consciousness* 3 (1978), p. 116.
9. Terry Eagleton, 'Ideology, fiction, narrative', *Social Text*, 1980.
10. Griselda Pollock, 'What's wrong with images of women?', *Screen Education* 24 (1977).
11. T. E. Perkins, 'Rethinking stereotypes', in *Ideology and Cultural Production*, ed. Barrett, Corrigan, Kuhn and Wolff.
12. 'A note on the distinction between sexual division and sexual differences', p. 57.
13. The problem is addressed explicitly by Mary McIntosh in 'The state and the oppression of women', in *Feminism and Materialism: Women and modes of production*, ed. Annette Kuhn and AnnMarie Wolpe (London: Routledge & Kegan Paul, 1978).
14. 'A note on the distinction between sexual division and sexual differences', p. 52.
15. *m/f* 4 (1980), p. 92.
16. 'Histories of culture/theories of ideology', p. 74.
17. See Parveen Adams and Jeff Minson, 'The "subject" of feminism', *m/f* 2 (1978); Beverley Brown and Parveen Adams, 'The feminine body and feminist politics', *m/f* 3, (1979).
18. For further discussion on this point see *m/f* 7 (1983), containing a critical letter from Rosalind Coward and myself and a response by the editors in defence of their theoretico-political position.
19. Terry Eagleton, 'Ideology, fiction, narrative'.

20. Pierre Macherey, *A Theory of Literary Production* (London: Routledge & Kegan Paul, 1978).
21. Colin Sumner, *Reading Ideologies: An investigation into the Marxist theory of ideology and law* (London: Academic Press, 1979).
22. 'Representation and cultural production', in *Ideology and Cultural Production*, p. 11.
23. Sumner, *Reading Ideologies*, pp. 172–3.
24. Terry Eagleton, *Criticism and Ideology* (London: Verso, 1976).
25. ibid., p. 48.
26. (Harmondsworth: Penguin, 1970; first published 1929.)
27. A selection of these may be found in Virginia Woolf, *Women and Writing*, ed. Michèle Barrett (London: Women's Press, 1979).
28. 'Women's writing: *Jane Eyre, Shirley, Villette, Aurora Leigh*', *Ideology and Consciousness* 3 (1978), p. 31.
29. Rachel Harrison, '*Shirley*: relations of reproduction and the ideology of romance', *Women Take Issue* (London: 1978), pp. 185–6, 187.
30. Cora Kaplan, 'Radical feminism and literature', p. 10.
31. Trevor Millum, *Images of Women: Advertising in Women's Magazines* (London: Chatto, 1975).
32. Camilla Nightingale, 'Boys will be boys but what will girls be?' in *The Politics of Literacy*, ed. Martin Hoyles (London: Writers' & Readers', 1977). See also Bob Dixon, *Catching Them Young: Sex, race and class in children's fiction* (London: Pluto Press, 1977).
33. Rosemary Radford Ruether, 'Misogynism and virginal feminism in the Fathers of the Church' in *Religion and Sexism*, ed. Rosemary Radford Ruether (New York: Touchstone Books, 1974).
34. Hilary Graham, 'Images of pregnancy in ante-natal literature', in *Health Care and Health Knowledge*, ed. R. Dingwall *et al.* (London: Croom Helm, 1977).
35. Catherine Hall, 'The early formation of Victorian domestic ideology', in *Fit Work for Women*, ed. S. Burman (London: Croom Helm, 1979); Catherine Hall, 'Married women at home in Birmingham in the 1920s and 1930s', *Oral History* (Women's History Issue), 5:2 (Autumn 1977); Leonore Davidoff, 'The rationalization of housework', in *Dependence and Exploitation in Work and Marriage*, ed. D. Leonard Barker and S. Allen (Harlow: Longman, 1976); Leonore Davidoff *et al.*, 'Landscape with figures: home and community in English society', in *The Rights and Wrongs of Women*, ed. Juliet Mitchell and Ann Oakley (Harmondsworth: Penguin, 1976).
36. John Berger, *Ways of Seeing* (Harmondsworth: Penguin, 1977), p. 51.
37. Simone de Beauvoir, *The Second Sex* (Harmondsworth: Penguin, 1974), p. 21. I am not suggesting that de Beauvoir sees collusion as anything other than a *response*: she also argues that 'woman is shut up in a kitchen or boudoir, and astonishment is expressed that her horizon is limited. Her wings are clipped, and it is found deplorable that she cannot fly' (p. 616).
38. 'The popular film as a progressive text – a discussion of *Coma*', *m/f* 3 (1979) and 4 (1980).
39. Helen Roberts, 'Propaganda and ideology in women's fiction', in *The Sociology of Literature: Applied studies*, ed. D. Laurenson, Sociological Review Monograph no. 26 (University of Keele, 1978).

FIVE

Writing the body: toward an understanding of l'écriture féminine

ANN ROSALIND JONES

France is today the scene of feminisms. The Mouvement de libération des femmes (MLF) grows every year, but so do the factions within it: feminist journals carry on bitter debates, a group of women writers boycotts a feminist publishing house, French women at conferences in the United States contradict each other's positions at top volume (Monique Wittig to Hélène Cixous: 'Ceci est un scandale!'). But in the realm of theory, the French share a deep critique of the modes through which the west has claimed to discern evidence – or reality – and a suspicion concerning efforts to change the position of women that fail to address the forces in the body, in the unconscious, in the basic structures of culture that are invisible to the empirical eye. Briefly, French feminists in general believe that western thought has been based on a systematic repression of women's experience. Thus their assertion of a bedrock female nature makes sense as a point from which to deconstruct language, philosophy, psychoanalysis, the social practices, and direction of patriarchal culture as we live in and resist it.

This position, the turn to *féminité* as a challenge to male-centered thinking, has stirred up curiosity and set off resonances among American feminists, who are increasingly open to theory, to philosophical, psychoanalytic and Marxist critiques of masculinist ways of seeing the world. (Speakers at recent US feminist conferences have, indeed, been accused of being too theoretical.) And it seems to me that it is precisely through theory that some of the positions of the French feminists need to be questioned – as they have been in France since the beginnings of the MLF. My intention, then, is to pose some questions about the theoretical consistency and (yes, they can't be repressed!) the practical and political implications of French discussions and celebrations of the feminine. For if one posits that female subjectivity is derived from women's physiology and bodily instincts as they affect sexual experience and the unconscious, both theoretical and practical problems can and do arise.

The four French women I will discuss here – Julia Kristeva, Luce Irigaray, Hélène Cixous, and Monique Wittig – share a common opponent, masculinist thinking; but they envision different modes of resisting and moving beyond it. Their common ground is an analysis of western culture as fundamentally oppressive, as phallogocentric. 'I am the unified, self-controlled center of the universe,' man (white, European and ruling class) has claimed. 'The rest of the world, which I define as the Other, has meaning only in relation to me, as man/father, possessor of the phallus.'[1] This claim to centrality has been supported not only by religion and philosophy, but also by language. To speak and especially to write from such a position is to appropriate the world, to dominate it through verbal mastery. Symbolic discourse (language, in various contexts) is another means through which man objectifies the world, reduces it to his terms, speaks in place of everything and everyone else – including women.

How, then, are the institutions and signifying practices (speech, writing, images, myths and rituals) of such a culture to be resisted? These French women agree that resistance does take place in the form of *jouissance*, that is, in the direct re-experience of the physical pleasures of infancy and of later sexuality, repressed but not obliterated by the Law of the Father.[2] Kristeva stops here; but Irigaray and Cixous go on to emphasize that women, historically limited to being sexual objects for men (virgins or prostitutes, wives or mothers), have been prevented from expressing their sexuality in itself or for themselves. If they can do this, and if they can speak about it in the new language it calls for, they will establish a point of view (a site of *différence*) from which phallogocentric concepts and controls can be seen through and taken apart, not only in theory, but also in practice. Like Cixous, Wittig has produced a number of *textes féminins*, but she insists that the theory and practice of *féminité* must be focused on women among themselves, rather than on their divergence from men or from men's views of them. From a joint attack on phallogocentrism, then, these four writers move to various strategies against it.

Julia Kristeva, a founding member of the semiotic-Marxist journal *Tel Quel*, and the writer of several books on avant-garde writers, language and philosophy, finds in psychoanalysis the concept of the bodily drives that survive cultural pressures towards sublimation and surface in what she calls 'semiotic discourse': the gestural, rhythmic, preferential language of such writers as Joyce, Mallarmé and Artaud.[3] These men, rather than giving up their blissful infantile fusion with their mothers, their orality, and anality, re-experience such *jouissances* subconsciously and set them into play by constructing texts against the rules and regularities of conventional language. How do women fit into this scheme of semiotic liberation? Indirectly, as mothers, because they are the first love objects from which the child is typically separated and turned away in the course of his initiation into society. In fact, Kristeva sees semiotic discourse as an incestuous challenge to the symbolic order, asserting as it does the writer's return to the pleasures of his preverbal identification with his mother and his refusal to identify with his father and the logic of paternal discourse. Women, for Kristeva, also speak and write as 'hysterics', as outsiders to male-dominated discourse, for two reasons: the predominance in them of drives related to anality and childbirth, and their marginal position vis-à-vis masculine culture. Their semiotic style is likely to involve repetitive, spasmodic separations from the dominating discourse, which, more often, they are forced to imitate.[4]

Kristeva doubts, however, whether women should aim to work out alternative discourses. She sees certain liberatory potentials in their marginal position, which is (admirably) unlikely to produce a fixed, authority-claiming subject/speaker or language: 'In social, sexual and symbolic experiences, being a woman has always provided a means to another end, to becoming something else: a subject-in-the-making, a subject on trial.' Rather than formulating a new discourse, women should persist in challenging the discourses that stand: 'If women have a role to play ... it is only in assuming a *negative* function: reject everything finite, definite, structured, loaded with meaning, in the existing state of society. Such an attitude places women on the side of the explosion of social codes: with revolutionary movements.'[5] In fact, 'woman' to Kristeva represents not so much a sex as an attitude, any resistance to conventional culture and language; men, too, have access to the *jouissance* that opposes phallogocentrism:

> A feminist practice can only be ... at odds with what already exists so that we may say 'that's not it' and 'that's still not it.' By 'woman' I mean that which cannot be represented, what is not said, what remains above and beyond nomenclatures and ideologies. There are certain 'men' who are familiar with this phenomenon.[6]

For Luce Irigaray, on the contrary, women have a specificity that distinguishes them sharply from men. A psychoanalyst and former member of l'Ecole freudienne at the University of Paris (Vincennes), she was fired from her teaching position in the fall of 1974, three weeks after the publication of her study of the phallocentric bias in Freud. *Speculum de l'autre femme* is this study, a profound and wittily sarcastic demonstration of the ways in which Plato and Freud define woman: as irrational and invisible, as imperfect (castrated) man. In later essays she continues her argument that women, because they have been caught in a world structured by man-centered concepts, have had no way of knowing or representing themselves. But she offers as the starting point for a female self-consciousness the facts of women's bodies and women's sexual pleasure, precisely because they have been so absent or so misrepresented in male discourse. Women, she says, experience a diffuse sexuality arising, for example, from the 'two lips' of the vulva, and a multiplicity of libidinal energies that cannot be expressed or understood within the identity-claiming assumptions of phallocentric discourse: 'I am a unified, coherent being, and what is significant in the world reflects my male image').[7] Irigaray argues further that female sexuality explains women's problematic relationship to (masculine) logic and language:

> *woman has sex organs just about everywhere.* She experiences pleasure almost everywhere. ... The geography of her pleasure is much more diversified, more multiple in its differences, more complex, more subtle, than is imagined – in an imaginary [system] centered a bit too much on one and the same.
>
> 'She' is infinitely other in herself. That is undoubtedly the reason she is called temperamental, incomprehensible, perturbed, capricious – not to mention her language in which 'she' goes off in all directions and in which 'he' is unable to discern the coherence of any meaning. Contradictory words seem a little crazy to the logic of reason, and inaudible for him who listens with ready-made grids, a code prepared in advance. In her statements – at least when she dares to speak out – woman retouches herself constantly.[8]

Irigaray concedes that women's discovery of their autoeroticism will not, by itself, arrive automatically or enable them to transform the existing order: 'For a woman to arrive at the point where she can enjoy her pleasure as a woman, a long detour by the analysis of the various systems that oppress her is certainly necessary.'[9] Irigaray herself writes essays using Marxist categories to analyze men's use and exchange of women, and in others she uses female physiology as a source of critical metaphors and counterconcepts (against physics, pornography, Nietzsche's misogyny, myth),[10] rather than literally. Yet her focus on the physical bases for the difference between male and physical sexuality remains the same: women must recognize and assert their *jouissance* if they are to subvert phallocentric oppression at its deepest levels.

Since 1975, when she founded women's studies at Vincennes, Hélène Cixous has been a spokeswoman for the group Psychanalyse et politique and a prolific writer of texts for their publishing house, des femmes. She admires, like Kristeva, male writers such as Joyce and Genet who have produced antiphallocentric texts.[11] But she is convinced that women's unconscious is totally different from men's, and that it is their psychosexual specificity that will empower women to overthrow masculinist ideologies and to create new female discourses. Of her own writing she says, 'Je suis là où ça parle' ('I am there where it/id/the female unconscious speaks.').[12] She has produced a series of analyses of women's suffering under the laws of male sexuality (the first-person narrative *Angst*, the play *Portrait de Dora*, the libretto for the opera *Le Nom d'Oedipe*) and a growing collection of demonstrations of what idliberated female discourses might be: *La, Ananké* and *Illa*. In her recent *Vivre l'orange* (des femmes, 1979), she celebrates the Brazilian writer Clarice Lispector for what she sees as a peculiarly female attentiveness to objects, the ability to perceive and represent them in a nurturing rather than dominating way. She believes that this empathetic attentiveness and the literary modes to which it gives rise, arise from libidinal rather than social-cultural sources: the 'typically feminine gesture, not culturally but libidinally, [is] to produce in order to bring about life, pleasure, not in order to accumulate'.[13]

Cixous criticizes psychoanalysis for its 'thesis of a "natural" anatomical determination of sexual difference-opposition', focusing on physical drives rather than body parts for her definition of male female contrasts: 'It is at the level of sexual pleasure in my opinion that the difference makes itself most clearly apparent in as far as woman's libidinal economy is neither identifiable by a man nor referable to the masculine economy.'[14] In her manifesto for *l'écriture féminine*, 'The laugh of the Medusa' (1975), her comparisons and lyricism suggest that she admires in women a sexuality that is remarkably constant and almost mystically superior to the phallic single-mindedness it transcends:

> Though masculine sexuality gravitates around the penis, engendering that centralized body (in political anatomy) under the dictatorship of its parts, woman does not bring about the same regionalization which serves the couple head/genitals and which is inscribed only within boundaries. Her libido is cosmic, just as her unconscious is worldwide.

She goes on immediately, in terms close to Irigaray's, to link women's diffuse sexuality to women's language – written language, in this case:

> Her writing can only keep going, without ever inscribing or discerning contours. ... She lets the other language speak – the language of 1000 tongues which knows neither enclosure nor death. ... Her language does not contain, it carries; it does not hold back, it makes possible.[15]

The passage ends with her invocation of other bodily drives (*pulsions* in the French) in a continuum with women's self-expression:

> Oral drive, anal drive, vocal drive – all these drives are our strengths, and among them is the gestation drive – just like the desire to write: a desire to live self from within, a desire for the swollen belly, for language, for blood.

In her theoretical and imaginative writing alike (*La jeune née*, 1975, typically combines the two) Cixous insists on the primacy of multiple, specifically female libidinal impulses, in women's unconscious and in the writing of the liberatory female discourses of the future.

What Kristeva, Irigaray and Cixous do in common, then, is to oppose women's bodily experience (or, in Kristeva's case, women's bodily effect as mothers) to the phallic/symbolic patterns embedded in western thought.

Although Kristeva does not privilege women as the only possessors of pre-phallocentric discourse, Irigaray and Cixous go further: if women are to discover and express who they are, to bring to the surface what masculine history has repressed in them, they must begin with their sexuality. And their sexuality begins with their bodies, with their genital and libidinal difference from men.

For various reasons, this is a powerful argument. We have seen versions of it in the radical feminism of the United States, too. In the French context, it offers an island of hope in the void left by the deconstruction of humanism, which has been revealed as an ideologically suspect invention by men. If men are responsible for the reigning binary system of meaning – identity/other, man/nature, reason/chaos, man/woman – women, relegated to the negative and passive pole of this hierarchy, are not implicated in the creation of its myths. (Certainly, they are no longer impressed by them!) And the immediacy with which the body, the id, *jouissance*, are supposedly experienced promises a clarity of perception and a vitality that can bring down mountains of phallo-centric delusion. Finally, to the extent that the female body is seen as a direct source of female writing, a powerful alternative discourse seems possible: to write from the body is to recreate the world.

But *féminité* and *écriture féminine* are problematic as well as powerful con-cepts. They have been criticized as idealist and essentialist, bound up in the very system they claim to undermine; they have been attacked as theoretically fuzzy and as fatal to constructive political action.[16] I think all these objections are worth making. What's more, they must be made if American women are to sift out and use the positive elements in French thinking about *féminité*.

First off, the basic theoretical question: can the body be a source of self-knowledge? Does female sexuality exist prior to or in spite of social ex-perience? Do women in fact experience their bodies purely or essentially, outside the damaging acculturation so sharply analyzed by women in France and elsewhere? The answer is no, even in terms of the psychoanalytic theory on which many elements in the concept of *féminité* depend. Feminists reread-ing Freud and Jacques Lacan, and feminists doing new research on the construction of sexuality all agree that sexuality is not an innate quality in women or in men; it is developed through the individual's encounters with the nuclear family and with the symbolic systems set into motion by the mother-father pair as the parents themselves carry out socially imposed roles toward the child. Freud, Juliet Mitchell has shown, describes the process through which girls in our society shift their first love for their mothers to a compen-satory love for their fathers and develop a sense of their own anatomy as less valued socially than that of boys.[17] Nancy Chodorow has documented and theorized the difficulty of this shift and used it to account for the complex affective needs of girls and women.[18] To the analysis of the process through which sexual identity is formed Lacan adds the role of the father as bearer of language and culture; he identifies the symbolic value attributed to the phallus as the basis for contrasts and contrasting values that the child incorporates as she attempts to make sense of and fit herself into the phallocentric world. So if early gender identity comes into being in response to patriarchal structures – as, for example, Chodorow, Lacan and Dorothy Dinnerstein argue[19] – and if even the unconscious is sexed in accordance with the nuclear family, then there seems to be no essential stratum of sexuality unsaturated with social arrangements and symbolic systems. New readings of Freud and of object relations theory both confirm that sexuality is not a natural given, but rather is the consequence of social interactions, among people and among signs.

Theoretical work and practical evidence strongly suggest that sexual identity ('I am a woman, I experience my body as sexual in this way') never takes shape in isolation or in a simply physical context. The child becomes male or female in response to the females and males she encounters in her family and to the male and female images she constructs according to her experience – especially her loss of direct access to either parent.[20] The desires of the child and of the adult who grows out of the child finally result not from the isolated erotic sensitivities of the child's body; these sensitivities are interpreted through the meanings the child attaches to her body through early experience in a sexed world. To take from psychoanalysis the concepts of drive and libido without talking about what happens later to the child's systems of self-perception is to drop out the deepest level at which phallocentric society asserts its power: the sexed family as it imprints itself on the child's sense of herself as a sexed being.

Psychoanalytic theory is not feminist dogma, and feminists have also analyzed the sexist ideologies that confront women past the age of childhood in the family. Not surprisingly, these ideologies make their way into many women's day-to-day experience of their bodies, even in situations that we have designed to be free of male domination. For instance, liberatory practices such as masturbation, lesbianism and woman-centered medicine coexist with thoroughly phallocentric habits of thought and feeling; they are not liberatory simply because they aspire to be. Some women discover, for example, that their masturbation is accompanied by puzzlingly unenlightened fantasies; contrary to the claims of *féminité*, women's autoeroticism, at least in these decades, is shot through with images from a phallically dominated world. Similarly, many lesbians recognize their need to resist roles of domination and submission that bear a grim, even parodic resemblance to heterosexual relationships. Women giving birth may wonder whether the optimistic, even heroic terminology of natural childbirth is not related to the suspect ideal of 'taking it like a man'. Even in the self-help clinics set up to spare women the sexist bias of the male gynecological establishment, a phallocentric *magasin des images* may prevail. A counselor at such a clinic, showing a friend of mine her cervix for the first time in a mirror, made a remark (unintentionally, that's the point) that struck us both as far less liberating than it was intended to be: 'Big, isn't it? Doesn't it look powerful? As good as a penis any day.' All in all, at this point in history, most of us perceive our bodies through a jumpy, contradictory mesh of hoary sexual symbolization and political counter-response. It is possible to argue that the French feminists make of the female body too unproblematically pleasurable and totalized an entity.

Certainly, women's physiology has important meanings for women in various cultures, and it is essential for us to express those meanings rather than to submit to male definitions – that is, appropriations – of our sexuality. But the female body hardly seems the best site to launch an attack on the forces that have alienated us from what our sexuality might become. For if we argue for an innate, precultural femininity, where does that position (though in *content* it obviously diverges from masculinist dogma) leave us in relation to earlier theories about women's 'nature'? I myself feel highly flattered by Cixous's praise for the nurturant perceptions of women, but when she speaks of a drive toward gestation, I begin to hear echoes of the coercive glorification of motherhood that has plagued women for centuries. If we define female subjectivity through universal biological/libidinal givens, what happens to the project of changing the world in feminist directions? Further, is women's sexuality so monolithic that a notion of a shared, typical femininity does justice to it? What about variations in class, in race and in culture among women? What about changes over time in *one* woman's sexuality (with men, with women, by herself)? How can one libidinal voice – or the two vulval lips so startlingly presented by Irigaray – speak for all women?

The psychoanalytic critique of *féminité* as a concept that overlooks important psychosocial realities is not the only critique that can be brought against positions like Irigaray's and Cixous's. Other French women have made a strong, materialist attack on what they call *néo-féminité*, objecting to it as an ideal bound up through symmetrical opposition in the very ideological system feminists want to destroy. (*Questions féministes*, the journal founded in 1977 with Simone de Beauvoir as titular editor, is a central source for this kind of thinking in France.) Materialist feminists such as Christine Delphy and Colette Guillaumin are suspicious of the logic through which *féminité* defines men as phallic – solipsistic, aggressive, excessively rational – and then praises women, who, by nature of their contrasting sexuality, are other-oriented, empathetic, multi-imaginative. Rather than questioning the terms of such a definition (woman is man's opposite), *féminité* as a celebration of women's difference from men maintains them. It reverses the values assigned to each side of the polarity, but it still leaves man as the determining referent, not departing from the opposition male/female, but participating in it.

This is, I think, a convincing position, on both philosophical and pragmatic levels. What we need to do is to move outside that male-centered, binary logic altogether. We need to ask not how Woman is different from Man (though the question of how women differ from what men *think* they are is important). We need to know how women have come to be who they are through history, which is the history of their oppression by men and male-designed institutions. Only through an analysis of the power relationships between men and women, and practices based on that analysis, will we put an end to our oppression – and only then will we discover what women are or can be. More strategically, we need to know whether the assertion of a shared female nature made by *féminité* can help us in feminist action toward a variety of goals: the possibility of working, or working in marginal or newly defined ways, or of not working in the public world at all; the freedom for a diversity of sexual practices; the right to motherhood, childlessness, or some as yet untheorized participation in reproduction; the affirmation of historically conditioned female values (nurturance, communal rather than individualistic ambitions, insistence on improving the quality cf private life); *and* the exploration of new ones. If we concentrate our energies on opposing a counterview of Woman to the view held by men in the past and the present, what happens to our ability to support the multiplicity of women and the various life possibilities they are fighting for in the future?

In a critique of *féminité* as praise of women's difference from men, the name of Monique Wittig must be mentioned. Active in the early 1970s in the Féministes révolutionnaires and a contributor from the beginning to *Questions féministes*, Wittig has written four quite different books, which are none the less related through her focus on women among themselves: the schoolgirls of *L'Opoponax*, the tribal sisterhood of *Les Guérrillères*, the passionate couple of *Le Corps lesbien*, the users of the postphallocentric vocabulary laid out in *Brouillon pour un dictionnaire des amantes*. Wittig writes her novels, her monologues and histories to explore what social relationships among women-identified women are or might be.[21] She rewrites traditional culture in mocking takeovers: one entry in *Brouillon pour un dictionnaire* is 'Ainsi parlait Frederika, conte pour enfants' ('Thus Spake Frederika, children's story'), surely one of the least reverent allusions to Friedrich Nietzsche to come out of French critiques of culture. She also invents new settings, such as the ceremonies and festivals of *Les Guérrillères* and *Le Corps lesbien*, and new modes, such as the feminized epic of *Les Guérrillères* and the lyric dialogue of *Le Corps lesbien*, to represent what a female/female life – separatist but not isolationist – might be.

As Wittig's talks at recent conferences in the United States show, she is suspicious both of the oppositional thinking that defines woman in terms of man and of the mythical/idealist strain in certain formulations of *féminité*.[22] In her argument for a more politically centered understanding of women at the Second Sex Conference in New York (September 1979), she used a Marxist vocabulary which may be more familiar to US feminists than the philosophical and psychoanalytic frameworks in which Irigaray and Cixous work:

It remains ... for us to define our oppression in materialist terms, to say that women are a class, which is to say that the category 'woman', as well as 'man', is a political and economic category, not an eternal one. ... Our first task ... is thoroughly to dissociate 'women' (the class within which we fight) and 'woman', the myth. For 'woman' does not exist for us; it is only an imaginary formation, while 'women' is the product of a social relationship.[23]

Colette Guillaumin, arguing along similar lines in *Questions féministes*, points out that the psychic characteristics praised by advocates of *féminité* have in fact been determined by the familial and economic roles imposed on women by men. There is nothing liberatory, she insists, in women's claiming as virtues qualities that men have always found convenient. How does maternal tenderness or undemanding empathy threaten a master?[24] The liberating stance is, rather, the determination to analyze and put an end to the patriarchal structures that have produced those qualities without reference to the needs of women.

I have another political objection to the concept of *féminité* as a bundle of Everywoman's psychosexual characteristics: it flattens out the lived differences among women. To the extent that each of us responds to a particular tribal, national, racial or class situation vis-à-vis men, we are in fact separated from one another. As the painful and counterproductive splits along class and racial lines in the American women's movement have shown, we need to understand and respect the diversity in our concrete social situations. A monolithic vision of shared female sexuality, rather than defeating phallocentrism as doctrine and practice, is more likely to blind us to our varied and immediate needs and to the specific struggles we must coordinate in order to meet them. What is the meaning of 'two lips' to heterosexual women who want men to recognize their clitoral pleasure – or to African or Middle Eastern women who, as a result of pharaonic clitoridectomies, have neither lips nor clitoris through which to *jouir*? Does a celebration of the Maternal versus the Patriarchal make the same kind of sense, or any sense, to white, middle-class women who are fighting to maintain the right to abortion, to black and Third World women resisting enforced sterilization, to women in subsistence-farming economies where the livelihood of the family depends on the work of every child who is born and survives? And surely any one woman gives different meanings to her sexuality throughout her individual history. Freedom from sexual expectations and activity may well be what girls in the western world most need because they are typically sexualized all too soon by media, advertising, peer pressures and child pornography; women of various ages undergo radical changes in sexual identity and response as they enter relationships with men, with women, or choose celibacy and friendship as alternatives. And it is hard to see how the situations of old women, consigned to sexual inactivity because of their age or, if they are widowed, to unpaid work in others' families or to isolated poverty, can be understood or changed through a concept of *jouissance*. I wonder again whether one libidinal voice, however non-phallocentrically defined, can speak to the economic and cultural problems of all women.

Hence, I would argue that we need the theoretical depth and polemical energy of *féminité* as an alternative idea. But a historically responsive and powerful unity among women will come from our ongoing, shared practice, our experience in and against the material world. As a lens and a partial strategy, *féminité* and *écriture féminine* are vital. Certainly, women need to shake off the mistaken and contemptuous attitudes toward their sexuality that permeate western (and other) cultures and languages at their deepest levels, and working out self-representations that challenge phallocentric discourses is an important part of that ideological struggle. Women have already begun to transform not only the subject matter, but also the ways of producing meaning in poetry, fiction, film and the visual arts. (Indeed, feminist research suggests that the French may have been too hasty in their claim that women are only now beginning to challenge the symbolic order.) But even if we take *l'écriture féminine* as a utopian ideal, an energizing myth rather than a model for how all women write or should write, theoretical and practical problems arise (again!) from an ideal defined in this way. Can the body be the source of a new discourse? Is it possible, assuming an unmediated and *jouissant* (or, more likely, a positively reconstructed) sense of one's body, to move from that state of unconscious excitation directly to a written female text?

Madeleine Gagnon says yes, in *La Venue à l'écriture*, written with Cixous in 1977. Her view is that women, free from the self-limiting economy of male libido ('I will come once and once only, through one organ alone; once it's up and over, that's it; so I must beware, save up, avoid premature overflow'), have a greater spontaneity and abundance in body and language both:

> We have never been the masters of others or of ourselves. We don't have to confront ourselves in order to free ourselves. We don't have to keep watch on ourselves, or to set up some other erected self in order to understand ourselves. All we have to do is let the body flow, from the inside; all we have to do is erase ... whatever may hinder or harm the new forms of writing; we retain whatever fits, whatever suits us. Whereas man confronts himself constantly. He pits himself against and stumbles over his erected self.[25]

But psychoanalytic theory and social experience both suggest that the leap from body to language is especially difficult for women.[26] Lacanian theory holds that a girl's introduction into language (the symbolic order represented by the father and built on phallic/non-phallic oppositions) is complex, because she cannot identify directly with the positive poles of that order. And in many preliterate and postliterate cultures, taboos against female speech are enforced: injunctions to silence, mockery of women's chatter or 'women's books' abound. The turn taking in early consciousness-raising groups in the United States was meant precisely to overcome the verbal hesitancy induced in women by a society in which men have had the first and the last word. Moreover, for women with jobs, husbands or lovers, children, activist political commitments, finding the time and justification to write at all presents an enormous practical and ideological problem.[27] We are more likely to write, and to read each other's writing, if we begin by working against the concrete difficulties and the prejudices surrounding women's writing than if we simplify and idealize the process by locating writing as a spontaneous outpouring from the body.

Calls for a verbal return to nature seem especially surprising coming from women who are otherwise (and rightly!) suspicious of language as penetrated by phallocentric dogma. True, conventional narrative techniques, as well as grammar and syntax, imply the unified viewpoint and mastery of outer reality that men have claimed for themselves. But literary modes and language itself cannot be the only targets for transformation; the *context* for women's discourses needs to be thought through and broadened out. A woman may experience *jouissance* in a private relationship to her own body, but she writes for others. Who writes? Who reads? Who makes women's texts available to women? What do women want to read about other women's experience? To take a stance as a woman poet or novelist is to enter into a role crisscrossed with questions of authority, of audience, of the modes of publication and distribution. I belive that we are more indebted to the 'body' of earlier women writers and to feminist publishers and booksellers than to any woman writer's libidinal/body flow. The novelist Christiane Rochefort sums up with amusing directness the conflicting public forces and voices that create the dilemma of the French woman who wants to write:

> Well. So here you are now, sitting at your writing table, alone, not allowing anybody anymore to interfere. Are you free?
>
> First, after this long quest, you are swimming in a terrible soup of values – for, to be safe, you had to refuse the so-called female values, which are not female but a social scheme, and to identify with male values, which are not male, but an appropriation by men – or an attribution to men – of all human values, mixed up with the anti-values of domination-violence-oppression and the like. In this mixture, where is your real identity?
>
> Second, you are supposed to write in certain forms, preferably: I mean you feel that in certain forms you are not too much seen as a usurper. Novels. Minor poetry, in which case you will be stigmatized in French by the name of 'poetesse': not everybody can afford it. ...
>
> You are supposed, too, to write *about* certain things: house, children, love. Until recently there was in France a so-called *littérature féminine*.
>
> Maybe you don't want to write *about*, but to write, period. And of course,

you don't want to obey this social order. So, you tend to react against it. It is not easy to be genuine.[28]

Whatever the difficulties, women are inventing new kinds of writing. But as Irigaray's erudition and plays with the speaking voice show (as do Cixous's mischievous puns and citations of languages from Greek through German to Portuguese, and Wittig's fantastic neologisms and revision of conventional genres), they are doing so deliberately, on a level of feminist theory and literary self-consciousness that goes far beyond the body and the unconscious. That is also how they need to be read. It takes a thoroughgoing familiarity with *male* figureheads of western culture to recognize the intertextual games played by all these writers; their work shows that a resistance to culture is always built, at first, of bits and pieces of that culture, however they are disassembled, criticized and transcended. Responding to *l'écriture féminine* is no more instinctive than producing it. Women's writing will be more accessible to writers and readers alike if we recognize it as a conscious response to socioliterary realities, rather than accept it as an overflow of one woman's unmediated communication with her body. Eventually, certainly, the practice of women writers will transform what we can see and understand in a literary text; but even a woman setting out to write about her body will do so against and through her socioliterary mothers, midwives and sisters. We need to recognize, too, that there is nothing universal about French versions of *écriture féminine*. The speaking, singing, tale-telling and writing of women in cultures besides that of the Ile-de-France need to be looked at and understood in their social context if we are to fill in an adequate and genuinely empowering picture of women's creativity.

But I risk, after all this, overstating the case against *féminité* and *l'écriture féminine*, and that would mean a real loss. American feminists can appropriate two important elements, at least, from the French position: the critique of phallocentrism in all the material and ideological forms it has taken, and the call for new representations of women's consciousness. It is not enough to uncover old heroines or to imagine new ones. Like the French, we need to examine the words, the syntax, the genres, the archaic and élitist attitudes toward language and representation that have limited women's self-knowledge and expression during the long centuries of patriarchy. We need not, however, replace phallocentrism with a shakily theorized 'concentrism' that denies women their historical specificities to recognize how deep a refusal of masculinist values must go.[29] If we remember that what women really share is an oppression on all levels, although it affects us each in different ways – if we can translate *féminité* into a concerted attack not only on language, but also directly upon the sociosexual arrangements that keep us from our own potentials and from each other – then we are on our way to becoming *'les jeunes nées'* envisioned by French feminisms at their best.

NOTES

1. For a summary of the intellectual background of French feminism, see Elaine Marks, 'Women and literature in France', *Signs* 3:4 (Summer 1978), pp. 832–42. Phallogocentrism at work is powerfully analyzed by Shoshanna Felman in her study of the characters and critics of a short story by Balzac, 'Women and madness: the critical phallacy', *Diacritics* 5:4 (Winter 1975), pp. 2–10.
2. *Jouissance* is a word rich in connotations. 'Pleasure' is the simplest translation. The noun comes from the verb *jouir*, meaning 'to enjoy', to revel in without fear of the cost; also, to have an orgasm. See Stephen Heath's Translator's Note in Roland Barthes's *Image-Music-Text* (New York: Hill and Wang, 1978), p. 9. A note to Introduction 3 in *New French Feminisms: An anthology*, ed. Elaine Marks and Isabelle de Courtivron (Amherst: University of Massachusetts Press, 1980), explains feminist connotations of *jouissance* as follows:

   > This pleasure, when attributed to a woman, is considered to be of a different order from the pleasure that is represented within the male libidinal economy often described in terms of the capitalist gain and profit motive. Women's jouissance carries with it the notion of fluidity, diffusion, duration. It is a kind of potlatch in the world of orgasms, a giving, expending, dispensing of pleasure without concern about ends or closure. (p. 36, n. 8)

   The Law of the Father is Lacan's formulation for language as the medium through which human beings are placed in culture, a medium represented and enforced by the figure of the father in the family. See Anika Lemaire, *Jacques Lacan*, trans. David Macey (London: Routlege & Kegan Paul, 1977), especially Part 7, 'The role of the Oedipus in accession to the symbolic'.
3. Julia Kristeva's books include *Semiotike: Recherches pour une semanalyse* (Paris: Tel Quel, 1969); *Le Texte du roman* (The Hague: Mouton, 1970); *Des Chinoises* (Paris: des femmes, 1974); *La Révolution du langage poétique* (Paris: Seuil, 1974); *Polylogue* (Paris: Seuil, 1977); and *Pouvoirs de l'horreur: Essai sur l'abjection* (Paris: Seuil, 1980). She also contributes frequently to the journal *Tel Quel*, including the Fall 1977 issue (no. 74) on women and women's writing. For her criticism of certain notions of *féminité*, see her interview with Françoise van Rossum-Guyon, 'A partir de *Polylogue*', in *Revue des sciences humaines* 168:4 (December 1977), pp. 495–501.
4. Kristeva, 'Le sujet en procès', in *Polylogue*, p. 77. See, in the same volume, her discussion of maternity as an experience that breaks down the categories of masculinist thought, in 'Maternité selon Giovanni Bellini', pp. 409–38. She expands her argument about the meanings of maternity for women's creativity, in 'Un nouveau type d'intellectuel: le dissident' and 'Héréthique de l'amour', *Tel Quel* 74 (Fall 1977), pp. 3–8, 30–49. For an explanation of her theory of the semiotic and of Irigaray's concepts of *l'écriture féminine*, see Josette Féral, 'Antigone, or the irony of the tribe', *Diacritics* 8:2 (Fall 1978), pp. 2–14.
5. 'Oscillation de "pouvoir" au "refus"', an interview by Xavière Gauthier in *Tel Quel* 58 (Summer 1974), translated in *New French Feminisms*, pp. 166–7. This collection of translated excerpts from French feminist writers is likely to be very useful to English-language readers.
6. Kristeva, 'La femme, ce n'est jamais ça', an interview in *Tel Quel* 59 (Fall 1974),

translated in *New French Feminisms*, pp. 134–8. Kristeva has written mainly about male writers, but see her comments on some typically feminine themes in a dozen recent French women writers in 'Oscillation', *Tel Quel* 58 (Summer 1974), pp. 100–2. She comments on certain elements of women's style in her interview with van Rossum-Guyon (see n. 3), although she derives them from social rather than libidinal sources.

7. Luce Irigaray, an interview, 'Women's exile', in *Ideology and Consciousness* 1 (1977), pp. 62–7, translated and introduced by Diana Adlam and Couze Venn.

8. Irigaray, 'Ce Sexe qui n'en est pas un', in *Ce Sexe qui n'en est pas un* (Paris: Minuit, 1977), translated in *New French Feminisms*, p. 103. Irigaray's subsequent books are *Et l'une ne bouge sans l'autre* (Paris: Minuit, 1979) and *Amante marine* (Paris: Minuit, 1980). Her first book was a clinical study, *Le Langage des déments* (The Hague: Mouton, 1973).

9. *New French Feminisms*, p. 105.

10. Irigaray discusses the historical position of women in Marxist terms in 'Le Marché aux femmes', in *Ce Sexe*. Her responses to Nietzsche are in *Amante marine*.

11. Hélène Cixous's studies of male writers include her doctoral thesis, *L'Exil de Joyce ou l'art du remplacement* (Paris: Grasset, 1968); *Prénoms de personne (sur Hoffman, Kleist, Poe, Joyce)* (Paris: Seuil, 1974); and introductions to James Joyce and Lewis Carroll for Aubier. Since 1975, all her books have been published by des femmes.

12. Cixous, 'Entretien avec Françoise van Rossum-Guyon', *RSH* 168 (December 1977), pp. 488. 'Ça parle' is a Lacanian formula, but elsewhere (in her fiction/essay *Partie* (Paris: des femmes, 1976), for example) she mocks what she sees as the Father/phallus obsession of recent psychoanalysis.

13. Cixous, 'Entretien', p. 487; and *Vivre l'orange* (includes an English version by Cixous with Ann Liddle and Sarah Cornell) (Paris: des femmes, 1980), pp. 9, 105–7.

14. Cixous, 'Sorties', in *La jeune née* (Paris: Bibliotheque 10/18, 1975), translated in *New French Feminisms*, p. 98.

15. *New French Feminisms*, pp. 259–60.

16. The opening manifesto of *Questions féministes* is a long and persuasive critique of *néo-féminité*, translated in *New French Feminisms* as 'Variations on common themes', pp. 212–30. See also the appraisal by Beverley Brown and Parveen Adams, 'The feminine body and feminist politics', *m/f* 3 (1979), pp. 33–7.

17. Juliet Mitchell, *Psychoanalysis and Feminism* (New York: Vintage, 1975). See especially 'The Holy Family, Part 4; The different self, the phallus and the father', pp. 382–98.

18. Nancy Chodorow, *The Reproduction of Mothering* (Berkeley: University of California Press, 1978).

19. Dorothy Dinnerstein, *The Mermaid and the Minotaur: sexual arrangements and human malaise* (New York: Harper & Row, 1977).

20. Jacqueline Rose, in an article on Freud's analysis of the hysteric Dora, emphasizes that the male/female roles internalized by the child enter the unconscious at such a deep level that they govern the production of dreams. Dora, who desires a woman, represents herself as a man – a striking example of the socialized image of desire, ' "Dora" – fragment of an analysis', *m/f* 3 (1979), pp. 5–21.

21. Wittig's books have all been translated into English: *L'Opoponax*, tr. Helen Weaver

(Plainfield, Vt: Daughter's Press Reprint, 1976); *Les Guérrillères*, tr. David Le Vay (New York: Avon, 1973); *The Lesbian Body*, tr. David Le Vay (New York: Avon, 1976); *Lesbian Peoples: Material for a dictionary* (with substantial revisions), tr. Wittig and Sande Zeig (New York: Avon, 1979).

22. Wittig, 'The straight mind', speech given at the Feminist as Scholar Conference in May 1979 at Barnard College, New York, NY.

23. Wittig, 'One is not born a woman', text of the speech given at the City University of New York Graduate Center, September 1979.

24. Colette Guillaumin, 'Question de différence', *Questions féministes* 6 (September 1979), pp. 3–21. Guillaumin points out that the claim to 'difference' comes from other oppressed groups as well (Third World and US blacks, for example), who have not yet succeeded in putting their desire for political self-determination into effect. To assert their difference against the ruling class strengthens their group solidarity, but at the expense of an analysis of the political sources of that difference.

25. Madeleine Gagnon, 'Corps I', *New French Feminisms*, p. 180. See Chantal Chawaf for a similar statement, in 'La Chair linguistique', *New French Feminisms*, pp. 177–8.

26. Cora Kaplan combines psychoanalytic and anthropological accounts of women's hesitations to speak, in 'Language and gender', *Papers on Patriarchy* (Brighton, Sussex: Women's Publishing Collective, 1976). Similarly, Sandra M. Gilbert and Susan Gubar demonstrate how socially derived ambivalence toward the role of writer has acted upon women's writing in English, in *The Madwoman in the Attic: The woman writer and the nineteenth-century literary imagination* (New Haven: Yale University Press, 1979).

27. See Tillie Olsen's *Silences* (New York: Delacorte, 1979) for a discussion of the practical demands and self-doubts that have hindered women's writing, especially 'The writer-woman: one out of twelve', pp. 177–258.

28. Christiane Rochefort, 'Are women writers still monsters?' a speech given at the University of Wisconsin, Madison, February 1975, translated in *New French Feminisms*, pp. 185–6.

29. 'Concentrism' is Elaine Showalter's term, used in a speech, 'Feminist literary theory and other impossibilities', given at the Smith College Conference on Feminist Literary Criticism, Northampton, Mass., 25 October 1980.

PART TWO
APPLIED CRITICISM

— SIX —
Villette

JUDITH NEWTON

Villette begins in that ideal interior, those 'large' and 'well-proportioned'[1] rooms, which in *Pride and Prejudice* and in much fiction by women functions as an emblem of the heroine's reward at the end of the novel – the life of comfort, quiet and order conventionally supposed to define the experience of a genteel married woman. Like many heroines before her, Lucy Snowe appears well pleased at first with the emotional tenor of this life, a tenor suggested by the calm interior of the Bretton house, by 'the large, peaceful rooms, the well-arranged funiture, the clear, wide windows', and by the housewife herself, a figure most pointedly represented by Polly Home.[2] Polly, of course, is only a child of 7, but she is a child who is learning how to be a woman, and in great measure she already behaves like an upper-middle-class housewife – stirring cream and sugar into papa's tea and meeting Graham at the end of a hard day with a warning to wipe his shoes properly upon the mat. Scolding, comforting, attending, Polly is intensely familiar, a doll-sized version of the genteel married woman and a figure in whom all the daily business and daily relations of a dependent female appear officially charming.

Many readers of *Villette* have responded to this charm and have been inclined to see in the first three chapters one of the least unpleasant episodes in the troubled history of Lucy Snowe – Andrew Hook, for example, finds the Bretton house 'an asylum of peace and tranquillity'.[3] But, for all its surface attractions, the Bretton household is not as tranquil as it has been seen: the very quiet of its interior is the quiet of muted suffering, and at the base of Polly's ostensibly charming relation to Graham is a power dynamic which is distinctly unpleasant. Charlotte Brontë, in fact, without making any overt comment to the effect, quietly presents the dependent life, the traditional end point of a marriage plot, as a condensation of powerlessness and pain.

Although there is much in Brontë's portrait of the dependent life that is familiar from Jane Austen, the inequities of money and power which Brontë subtly evokes are more permanent, more radical and more painful than the inequities of money and power which Austen establishes and then subverts in *Pride and Prejudice*. In Brontë, for example, the economic inequity between men and women, which is based not on men's access to money but on their access to work that pays, is never mystified or subverted. Men's work and most women's lack of work are real to us in this novel, and, because they are real, we are made to experience what we are never really permitted to feel in *Pride and Prejudice*, that the division of labor between genteel women and genteel men is the source of profound and daily differences in powerlessness and power.

As in Austen, we are aware early in the novel of the traditional difference in men's and women's mobility – Graham comes and goes while Polly sits on a stool 'all day long' – but we are also made to feel, as we are not in Austen, that men come and go because they have work that requires it, while genteel dependent women sit on a stool all day long because there is little else that they are required or allowed to do (20). As in Burney and Austen, men's economic privilege in *Villette* is also a source of status and of control over women in that it gives men the means of bestowing benefits. Graham is not yet earning a living, but he does have treasures that little Polly covets, and, in his use of them as a mode of securing her attention, he anticipates the emotional control which work that pays will give him as a man: 'Yes, yes; you will stay with me, I am sure. I have a pony on which you shall ride, and no end of books with pictures to show you' (15). But in *Villette* men's privilege, especially their access to work in public spheres, allows them the further status of providing women with the vicarious experience of a larger world. Graham's every entry into the Bretton household introduces the eventfulness and energy of the world outside, a world which the women of *this* interior can't even see from their windows: 'The evening, by restoring Graham to the maternal roof ... brought us an accession of animation' (16).

Graham as well as Mr Home denies women the right to explore this world on their own. Mr Home warns Polly that 'only great, strong people' – that is, men – are fit for travel, and Graham reinforces this message by lending her a book in which the world is described as a place full of dangers for women – wild men with scarcely any clothes on, wild horses and a goblin which might 'trample me down amongst the bushes, as I might tread on a grasshopper in a hayfield without knowing it' (18, 25). No wonder Polly means to postpone traveling until she is as tall as Mrs Bretton and can command Graham's protection. In the meantime, her experience of the world is more confined than Elizabeth's, consisting only of secondhand participation in the world of males.

In *Villette*, men's access to work that pays is not just the source of power to move or power to assume control over women; it is the source of a vital autonomy – the power to define the self and to feel approved. We are made to understand that young Graham is identified by his work as a student, the mature Graham by his professional career, and we are told that both have their share of prizes or esteem. But dependent women cannot be identified by their work at all since Brontë all but omits genteel domestic labor from the novel. Indeed, no dependent woman is ever more productively employed than little Polly, in whom domestic work is seen as miniature and, therefore, as absurd: 'I found her seated, like a little Odalisque, on a couch. . . . She seemed happy; all her appliances for occupation were about her; the white wood work-box, a shred or two of muslin, an end or two of ribbon, collected for conversion into doll-millinery' (25). It is this division of labor between women and men that prompts women to see men as superior: Polly secures Graham a piece of cake on the grounds that 'he goes to school: girls – such as me and Miss Snowe – don't need treats, but *he* would like it' (21).

Of course dependent women do labor in this novel, but not at anything so visible as the performance of domestic chores, for their real job is to be self-sacrificing, to love and serve. Thus Polly entertains Graham; she soothes him; she hands him his tea; she secures him cake while she goes without. Graham, in fact, 'could not be sufficiently well waited on, nor carefully enough looked after' (21). It is as if Polly had already read a spate of manuals on the true nature of woman's sphere.

It is in sacrificing herself to Graham and her father, moreover, that Polly finds what worth and identity she can feel; but to be identified through love and sacrifice in this novel is barely to be there. Polly's very self is 'forgotten' in serving Graham, and 'with curious readiness' she so completely adapts herself 'to such themes as interested him' that 'one would have thought the child had no mind or life of her own, but must necessarily live, move and have her being in another: . . . she nestled to Graham, and seemed to feel by his feelings: to exist in his existence' (21–2).

It is Polly's immersion in an ideologically prescribed self-sacrifice and her consequent lack of autonomy which is at the root of the suffering which so permeates the Bretton chapters. For the emotionally dependent female needs men as men do not need her, and separation, loss, suffering are inevitable. Polly is separated twice from the men who sustain her sense of being, and separation, in each case, submits her to something that resembles the agonies of dying. To be divided from Graham or her father is to ask 'Why hast thou forsaken me?'; is to lie 'mute and motionless' by Graham's foot; is to feel 'in this way I cannot – cannot live!' (19, 27). The scene in which Graham sits 'wholly unconscious' of Polly, pushing her with his 'restless foot' while she lies on the floor softly caressing his shoe, is one of the more painful scenes in literature (27).

One further consequence of Polly's immersion in self-sacrifice is not only that it submits her to pain but that it enforces her low status and lack of power in relation to Graham. Graham, of course, is perfectly content to let her wait on him and is fond of treating her as a kind of serving maid, asking her to 'bring me something particularly nice; that's a kind little woman' or 'promising that, when he had a house of his own, she should be his housekeeper, and perhaps – if she showed any culinary genius – his cook' (20). Lucky Polly. But while men like Graham may enjoy being served, may adore being worshiped, at base they view women who do both as inferior, less fully human than themselves, and naturally more subject to control.

This attitude was conventionally buried in mid-nineteenth-century life by an ideology which assured women of the middle class that they were both superior to men and mysteriously more powerful as well, but the contradictions between this ideology and the realities of status and power are writ large in Graham's first encounter with Polly Home. The encounter begins playfully with a homage that is patently insincere – 'Miss Home. ... Your slave, John Graham Bretton' – and ends with a display of Graham's control that effectively reduces Polly to the less than human (15). Even Polly protests after Graham casually lifts her over his head with one hand: 'I wonder what you would think of me if I were to treat you in that way, lifting you with my hand ... as Warren lifts the little cat' (16).

The Miss Marchmont episode repeats on an adult scale, but with little essential variation, the elements first broached in the relation of Polly and Graham. Once again there is the 'handsome residence', the quiet interior of the leisured genteel woman (30). But once again the ground note of this quiet interior is that of suffering, and the suffering is linked with a lack of autonomy, with emotional dependence on a man: Maria Marchmont has mourned the death of her fiancé for thirty years, and that grief – since she has been a cripple for the last two decades – has been quite literally paralyzing. Like little Polly's, Maria Marchmont's dependence and emotional powerlessness are indirectly connected with the division between women's and men's spheres, for our only view of her past reminds us of that traditional division between action and inaction in the lives of genteel men and women. We see Maria indoors, 'dressed and decorated', sitting by the fireside to wait, while Frank, the lover, the *man*, is riding about somewhere in the world (34). Like Polly, too, Maria looks up to the man, the active one, as her superior: 'O my noble Frank – my faithful Frank – my *good* Frank! so much better than myself – his standard in all things so much higher!' (33). Like Polly, in fact, she sees him as a kind of god and as a giver of life itself: 'You see I still think of Frank more than of God'; 'while I loved, and while I was loved, what an existence I enjoyed!' (35, 33). Logically, then, deprivation of Frank means death or a deathlike existence, means 'thirty years of sorrow' and 'twenty years' of 'impotence' as a 'rheumatic cripple' (31, 30).

What Lucy feels about this, her first exposure to the lives of dependent women, is suggested obliquely at best, but Brontë does give her some ironic consciousness of the division between ideologies about women's lives and the potentially painful realities. Eight years of Lucy's own life have been full of storm and loss and suffering, yet she withholds the details, wryly permitting

> the reader to picture me, for the next eight years, as a bark slumbering through halcyon weather, in a harbour still as glass – the steersman stretched on the little deck, his face up to heaven, his eyes closed: buried, if you will, in a long prayer. A great many women and girls are supposed to pass their lives something in that fashion; why not I with the rest? (29)

What Lucy suggests, of course, is that women's lives are often more troubled than they seem, but the image of women's lives as they should be, with its emphasis on idleness and inactivity, also betrays an aversion to the very ideal of woman's sphere. The image, for example, makes us feel that idleness is unnatural. It is not natural, after all, for a steersman to be inert, 'buried' in a prayer, for men and steersmen in particular are supposed to be active. Even the pleasant variation of the image which follows – 'Picture me then idle, basking, plump and happy, stretched on a cushioned deck' – strikes us as wrong (30). Steersmen are supposed to steer, not bask in the sun. It is by asking us to imagine a *man* undergoing the idleness assigned to the life of a genteel woman that Brontë emphasizes the feeling that even the ideal for women is unpleasant and unnatural.

But if the ideal is unpleasant in the abstract it is much more unpleasant in the concrete, for the lives of dependent genteel women are not simply inactive, as the image suggests. They are potentially full of pain. The real image of women's life is not that of burial in a prayer or of basking in the sun but that of little Polly Home pricking her fingers and bleeding away on the handkerchief she is hemming as a 'keepsake for "papa"' (16). Lucy Snowe, of course, despite her name and her pretensions to calm, participates vicariously in Polly's suffering, and this participation subtly enforces Brontë's oblique criticism of woman's sphere. When Polly mopes, Lucy's tranquility is broken. When Polly loses herself in her father, Lucy is oppressed by the intensity of her feelings: 'it was a scene of feeling too brimful, and which, because the cup did not foam up high or furiously overflow, only oppressed one the more' (12). To love Mr Home, to love any male with Polly's self-submerging devotion, is clearly hazardous from Lucy's point of view, and Graham in particular strikes her as 'an animal dangerous by nature, and but half-tamed by art' (25).[4]

Like Austen, then, Brontë evokes a causal relation between economic dependence and lack of power, but in contrast to Austen she does not subvert this relation. In *Villette*, moreover, the modes of powerlessness with which economic dependency is linked are more radical and more painful than those which we encounter in Jane Austen. Indeed, the dependent life, which in *Pride and Prejudice* constitutes the heroine's reward and which appears protectively enclosed by Pemberley at the end of the novel, reappears in *Villette* as both painful and claustrophobic. What Brontë appears to arrive at, in fact, is that to be denied work, to be dependent, is to be denied power even to define one's self, and this is to be denied a vital form of autonomy. The novel begins, therefore, by obliquely rejecting dependency, the traditional happy ending, and by rewriting a conventional fictional script: the real history of Lucy Snowe, in contrast to the histories of Elizabeth and Evelina, begins not with an entry onto the marriage mart but with an entry onto the labor market. It begins with a reordering of the priorities previously assigned to love and quest.

Of course, by covertly rejecting the traditional love and marriage plot, the opening of *Villette* strains against ideology – as it informed literature as well as life. And it is this tension with ideology which accounts for the extensive mystification in this novel. Brontë's critique of the dependent life, for example, is disguised in these opening chapters by the fact that Polly is officially a girl of 7, and Polly's unpleasant power relation with Graham is masked by the charm which Lucy Snowe attaches to this officially childlike relationship. The ideological source of Polly's role, indeed the very existence of an ideology, is also mystified by the peculiar absence of community. Elizabeth Bennet and Maggie Tulliver live in the midst of societies that are well defined; we feel the weight of their shared assumptions, the universality of their 'truths'. But English society in *Villette*, the society to which Lucy Snowe belongs, seems to be no society at all and seems therefore to make no demands upon the heroine. What passes for English society is a handful of characters – and peripatetic characters at that. They appear in England and then disappear, relocate, reassemble in Belgium, and seem unrelated on the whole to any larger body. This English network, moreover – the Brettons, the Homes and Ginevra Fanshawe – is not family or even properly kin to Lucy Snowe. Their notions about women are not officially binding upon her, and their relation to her anyway is so tangential that they seldom appear to exert any influence. The second community in the novel, a community represented by Villette, is more cohesive but is also foreign, and what is foreign may be rejected. In this novel, it usually is. Villette ('small town') and Labassecour ('farmyard'), far from binding Lucy with their provincial notions about woman's fate, are generally just the locus of certain highly traditional attitudes toward genteel women which have been half consciously projected onto the Catholic and the foreign that they may be discredited by Lucy, and by Brontë too, for the benefit of an English and Protestant reader. In effect, then, *Villette* disguises the communal source and therefore the very existence of the ideology whose oppressive weight it nevertheless records.

But if Brontë's resistance to the ideology of woman's sphere prompts her to mystify this ideology – and Lucy Snowe at times seems remarkably free of those 'universal' truths which Elizabeth Bennet must overcome – her resistance also appears to generate counter-longings for what has been denied. These are longings which inform the experience of her heroine and which ultimately deform the very shape of her narrative, and they make Lucy Snowe in some ways more fiercely bounded by ideology than Elizabeth Bennet. At the beginning of the novel, for example, Brontë, having obliquely exposed Lucy to some of the unnatural ideals and painful realities of a dependent woman's traditional existence – the confinement, the inactivity, the painful emotional dependency on men – having emphasized the claustrophic quality of a woman's life without men or occupation,[5] turns around and stresses the difficulty with which any of this can be given up. Lucy does leave the quiet interiors of genteel women for a life of labor, economic independence and self-enhancing power, but she does not leave them out of distaste for what she has observed. She leaves because she has to. Far from casting herself romantically into the arms of the unknown, she 'must be goaded, driven, stung, forced to energy' (32). Indeed, so alien is the notion of leaving the genteel dependent life that the decision to seek London appears to come from some source other than herself: the aurora borealis. 'Some new power it seemed to bring. I drew in energy with the keen, low breeze that blew on its path. A bold thought was sent to my mind; my mind was made strong to receive it' (36). And so foreign does the independent life appear that from the time Lucy leaves for London *every* landscape, even English landscapes, appears dark, foreign and often sinister.

That Charlotte Brontë could take so critical, though finally so ambivalent, a view of the dependent life and the ideology of woman's sphere owes much to the fact that she could afford to do so, for she had a sense of option which Burney and Austen did not. For one thing, Brontë lived in an age which valorized work. The ideal of earning one's own way rather than of being born into independency, the ideology that any man *could* earn his own way, the equation of work and duty had all gained ascendancy by 1853, and they had gained ascendancy in part because men of the bourgeoisie had acquired money and status through their own labor and were gaining social and political influence as well.[6] This shift in wealth and influence is partially evoked in *Villette* by the fact that the creatures of 'sunshine', the persons of highest status and greatest income, are not landed gentry as in *Evelina* or *Pride and Prejudice* but men who have essentially earned their own way (357). Mr Home is a scientist before he becomes the Comte de Bassompierre, and John Graham Bretton is a doctor whose family fortune gets misplaced and who regains his wealth by establishing a successful practice.

Brontë's sense of option must also have been enforced by the fact that protest over the economic contradiction between middle-class men and middle-class women, especially over the plight of genteel working women, had surfaced in the 1830s and 1840s. It had become impossible to ignore the fact that, while the doors of professions and trade were opening to men of the middle class, independent women of the same class background were still confined to the totally glutted and low-status positions of teacher and governess. Protests against this inequity, demands that single women be admitted into occupations normally reserved for men, were lending new legitimacy to the idea of genteel working women, were opening new spheres of work and education, and were inevitably casting doubt upon the desirability of the leisured economically dependent life, or so literature on the 'woman question' and on the status of dependent middle-class women would suggest. But, even as manuals and periodical literature of that time legitimated genteel working women,[7] they appeared compelled to defend dependency. Both suggested the consolidation of an essentially defensive ideology, an ideology which assured dependent middle-class women that they too had significant work and significant power but which restricted them to the home, identified their work with love and sacrifice, and limited their power to 'influence' or their ability to manipulate and improve others.

Brontë's particular insertion into this historical situation inclined her both to reject and embrace this ideology. Some of the circumstances of her life required her to respect the genteel working woman; her economic situation, for example, required her to tolerate the kind of drudgery which Austen could afford to dismiss with a shudder. Charlotte had to work – the career of her brother and the education of her sisters demanded it – and so she was forced to have respect for work that paid. This respect, moreover, was grounded in her social position. Patrick Brontë had worked his way up from peasantry to country clergy, and the Brontë family as a whole felt some lingering though uneasy adherence to the idea of work and rising.[8] Certainly there is genuine admiration for the independent life in Brontë's letters. In August 1850 she writes that 'there is no more respectable character on this earth than an unmarried woman who makes her own way through life – without support of husband or brother.'[9]

Villette, to some extent, is the story of a 'respectable character', the story of an independent life. But it is in no way a simple endorsement of work and rising. For one thing, Brontë knew too well how arduous and how barren of achievement the working life could be. As governess and teacher she had to contend with children of the upper class, children who were most often spoiled and undisciplined, and she also had to contend with the lower-class labors imposed upon this teaching, the 'oceans of needlework' which convinced her that her employer cared 'nothing in the world about [her] except to contrive how the greatest possible quantity of labour [might] be squeezed out'.[10] The salary too was miserably low (£20 a year from Mr and Mrs White, with £4 deducted for laundry), but most painful was the experience of being declassed and disregarded: 'I see now more clearly than I ever have done before that a private governess has no existence, is not considered as a living and rational being except as connected with the wearisome duties she has to fulfil.'[11] It is no wonder that as a novel about the independent life *Villette* is often bitter, for Brontë understood too well that for genteel women work might be a barrier against rather than an avenue to power.

Still, it is not the hardships of the working life which are given emphasis in *Villette*, and for the most part Brontë's ambivalence toward independence has other sources. There is, in part, some uneasiness about the idea of economic achievement in itself, for, as Terry Eagleton suggests, Brontë felt critical of the very bourgeois comforts to which she and Lucy Snowe aspired.[12] But in the novel's unflattering portraits of ambitious women there is also a very strong element of aversion to the idea of a *woman's* making her own self-interest the center of her life, some adherence to the ideology that self-sacrifice really is a woman's virtue, some lingering fear that the 'selfish woman may not improperly be regarded as a monster'.[13] Connected to this is Brontë's immersion in the ideological valorization of love, her longing for the love of a good man and for the identity which such a love might confer. And this longing is sustained in confusing tension with her desire for autonomy or for self-identification. As Helene Moglen has convincingly argued, Charlotte's early feelings of guilt and inadequacy prompted her to embrace the domination of her father and brother and to depend on them, as she depended in later life on Monsieur Héger, to confirm her sense of self.[14] In this way, she was particularly vulnerable to the ideology which urged middle-class women in general to submerge themselves in the lives of men because submerging self was in their nature. It is this contradiction between her desire for autonomy and her loyalty to an ideology of love and sacrifice which Brontë encounters in *Villette*.[15]

Despite Brontë's finely intuited perceptions of the pain and powerlessness which love and sacrifice entail, perceptions subtly embodied in the first three chapters, Lucy's longing for love and sacrifice continues. It is this longing above all which makes the independent life untenable in *Villette*, and it is a longing which Brontë cannot analyze because she shares it. Indeed, the very intensity of her resistance appears to generate desire for what is being resisted. It is this contradiction in Brontë which prompts her to qualify and displace her initial criticism of the dependent life by projecting it onto the figure of a child. It is this contradiction which impels her almost compulsively to examine and re-examine the dependent existence and, in the process, to disrupt the progress of her narrative, and it is this contradiction which seduces her into creating her own untenable 'happy' ending. It is this contradiction, in short, which makes of *Villette* a lesson in the virulence of the enemy within and a demonstration of the fact that intuition of oppression does not make for easy protest.

The tension in *Villette* between resistance to ideology and counter-longing is evident, as I have noted, in the difficulty with which Lucy separates herself from the genteel but stifling interiors in the first part of the novel. The same tension shapes Brontë's management of Lucy's entry into the world of work. The chapters which deal with this entry are the most vigorous and the most exhilarating in the novel and they mark the beginning of an autonomy (an existence!) in Lucy that we have not yet seen. Lucy, for example, appears to take on life as she draws nearer to people who are earning their way: 'I have seen the West-end, the parks, the fine squares; but I love the city far better. . . . The city is getting its living – the West-end but enjoying its pleasure' (41). The effect of this work environment is to make Lucy powerful, is to give her both autonomy and control. Lucy's departure for the continent, in fact, is one of the high points of female power in *Villette*. Here we find Lucy utterly alone on a wharf at night, ordering workmen to take their hands off her and to place her trunk at her side. Then, having heard her assert herself against a 'throng of watermen', we witness her gliding off in the midst of wind, rain and 'insane oaths', feeling 'animated and alert' and fully ready to sail aboard *The Vivid* (42, 43). Lucy, instead of being trampled on by one of Graham's goblins, begins to experience the kinds of power usually reserved for men.

Of course the autonomy and control that Lucy feels on being plunged into the world outside, the world of men, are really momentary, only part of that happy interlude in which the world to be explored appears 'like a wide dreamland, far away', and in a touch of unsubtle foreboding she spies a rainbow over the European continent and is immediately seasick (48).[16] But, short-lived as this spell of power and daring is, it is quite in conflict with a genteel woman's proper role, and Brontë herself is in such conflict that she feels called upon to apologize for and justify it to the reader. The influence of the aurora borealis, for example, which on one level suggests Lucy's difficulty in leaving what is known, functions on another level to assure the reader that Lucy is not as unfeminine and daring as she seems: reader, the aurora borealis made me do it. A 'grave, judicious' Mrs Barrett is also drummed up as a kind of role model for the reader – 'grave and judicious as she was, she did not charge me with being out of my senses' (37). And then, we are assured, Lucy herself is moderate in her conscious motivations: 'In going to London, I ran less risk and evinced less enterprise than the reader may think' (38). So anxious is Brontë, like Austen and Burney before her, to qualify, justify and in part deny the power of her heroine that she also very speciously assures us that Lucy's boldness is characteristic of English women and that only foreigners would find it strange.

This same tension between enjoyment of self-enhancing power and the ideological necessity of disguising and disowning it must account for the vacillations of judgment which mark Brontë's portraits of other independent women in the world which Lucy is about to enter. Madame Beck, for example, is a vicarious quest figure, a substitute for Lucy Snowe, and an embodiment of self-enhancing power.[17] She is also a character whom Brontë treats with deep ambivalence. Beck's function as a quest figure is somewhat masked by the fact that she is 'motherly' in function and appearance and by the fact that some of her powers are traditionally feminine; that is, she is manipulative and indirect: '"Surveillance", "espionage", – these were her watchwords' (55, 61). But if Madame Beck is familiar, she is also foreign; she is something other than the Miss Marchmonts and little Pollys of the world's firesides. For one thing, she has work that pays and that pays enough to be valued, and Charlotte Brontë and Lucy Snowe frankly admire both the work and the benefits: 'All these premises and this garden are hers, bought with her money; she has a competency already secured for old age and a flourishing establishment under her direction, which will furnish a career for her children' (306). Unlike Maria Marchmont and Paulina Mary, moreover, Maria Beck can find identity in her work. She *is* the 'directress' of the Rue Fossette; she is a 'first-rate *surveillante*,' and in her capacity as both she has the power of control: 'she rules all [120 pupils], together with four teachers, eight masters, six servants and three children, managing at the same time to perfection the pupils' parents and friends' (123, 61). Control is another quality that Brontë and Lucy Snowe admire: 'Madame was a very great and a very capable woman. That school offered for her powers too limited a sphere; she ought to have swayed a nation: she should have been the leader of a turbulent legislative assembly' (63).

Both Beck's work and the autonomy and control it affords her account for her untraditional relation to men. Although she does allow Monsieur Paul to disobey orders and although she is susceptible to the charm of Graham, now Dr John, she is never tempted into real submission or dependency. In fact, when Lucy speculates about a future for Madame Beck she imagines Dr John in the role of dependent, a reversal of the traditional love and marriage plot: 'Had she, indeed, floating visions of adopting Dr John as a husband, taking him to her well-furnished home, endowing him with her savings ... and making him comfortable for the rest of his life?' (86–7). When Madame Beck finds herself rejected, she does not lie at Dr John's feet or take to her room for thirty years. She reasons with herself; she behaves 'wisely', and it is her access to paid labor, at least in part, that permits her to do this: 'she had an important avocation, a real business to fill her time, divert her thoughts, and divide her interest' (90). More than any other quality it is this emotional independence of men that Charlotte and Lucy admire: 'Brava! once more, Madame Beck. I saw you matched against an Apollyon of a predilection; you fought a good fight, and you overcame!' (90).

From some perspectives Madame Beck is an intensely attractive woman – autonomous, achieving, controlling and emotionally independent of men – a woman whom Lucy describes more than once as having 'very good sense' and 'very sound opinions' (62). And yet none of her good qualities is permitted to sit well. As in much of women's fiction there is something wrong, something alien, about the woman who really does make self-enhancing work the center of her existence.[18] In *Villette* she is at first a 'little bourgeoise', a little scheming, a little lacking in passion, and by the end of the novel she is a monster of avarice, heartlessness and intrigue (61).

What lies behind Brontë's initial ambivalence toward Madame Beck, and behind the ultimate aberrant reduction of her to a villain, is Brontë's ambivalence toward the life of work and self-enhancing power which is the quest of Lucy Snowe; and it is not the drawbacks of that life, as Kate Millett has suggested,[19] but its very goals which give her most unease. Work that pays is certainly the key to autonomy and control in this novel, but as much as Lucy may aspire to both, as much as she may admire these self-enhancing powers in Madame Beck, they are not powers which she herself can easily embrace. To hanker after them is to desire what stands in conflict with the ideology of woman's sphere, an ideology which required the middle-class female to be self-sacrificing rather than self-interested. And for all its discomforts this is an ideology which Charlotte Brontë cannot abandon, and cannot abandon in part, it would seem, because she so deeply resists it. Try as she will, Brontë cannot approve a woman who is successful at making self-interest the center of her existence, and 'interest was the master-key of Madame's nature' (63). Madame Beck, therefore, is made to suffer from a malady traditional to the independent woman in nineteenth-century fiction. She is made radically lacking in feeling and heart, and these are deficiencies which make her unattractive and unacceptable as a model for the heroine: 'to attempt to touch her heart was the surest way to rouse her antipathy. ... It proved to her she had no heart to be touched: it reminded her where she was impotent and dead' (63). It is still some leap from this portrait to the Madame Beck of the final chapters, to that 'heartless, self-indulgent and ignoble' villain whose 'money reasons' and self-seeking are so exaggerated that she would rather destroy Monsieur Paul than allow another to have him; but the reduction of Beck to a villain is, to a great extent, a final anxious renunciation of the working life and of self-enhancing power, unredeemed by the Victorian woman's traditional virtues – love and self-sacrifice (377, 389).

Brontë's rejection of and counter-adherence to the ideology of woman's sphere are further suggested in her overt criticism of and lurking admiration for Ginevra Fanshawe, a quest figure disguised as the thoughtless heroine of a love and marriage plot. The daughter of an 'officer on half-pay', 'well descended' but essentially middle-class, Ginevra is actually a woman who must earn her way. Ginevra, of course, plans to earn *her* fortune through conventional methods – marriage and dependency – and this obscures her relation to Madame Beck and Lucy Snowe. But Ginevra, none the less, in her unvarnished quest after economic gain, may still be seen as a version of the woman who makes self-interest rather than self-sacrifice the conscious center of her life.

Brontë's judgment of this quest is deeply ambivalent. On the one hand, Ginevra's nonchalance about marrying a rather elderly gentleman 'with cash' is meant to be shocking, but, on the other, Ginevra, in all her money grubbing, is still an appealing and vigorous character, and it is precisely her ambition, her frank selfishness, that makes her so (47). Brontë may invite us to disapprove of Ginevra for being class-conscious and a snob, and she may invite us to agree with Lucy when Lucy castigates her for taking presents from a man she doesn't love, but she also permits Lucy to sympathize with Ginevra's economic needs and even to enjoy her vigor and honesty about her own self-serving ambition: 'Ginevra ever stuck to the substantial; I always thought there was a good trading element in her composition, much as she scorned the "bourgeoise"' (401).

For all her scolding, Lucy actually indulges Ginevra's selfishness as if she participated in it too.[20] She stands with Ginevra in front of the mirror: 'I let her selflove have its feast' (104). She gives her breakfast rolls, and she rather likes to 'let her take the lion's share, whether of the white beer, the sweet wine or the new milk' (200). Ginevra is also rather consciously admired for her attempts at autonomy, for her refusal to please men by becoming what they want her to be: 'the man is too romantic and devoted, for he expects something more of me than I find it convenient to be. He thinks I am perfect ... and it does so tire one to be goody, and to talk sense, – for he really thinks I am sensible' (78). Although we are meant to feel that Ginevra settles for too little – she should want to *be* sensible whether Dr John thinks her so or not – Lucy almost laughs with approval at her 'whimsical candour' and rather sympathizes than not with her complaint that Dr John is always 'preaching ... always coddling and admonishing' (78, 127).

Ginevra, in fact, far from wanting to serve men, like little Polly, far from simply granting them control over her mind or feelings, is bent on having power herself. Ever practical, she opts for the only kind of control immediately available: the transient and finally illusory power of the unattainable beauty. Like Graham, Ginevra enjoys her partially imagined control: she is as 'well amused' by Graham as Graham is amused by Polly, and it pleases her to feel that 'I can wind him round my little finger' (74). She is also a bit sadistic, and like Graham she finds opportunities to inflict suffering: she flirts with Lucy here or de Hamal there, rejoices when she imagines having seen Graham 'sulking and dying in the distance', and declares bluntly that 'of course he will break his heart. I should be shocked and disappointed if he didn't' (202, 74). Once again, moreover, Lucy Snowe both criticizes Ginevra and participates in the quality about which she is implicitly critical. In the school play, for example, Lucy conspires with her to make Graham himself feel powerless: 'my longing was to eclipse the "Ours": i.e. Dr John' (121).

But Ginevra's control over Graham is transient and in part illusory, for from the beginning her power is the power of a subordinate. Graham may elevate her to the position of someone he can worship, but he is always half-aware of his own fictions. Ginevra is at once an 'angel' and an inferior, a perfect lady and a greedy middle-class girl whom he plans to 'mold' into something better (192). It is not surprising, then, that Graham can recover from his emotional bondage in an instant, for his bondage has been a function less of Ginevra's control than of his own will. Graham has merely indulged himself in a courtly mood, and 'the mood of one hour is sometimes the mockery of the next' (215).

Ginevra's designs, then, are not designs that Lucy can take seriously, and this is precisely what makes Ginevra so handy. For the shapes taken by her ambition, the vehicles of *her* selfishness and desire for autonomy and control, are so patently different from any which Lucy officially aspires to that Lucy can be allowed covertly to admire Ginevra, to identify with her, and to participate in her selfishness without ever being identified with her in a serious way. Ginevra provides Brontë with a safe and nonconscious mode of exploring the self-enhancing power and ambition which she cannot consciously embrace. Because Madame Beck's ambitions take a form almost identical to Lucy's – Lucy, like Beck (and Brontë herself), eventually aspires to having a school of her own – she must be carefully dissociated from Brontë's heroine and rejected, while Ginevra, who is no less ambitious or unfeeling, can be spoken of with favor to the end.

Despite Brontë's ambivalence toward self-enhancing power, Lucy's own attempts at acquiring it are initially as vigorous as those of Ginevra or Madame Beck, and they are seen, in the beginning at least, as energizing and healthy. Lucy *is* confined to another interior and to women's work, but this interior is more continuously lively than those of Maria Marchmont and Polly Home, and although Lucy, like any genteel woman, is at first properly 'inadventurous, unstirred by impulses of practical ambition', when challenged to do more she responds with characteristic reserves of strategy and power (65). Lucy day-dreaming over silk dresses is almost instantly transformed into Miss Snowe taking 'command' over a 'wild herd' of schoolgirls by ripping up exam books and thrusting unruly pupils into closets (68–9). She is instantly a 'good deal bent on success', and she is happier: 'I felt I was getting on; not lying the stagnant prey of mould and rust, but polishing my faculties and whetting them to a keen edge with constant use (70, 69). 'Getting on' makes Lucy feel good.

But Lucy's first year as an independent woman does not culminate in satisfaction or in feeling good – it culminates in a symbolic outbreak of rebellion, the rage of rebellion turned inward in the form of illness, depression and hysteria. The explanation, moreover, is not simply that her job is ill paid, isolated, and confined, although all are true; it is also that a familiar craving for love and sacrifice reasserts itself on every hand. Despite the autonomy, the achievement and the control associated with her passage to Villette, Lucy arrives at no inner or outer space which is new. She leaves two male-centered interiors for a third, and within the third, an interior seething with stifled romance and sexual passion, an obsession with men like commitment to self-sacrifice returns with all the force of the repressed.

This longing for love is conveyed in the pensionnat chapters through a series of references to feminine interiors, interiors which represent Lucy's life or Lucy herself as an independent woman. Like the interiors which initially represent the lives of genteel dependent women, the interiors now representing Lucy's life become pointed in their emphasis upon confinement and upon painful and hidden desire. Among the emblems of this life, for example, is the pensionnat itself, once a convent inside which a nun sinned in passion against her vows. There is the nun herself, hiding a secret passion, and there is the nun's grave, where the nun and her passions have both been buried alive. There is also the enclosed garden of the pensionnat, where clusters of vines hang in 'loving profusion', where jasmine and ivy met and 'married', where Lucy herself keeps 'tryste' with the rising moon and tastes one 'kiss of the evening breeze' (91). There is the alley within the garden, an alley forbidden to the nubile pupils but haunted by Lucy Snowe, and finally there is Lucy herself, with her cold name and passive exterior holding the 'quick' of her nature in a 'dead trance' but giving way to 'craving' cries and driving nails into the head of her 'longing' for 'something to fetch me out of my present existence' (93).

That Lucy's hidden longings are both sexual and romantic is suggested by the sensuous imagery of the garden – trysts with the moon, kisses from the breeze – and also by the figure of the nun who has sinned against her vows. That Lucy's feelings are specifically centered on males, or that they will be, is implied by the fact that her interiors are broken in upon by male figures in pursuit of romance. The image of male intrusion is sexual, but what it suggests most directly is that men, specifically men as objects of love and romance, are impinging upon Lucy's consciousness. The suppressed love plot, in effect, inserts itself into the quest.

Lucy's alley is disturbed by a billet-doux only a few paragraphs after she describes her longing for something to take her out of her present existence. What follows the intrusion of the billet-doux is the reflection that she has not had the experience of other teachers in feeling 'power to strike and to attract' the opposite sex, and what follows this reflection is Dr John, who intrudes upon the garden and wanders through the alleys until he 'penetrated at last the "forbidden walk"' (95, 96). Dr John leaves footprints on that walk which Lucy takes pains to erase, but, emotionally at least, they are not obliterated. When Madame Beck rifles Lucy's possessions for signs of a romantic liaison, Lucy 'loverless and inexpectant of love' suffers an attack of 'bitterness' and 'inward tumult', of 'soreness and laughter, and fire, and grief' (101, 102). Her hold upon herself as the calm, the independent Lucy Snowe is permanently in jeopardy, and the effect is both exciting and deeply unsettling – for Lucy has witnessed the pain and powerlessness of passion in Maria Marchmont and in Polly Home.

Lucy's foray into acting – the play, like everything else in this school for girls, has to do with love – clearly functions as an outlet for her conflicting responses to women's obsession with men, sex and romance. On the one hand, her repressed sexual and romantic feelings are released for the moment in a love and marriage plot which casts her as Ginevra's foppish wooer – it is always less painful in this novel to love women than to love men. But, on the other hand, Lucy expresses rebellion against the hold that sex and romance have upon her. She wishes, for example, to strike back at Dr John for his power over her own feelings and perhaps for his control over the feelings of women in general, so she acts as if 'resolute to win and conquer' (121). But, immediately after this display of self-assertion, Lucy swears off: 'the strength and longing must be put by' (121). It is not possible in the world of *Villette* to defy men's emotional control in this way – or to direct romantic and sexual feeling toward women – and having acted out a measure of resistance to men's emotional supremacy Lucy returns at once to a state of susceptibility, half participating in Ginevra's hysterical self-worship and half empathizing with Dr John.

Thus, although it promises at first to be a novel about quest, about a life of independence and of making one's own way, *Villette* devotes much of its energy to depicting the heroine's longing for the love of a good man – and Lucy's work, we should note, is not the only thing that drives her to this. *We* may notice that she works for starvation wages in an occupation little better than that of a servant, but Lucy herself thinks very little about such matters, and Brontë simply does not draw attention to the insufficiency of Lucy's labor as a means either of financial or of personal gain. What the novel does focus upon is the persistence of a romantic and self-sacrificing ideology, an ideology all the more persistent because suppressed. And it is this ideology that makes work and independence seem inadequate:

> be content to labour for independence until you have proved, by winning that prize, your right to look higher. But afterwards, is there nothing more for me in life. ... Nothing, at whose feet I can willingly lay down the whole burden of human egotism, and gloriously take up the nobler charge of labouring and living for others? (306)

In the long vacation even the meager distractions of Lucy's independent existence are suspended; 'the prop of employment' is withdrawn, and the life of the demiconvent is cut off (135). But what might pass here as a nightmare of generalized loneliness – who wouldn't suffer by being shut up for several weeks with a cretin for company – seems in reality the ideological nightmare of having to do without male love. Lucy envies Madame Beck for being at a 'cheerful watering-place' with her children, and Zélie for being at Paris with her relatives, but it is Ginevra to whom her thoughts turn and return, Ginevra who 'seemed to me the happiest', for Ginevra is followed by 'True', that is to say, by male, 'Love': 'I pictured her faithful hero half conscious of her coy fondness, and comforted by that consciousness: I conceived an electric chord of sympathy between them' (136, 137). Ginevra, as the woman who commands male devotion, becomes for Lucy 'a sort of heroine' (137).

Ironically, Lucy's attempt to deal with the agonies of her loveless lot – she tries to get away from the pensionnat to a 'certain quiet hill' – takes her out of the virginal dormitory to a Catholic confessional where she encounters still another unattractive option for the genteel woman, another celibate life spent in still another interior, doing more repetitious, ill-paid women's labor (138). Had she visited Père Silas at home she might, 'instead of writing this heretic narrative, be counting my beads in the cell of a certain Carmelite convent' (140–1). Here is a life of 'labouring and living for others', but it is without the love of a man, and finally that is no life at all for Lucy Snowe. The long vacation ends, then, in an impasse and with symbolic death. Lucy succumbs to a wind so cold that it pierces her to the vitals and then pitches her 'headlong down an abyss' (141). In the next section of the novel, Brontë removes her from the world of work and quest and in a trance of wish fulfilment and regression returns her to a familiar English interior and a familiar life, the life of love and sacrifice, the life of the genteel dependent woman.

Readers of *Villette* sometimes complain that the novel is ill structured. Characters – major characters – are introduced in the opening chapters only to be mislaid for the entire first volume before being dredged up again without warning in the second and the third. This reintroduction is particularly striking because the mislaid characters are English and the site of their resurrection is Labassecour. We are not precisely expecting them, and this reconstruction of England upon foreign soil does give the novel the curious quality of moving forward and then lurching suddenly into reverse. This arrest, this reversal, of forward movement, of course, tells us something familiar about the quest of the independent woman: it is all too easy for her, spiritually at least, to give it up.

The man who seeks his fortune is also subject to reversals, to the feeling that he'd like to throw it over, but he cannot do so with the same emotional comfort. He cannot abruptly choose to go home and sit by the fire, tempting as that prospect might be, because a sense of being destined for movement must assail him as a man. The fate of the genteel independent woman, however, is that she may always return, at least in feeling, and that her failure to make it in the world will seem no failure at all but a mode of coming to her senses. Lucy's sojourn at La Terrasse begins literally with her coming to her senses, and the imagery is not of rebirth, which is a movement forward, but of re-entry, reunion, and return. In her ambivalence toward a life of self-enhancing power, in her resistance and countering adherence to the ideology of woman's sphere, Brontë simply arrests the progress of her novel and restores Lucy Snowe to the familiar world of the dependent woman. Here, quest gives way to love, and like many a working woman before her Lucy takes another look at what she has been forced to do without.[21]

What is interesting about Lucy's reunion with the dependent woman's life, and with the love plot of the novel, is that the focus for the first time is upon material comfort and luxury, and this focus does not characterize the earlier Polly–Graham chapters. It is as if Lucy's encounter with the world of work and quest had made her newly sensitive to the most traditional rewards of dependency and love – economic security and comfort of a material kind. Lucy Snowe, the hard-working independent woman, accustomed to cold rooms and bare chambers, now lies in a French bed, takes tea from a silver urn, sits before English fires and does not work – and it is all very appealing.

One effect of this focus on comfort is to bring into the foreground the material base of the traditional power relations between women and men, for like the earlier English interiors this secure world is dominated by a man: Graham has purchased the château, Graham is its master, and Lucy takes immediately to the dependent woman's traditional power relation with the male provider. Graham becomes the dispenser of benefits, a 'cozy arrange-ment' of pillows, a tour of Villette, a night at the concert and some easily given attention, and in return Lucy offers him a generous dose of love and sacrifice: 'I kept my ear and mind in perpetual readiness ... my patience was ordered to be permanently under arms, and my sympathy desired to keep its cornucopia replenished and ready for outpouring'; 'he seemed to know that if he would but talk about himself, and about that in which he was most interested, my expectation would always be answered, my wish always satisfied'; 'I grew almost selfish, and quite powerless to deny myself the delight of indulging his mood, and being pliant to his will' (151, 161, 165).

Unlike little Polly, Lucy is not entirely committed to this powerless role, and it is not merely that she knows her own playing of it must be temporary, that she feels the 'shadow of the future', or that 'a pink dress and black lace mantle' cannot transform her into the kind of beauty capable of holding Graham's attention (179). It is not just that she finds herself in a fairy-tale love plot. It is in part that there is something wrong with the love plot itself and that Lucy is allowed to know it. The prince, for example, is an egoist and a bit of a sadist too, and this makes love and sacrifice potentially painful. The very privilege Graham enjoys as an upper middle-class male, the privilege of access to a lucrative profession, the privilege of achieving 'a world of active good', may make him strong and cheerful, but it also inclines him to elevate himself even further at the cost of those who are less privileged than himself (169). Lucy is aware that Graham feeds his masculine self-love at women's expense without care for 'the price of provender' and that at the fireside there is 'expressed consciousness of what he has and what he is; pleasure in homage, some recklessness in exciting, some vanity in receiving the same' (169). She is also aware that a desire for ego gratification prompts him to inflict suffering, to pocket the letter that she drops in the attic and to withhold it until he has exacted a full and tearful tribute to its importance and the importance of the writer too.

Lucy also sees that, when Graham is not exacting praise or exhibiting control over her feelings, he is often merely insensitive or uncomprehending. The privilege he enjoys gives him remarkable resilience and energy, and like many privileged people he assumes that everyone has access to the same emotional resources. Witness Graham, with his 'all-sufficing strength', 'bountiful cheerfulness of high and unbroken energies', blithely advising the isolated, impoverished, and classless Lucy to '*cultivate* happiness' and 'a cheerful' mind, while she protests silently that 'happiness is not a potato' (168, 214). Witness Graham demanding to know why a plain declassed woman can't be more like a handsome upper-class man: 'And why, Lucy, can't you look and feel as I do – buoyant, courageous, and fit to defy all the nuns and flirts in Christendom?' (215). Graham may exhibit 'delicacy' in being wounded, but he has a privileged man's insensitivity to wounding others, and as Lucy puts it 'the sympathetic faculty was not prominent in him' (163).

But Lucy's response to Graham's privilege, egoism and control is far more charitable than one might expect, and here is another expression of Brontë's ambivalence toward the ideology of woman's sphere – and toward the divisions of money and power which it defends. Lucy, for example, does not overtly resent Graham's privileged access to money and work. Men in *Villette*, as in *Evelina* and *Pride and Prejudice* as well, are simply granted an unequal access to both. Nor does Lucy completely resent Graham's desire for ego gratification or even his power to hurt her. What she most resents is, in some ways, not the powerlessness or pain of the dependent role itself but her inability to *be* the dependent woman, the Cinderella who captures the prince's heart. This pain is directed into anger at Graham, but it is not precisely an expression of anger at his control. Lucy is less resentful of Graham when he is conscious of his control over her, when he is sadistic, than when he ignores her, and her most bitter comments have to do with his failure to pay her attention: 'He did not at all guess what I felt: he did not read my eyes, or face, or gestures; though, I doubt not, all spoke' (270).

Thus, the unpleasant power relations between women and men, and their economic base, are presented more overtly in this section of the novel than in the Polly–Graham chapters, where they are masked by the fact that Polly is still a child. But overt as the oppressions of these power relations are, and as closely as she explores them in Lucy Snowe, Brontë still cannot criticize the dependent role without ambivalence and disguise. Ultimately, unable either to embrace or to reject the dependent role, she attempts to reconcile contradiction by projecting all resentment of the inequities of gender onto disapproval of Graham's class feeling and bourgeois materialism.[22] This is at once a more familiar and a less threatening focus: 'Had Lucy been intrinsically the same, but possessing the additional advantages of wealth and station, would your manner to her, your value for her have been quite what they actually were?' (268).

Brontë's contradictory relation to the ideology of woman's sphere is also evident in her judgments of Louisa Bretton and Polly, now Paulina, Home. In some measure these women are attractive. In fact, for the first time in the novel, during Lucy's stay at La Terrasse, we see at length a dependent woman who seems satisfied and at peace. In contrast to the oversensitive Polly Home or the remorseful Maria Marchmont, Mrs Bretton suggests all that is healthy and untroubled. She is a 'hale, serene nature', a 'summer day', a 'stately ship, cruising safe on smooth seas' (155). Still, the attractiveness of Louisa's situation is qualified for the reader by a power relation that is by now entirely familiar. It is Graham who provides the house and all its comforts, who supplies vicarious contact with the larger world, who affords in effect his mother's life: 'at night he still comes home to me in such kindly, pleasant mood, that really I seem to live in a sort of moral antipodes, and on these January evenings my day rises when other people's night sets in' (233). It is Graham, therefore, who has emotional control, and Graham, for his part, rather sadistically enjoys it: 'All of a sudden, when you think you are most secure, I shall go forth like Jacob or Esau, or any other patriarch, and take me a wife; ... Mamma, she would fill your blue chair so admirably!' (181).

Paulina Mary, like Louisa Bretton, is also engaged in an entirely familiar power relation with the man on whom she is dependent, and it is at this point in the novel that Brontë suggests overtly what has been latent in the early chapters: the child Polly Home has been acting out the role that will be hers as an officially adult woman. Her role is to love and sacrifice to men who act as givers of material and emotional benefits. In Paulina Mary this traditional role is seen clearly, for the first time, as a barrier to autonomy, adulthood and even humanity. The 17-year-old Paulina Mary is still waiting on papa, still thinking only of his needs, still acknowledging her willingness to do and be whatever he asks. When she dances about him and claps her hands like a 'sprite', a 'chamois', a 'kitten' and a 'child', papa looks 'down on her as men *do* look on what is the apple of their eye' (239). Paulina is 'nearly as much the child as she was ten years ago', and it is all charming, the object of nothing more than playful protest or concern (239).

Paulina's relation to her father is also directly compared with her relation to Graham, enforcing the parallel already implied early in the novel between the dominant–subordinate roles of parent–child and husband–wife. Although Paulina, as an heiress, scarcely needs Graham for economic survival, her relation to him as a wife promises to carry on the traditions of sacrifice and powerlessness which have characterized her relation to her father and her early relation to Graham as little Polly. Graham, in fact, is most pleased with her when she regresses, which is often. With Paulina dimpling, lisping and forgetting to correct herself, Graham's 'position seemed to become one of more pleasure to himself' (246). All that has really changed about little Polly is that she has acquired an ability sometimes to *seem* the adult that she is not. Her workbox is now inlaid with mosaic, but she retains the same 'dainty mannerisms' of the child (247).

Although Graham and Paulina both are officially creatures of 'sunshine', anticipating the 'happiness of Heaven' here on earth, Paulina's sunshine seems lukewarm at best (368). Indeed, she is most often linked with white and winter, not with warmth or the sun, and in our last view of her she appears rather less like the sun than the moon: she is all 'white and light and bridal' and her face takes its luster from Graham's (382). Paulina's fate, moreover, in pointed contrast to Ginevra's, is to disappear from the novel like the little satellite she is. The last we hear of Paulina and Graham is that *both* their son and daughters look like Graham and that *he* reared them all with 'a firm hand' (369).

Paulina's vanishing act somewhat belies Lucy's insistence that she really is a creature of some substance after all, and it is Brontë's characterization of Paulina which most overtly suggests what Brontë felt the role of a dependent gentlewoman to be – one of powerlessness and dehumanization. But, once again, Brontë's resistance to the ideology of woman's sphere seems to evoke a countering adherence, and despite her fine perceptions about sexual politics and the inequities of gender, Brontë, for the second time in the novel, displaces her veiled criticism of woman's sphere onto a form of class protest. Louisa Bretton and Paulina Home are summarily lumped with Dr John into a single category – creatures of sunshine – and both are criticized, in the end, not because they are subordinate and half-existent but because, like Graham, they enjoy the privileges of their class.

As a creature of sunshine, Brontë implies, Louisa Bretton *cannot* understand the pain of Lucy, the pain of persons liable to go 'mad from solitary confinement' (234). And it is on the grounds of her class privilege and class insensitivity that Louisa's situation in life is finally criticized in *Villette*. Lucy is made to compare herself to abandoned hermits, starving animals and frozen dormice – all expressions chiefly of her suffering at having lost Graham's attention – and these comparisons are duly followed by a letter from Louisa Bretton in which she cheerfully tallies her own joy in Graham's comfort and blithely asserts that Lucy must have been 'just as busy and happy as ourselves' (233). All this is meant to strike us as cruel in its lack of comprehension. Paulina Home is also obtuse and, despite Lucy's official admiration of her, less sympathetic than Louisa Bretton. Paulina assumes that everyone well bred must be supported in life, but she appears least to her advantage when, like Louisa, she insists that Lucy bear witness to her relationship with Graham. Paulina 'showed me these letters; with something of the spoiled child's wilfulness, and of the heiress's imperiousness, she *made* me read them' (360).

Lucy's later association of Paulina with a pampered spaniel certainly enforces the element of class protest which winds like an underground marsh stream through her portrait of dependent women in this section of the novel. But ultimately this incipient protest, like the protest over woman's sphere, is never developed. In fact, protest of any kind is arrested by Lucy's counterinsistence that it is Fate or the Will of God or Providence – and not the working of an inequitable social and economic system – which must account for the differences between her own life and that of Paulina: 'Some lives *are* thus blessed: it is God's will' (318). Brontë's overt analysis, once again, is simply inadequate to the intensity with which she captures the experience of social and economic inequities, for we have felt the weight of class feeling and of class insensitivity in Paulina and Louisa Bretton just as we have felt the tyrannies of male supremacy in Graham.

It is not, of course, that Brontë did not know that systematic class and gender oppressions were at work, for in her positions as governess she experienced both with great directness. It is in part, as Carol Ohmann has argued, that Brontë's radical impulses – like her desire for power – 'come into very sharp collision with the ideal of Victorian womanhood which she herself internalized'.[23] The ideal required that she be accepting rather than rebellious, just as it required her to desire self-sacrifice instead of self-enhancing power. But Brontë's protest stops short as well because it is difficult systematically to criticize what one rejects on one level and longs for on another, and Brontë harbored longings for both the bourgeois comforts of class privilege and the dependency, love and self-sacrifice which such comforts purchased in middle-class females. The degree of her longing was commensurate, perhaps, with the degree of her rebellion.

Lucy officially separates herself from a woman's proper sphere and from a love and marriage plot, for the second time in the novel, when she buries Graham's letters, and it is noteworthy that her second separation is more consciously achieved than the first: Lucy seals the letters in an airtight bottle, buries them, and then covers the hole with slate and cement. What follows this second farewell is still another excess of energy. Lucy makes a deft job of mortaring and then falls under the influence of an 'electrical' mist which, like the aurora borealis, makes her strong with reinforced strength (253). And for the first time she encounters the nun – as an emblem of the isolated life – with courage and self-assertion: 'If you have any errand to me, come back and deliver it' (254). Playing Cinderella has been a debilitating business as Lucy now observes – 'The Hope I am bemoaning suffered and made me suffer much' – and it is in response to her experience of genteel female dependency and self-sacrifice that she embarks on another quest plot and on another step toward self-enhancing power: acquiring a school of her own (251).

It is at this point in the novel that Brontë attempts to pair off Lucy with Monsieur Paul, and this final love plot, we should note, actually moves the quest plot forward. Instead of curtailing the powers of the heroine, as it does in *Evelina* and *Pride and Prejudice*, the final love plot in *Villette* functions as a mode of completing and justifying the life of self-enhancing power which Lucy has been aspiring to and in part rejecting throughout the novel. Thus, it carries out the revision of scripts with which *Villette* begins – that reordering of the priorities traditionally assigned to love and quest. This use of the love plot also requires a recasting of the princely hero, a recasting in which a systematic economic contradiction between middle-class men and middle-class women is firmly reconstituted as individual and is then eroded. Ultimately, the fulfillment of Lucy's quest requires no confrontation with the ideological and material restrictions of a communal order, for both have been mystified throughout the novel, and in the end both are evoked only to be defined and thereby managed as individual.

Thus, where Orville, Darcy and Dr John are wealthy and class-privileged, Paul is impoverished and declassed. Paul is not the best that Lucy's culture has to offer, and the very construction of his character represents a deformation of the traditional love and marriage plot. But the degree to which he is deficient by the conventions of a love and marriage plot is the degree to which he is efficient by the standards of Lucy's quest. Paul's impoverishment and declassment, for example, alter the traditional power balance between middle-class man and middle-class woman and between conventional heroine and hero. Paul, since he lacks Graham's money and class position, lacks Graham's ease in assuming control over women. We are allowed to see the effort that goes into this attempt at domination, and this effort encourages us, as it encourages Lucy, to entertain an essentially patronizing attitude toward him: 'I knew that it was his love of display and authority which had brought him there – a love not offensive, only because so naïve' (182). Rather than giving him control over Lucy, Paul's class position, his economic situation, and his looks and temperament as well, tend to identify him with her. Paul, in fact, is a kind of double for Lucy Snowe, and this identification between hero and heroine is allowed to outweigh the very real privilege and power he enjoys as a male – for poor, declassed and struggling as he may be, Paul has a better job, more money, more status, more control and a greater scope for achievement than does Lucy Snowe.[24]

Paul is also stripped of ideological support in his attempts to dominate Lucy, for the fact that he is foreign and Catholic rather than British and Protestant – like Orville, Darcy and Dr John – undermines the validity of his traditional attitudes toward women and the effectiveness of his efforts to control them. Once again, of course, a communal or systematic force – in this case that of ideology – is reconstituted in the hero as individual and idiosyncratic. Ideology, in effect, is recast in a form which allows it to be managed. Thus when Paul, as a Catholic and a foreigner, fulminates against Lucy for unfeminine ambition and power, when he throws barriers in the way of her progress, the effect is only to endorse what ambition and power Lucy does have and to absolve her of selfishness: 'his injustice stirred in me ambitious wishes – it imparted a strong stimulus – it gave wings to aspiration. ... Whatever my powers – feminine or the contrary – God had given them, and I felt resolute to be ashamed of no faculty of His bestowal' (298). Ultimately, this ideological barrier, which has been displaced from the communal to the individual, is displaced once again. An ideological struggle between female and male becomes a religious war. Lucy's desire for self-enhancing power is identified as an expression of her 'terrible, proud' Protestantism, and Paul, in the guise of religious toleration, is allowed to grant her her way (353).

Charlotte Brontë's manipulation of the love plot for the purposes of quest involves a diminution of the hero's traditional privileges and, in the process, a reduction to the individual of the material and ideological forces which have operated in a systematic, if mystified, way throughout the novel. But this revision of fictional scripts involves more than a denial of the hero's traditional resources. It involves a reharnessing of them for the purposes of Lucy's quest: Paul is not only ineffective in controlling Lucy Snowe, he is made to validate her quest and to help her on her way. At the end of the novel, for example, Brontë makes use of a standard love- and fairy-tale device: she erects barriers to the happiness of her lovers and allows the hero, in coming to the rescue, to demonstrate both love and power. Paul's intervention on behalf of Lucy is certainly reminiscent of Lord Orville's on behalf of Evelina or of Darcy's on behalf of Elizabeth's errant sister – yet the barriers between Paul and Lucy take a puzzling form. Madame Beck, Père Silas and Madame Walravens – suddenly endowed with a rampant selfishness and materialism not before noted as a feature of their makeup – are abruptly posed as obstructions to the union of the lovers. The barriers are so unexpected and so grotesque – a middle-class woman, an ageing priest and a landed crone – that they call their own significance into question, and, on a closer look, the barriers to love take the shape of barriers to quest.

On one level, what Brontë betrays here by drumming up this 'secret junta' of 'self-seekers' as barriers to the happiness of Lucy Snowe is her awareness that the haves of society and an inequitable social system really do stand in Lucy's way (388, 390). And to an extent Walravens, Silas and Beck do allow

Brontë to criticize bourgeois society for its materialism and its exclusion of the many by the few. Still, the haves of society are very curiously represented. They are not represented by a Graham Bretton or by an industrial capitalist; they are not represented by anyone actually enjoying the privileges of gender or of class at the moment Brontë wrote. In two cases the haves are dimly feudal figures who make very little sense as representatives of privilege and power in 1853. The third enemy, Madame Beck, is successful, but she is female and middle-class, and as such she is a more fitting representative of one who has had to struggle against the privileges of gender and class than of one who has enjoyed an unequal share of either. All three of these characters, moreover, are Catholic and foreign, and thus they cannot involve Brontë in any overt protest of the inequities of the British system. Once again, the social has been displaced onto the private, where it can be resolved by individual action.

But the major function of Walravens, Silas and Beck is not to provide criticism of a social and economic system at all. It is to establish generalized emblems of self-seeking against which Paul and especially Lucy Snowe can be defined.[25] Because Walravens, Silas and Beck are made to stand in Lucy's way, Lucy's union with Paul and with achievement may be seen as something distinct from and triumphant over, unfeminine selfishness and desire for gain, and this removes one of the major barriers to Brontë's acceptance of the life of work and self-enhancing power.

After Paul's rescue of Lucy, after the individual triumph over the social forces which that rescue represents, the novel closes with another moment familiar to a love and marriage plot. Paul, like Darcy before him, establishes Lucy in a new life and a new interior. This final interior is a bit of a dollhouse, in fact, but it is less luxurious, less upper-class, less claustrophobic than the other interiors we have seen. Most significantly, of course, and in marked contrast to Pemberley, it is also a place of business and it is Lucy's business at last. In this private world, Lucy is allowed to savor the fantasy of combining old and new, dependence and independence, self-sacrifice and self-enhancing power. She is allowed, that is, to combine love and quest, to be what a Victorian gentlewoman ought to be plus something more. Paul *gives* Lucy her school, but she must pay the rent from her own year's savings. She is properly self-sacrificing, but she is prosperous too: 'I worked hard. I deemed myself the steward of his property, and determined, God willing, to render a good account' (414). And Lucy is deferential, but she is powerful as well: 'The secret of my success did not lie so much in myself, in any endowment, any power of mine, as in a new state of circumstances. ... The spring which moved my energies lay far away beyond seas' (415).

Paul, of course, is still the giver of benefits and as such he is Lucy's 'king': 'royal for me had been that hand's bounty; to offer homage was both a joy and a duty' (410). But, far from objecting to this traditional power relation, Brontë approves it. Indeed, she celebrates it by surrounding it with Edenic imagery. It is not for his sexism that Paul Emanuel is drowned. He is sacrificed to Brontë's sense of possibilities. The combination of love and quest, of autonomy and subordination, of being what a woman should be and of being more, was simply too good to be true; it was a private fantasy, worked out in isolation from the forces of the larger world, and, finally, Brontë knew it.[26]

Throughout the novel, in fact, Brontë uses Edenic imagery to mark pleasant but transient interludes in Lucy's life only to counterpoint those interludes with imagery which insists that Lucy's life is really a pilgrimage – and an arduous pilgrimage at that. Social pilgrimage, not private paradise, is the real essence of existence for the genteel working woman, and Lucy's last evening with Paul in the Faubourg Clotilde is heavily endowed with images of Eden. Paul and Lucy sit outside; the gardens of the faubourg are around them; the air is mild and fresh; the roses look up at a halcyon moon; and Paul's voice blends harmoniously with the silver whisper 'in which light breeze, fountain, and foliage intoned their lulling vesper' (410). The two dine innocently on chocolate and rolls and summer fruit while Lucy feels 'delight inexpressible in tending' Paul (411). It is a 'happy hour', an hour like a 'White Angel', another happy ending, another version of the dependent life (411). 'The next day – he sailed.'

NOTES

1. Austen, *Pride and Prejudice*, (New York: Holt, Rinehart & Winston, 1949), p. 229.
2. Charlotte Brontë, *Villette*, ed. Geoffrey Tillotson and Donald Hawes (Boston: Houghton Mifflin, 1971), p. 5. Subsequent references appear in the text.
3. Andrew Hook, 'Charlotte Brontë, the imagination and *Villette*', in *The Brontës: A collection of critical essays*, ed. Ian Gregor (Englewood Cliffs, NJ: Prentice-Hall, 1970), p. 145.
4. I differ here from Helene Moglen, who finds the Bretton household 'a household warmed by love' and who attributes the focus on Polly, along with Lucy's distance from Polly's experience, to Lucy's inability to recognize in herself 'an overwhelming need and capacity for love'. See *Charlotte Brontë: The self conceived* (New York: W. W. Norton, 1976), pp. 199, 200.
5. *Villette*, in contrast to *Jane Eyre*, is not a novel that gives emphasis to the richness of relations between women. In every relation between Lucy and another woman in this novel, the other woman is preoccupied with a man and, what is more, without men the confined spaces of leisured female existence are made to seem cut off from life and even unhealthy. In the Miss Marchmont episode especially, women's world shrinks to 'two hot, close rooms', a narrowness which goes a long way toward making an emotional invalid of Lucy: 'I forgot that there were fields, woods, rivers, seas, an ever-changing sky outside the steam-dimmed lattice of this sick-chamber; I was almost content to forget it. All within me became narrowed to my lot' (31, 32).
6. According to Harold Perkin, 'entrepreneurial class society ... was based on the moral conception of work', and it was by persuading the rest of society to accept

this ideal, along with the primacy of capital and competition, that the capitalist middle class was able to achieve its aims. See *The Origins of Modern English Society: 1780–1880* (London: Routledge & Kegan Paul, 1969), pp. 277, 272.

7. Feminists like Josephine Butler, Bessie Parks and Frances Cobbe continued to endorse the notion that 'the immense majority of women are, and ought to be, employed in the noble duties which go to make up the Christian household'. See Bessie Rayner Parks, *Essays on Woman's Work*, 2nd edn (London: Alexander Strahan, 1865), p. 222. But they argued the necessity of opening traditionally masculine occupations to single women and they endorsed the respectability of the working life:

> Idleness, which is the root of all evil for men, is not particularly suited to be the root of all virtue for women. In truth, every woman of sense knows that it is precisely the want of suitable and hopeful work which is the great bane and peril of her sex. ... women who support themselves successfully, or aid their husbands by real work at home, are the happiest and most morally safe of their sex. (Cobbe, 'The final cause of woman', in *Women's Work and Women's Culture: A series of essays*, ed. Josephine E. Butler (London: Macmillan, 1869), pp. 20–1.)

8. According to Terry Eagleton, the Brontës felt both 'the simple imperative to earn a living – the need for energy and drive, the respect for whatever was hardy, shrewd and stoical' and 'fascination with the genteel coupled with a distaste for the brash and pushing'. See *Myths of Power: A Marxist study of the Brontës* (New York: Barnes & Noble, 1975), p. 13.

9. Charlotte Brontë, letter to Miss Wooler, 1846, quoted in Inga-Stina Ewbank, *Their Proper Sphere: A study of the Brontë sisters as early-Victorian novelists* (London: Edward Arnold, 1966), p. 157.

10. Charlotte Brontë, letter to Emily Brontë, 8 June 1839, quoted in Winifred Gerin, *Charlotte Brontë: The evolution of genius* (London: Oxford University Press, 1967), p. 144.

11. Quoted ibid.

12. Eagleton, for example, notes Lucy's 'ambiguous approval and resentment of those more successful than herself.' *Myths of Power*, p. 70.

13. Ellis, 'The Women of England: Their social duties and domestic habits', reprinted in *The Family Monitor and Domestic Guide* (New York: E. Walker, n.d.), p. 24.

14. Moglen says: 'Already plagued by the survivor's sense of inadequacy and guilt, Charlotte must easily have fallen prey to masochistic submission. She would have embraced the domination of her father and brother, accepted the social pressures as interpreted by her aunt.' Later, with Monsieur Héger, she is 'powerless: enslaved not by Héger but by herself: by her obsession, her need'. *Charlotte Brontë*, pp. 41, 73.

15. Helene Moglen sees this as the dominant conflict in Brontë's works and life: 'In [*Villette*], as in her three earlier books, it is Brontë who must try to reconcile the heroine's independent self-realization with her need to be submerged in the powerful, masculine "other". For Brontë it had always been impossible to accommodate these two commanding impulses which psychosexual conditioning and social reality place in extreme conflict.' ibid., p. 225.

16. It is interesting to note how much more difficult it is for Lucy to enter this world

than it is for her predecessor, William Crimsworth, in *The Professor*. Crimsworth journeys to Belgium with a letter of introduction, and, although he too arrives at night, there are no incidents. He alights from his diligence, is immediately directed to an inn, arrives there in a fiacre, eats supper and goes to bed. The next morning he sallies out into a fine day and presents his letter to a Mr B. Mr B. promptly assures him of a post as professor of English and Latin. What could be simpler? For Lucy Snowe, however, the world of work is far more foreign. She too arrives at night, but she loses her portmanteau, has no notion of where to put up, is given directions but is harassed by strange men, loses her way, lands at the pensionnat entirely by accident, and is hired, in the middle of the night, purely on a whim. In Lucy's case getting a job is both remarkable and haphazard. There are no letters of introduction and no network of old girls, and the job itself is not the classy position of professor but the low-paid, almost menial, position of children's governess and maid. But what is most striking about all this is that the adventure, daring and risk which mark Lucy's passage land her where they do – in another interior, foreign but finally familiar. A gentlewoman's place in a man's world is not to be where the action is – on the streets of London or Villette – but to be in relative seclusion, to inhabit an interior which is really an extension of the home, a 'demi-convent, secluded in the built-up core of a capital' (84).

17. Nina Auerbach and Sandra Gilbert and Susan Gubar make similar points about Lucy's allegiance or identification with Beck. See Auerbach, *Communities of Women: An idea in fiction* (Cambridge, Mass.: Harvard University Press, 1978), p. 103, and Gubar and Gilbert, *Madwoman in the Attic: The woman writer and the nineteenth-century literary imagination* (New Haven: Yale University Press, 1979), p. 408.

18. See Auerbach on the increasing unreality of Beck's power: *Communities of Women*, p. 107.

19. Kate Millett, *Sexual Politics* (Garden City, NY: Doubleday, 1976), p. 145.

20. See Gilbert and Gubar on Lucy's attraction to Ginevra's self-indulgence and freedom. *Madwoman in the Attic*, p. 409.

21. Moglen explains this regression psychoanalytically: 'Lucy can be moved into the future only through the medium of the past. Lucy awakens to the beginning ... the house at Bretton. We discover how deeply she cared for Graham, how Paulina had been her surrogate.' *Charlotte Brontë*, p. 210.

22. Eagleton observes that 'Lucy's bitterness at John's breezy treatment of her is clearly a class-issue', but he fails to note the sexual power relations for which the class issue is really a displacement. *Myths of Power*, p. 71.

23. Carol Ohmann, 'Historical reality and "divine appointment" in Charlotte Brontë's fiction', *Signs* 2 (Summer 1977), p. 767.

24. As Ohmann rightly notes, the conflict between a man who would dominate and a woman who'd rather he didn't is resolved with relative ease because of the terms in which Brontë poses their opposition: 'Brontë has Paul and Lucy collide not primarily as patriarchal man and subordinate woman ... but as *continental* man and *English* woman.' She also notes the essential likeness of the two: 'Although [Paul] is freer by far and better circumstanced than Lucy is, Paul none the less suffers her essential experience of deprivation.' ibid., p. 772.

25. Moglen suggests that the villainy of Silas and Walravens is an expression of Lucy's

irrational fears, but it is clear, I think, that they also function as part of Brontë's attempt to reconcile her own conflicts about the independence of her heroine; *Charlotte Brontë*, p. 221. Auerbach sees Walravens as an expression of female power, 'a preternatural female ruler'; *Communities of Women*, p. 107. Gilbert and Gubar see her as an image of Lucy's repressed anger; *Madwoman in the Attic*, p. 431.

26. I agree with Patricia Spacks that Lucy does not choose freedom over love, as Kate Millett suggests. She, and Brontë with her, attempt to choose both. See *The Female Imagination* (New York: Avon Books, 1972), p. 38. Nina Auerbach suggests that Lucy lives in a female community at the end and that the community is translated 'into a seal of her triumph'; *Communities of Women*, p. 113. My own reading is closer to Gilbert and Gubar's, who suggest that Brontë wishes to have an integrated sense of self, economic independence, and male affection for her heroine but who also suggest that Brontë leaves the conclusion open-ended and elusive, 'refraining from any deliberate message except to remind us of the continuing need for sustaining stories of survival'; *Madwoman in the Attic*, p. 438.

SEVEN
Aurora Leigh

CORA KAPLAN

> Never flinch,
> But still, unscrupulously epic, catch
> Upon the burning lava of a song
> The full-veined, heaving, double breasted Age:[1]

With this 'woman's figure' the doubled female voice of *Aurora Leigh*, its woman-poet-author and woman-poet-heroine, defines the poet's task. The age is Victoria's, but Elizabeth Barrett Browning calls back a looser Elizabethan speech to extend her image from matriarch to nursing mother, 'the paps from which we all have sucked'. Milk and lava pour from the poem in twin streams; *Aurora Leigh* (1857) produces the fullest and most violent exposition of the 'woman question' in mid-Victorian literature. In her discussion about self-determination Barrett Browning remembers and revises the work of other great women writers from Mme de Staël to George Sand and integrates the debate on gender relations, into which most eminent Victorians were drawn in the 1840s and 1850s, with other political and cultural issues of those years. *Aurora Leigh* is a collage of Romantic and Victorian texts reworked from a woman's perspective. Gender difference, class warfare, the relation of art to politics: these three subjects as they were argued by the English and continental intelligentsia are all engaged as intersecting issues in the poem. The longest poem of the decade, it is, to use another 'woman's figure', a vast quilt, made up of other garments, the pattern dazzling because, not in spite, of its irregularities.

Although Virginia Woolf was to write that 'fate has not been kind to Mrs Browning as a writer. Nobody reads her, nobody discusses her, nobody troubles to put her in her place',[2] Elizabeth Barrett Browning's place among eminent Victorians was so well assured in her lifetime that she was a prominent candidate for poet laureate when Wordsworth died at mid-century. Her place is empty today, the chairs having been moved up to hide her absence from that otherwise meticulously reconstructed feast Victorian studies have served up to us in the past twenty years, but her excision from the canon of great Victorian poets began relatively recently with the twentieth-century revision of literary taste. (Women writers like Woolf, however, never cut her out of *their* list.)

Aurora Leigh, Barrett Browning's 'art-novel' or 'novel-poem', was widely noticed and enjoyed an immediate and continuing popularity for at least a generation following its publication in 1857. It ran through thirteen editions in England by 1873 and was still read and republished up until the turn of the century. Conceived as early as 1845, just at the point of her meeting with Robert Browning, she saw it ambitiously if somewhat vaguely as a

> sort of novel-poem ... running into the midst of our conventions, and rushing into drawing rooms and the like 'where angels fear to tread'; and so, meeting face to face and without mask the Humanity of the age and speaking the truth of it out plainly. That is my intention.[3]

The intention lay fallow during the intense and artistically productive years of her early married life, but in 1853 she started to write it in great bursts and towards the end, some three years later, she wrote at the rate of thirty or forty lines a day – writing, revising and producing fair copy, sometimes simultaneously. Her dedication of the poem to her loved and admired friend John Kenyon shows how much she staked on 'the most mature of my works, and the one into which my highest convictions upon Life and Art have entered'.[4] To a correspondent in 1856 she wrote, 'I mean that when you have read my new book, you put away all my other poems ... and know me only by the new.'[5] The hectic composition and self-assurance are reflected in the finished poem whose 'Speed, energy, forthrightness and complete self-confidence', says Woolf, make us 'read to the end enthralled.'[6]

Aurora Leigh comes between two very explicitly political books: *Casa Guidi Windows* (1851) and *Poems Before Congress* (1860), verse which deals much more directly than *Aurora Leigh* with the revolutionary issues of 1848 and after. If Elizabeth Barrett was a lyric poet with an interest in political and social questions, Elizabeth Barrett Browning was primarily a political poet whose subjects were slavery, suppressed nationality (Italy), the plight of the poor and the position of women.

Aurora Leigh is Barrett Browning's fullest exploration of this last subject. In 1845, when the poem was forming in her mind, she did not directly relate it to the woman question, but saw the success of an earlier poem, 'Lady Geraldine's courtship' (about the love of a titled woman for a poor poet) as encouragement 'to go on, and touch this real everyday life of our age, and hold it with my two hands. I want to write a poem of a new class, in a measure – a

Don Juan, without the mockery and impurity.'[7] 'Lady Geraldine' touched on a subject central to most women novelists of the time: the ability of women to choose their own partners without the approval of kin or society, but *Aurora Leigh* includes this as a sub-theme only. Its more modern preoccupation is whether marriage itself is a good thing, especially for women with a vocation. Elizabeth Barrett Browning, justifying her elopement to Mary Russell Mitford, explains, 'It never was high up in my ideal, even before my illness brought myself so far down. A happy marriage was the happiest condition, I believed vaguely – but *where were the happy marriages?*'[8] Novels which concerned themselves only with happy marriages, Jane Austen's for example, struck her with their 'narrowness – the want of all aspiration towards, or instinct of the possibility of *enlargement* of any kind'. Yet she was equally dubious about the political implications of feminism. Again to Miss Mitford she wrote,

> I am *not*, as you are perhaps aware, a very strong partisan of the Rights-of-women-side of the argument – at least I have not been, since I was twelve years old. I believe that, considering men and women in the mass, there *is* an *inequality* of intellect, and that is proved by the very state of things of which gifted women complain; and more than proved by the manner in which their complaint is received by their own sisterhood.[9]

She thought the feminist views of her friends Anna Jameson or Harriet Martineau too advanced for ordinary middle-class women to take in, and that this prejudice 'proved' female inferiority. The conscious snobbery of this view is mitigated by her contradictory belief that 'the difference between men and women arose from the inferiority of education of the latter', and her strong defence of women as writers and reformers. But her chief sympathies were reserved for women who wrote: '*You*, who are a woman and man in one, judge if it isn't a hard and difficult process for a woman to get forgiven for her strength by her grace ... every woman of letters knows it is hard.'[10]

Aurora Leigh expresses this equivocal view of the woman question. The story of a young poet, the daughter of an English father and Italian mother, it is about the development of a woman writer. Aurora is brought up alone in Italy by her widower father. He dies when she is thirteen and she is sent back to England to live with his sister, a maiden lady, in the English countryside. The aunt tries to educate her as a perfect English lady, but the young woman resists and secretly constructs a syllabus of her own from her father's stored library. At 20 she receives a proposal from her cousin Romney, heir to the Leigh fortunes, who asks her to abandon poetry and join him in a life given over to social and political reform. She refuses, eloquently defending poetry and women's right to determine their own careers. Her aunt is furious; the marriage was blessed, even arranged, so that Aurora would inherit her share of the family fortune. The aunt dies with an unopened bequest from Romney in her hands. Aurora is left only £300 (she refuses Romney's money) and heads for London and a garret where she slowly builds herself a reputation as a writer. Romney pursues his own career, rescuing, in the course of his good works, a poor girl, Marian Erle, who has run away from her brutal and drunken parents. He sets her up as a sempstress in London and eventually decides to marry her, not for love but as a gesture towards the breakdown of class barriers. Aurora, who has seen little of her cousin in her years in London, is informed of this imminent marriage by Lady Waldemar, an aristocrat passionately in love with Romney. Lady Waldemar wishes Aurora to intervene in the marriage, but after meeting Marian, Aurora gives it her blessing. On the wedding day rich and poor gather for the ceremony. Marian stands her bridegroom up, explaining in a letter that she does not really love him. Distressed, Romney returns to his utopian projects. Aurora finishes a major book and goes to the continent to rest. There she glimpses and pursues Marian, whom she discovers with an illegitimate son. It appears that Marian had been persuaded against the marriage by Lady Waldemar, betrayed by her servant and raped and abandoned in France. Aurora persuades Marian to accompany her to Italy. In Florence the two women live in relative happiness and self-sufficiency with the child. Through a series of rather clumsy plot manipulations Aurora learns that Romney has been ill and is convinced he is married to Lady Waldemar to whom she has written an outraged letter. He arrives soon after, unwed, and ready to atone for Marian's misfortunes by marrying her. Marian will have none of it! She sees her early love for Romney as an unequal infatuation and her commitment to her child as excluding marriage which might produce legitimate siblings. Aurora learns that Romney has been blinded during a riot where local peasants and his London down-and-outs combine in the sacking and burning of Leigh Hall. He has given up his socialism and philanthropic schemes. There is a mutual confession of love. Romney accepts Aurora's 'art' as a higher good than politics and asks her to speak for them both in the future. Aurora, Marian and Lady Waldemar form the triptych through which Barrett Browning speaks her views on the woman question.

In the opening of Book V of *Aurora Leigh* there is a long discursive section on the poet's vocation where the author dismisses the lyric mode – ballad, pastoral and Barrett Browning's own favourite, the sonnet – as static forms: the poet 'can stand/Like Atlas in the sonnet and support/His own heavens pregnant with dynastic stars;/But then he must stand still, nor take a step.' The move into epic poetry chipped at her reputation in establishment circles, but enhanced her popularity. It was a venture into a male stronghold, epic and dramatic verse being associated with the classicists and with Shakespeare, Milton, Shelley and Tennyson, and later, Browning. In 1893 the influential critic Edmund Gosse wrote that women have achieved nothing 'in the great solid branches of poetry in epic, in tragedy, in didactic and philosophical verse. . . . The reason is apparently that the artistic nature is not strongly developed in her.'[11] This typical retrospective judgement may be a clue to *Aurora Leigh*'s modern oblivion, and one reason why such an important and diverse poet as Barrett Browning is now known almost exclusively as the author of *Sonnets from the Portuguese* (1850), her brilliant series of love lyrics to her husband. Twentieth-century male poet-critics echo Gosse's belief that women's voice in poetry, as in life, should be confined to the lyric. How can one account then for a sustained narrative poem that is both didactic and philosophical as well as passionate and female, an unmannerly intervention in the 'high' patriarchal discourse of bourgeois culture?

The taboo – it is stronger than prejudice – against women's entry into public discourse as speakers or writers, was in grave danger of being definitively broken in the mid-nineteenth century as more and more educated, literate women entered the arena as imaginative writers, social critics and reformers. The oppression of women within the dominant class was in no way as materially brutal as the oppression of women of the working class, but it had its own rationale and articulation. The mid-century saw the development of a liberal 'separate but equal' argument which sometimes included and some-times resisted the definition of woman's sphere and the development of the cult of true womanhood. The publicity given to the woman question hardly dented the continued elaboration of mores and manners which ensured that daughters were marriageable, i.e. virgins. Patriarchal dominance involved the suppression of women's speech outside the home and a rigorous censorship of what she could read or write. All the major women writers were both vulner-able to and sensitive about charges of 'coarseness'. The Brontë sisters, Sand and Barrett Browning were labelled coarse by their critics, and, occasionally, by other women – sexual impurity, even in thought, being *the* unforgivable sin, the social level through which Victorian culture controlled its females, and kept them from an alliance with their looser-lived working-class sisters.

The debates on the woman question which took up so many pages of leading British periodicals between 1830 and 1860 should not be seen as marginal to a male-dominated ruling class, increasingly threatened from below by an organizing proletariat. Caught between this and the need to accommodate a limited demand for equity from informed women of their own class, they were equally committed to the absolute necessity of maintaining social control of females, and its corollary, the sexual division of labour. To get a sense of the space and importance given to the issue, one only has to leaf through the major quarterlies for a given year. The winter 1857 issue of the *North British Review* had both a substantial review of *Aurora Leigh* and a long review article, dealing with eight books and titled 'The employment of women', which ranges from an abrupt dismissal of Margaret Fuller's *Woman in the Nineteenth Century* for its romantic obscurity, to a serious discussion of Anna Jameson's *The Communion of Labour*, a work which argued that middle-class women should be 'employed' in ameliorating the condition of the female poor. In support of Mrs Jameson the article quotes both Tennyson's *The Princess* and *Aurora Leigh*.[12]

The right to write was closely connected with every wider choice that women might wish to make. In an age characterized by the importance of the popular press as the place of ideological production and the spread of female literacy, it was of prime importance to warn women against questioning traditional sexual morality. Public writing and public speech, closely allied, were both real and symbolic acts of self-determination for women. Barrett Browning uses the phrase 'I write' four times in the first two stanzas of Book I, emphasizing the connection between the first person narrative and the 'act' of women's speech; between the expression of woman's feelings and thoughts and the legitimate professional exercise of that expression. Barrett Browning makes the link between women's intervention into political debate and her role as imaginative writer quite clear in her defence of Harriet Beecher Stowe's *Uncle Tom's Cabin*. She rejoices in Stowe's success as 'a woman and a human being' and pushes the message home to her timid female correspondent:

> Oh, and is it possible that you think a woman has no busines with questions like the question of slavery? Then she had better use a pen no more. She had better subside into slavery and concubinage herself I think as in the times of old, shut herself up with the Penelopes in the 'women's apartment', and take no rank among thinkers and speakers.[13]

Writing is a skilled task learnt at the expense of 'Long green days/Worn bare of grass and sunshine, – long calm nights/From which the silken sleeps were fretted out ... with no amateur's/Irreverent haste and busy idleness/I set myself to art!' *Aurora Leigh* enters, however tentatively, into debates on *all* the forbidden subjects. In the first person epic voice of a major poet, it breaks a very specific silence, almost a gentlemen's agreement between women authors and the arbiters of high culture in Victorian England, that allowed women to write if only they would shut up about it.

Barrett Browning makes the poem's very existence hinge on the fact that its protagonist is a woman and a poet. Aurora's biography is a detailed account both of the socialization of women and the making of a poet, and her rejection of her cousin's proposal is directly related to her sense of her own vocation. Books III and IV are full of the trivia of a young writer's daily life. Book V, the poem's centrepiece, begins as a long digression on the poet's task. Having established Aurora as artist so firmly in the first half of the poem, Barrett Browning can afford to let Books VI to IX take up the narrative line and extend the discussion of female autonomy to her working-class character, Marian Erle, and Marian's scheming opposite, Lady Waldemar. Aurora, having a vocation and a recognized status, can be identified by more than her sexual or emotional relationships within the poem, and the female voice, simultaneously the author's and Aurora's, speaks with authority on just those questions about politics and high culture from which women were generally excluded. *Aurora Leigh*'s other subject, the relationship between art and political change, is reformulated by the fact that, in the poem, the poet is female and the political reformer male. The poetic and all it stands for in *Aurora Leigh* – inspiration, Christian love, individual expression – becomes feminized as a consequence. The mechanical dogmas of utopian socialism, Romney's 'formulas', are straw theories with little chance against this warm wind. Abstract political discourse yields, at the end of the work, to poetry.

So much we can find in *Aurora Leigh* without situating the poem too precisely in the historical moment of its production. Read in the 1970s, it does at first seem to be, as Ellen Moers has said, '*the* feminist poem', radical in its celebration of the centrality of female experience. In spite of its conventional happy ending it is possible to see it as contributing to a feminist theory of art which argues that women's language, precisely because it has been suppressed by patriarchal societies, re-enters discourse with a shattering revolutionary force, speaking all that is repressed and forbidden in human experience. Certainly Elizabeth Barrett Browning saw herself as part of a submerged literary tradition of female writers. She compared herself physically to Sappho, 'little and black', intellectually to Mme de Staël her romantic pre-cursor, and among her contemporaries an intuitive sympathy bound her to George Sand. No woman poet in English after Emily Dickinson and before Sylvia Plath rang such extreme changes on the 'woman's figure'. Still the relation of women's writing to political change was problematic for Elizabeth Barrett Browning as it is problematic for us. We have only to look at the sections of the poem which are crude and alienating, the vicious picture of the rural and urban poor, to see that there are painful contradictions in a liberal feminist position on art or politics.

Both liberal and radical feminism insist that patriarchal domination is *the* problem of human culture. This position tends to ignore or diminish the importance of class conflict, race and the operations of capital, and to make small distinction between the oppressions of middle-class women and working-class or Third World women. The strains in *Aurora Leigh* which prefigure modern radical feminism are not only those which celebrate the heroine's relation to art but those which surface in Barrett Browning's manip-ulation of her working-class figure, Marian Erle. Marian is given the most brutal early history of any figure in the poem – drunken ignorant parents, a mother who 'sells' her to the first male buyer – but she enters the world of our genteel protagonists literate and unsullied. Taken up by Romney as a symbolic cause – his marriage to her is intended as a sort of virtuous miscegenation between the classes – she is betrayed, raped and abandoned in a series of villainies which suggest that sisterhood across class boundaries is a frail concept at best. When Aurora finds and rescues her in Book VII, a genuine alliance of female sympathy is formed between women of different classes who have the added complication of loving the same man.

But this sisterhood is bought in the narrative at the expense of a representation of the poor as a lumpen motley of thieves, drunkards, rapists and childbeaters, except for Marian, whose embourgeoisement in terms of language and understanding occurs at embarrassing speed. Only children (innocents) and prostitutes (exploited by men) escape with full sympathy. What is really missing is any adequate attempt at analysis of the intersecting oppressions of capitalism and patriarchy. Elizabeth Barrett Browning has as her particular political target in the poem the Christian Socialism adapted from Fourier and Owen and practised by F. D. Maurice, Charles Kingsley and others, but since she has no answer to the misery of the poor except her own brand of Christian love – and poetry – her solutions to class conflict are even less adequate than theirs. Inevitably a theory which identifies the radical practice of art with the achievement of radical social change, or asserts the unity of female experience without examining the forms taken by that experience in different social groups, will emerge with a theory of art and politics unconnected with material reality and deeply élitist. This is true of the book read in her time and ours.

Aurora Leigh, of course, is more than a single text. It is different as it is read and understood at each separate point in history, as it is inserted into historically particular ideological structures. There is a danger in either blaming the poem for its political incoherence by relegating those debates to history or in praising it only for the euphoria with which it ruptures and transforms female language. Works of art should not be attacked because they do not conform to notions of political correctness, but they must be understood in relation to the seductive ideologies and political possibilities both of the times in which they were written and the times in which they are read. Otherwise Barrett Browning's belief that the 'artist's part is both to do and to be' stands in place of, not on behalf of, political transformation.

When *Aurora Leigh* was published in 1857, its author was one of the leading literary figures in England, her reputation ensuring extended notices in the periodical and newspaper press. Ruskin called it 'the first perfect poetical expression of the Age', and there were delighted reponses from Swinburne, D. G. and William Rossetti, Walter Savage Landor and many other writers, critics and artists. Reviews in the major quarterlies were considerably less favourable. Most could not cope with the transitions from high to common language, 'wilfully alternated passages of sorry prose with bursts of splendid poetry', the ambitious scope of the subject matter and the obscure and violent imagery. The overriding technique of the reviewers was to quote passages 'of great beauty' next to lines they disliked. They wanted the plot to be either more realistic or more allegorical – either *Jane Eyre* or Tennyson's *Princess*, not both at once. A few radical critics, especially the *Westminster Review*, objected to her castration of Romney's socialist projects; a few conservative reviewers thought that the conventions 'which are society's unwritten laws, are condemned in too sweeping and unexamining a style'. The *National Review* found the imagery 'savage':

> Burning lava and a woman's breast! and concentrated in the latter the fullest ideas of life. It is absolute pain to read it. No man could have written it; for independently of its cruelty, there is a tinge in it of a sort of forward familiarity, with which Mrs. Browning sometimes, and never without uneasiness to her readers, touches upon things which the instinct of the other sex prevents them, when undebased, from approaching without reverence and tenderness.[14]

Several reviewers object to Aurora as being 'not a genuine woman', alternately cold and intellectual, and morbidly preoccupied with the 'misappreciation of woman by man'. *Blackwoods'* declared,

> We must maintain that woman was created to be dependent on the man, and not in the primary sense his lady and his mistress. The extreme independence of Aurora detracts from the feminine charm, and mars the interest which we otherwise might have felt in so intellectual a heroine.[15]

The *Dublin University Review* found her expression and thought 'coarse' and 'unfeminine': 'The days when such a woman as Aphra Behn can hope to be palatable to the female sex are gone forever.'[16] The *North American Review* was more enlightened about the poem's feminism:

> When we transfer Mrs. Browning from the ranks of female poets to those of the poets of England, we would not be understood to separate her from the first class. Mrs. Browning's poems are, in all respects, the utterance of a woman – of a woman of great learning, rich experience, and powerful genius, uniting to her woman's nature the strength which is sometimes thought peculiar to a man. She is like the Amazon in the midst of battle ... [and has] ... attained to such a height of poetic excellence, not in spite of her woman's nature, but by means of it.[17]

What is remarkable about even the most negative and chauvinist reviews is that they acknowledge the great power of the poem, recognize its importance in contemporary literature and place its author in the first rank of poets.

While the greatest part of these long reviews is given over to summary of the plot interspersed by quotation, there are occasional acute analyses of what it means to be a woman writer. *The National Review* said:

She gives no voice to the world around her. It is herself she is pressed to utter. And this is not only the unconscious but the direct and conscious aim of her striving. ... She is never the passive subject of that sort of inspiration by which some *men* almost unconsciously render back the impressions of things around them; what comes from her is part of her. It is the song of her own soul she 'struggles to outbear' and she grasps the outer world to make it yield her a language. (my italics)[18]

In this respect the critic may be confusing what is characteristically female in Barrett Browning's verse – the need to transform a metaphorical tradition and political perspective formed and dominated by the male voice – with the personal or individual elements in the poem. The critic who notes her popularity with women is close to the mark when writing that she 'speaks what is struggling for utterance in their own hearts and they find in her poems the revelation of themselves'.

What the critical reception indicates is how fully the poem, with all its dissonant and outrageous elements, was taken to the heart of Victorian culture. Everybody in polite society read it, even the Queen, and Barrett Browning was delighted by reports that it had corrupted women of 60 and been banned by horrified parents. The ways in which the poem is challenged and embraced is a comment on the contradictory presence of women writers on the woman question in mid-Victorian culture. It is as if they appear so prominently in the discourses of the ruling class in direct relation to their continued powerlessness in its social and political structures.

Aurora Leigh is a dense and complex text. Deliberately discursive and philosophical, the reflective sections of the poem state very clearly Barrett Browning's position on women's relation to self-determination, art, love, politics. The self-conscious didacticism of the poem includes some of its best 'poetic' passages: Aurora's description of her aunt; her bitter diatribe on female education; her definition of modern poetry. But these sections are complemented by a less visible polemic built into the poem's structure and narrative. The plot borrows elements from so many other literary sources, and reworks them in a semi-parodic and sometimes semi-conscious fashion, that one can find a cutting commentary on the literary and political culture through an analysis of the 'sources' of the plot alone. The narrative, often criticized for its lack of realism or simple credibility, is an elaborate collage of typical themes and motifs of the novels and long poems of the 1840s and 1850s. Years of ill-health, during which Elizabeth Barrett saw few people outside the Barrett household, had reinforced an early indiscriminate addiction to print, a habit that persisted through her married life. Characterizing her life as se-cluded even before her illness, she thought that living less in society than in books and poetry was 'a disadvantage to her art'. She compared herself in her late thirties to a 'blind poet' who would willingly exchange 'some of this lumbering, ponderous, helpless knowledge of books, for some experience of life and man'.[19] She lived with peculiar intensity through the written word, her own and other people's. Books substituted for the variety and pattern of social experience which make a novelist. Many social events in *Aurora Leigh*, as well as many of the social types, are drawn more from fiction than from life, but released through poetic licence from the demands of a realistic mode of representation. In the bed-sitting-room at Wimpole Street, and in the sequence of apartments in France and Italy after 1846, the Victorian world as represented in the social novel is reduced to a sort of essence and reconstituted in *Aurora Leigh* as a different brew altogether. Several times removed from the 'real', it is neither a distorted reflection of Victorian life nor a lifeless imitation of other literature, but a living critical commentary on both, full of its own ideological idiosyncrasies.

Victorian readers already familiar with Tennyson, Clough, Kingsley, the Brontës, Gaskell and Sand would have caught echoes that we are too far away to hear. Barrett Browning played very self-consciously too on earlier, Romantic sources. The growth of the poet in Books I and II takes us very naturally back to Wordsworth, and large parts of the poem play with themes and characters from a novel that every literate lady of Elizabeth Barrett's generation loved, Mme de Staël's *Corinne, or Italy* (1807). The narrative of *Aurora Leigh* is a critical revaluation of its multiple sources in which didactic asides are interleaved with the story, much as de Staël leavened her romance with long sections on Italian manners, culture and art.

Crucially, the seemingly fragmented, discursive poem (2000 lines longer than Paradise Lost as one reviewer noted sourly) is tightened and held by a rope of female imagery. One reviewer at least appreciated the 'command of imagery' which gave a 'vital continuity, through the whole of this immensely long work'. Approved and taboo subjects are slyly intertwined so that menstruation, childbirth, suckling, child-rearing, rape and prostitution are all braided together in the metaphorical language. The mother–child relationship – Aurora and her mother, Aurora and her father, Marian and her son – receives special emphasis. Suckling becomes a multi-purpose symbol of nurturing and growth. It links the narrative themes of Aurora's development as a poet and Marian's rehabilitation, to the philosophical and aesthetic themes: the relationship of art to its 'age'. Mothering and writing are identified as the process of 'stringing pretty words that make no sense/And kissing full sense into empty words' (I, 51–2).

The force of the 'woman's figure' is an argument for the genre Barrett Browning has chosen. The social and domestic novel that operated under the constraints of realism, as realism was defined in the middle of the nineteenth century, had little room for the rhetorical excesses acceptable in the female gothic novel written half a century earlier, and in the romance *Corinne*. After Jane Austen's reaction against the emotional and romantic in women's writing, heightened language became a dangerous tool for women novelists. Sneaked in as explosive interjections in Charlotte Brontë's novels, it immediately brought upon her the accusation of coarseness. More liberty was given to poets. Felicia Hemans, one of the most popular women poets in England before Elizabeth Barrett replaced her in the public eye, was rarely criticized for her passionate expression. Her love-crossed heroines could weep or commit suicide with impunity, while Brontë's Lucy Snowe or Jane Eyre were reproved for a private howl at bedtime.

Most charges of coarseness were directed at any indication that women had a self-centred, independent sexuality. In Charlotte Brontë's novels, women are characteristically made to repress these feelings. Elizabeth Barrett's inhibitions are reflected in her comment on Sand's 'disgusting tendency ... towards representing the passion of love under its physical aspects'.[20] Even Aurora resists and denies her passion for Romney lest he suppress or divert her sense of vocation. As a result, Aurora's sexuality is displaced into her poetry, projected onto landscapes, the age, art, through the 'woman's figure'. Love denied is rerouted through language. Comparing England, where her mind and spirit mature, to Italy which represents the body and passion, she describes England as a series of negations of the sexualized Italian panorama:

> Not my headlong leaps
> Of waters that cry out for joy or fear ...
> Not indeed
> My multitudinous mountains, sitting in
> The magic circle with the mutual touch
> Electric panting from their full deep hearts
> Beneath the influent heavens and waiting for
> Communion and commission. Italy
> Is one thing, England one. (I, 617–27)

This is straight out of *Corinne*, protected from censure by being suggestive, half-completed metaphor. Breasts, one is tempted to add, are one thing in verse, another in prose.

Aurora Leigh should be read as an overlapping sequence of dialogues with other texts, other writers. None of these debates is finished and some pursue contradictory arguments. The poem tries to make an overarching ideological statement by enlarging the personal to encompass the political, but the individual history interior to the poem – its 'novel' – cannot answer the questions which the work as a whole puts to discourses outside it. What is true of *Aurora Leigh* is, of course, true of all writing. The pauses and awkward jumps in the text, the sense that the speaker has turned abruptly from one discussion to another, has omitted some vital point or has clammed up just as the argument gets interesting – those moments should claim our attention as powerfully as the seeming integration of structure and symbol. The text's unity is that adult voice that does not permit interruption as it tells us how things should be: its unintegrated remarks and pointed silences remind us that the 'knowledge' of any one age is constantly open to rupture and revision. If we follow Elizabeth Barrett Browning through a select few of the debates in which she engaged we can understand the ways she could and could not meet 'face to face and without mask the Humanity of the age', and speak 'the truth of it out plainly'.

Corinne, or Italy was published in 1807, a year after Elizabeth Barrett's birth, when Mme de Staël was 41. Set between her already famous study of literature and society (*De la litterature* ... , 1800), and her equally well-known work on Germany in 1810, it enjoyed an immediate and dramatic popularity. Two English translations vied for popular favour, and for literary women of several generations reading it was a traumatic, even catalytic, experience. Elizabeth Barrett at 26 called it 'an immortal book' that deserved to be read 'once every year in the age of man'. Corinne is an idealised heroine. Ellen Moers calls her the 'fantasy-transposition of Mme de Staël's own speciality as woman of genius', a poly-artist, 'poet, improvisatrice, dancer, actress, translator, musician, painter, singer, lecturer'.[21] Born in Italy of an English father and Italian mother, she is orphaned at 10 when her mother dies, and left by her father in the care of her Florentine aunt until she is 15 when 'my talents, my taste, even my character, were formed'.[22] Sent back reluctantly to England to live in Northumberland with her father, Lord Edgermond, and his cold, correct second wife, she finds her manners and education improper by English standards. At a dinner party she quotes some 'pure' Italian verses on love and is roundly ticked off by her stepmother, who tells her 'that it was not the custom for young ladies to speak in company, and that above all they ought never to cite verses which contained the word love'. Her father too reproaches her: 'Women amongst us, have no other vocation than domestic duties; the talents which you possess will serve to relieve the irksomeness of solitude', or entertain a husband.[23] Lord Edgermond looks back on his first marriage as a youthful indulgence, although Corinne sees his transformation into a pompous English country gentleman as his 'bending beneath that leaden cloak which Dante describes in the infernal regions'. She compares the attitude towards her talents in Italy where they are regarded as 'celestial endowments' with their reception in England as a kind of deformation. De Staël takes revenge on her own dreary year in England by describing with savage minuteness the dulling and crippling effect of English ideas of female education and socialization. Corinne's step-mother monitors her thought as well as her behaviour, and de Staël makes the damp, cold climate a projected corollary of a world where 'Birth, marriage, and death' composed the whole history of society.[24]

Although Corinne spends some pleasant hours educating her young half-sister, she eventually defeats her own chance of happiness in England by displaying her talents too brilliantly to the father of a prospective suitor, Oswald, Lord Nelville. He decides against her on the grounds that she does not conform to an English idea of womanhood. Her own father dies, leaving her at the mercy of Lady Edgermond. Eventually, after refusing a proper marriage, she returns to her native Italy to pursue her career, promising to adopt a pseudonym rather than bring disgrace to the family. In Rome Oswald meets her, acknowledged now as the first lady of Italian arts. Travelling to dispel depression following his father's death, he falls in love with Corinne's beauty and genius. Much of the novel is taken up with their passionate but unconsummated courtship which gives de Staël her excuse for long asides on Italian culture. Corinne knows that Oswald was to have been her husband but puts off telling him her story for two-thirds of the tale. He is shaken to discover that his father may have disapproved the marriage and rushes back to England, promising fidelity, but in fact to discover how full and explicit was his father's interdiction. At first he remains faithful to Corinne but eventually yields to the attractions of her young half-sister, a conventional English virgin, and marries her. Corinne follows him to England and witnesses his betrayal. Back in Italy, she falls ill and gradually declines, hanging on for an improbable but somehow moving encounter with Oswald who, discontented with his marriage, returns in search of 'Italy' with his wife and little daughter. Corinne tutors the daughter in music and gives lessons to her half-sister in the art of becoming an adequate wife for the demanding Oswald. She dies and is mourned by all of Italy. De Staël leaves us considering the appropriateness of Oswald's choice.

Ellen Moers suggests that the first books of *Aurora Leigh* are a 'return to Corinne' because Barrett Browning borrows heavily from the earlier work for her conception of her poet-heroine, her description of Aurora's genealogy and early life, and above all, her indictment of the socialization of English women. It could be nearer the truth to say that *Aurora Leigh* carries on an extended debate with Corinne about all these matters. There is no single plot element that Barrett Browning uses that she does not change in some significant way. What Moers calls the 'myth of Corinne' became the private fantasy of two generations of genteel women readers. The primal scenes of the myth are its belief in the possibility of female genius and the rejection of the woman who embodies it by her chosen lover. It is powerful and painful. The most significant alteration made by Barrett Browning is the most vulgar one. Corinne dies of disappointed love; Barrett Browning makes damned sure that Aurora, her modern Corinne, survives.

Like Corinne, Aurora is the daughter of an 'austere Englishman' and a beautiful Florentine, but her father comes to Italy when 'no longer young' to study that subject of perennial interest to the English bourgeoisie, the 'secret of Da Vinci's drains'. Italy itself does not move him; rather it is Italy embodied in a beautiful young woman in a Catholic procession which 'shook with silent clangour brain and heart,/Transfiguring him to music' (I, 87–8). As in *Corinne*, and in so much Protestant writing about Italy, classical architecture, Catholicism and warm weather come to represent a blurred sensuality, missing in England, which opens the self to its permitted corollary, love. Aurora, like Corinne, is orphaned, but with a crucial difference in timing. Aurora's mother dies when she is 4 not 10, leaving her unreconciled and unfraternized to 'the new order'. 'As it was ... I felt a mother-want about the world,/And still went seeking, like a bleating lamb/Left out at night in shutting up the fold,–/As restless as a nest-deserted bird' (I, 39–43). There is no woman to socialize Aurora, no mother to be cuddled by or imitate. Her loss is, however, a tragedy mixed with blessing. Although she forgoes an early and desirable experience of love and loving, to make her 'unafraid of Love' she also avoids, if we adopt a Freudian schema for the socialization of children, the full conflict of the oedipal crisis which occurs at about 4 or 5 since she does not have to 'give up' her father to her mother and identify with the weaker sex. Aurora's 'mother-lack' makes her less conventionally feminine, perhaps less spontaneously affectionate, but also inclines her to identify with Marian, another semi-orphan, to protect and defend at all costs the maternal experience. Aurora is raised not by a Florentine aunt, but by her bereaved father 'Whom love had unmade from a common man/But not completed to an uncommon man' (I, 183–4). This unfinished man, seduced from an absorption of patriarchal duties, 'law and parish matters', teaches Aurora 'all the ignorance of men,/And how God laughs in heaven when any man/Says "Here I'm learned: this, I understand;/In that I am never caught at fault or doubt"' (I, 190–3). Unlike Corinne, Aurora does not display any precocious talents except a fine intelligence. As if to prove that she had read Freud Barrett Browning conveniently kills off Aurora's father at the onset of puberty:

> I was just thirteen,
> Still growing like the plants from unseen roots
> In tongue-tied Springs, – and suddenly awoke
> To full life and life's needs and agonies
> With an intense, strong, struggling heart beside
> A stone-dead father. Life, struck sharp on death,
> Makes awful lightning. (I, 205–11)

Discreet as this passage may now sound, it is probably the closest any English woman writer had come to an explicit reference to menstruation and the stirrings of sexual desire. What is even more important is that this awakening is not provoked by a romantic encounter with a male object (except of course the forbidden one, the father). 'Life's needs and agonies' are assumed to be part of the natural development of female personality, not a set of feelings inspired by a marriageable male. In this subversive assertion of the autonomy of female sexuality Barrett Browning follows the spirit of Corinne. Her version of orphaning is one of the most interesting narrative inventions in the poem. The deaths of Corinne's parents deprive her of certain essential protection; she is allowed to stay in Italy until her character and talents are fully formed. De Staël makes the point that in a world where women's only option is to marry, the absence of the appropriate kinship structures makes women seriously vulnerable. Corinne goes back to Italy where her genius gives her a protective immunity, and where, in any case, manners and morals are more relaxed. Elizabeth Barrett Browning is making a slightly different statement. Aurora's eccentric education in anti-patriarchal attitudes equips her more fully for the life she will eventually lead than a traditional upbringing. Her mother's picture becomes the glassed image of the representation of women in western culture 'mixed, confused, unconsciously' with 'Whatever I last read or heard or dreamed/Abhorrent, admirable, beautiful,/Pathetical, or ghastly, or grotesque' (I, 146–50). Her father's rejection of the conventional wisdom of patriarchal discourse mingled with her 'restless', 'seeking' 'mother-want' is precisely the proper education for a poet who will take over the mother function of 'stringing pretty words that makes no sense,/And kissing full sense into empty words' (I, 51–2). De Staël was interested in describing the evolution of natural genius in women, in refuting Rousseau's claim that women could not express the thoughts they inspired. Barrett Browning adds to that point a whole psychological dimension about the making of a woman writer, rejecting a romantic view of the evolution of genius and emphasizing instead through a negative example, the role of family and early education in woman's development. Corinne's genius is nurtured in Italy, thrives only on Italian soil. Barrett Browning, loyal to her native England, does not allow Italy to take the credit for Aurora's poetic gifts. These are drawn out in green England which she comes to love. Elizabeth Barrett's country childhood at Hope End is preserved in her description of the Leigh's estate. England's 'sweet familiar nature' provided a substitute for loving family 'presence and affection' for the growth of the spirit. England nurtured the spirit and the mind; Italy the passions. Barrett Browning was a faithful English romantic, bred on Wordsworth and Keats. Accordingly *Aurora Leigh* is *Corinne* anglicized, the radical opposition between feminine poetic Italy and masculine England modified. Corinne finds no asylum in England; her two sojourns there are disastrous. Aurora finds her vocation in England and is recognized *there* (though without the exotic fanfare accorded Corinne) as a major poet. Italy remains the 'magic circle' where love can be expressed and experienced.

Even in what seem direct steals from de Staël, important changes have been made. Aurora's spinster aunt who 'liked a woman to be womanly' is a fair copy of Lady Edgermond; the ridiculous education she imposes on Aurora is an updated version of the tasks given to Corinne. Aurora is taught a jumble of useless facts and dates and a set of accomplishments: to play and draw, dance, spin glass, stuff birds and model flowers. No Corinne, Aurora does it all badly; she has only one gift which she develops herself, helped by her father's early instruction in the classics, 'He wrapt his little daughter in his large/ Man's doublet, careless did it fit or not', and her own secret borrowing from the remains of his library. The savage passage on female education jumps out at us from the poem; the aunt who, caged herself, kept that wild bird Aurora caged, owes something to Elizabeth Barrett's maternal maiden aunt 'Bummy'. She is, however, an older generation of Englishwoman, and Barrett Browning's critique of female education is not sustained throughout the poem, nor is an alternative system described. The point of that critique, like de Staël's, is that all female training, whether adequate or hopelessly faulty, is directed at making women better wives so that they may assert 'their right of comprehending husband's talk ... their, in brief,/Potential faculty in everything/Of abdicating power in it' (I, 431, 440–2). Self-realization is the issue here, not only for women of genius but for all women. Barrett Browning is engaging with quite another set of adversaries than those de Staël routed in *Corinne*. Corinne was an unacceptable wife because she was an artist. Aurora, initially, wants no part of a marriage which will not accept her aspirations as valuable and give them space; but she is not unmarriageable in the same sense. Contemporary male enlightenment allowed women of Elizabeth Barrett Browning's generation any amount of literary talent and intelligence (though the stage and the platform were still forbidden arenas), but clever wives were seen as an asset to a man's career, which naturally took precedence. Aurora and Marian are capable of surviving as Corinne is not without marriage or love, although in the end Aurora triumphs over her rivals and has her career *and* her man.

Aurora Leigh is superficially more 'realistic' than *Corinne* but the reconstructed ending suggests a desire to repair, through rewriting, a tragic story that bit deep into the consciousness of the young Elizabeth Barrett. There is an evangelical note in her revision reinforced by the fact, known to her readers, that her personal history suggested a happy ending was possible. *Corinne*, as inspiration, myth and prophecy, was tangled up in so many ways in Elizabeth Barrett Browning's life and work and more subtle points in the text of *Aurora Leigh* reflect its influence. In both works Italy is the social landscape for 'light' amours. In *Aurora Leigh* the passions released by the Italian setting are enduring, sanctified, while Oswald's early history included a sordid affair with a French aristocrat. Unscrupulous and scheming, she provides the model for *Aurora Leigh*'s Lady Waldemar. De Staël's version of English patriarchal puritanism comes dangerously near parody. The alterations Barrett Browning incorporates show how deeply the patriarch–ungrateful-child theme cut. On one level she accepts de Staël's version of a desexualized England. Sexuality, even in the brutal instance of Marian's rape, occurs across the Channel.

The Brownings' own marriage took place in England but was consummated abroad. But consciously Barrett Browning rejects the sort of national stereo-typing indulged in by de Staël. Lady Waldemar is a light *English* aristocrat. Romney's father is a shadowy figure who positively wants the cousins to marry. There is also transposition of the close relationship between Oswald and *his* father to that between Aurora and her father. The portrait of the elder Lord Nelville as a kind but autocratic patriarch who directs his children's marital choices from the grave was too close to the reality of Edward Barrett Moulton Barrett who barred his ailing daughter's passage to Italy, that land of health and passion, and never forgave her for marrying Browning. In the world of the poem things are otherwise and better. Aurora's father is consti-tuted as an anti-type to the figure of a patriarchal tyrant. At his death he explicitly frees his daughter from the constraints of the oedipal tie with the injunction that rings through the body of the poem: 'His last word was "Love – "/"Love, my child, love, love"!' (I, 210–11).

The most bizarre echo of the novel occurred after Barrett Browning's death in Florence in 1861, which occasioned a day of mourning throughout her adopted city. Robert Browning described it in a letter to Elizabeth's brother George:

> She was buried yesterday, with the shops in the streets shut, a crowd of people following sobbing, another crowd of Italians, Americans, and English crying like children at the cemetery, for they knew who she was, the 'greatest English poet of the Day, writer of the sublimest poems ever penned by woman, and Italy's truest and dearest of friends', as the morning and evening papers told them.[25]

'The love-affair of Elizabeth Barrett with George Sand is much less cele-brated than her romance with Browning, but in its own way it was as intense, as liberating and as clearly, if not as fully, documented.'[26] Patricia Thomson's excellent account of that relationship leaves so little out that it is almost enough to summarize her essay. Sand's life and work represented for Barrett Browning an excursion into the forbidden world of 'immortal improprieties'. Hugo, Sand, Balzac were her 'triumvirate' of French writers, but she also read Sue, Soulie, de Quilhe and came away exhilarated and disappointed with *home* for being 'so neutral tinted and dull and cold by comparison'.[27] Her sonnets on Sand reflect her wish that the Frenchwoman could be passionate and pure 'true genius and true woman'. Elizabeth Barrett was fascinated and repelled by the androgyny involved in Sand's masculine charade; much more import-ant, she found in Sand, only three years her senior, an emotional, intellectual and political affinity and a passionate literary style missing in her English contemporaries. As Thomson points out, both 'were warm, impulsive, emo-tional; both were Romantics, Byron-worshippers in their youth, radicals, moderate feminists; both were genuinely and effortlessly creative, enthusiastic reformers – but for both, literary creation came first'.[28] No single Sand novel can be produced as a source for *Aurora Leigh*; rather the whole Sand oeuvre, her philosophy and a modified version of her life, play into Barrett Browning's conception of her poet heroine. Aurora as a name was chosen after some debate – she hovered between Laura and Aurora – with her friend Harriet Hosmer throwing in her vote for the name with more 'backbone'. Aurore Dudevant was the 'woman' in George Sand, the woman that Barrett Browning wanted Sand to acknowledge. Aurora's garret in London is modelled on Sand's attic in the *quai* St Michel and her unequivocal equality with her male contemporaries mimics Sand. But Aurora is 'a woman of repute'; just as Barrett Browning has given Corinne a new ending, so she has restored her living idol's lost reputation. When Barrett Browning chose to evoke specific references to contemporary works, she kept her audience and its reading habits carefully in mind. *Corinne* was an old favourite with the English reading public. George Sand might have been thought a subversive taste. Her novel *Consuelo* provoked Robert Browning to label Sand insultingly 'la femme qui parle'.[29] Elizabeth Barrett rejected this judgement but incorporates it in a curious way in *Aurora Leigh*, transferring it from the woman writer whom she most admired to the feminist polemicists, like her friends Anna Jameson or Margaret Fuller, and placing the accusation 'A woman's function plainly is – to talk' in Aurora's mouth, not Romney's. Finally, it is in the sexual metaphor, as Thomson shows, that Sand's liberating effect on Barrett Browning is most apparent. Although Aurora's love must be sanctified, the poet Aurora can speak freely of 'Spring's delicious trouble in the ground,/Tormented by the quickened blood of roots,/And softly pricked by golden crocus-sheaves' (V, 8-10), a passage that anticipates in its boldness and modernity both T. S. Eliot and Dylan Thomas and matches the erotic eloquence of Barrett Browning's unknown contemporary, Walt Whitman.

In her celebration of 'sexual passion' and woman's right to feel it, Barrett Browning is clearly on the side of Sand and the Brontë sisters, 'coarse' to the bone. She presses the contemporary argument for the legitimacy of passion one crucial stage further, insisting on the ultimate compatibility of passion and vocation. Little wonder then that in spite of its tragic resolution she preferred *Villette*, 'a strong book', to either *Shirley* or *Jane Eyre*.[30] Yet of all Charlotte Brontë's novels it is *Jane Eyre* whose plot and characters are cannibalized and reworked in *Aurora Leigh*; *Jane Eyre* with which the poem is in dialogue over the issue of creativity, passion and companionate marriage. In fact, Barrett Browning claimed to have forgotten *Jane Eyre* when writing *Aurora Leigh*, forgotten it so completely that when a friend challenged her for reproducing Rochester's fate in Romney's accident she had to send for the novel from a lending library to refresh her memory. Romney is merely blinded, she points out, not disfigured. 'As far as I recall the facts, the hero was monstrously disfigured and blinded in a fire the particulars of which escape me, and the circumstances of his being hideously scarred is the thing impressed chiefly on the reader's mind, certainly it remains innermost in mine.' [31] Both Barrett Browning's lapse of memory and her selective recall of the novel point towards, not away from the powerful influence of *Jane Eyre* and mark out her different but related use of male blindness. The reasons for her decisive distinction between blindness and disfigurement lie partly in the very personal associations that blindness had for her. Elizabeth Barrett's first mentor outside her immediate family was the blind classical scholar, Hugh Stuart Boyd. Their friendship, which began when Elizabeth was in her twenties and Boyd in his forties had strong romantic and erotic undertones which the young poet recorded in her diary of the year 1831–2.[32] Her anguish at Boyd's lack of enthusiasm for her work which can be found there is, in *Aurora Leigh*, transposed into Romney's slighting remarks in Book II. In the plot of her poem cause and effect are reversed, and the hero/lover's blindness becomes an indirect consequence of his inability to place a correct value on his cousin and her art. But Barrett Browning's affection for and trust in Boyd was as strong and enduring as her desire for literary revenge. In the last months of her secret courtship with Browning, the aged and ailing scholar was her only confidant. Blindness must thus stop short of 'hideous disfigurement', which, in *Jane Eyre*, is in great part a punishment for Rochester's sexual excesses. In the poem, Romney is painlessly deprived of his vision, in his own words 'mulcted as a man', but this milder symbolic castration punishes his political and intellectual deviations rather than his sexual ones. There is one more, rather poignant reason why Barrett Browning may have found the 'hideous disfigurement' coupled with blinding deeply repugnant, even threatening. The image of the 'blind poet' shut out from the world but with an intense inner life is also one which Elizabeth Barrett used about herself.

These multiple determinants make the blinding of Romney a very complex, even contradictory, symbolic event. Barrett Browning's horrified rejection of a castration motif in her poem as opposed to its undeniable presence in *Jane Eyre*, only confirms the reader's sense of the sexual overtones also present in *Aurora Leigh*. Romney's blinding simultaneously robs him of his 'manly' image and his masculine, mechanical projects for social improvement. His blindness brings spiritual enlightenment and forces Aurora's love out into the open. His helplessness gives the cousins a parity they did not have before, but it also symbolizes the exchange of insight and merging of sexual identity in sexual passion. Romney is made a sort of poet through the loss of his natural sight. Aurora's speech must now substitute for his vision. Contemporary critics complained of the fashion women writers were falling into of disfiguring their heroes. The fashion was not casual, for in the imaginary world of fiction and poetry, disfigurement was the punitive equalizer which ensured that the male partners would not easily reassert their dominant functions. The analogy to *Jane Eyre* stands, but with the added meanings which resolve the man of action into the enlightened lover, and allow the speaker of the poem to become the only doer. All the oppositions which Romney and Aurora separately represent – male and female, poet and reformer, speaker and actor – are dispersed and merged through the light, dark, sight, sound imagery of the final pages of the poem.

The question of innocence and atonement for sexual deviation is a vexed one for women authors, as suggested by Barrett Browning's reworking of *Ruth* (1853), Mrs Gaskell's latest novel. Barrett Browning read this story of an unmarried mother with much greater enthusiasm than she had shown for *Mary Barton* (1848). Of the earlier book she said, 'There is power and truth – she can shake and she can pierce – but I wish half the book away, it is so tedious every now and then; and besides I want more beauty, more air from the universal world – these class-books must always be defective as work of art.'[33] The style was 'slovenly' and later, reading *Ruth*, she thought it 'a great advance on *Mary Barton*', an opinion which shows Barrett Browning's élitism as well as her weakness as a critic. This preference tallies with her resistance to books which dealt intimately and sympathetically with working-class characters. She thought *Ruth* 'strong and healthy at once, teaching a moral frightfully wanted in English society', a moral so important she incorporated it into *Aurora Leigh* through the second part of Marian's history.[34] *Ruth*'s passage to unmarried motherhood is very different from Marian's. The beautiful daughter of a respectable farmer, she is sent, after her parent's death, to an establishment which trains sempstresses. Seduced by a young gentleman who whisks her to Wales and heartlessly abandons her, she is taken up and protected by a kind, dissenting clergyman. She moves in with him and his sister in their northern manufacturing town where they pass her off as a young widow. Eventually she is discovered. Disgraced in the eyes of the town, she becomes its saviour by turning to nursing. After heroic service in a typhoid epidemic she dies, and is canonized by the community. Mrs Gaskell is at pains to defend the unmarried mother against permanent stigma, although Ruth must atone for her sin through service, rather like Hester in Nathaniel Hawthorne's *The Scarlet Letter* (1852), a book also known to Barrett Browning. Marian, in contrast to Ruth, has to be raped while unconscious in order to free her from any responsibility for her loss of virginity and is thus a 'pure' victim of male violence. However, in order for the author to absolve her she must be denied the self-generated sexuality which is permitted to upper-class women in *Aurora Leigh* but which taints all working-class women except Marian. Barrett Browning was no more liberated about expressed female sexuality outside marriage than most of her readers, and the right to a passionate consummation within marriage is seemingly reserved for the well-born. Through the trauma of her rape Marian becomes a virtuous untouchable, at once transformed from a good child into a self-determining woman (like Ruth), but an unmarriageable one. The instinctive horror of the defiled woman evoked in *Aurora Leigh*, as it is in *Ruth* and in most Victorian fiction, suggests how deeply internalized were the rules of sexual conduct. Barrett Browning's aversion to realistic portrayals of working-class women is apparent in her idealization of Marian, and the equally heroicized slave mother in 'The runaway slave at Pilgrim's Point' (1848). The conflict and contradiction in her position on female sexuality and class is poignantly suggested by her use of the *Ruth* theme in *Aurora Leigh*.

If *Aurora Leigh* reworks the literary production of women writers, however, it also deconstructs the work of men. At the beginning of 1846, for example, Barrett Browning told Robert Browning she had heard Tennyson was

> writing a new poem – he has finished the second book of it – and it is in blank verse and a fairy tale, and called *The University*, the university-members being all females. ... I don't know what to think – it makes me open my eyes. Now isn't the world too old and fond of steam for blank verse poems, in ever so many books to be written on the fairies?[35]

Tennyson's poem, renamed *The Princess*, appeared on Christmas Day, 1847, one of the two major poetic works of the decade before *Aurora Leigh* which deal centrally with the woman question. (The other is Arthur Gordon Clough's *The Bothie of Tober-Na-Vuolich* published in the revolutionary year, 1848.)

The Princess vacillates between burlesque and high-seriousness, and despite the fact that Tennyson was highly critical of its unevenness in later years, it is the absence of his usual coherent manner which supplies part of its pleasures. Large sections of *The Princess* read like an Asterix cartoon version of the war of the sexes. Tennyson, however, was influenced by contemporary debates on feminism and women's place, and modern Tennyson critics argue plausibly that his conscious intention was serious and that he wished to write a poem which dealt with modern problems.[36] *The Princess* presents us with a spectre of a doomed feminist separatism, symbolized by the motto of the University which threatens death to any man who enters its grounds. The all-female university cannot of course be allowed to survive, since it constitutes a serious challenge to patriarchal power and discourse. Princess Ida tries in vain to defend her heroic experiment, but women's nature, their maternal instinct, natural jealousy of each other and desire for the opposite sex all contribute to the downfall of the project. Once the men have penetrated the sacred ground the end is near; the threat dissolves in liberal compromise. Happy couples, the Princess and her Prince, will work together to improve the condition of women.

Elizabeth Barrett Browning knew the poem well and was directing her work at the same audience, but the dialogue between *The Princess* and *Aurora Leigh* is both more inhibited and more oblique than that between *Corinne* and *Aurora Leigh*. There are, of course, many points of agreement between Tennyson's and Barrett Browning's view of Victorian feminism. Barrett Browning rejects the 'mapping out of masses to be saved/By nations or by sexes' (IX, 867–8). Neither poet had any time for militant or separatist feminism; both offer similar resolutions to gender antagonism. Ida and Aurora are two formidable women, educated and autonomous, who reject marriages arranged by their male kin. Each has an individually developed philosophy, Ida on feminism and Aurora on art, which they are unwilling to compromise to please a suitor. Each assumes, mistakenly, that since they cannot find male approval for their vocations they will live without love. In the end both discover they have been loved as much for their independence as in spite of it. Their enlightened lovers, the Prince and Romney, are converted to their cause. Most important, the political resolution of both poems transforms the private marriage into the public act. The Prince promises Ida: 'Henceforth thou has a helper, me, that know/The woman's cause is man's: ... We two will serve them both in aiding her ... /Will leave her space to burgeon out of all/Within her'.[37] Aurora echoes this worthy sentiment in Book II when she argues with Romney 'That every creature, female as the male,/Stands single in responsible act and thought/As also in birth and death' (II, 437–9). Where Barrett Browning quarrels with Tennyson is over the concept of ideal marriage as gender complementarity. 'You misconceive the question like a man,/Who sees a woman as the complement/Of his sex merely' (II, 434–6), Aurora says to Romney, answering Tennyson's formulation in the words of the Prince: 'Either sex alone/Is half itself and in true marriage lies/Nor equal nor unequal: each fulfils/Defects in each'.[38] Romney's symbolization of married love resists the two-halves-make-a-whole imagery. Instead he concentrates on the special quality of 'the love of wedded souls', a concept which does not depend on oppositional images of sexual identity. He calls it the 'human, vital fructuous rose/Whose calyx holds the multitude of leaves,/Loves filial, loves fraternal, neighbour-loves/And civic' (IX, 886–9). *Aurora Leigh* avoids a discussion which locates and fixes social biological definitions of the feminine or the masculine, a subject which Tennyson dwells on at dismaying length. His feminism stops this side of redefining gender difference. Woman may change only:

All that not harms distinctive womanhood ...
Yet in the long years liker must they grow;
The man be more of woman she of man;
He gain in sweetness and in moral height
Nor lose the wrestling thews that throw the world;
She mental breadth nor fail in childward care
Nor lose the childlike in the larger mind;
Till at the last she set herself to man
Like perfect music unto noble words.[39]

Romney, on the other hand, yields the speaker's role to Aurora: 'Now press the clarion on thy woman's lip ... And breathe thy fine keen breath along the brass' (IX, 929, 931). Tennyson's attachment to woman's traditional role is clear. His wife of the future still minds the kids and hums the tunes without the words.

The love scene between Aurora and Romney in Book IX owes something to the final pages of *The Princess*. Having brought the shadow text into consciousness, Barrett Browning criticizes some of its arguments. The 'fairy story' frame was not what she was looking for. Poets should 'represent the age,/ Their age, not Charlemagne's . . . To flinch from modern varnish, coat of flounce,/Cry out for togas and the picturesque/Is fatal, – foolish too' (V, 202, 203, 208–10). As wary of political feminism as she was of socialism, her silence about the central polemic in *The Princess*, the recuperation of an autonomous women's movement into a liberalized version of kinship and marriage structures, can be reckoned as a kind of agreement.

Barrett Browning's critique of Tennyson reflects her refusal to accept male versions of female experience and the co-option by liberal men of the women's issue. But the male writer who engaged her critical attention most completely during the writing of *Aurora Leigh* was Charles Kingsley, the utopian socialist to whose novel *Alton Locke, Tailor and Poet* (1850), *Aurora Leigh* is a sort of counter-text. *Alton Locke* was greeted by a critical reception that was both noisy and scathing. Because it dealt sympathetically with Chartism and had a working-class hero it was an easy target for establishment periodicals. Kingsley was 31 at the time of its publication, a Church of England parson already well-known as one of a band of liberals who called themselves Christian Socialists and had been influenced by the utopian socialism of Fourier and Owen. Their desire to 'Christianise socialism, and socialise Christianity' was deliciously vague, but the projects in which they involved themselves were more concrete. In the mid-1840s the group, whose leading theorist was F. D. Maurice, was involved in the setting up of Queens College, London, the first institution of higher learning for women, and Kingsley, an effective muckraking journalist, wrote an excellent pamphlet for their series 'Politics for the people' on the immiseration of artisans in the garment trade, *Cheap Clothes and Nasty*.

Elizabeth Barrett Browning had read *Alton Locke* and Kingsley's other novel *Yeast*. In 1852 she met Kingsley and told Mrs Martin that:

Few men have impressed me more agreeably than Mr. Kingsley. He is original and earnest and full of a genial and almost tender kindliness which is delightful to me. Wild and theoretical in many ways he is of course, but I believe he could not be otherwise than good and noble let him say or dream what he will.[40]

A year later, to Miss Mitford, she enlarged on her praise:

> I am glad he spoke kindly of us because really I like him and admire him.
> Few people have struck me as much as he did last year in England. 'Manly,'
> do you say? But I am not very fond of praising men by calling them *manly*. I
> hate and detest a masculine man. *Humanly* bold, brave, true, direct, Mr.
> Kingsley is – a moral cordiality and an original intellect uniting in him.[41]

This passage is written in the year she began work on *Aurora Leigh*, so much of
which is given over to a refutation of the politics Kingsley espoused in his life
and work. A comparison of Aurora's description of Romney in Book V and her
assessment of him in Book II shows how Kingsley figures in the poem.

> One man – and he my cousin and he my friend
> And he born tender made intelligent
> Inclined to ponder the precipitous sides
> Of difficult questions ...
> With kindness, with a tolerant gentleness. (V, 32–5, 40).

Romney, like Aurora, is a synthesis of real-life and literary models. The
quoted passage reminds us too of Barrett Browning's honorary cousin and
lifelong friend John Kenyon to whom the poem is dedicated.

However, her liking for Kingsley and her hostility to his ideas make him a
perfect pattern for her 'wild and theoretical' hero who must be converted from
socialism to Art. Kingsley was the richest contemporary resource for Barrett
Browning because his reformist programme included attention to the woman
question, explicity treated in *Yeast* and dealt with marginally but seriously in
Alton Locke, Tailor and Poet.[42] The latter book forms the ideal foil for *Aurora
Leigh*. The problems of social identity and self-determination for both
working-class men and middle-class women were temptingly parallel.
Charlotte Brontë had touched on the subject in *Shirley*, Mrs Gaskell in *North
and South*, but Kingsley's creation of a working-class *poet* was a gift to Barrett
Browning. *Aurora Leigh* might well be subtitled *Woman and Poet* and a later
poem, *Mother and Poet*, picks up on the dissonance between the two descriptions. The self-taught hero of *Alton Locke* shares the same initials with our
heroine. In his evolution as a poet he meets similar prejudice and encounters
similar difficulties in finding an individual voice.

The high points of the novel aesthetically and politically are the scenes
among the poor. The description of St Giles is genuinely harrowing, and
worth quoting since it is these scenes that Barrett Browning cannibalizes for
her picture of the London poor. Mackaye, Alton's radical patron and a loving
caricature of Thomas Carlyle, calls it the mouth of hell and points Locke at
the gin shop where he can see an 'Irishwoman pouring the gin down the
babbie's throat ... Drunkards frae the breast! – harlots frae the cradle!'
Mackaye drags him to 'a phalanstery of all fiends. ... Up stair after stair ...

while wails of children and curses of men steamed out upon the hot stifling rush of air from every doorway, till at the topmost story, we knocked at a garret door.'[43] There Mackaye introduces Locke to a family of girls who keep themselves and a sick sister alive by sewing and whoring alternately. Kingsley's inferno is drawn to evoke pity, horror and indignation. If a cause and a solution are not offered at least Kingsley does not suggest that it lies in the original sin of the poor. When Elizabeth Barrett Browning picks up and imitates this scene, compassion and any pretence at social analysis have dropped out of it. Aurora notes 'a woman rouged/Upon the angular cheek-bones, kerchief torn/Thin dangling locks, and flat lascivious mouth/Cursed at the window both ways, in and out/By turns some bed-red creature and myself–/Lie still there mother! like the dead dog/You'll be tomorrow' (II, 764–70). This description is typical of Barrett Browning's portrait of the poor. Kingsley concentrates on poverty and ignorance; Barrett Browning prefers a close-up which emphasizes an almost racial distinction between whore and lady and the total absence of affectionate bonds of kinship, particularly between mothers and daughters.

Barrett Browning also uses *Alton Locke* for her description of the riot at Leigh Hall. In Kingsley's novel Lord Lynedale gives his estate over to socialist experiment. Barrett Browning makes Romney's phalanstery the scene of social disorder, cleverly transferring the description of the riot in which Alton gets arrested to the incident at Leigh Hall. It is a reactionary running together of two very different episodes in Kingsley's novel in order to drive home the point that utopian socialism cannot alter the natural depravity of the lower orders.[44]

Kingsley's panaceas for the class conflict he describes are particularly wet and weak and *Alton Locke* has passages of ugly racism and anti-semitism of which Barrett Browning could never be guilty. Nevertheless, Barrett Browning's handling of the working class suggests just how her lack of first-hand knowledge of the world had damaged her political sensibility. Her only excursion into the London slums was made to redeem her dog Flush from dog thieves. Yet she was interested in social questions and wrote several compassionate poems, *The Cry of The Human, The Cry of the Children, A Plea for the Ragged Schools of London*. She saw herself as a 'democrat', but her response to the failure of the 1848 revolutions suggests this veneer of democracy was easily scratched. The years between 1848 and 1856 had left her deeply cynical about the ability of the working classes to transform themselves into good bourgeois republicans. Her faith in leaders of Italian nationalist movements became directly in proportion to their aristocratic position and élitist aims. The picture of natural depravity set against natural virtue in *Aurora Leigh* confirms this disillusionment.

Also taken up and argued in *Aurora Leigh* are the role of the poet and the proper vocation for intelligent women. Kingsley was committed to the idea that Locke should remain loyal to his class as a 'people's poet' rather than enter the bourgeoisie. When Locke discovers Tennyson he describes him as a model of the democratic poet, not in his political opinions 'but in his handling of the trivial everyday sights and sounds of nature'.[45] Aurora's version is identical. 'For poets ... half poets even are still whole democrats'. Both descriptions take poetic licence with the meaning of 'democrat'; the sentiment is straight out of Carlyle.

Kingsley rejects class mobility for Locke as Barrett Browning's Aurora rejects androgyny as a masque or aspiration for women writers. She refuses all current definitions of women's roles and rejects the notion that there is a creative limitation on women as artists. Women should tackle epic as naturally as the ballad. One of Elizabeth Barrett Browning's closest friends was the American sculptor, Harriet Hosmer, whose giant figures were also epic attempts. However Barrett Browning did see women as constrained by their mediated relation to patriarchal power. Self-determination about work was more important than the right to choose one's own mate, and was always a struggle. This argument appears at various points in the poem and has a particular relation to Kingsley's view of the liberated woman represented by Eleanor, Alton's upper-class patron, who explains that she was an only child and an heiress, 'highly educated'.

> Every circumstance of humanity which could pamper pride was mine. ... I painted, I sang, I wrote in prose and verse – they told me, not without success. Men said that I was beautiful ... I worshipped all that was pleasurable to the intellect and the taste. The beautiful was my God. I lived in deliberate intoxication, on poetry, music, painting and every antitype of them which I could find in the world around. At last I met with one whom you once saw. He first awoke in me the sense of the vast duties and responsibilities of my station – his example first taught me to care for the many rather than the few.[46]

Proud of her intellect she delves into Bentham, Malthus, Fourier and Proudhon and helps her husband with his social experiments. When Lynedale died the 'blow came. My idol – ... To please him I had begun – To please myself in pleasing him I was trying to become great'.[47] Eleanor ends up living with a household of ex-prostitutes where the women work for each other and the workrooms 'were not a machinery but a family'. Here, in brief, is Corinne converted into a female reformer.

Eleanor's history is replied to in *Aurora Leigh* through the angry disagreement between Romney and Aurora in Book II. Romney suggests that art is an inappropriate and vaguely unworthy occupation for a woman. Aurora replies, 'Whoever says/To a loyal woman, "Love and work with me,"/Will get fair answers if the work and love/Being good themselves, are good for her – the best/She was born for' (II, 339, 443). It is precisely Kingsley's notion of higher good for Eleanor that is rejected and eroded throughout *Aurora Leigh* so that Romney finally accepts Aurora's art and love as the combined forces which will 'blow all class-walls level as Jericho's' (IX, 932).

A point that Barrett Browning accepts, reluctantly, however, is the notion that women cannot do without male approval for their work or rely on their own assessment of their talents or deal with material outside of the personal. Some of the most acute and enduring passages in *Aurora Leigh* are given over to discussing this problem.

> We women are too apt to look to one,
> Which proves a certain impotence in art.
> We strain our natures at doing something great
> Far less because it's something great to do,
> Than haply that we, so, commend ourselves
> As being not small and more appreciable
> To some one friend. We must have mediators
> Betwixt our highest conscience and the judge:
> Some sweet saint's blood must quicken in our palms
> Or all the life in heaven seems slow and cold. (V, 43–52).

Women's achievement in art is hindered by this seeming inability to perceive 'Good only ... as the end of good'. The manifesto of liberation is placed in the very centre of the poem and is the heart of its plea for women to attempt emotional and intellectual autonomy.

> Yet so I will not. – This vile woman's way
> Of trailing garments shall not trip me up:
> I'll have no traffic with the personal thought
> In Art's pure temple. *Must I work in vain*
> *Without the approbation of a man?*
> *It cannot be; it shall not.* ...
> We'll keep our aims sublime, our eyes erect,
> Although our woman-hands should shake and fail.
>   (V, 59–64, 65–6; my italics)

No woman engaged in work traditionally defined as male can read this passage without being touched by it. 'Love' is quite pointedly not mentioned in these lines for Barrett Browning is distinguishing between Corinne's disease, the loss of genius through the loss of a lover, and the more general anxiety about male approval in patriarchal culture.

The feminism of *Aurora Leigh* is produced as a complex of objections to a liberal male response to the 'woman question' as well as a revaluation of the concepts of self-determination as they were dealt with by contemporary women writers and feminists. The rejection of male left politics, 'Fourier's void,/And Comte absurd, – and Cabet puerile./Subsist no rules of life outside of life' is marked by Romney's failure and his capitulation to a new trinity: Art, a very feminized Christianity and Love. A male discourse denying female experience and wisdom, which attempts to co-opt women into a male-designed version of utopia, must fail as certainly as Ida's University. However, there is congruence between Barrett Browning's feminist perspective and that of the utopian socialists, for both deny to the working classes any self-generating consciousness, a fact which Marx notes in *The Communist Manifesto*. Nowhere in the literature of the mid-century is the bourgeois rejection of working-class consciousness more glaring than in *Aurora Leigh*, though it is certainly present in Charlotte Brontë, Gaskell and Stowe, among others. *Aurora Leigh* reminds us that there is a female as well as a male version of liberal bourgeois ideology. The feminist analysis in the poem is in some ways so advanced and so piercing that we forget it is central partly because the political analysis of the poem is so weak, so over-dependent on the vacillations of Barrett Browning's favourite thinker, Carlyle. It exists by creating a vacuum around it which whirls away problems of class oppression.

Yet for all its difficulties the poem remains radical and rupturing, a major confrontation of patriarchal attitudes unique in the imaginative literature of its day. For the woman as speaker poet has virtually replaced all male prophets, and the 'woman's figure' dominates the symbolic language of the poem just as women's experience dominates its narrative. The description of Aurora as an independent author living and working in London was possibly the most 'revolutionary' assertion in the poem, an item more likely to corrupt the daughters of the gentry than Barrett Browning's sympathetic reference to the plight of prostitutes, for it affected the real possibilities and conditions of the lives of middle-class women. She does not, of course, suggest that the literary life lived single is romantic or exciting. More subversively and seductively she indicates that it is possible, interesting and productive – something that was beginning to be true for the generation of women who came after the mid-century.

NOTES

1. Elizabeth Barrett Browning, *Aurora Leigh*, in *Aurora Leigh and Other Poems*, intr. Cora Kaplan (London: Women's Press, 1977), bk V, lines 214–17. All subsequent references to the poem are cited in the text and are to this edition (they are consistent, however, with most editions of *Aurora Leigh*).
2. See Virginia Woolf, 'Aurora Leigh', *The Common Reader*, 2nd series (London: Hogarth Press, 1932), pp. 202–13.
3. Elizabeth Barrett to Robert Browning, 27 February 1845, in *The Letters of Robert Browning and Elizabeth Barrett Browning 1845–1846*, 2 vols (New York: Harper, 1898), p. 32. hereafter *RB and EBB*.
4. Quoted in Woolf, 'Aurora Leigh', p. 203.
5. Elizabeth Barrett Browning to Anna Jameson, 28 February 1856, in *The Letters of*

Elizabeth Barrett Browning, ed. Fredric G. Kenyon, 2 vols (London: Smith, Elder, 1897), p. 228, hereafter *LEBB*.

6. Woolf, 'Aurora Leigh', p. 213.
7. Elizabeth Barrett to Miss Mitford, 30 December 1844, in *Elizabeth Barrett to Miss Mitford: The Unpublished Letters of Elizabeth Barrett Browning to Mary Russell Mitford*, ed. Betty Miller (London: John Murray, 1954), pp. 231–2, hereafter *EBB to MRM*.
8. *EBB to MRM*, 18 September 1846, pp. 274–5.
9. *EBB to MRM*, February 1845, p. 235.
10. *EBB to MRM*, Monday 14 December 1844, pp. 228–9.
11. Edmund Gosse, in *The Critic* (January 1893).
12. *North British Review* 26 (February 1857).
13. *LEBB*, 12 April 1853, 2, pp. 110–11.
14. *National Review* 4 (April 1857), p. 245.
15. *Blackwood's Magazine* 81 (January 1857), p. 33.
16. *Dublin University Review* 49 (April 1857), p. 470.
17. *North American Review* 85 (October 1857), pp. 418–19.
18. *National Review* 4, pp. 243–4.
19. *RB and EBB*, 20 March 1845, 1, p. 43.
20. *EBB to MRM*, 1 October 1844, pp. 227–8.
21. Ellen Moers, *Literary Women* (Garden City: Doubleday, 1976), p. 185. See the whole of Moers' chapter, 'Performing heroinism: the myth of Corinne', pp. 173–210, for a brilliant and wide-ranging discussion of the novel and its contemporary influence.
22. Madame de Staël, *Corinne, or Italy* (London: Samuel Tupper, 1807), bk 14, ch. 1, pp. 353–76.
23. *Corinne*, p. 356–8.
24. *Corinne*, p. 366.
25. Robert Browning to George Barrett, Tuesday 2 July 1861, in *Letters of the Brownings to George Barrett*, ed. Paul Lands (Urbana: University of Illinois Press, 1958), p. 272.
26. Patricia Thomson, *George Sand and the Victorians* (London: Macmillan, 1977), p. 43. See the whole of the chapter on Sand and Elizabeth Barrett Browning, 'Through the prison bars ...', pp. 43–60.
27. *EBB to MRM*, 21 November 1842, p. 145.
28. Thomson, *George Sand and the Victorians*, p. 46.
29. Quoted in *RB and EBB*, 16 August 1845, p. 164.
30. EBB to Mr Westwood, September 1853, *LEBB* 2, p. 139.
31. EBB to Anna Jameson, 26 December 1856, *LEBB* 2, pp. 245–6.
32. See *The Barretts at Hope End: The Early Diary of Elizabeth Barrett Browning*, ed. Elizabeth Berridge (London: John Murray, 1974), and *Elizabeth Barrett to Mr. Boyd: Unpublished Letters of Elizabeth Barrett Browning to Hugh Stuart Boyd*, ed. Barbara P. McCarthy (London: John Murray, 1955).
33. EBB to Miss Mitford, *LEBB* 1, pp. 471–2.
34. EBB to Mrs Martin, 5 October 1853, *LEBB* 2, p. 141.
35. *RB and EBB*, 31 January 1846, 1, p. 441.
36. See John Killham, *Tennyson and 'The Princess'* (London, 1958).

37. Alfred Tennyson, *The Princess: A Medley* (London: Edward Moxon, 1847), p. 155.
38. *The Princess*, p. 156.
39. *The Princess*, p. 157.
40. EBB to Mrs Martin, 2 September 1852, *LEBB* 2.
41. EBB to Miss Mitford, 20/21 August 1853, *LEBB* 2, p. 134.
42. Charles Kingsley, *Alton Locke, Tailor and Poet: An Autobiography*, (London: Chapman & Hall, 1850).
43. ibid., pp. 126–9.
44. ibid., ch. VII, pp. 77–107.
45. ibid., p. 140.
46. ibid., pp. 272, 273.
47. ibid., p. 275.

EIGHT
Inverts and experts: Radclyffe Hall and the lesbian identity

SONJA RUEHL

Radclyffe Hall published her explicitly lesbian novel, *The Well of Loneliness*, in 1928. It is a work of polemical fiction setting out her view that lesbianism is inborn, an 'inversion' of normal sexuality which ought to be tolerated by society because it cannot be helped. When it was published, the book was immediately denounced by the *Sunday Express* as an insidious moral poison and within six weeks it was being prosecuted for obscenity. The trial and surrounding publicity about the book put lesbianism on the map. A battle over competing definitions of lesbianism was engaged and, for the first time, the idea of 'the lesbian' as a specific identity and image was given wide public currency.

Radclyffe Hall's public stance was that she wrote as a lesbian herself and the reports, photographs and cartoons of her in the press turned her into the paradigm of lesbianism in appearance and manner. Her notoriety was the greater because by this time she was already an established novelist and literary prizewinner. Her upper-class provenance and aura of exotic masculinity contributed to public interest in her as a notorious personality. Both she and her fictional heroine, Stephen, became points of reference for women who, in a time when landmarks were few, were struggling to make sense of their attraction to other women and to find a social identity by which to live.

What affected the way women were able to live and construe their lives was not simply that lesbianism could be talked about, but the way it could be talked about. And I want to examine how lesbianism came to be defined as a sexual identity. As press reaction of the time illustrated, lesbianism before 1928 had commonly been situated predominantly within a rhetoric of sin, if it was discussed at all. The sinful perspective had already been challenged from within a restricted medical discourse by 'sexologists' such as Havelock Ellis, who had established lesbianism as a medical-psychological category. Radclyffe Hall used Ellis's category but deployed it in a different kind of discourse, a literary and fictional one. This in itself, together with her own public identification as a lesbian, contributed to the beginning of a transformation of Ellis's category and a shift in the definition of lesbianism. The events surrounding her book and its trial enable us to see competing definitions of lesbianism within the discourses of science, fiction and the popular press.

Where scientific definitions are concerned, a strand of medical-psychological opinion in the nineteenth century had begun to develop the idea that people could actually be defined by their sexual natures – that lesbians, say, could actually be thought of as a separate type of person. 'Sexology' had started to classify and differentiate aberrant forms of sexuality more minutely than the moral and religious language of sin had done and also to categorize these sexual aberrations in biological terms. Havelock Ellis was the most influential of sexologists in England. His work on homosexuality, entitled *Sexual Inversion*, had been published in 1897. The book had been prosecuted and found 'obscene' under the same law from which Hall later suffered, and the remainder of his series, *Studies in the Psychology of Sex*, had to be published in America.

Ellis developed the category of 'congenital inversion' to describe homosexuality. He viewed it as neither sin nor sickness: what was inborn could not be helped or passed on to others. Although he realized that a theory of innateness provided a basis for public tolerance of homosexuality he never actively campaigned on the issue. Congenital inversion remained a definition restricted to scientific discourse until given wide publicity through *The Well of Loneliness*. In order to consider how Hall's categorization of homosexuality relates to that of Ellis – and what its political consequences might be – I want to draw on the work of the French philosopher, Michel Foucault.

FROM IMPRISONING CATEGORIES TO SELF-DEFINITION

In *The History of Sexuality* (1979) Foucault argues the need to examine sexuality in terms of historically specific discourses and their methods of classification. He challenges the view that sexuality has a coherent, unitary existence, at one moment repressed, at another liberated. In his view, any coherence sexual activities may have derives entirely from the concepts and definitions that organize our knowledge of them. When he examines the work of nineteenth-century sexologists like Ellis he notes how they create a medical-psychological discourse whereby 'peripheral' sexualities, like homosexuality, are organized into a scientific taxonomy, or classification system. The categories created by the system, such as Ellis's inversion, are then interpreted as permanent attributes of individuals.

Furthermore, these categories do not merely compose a person's identity: they *are* what defines it. Thus, from being an undifferentiated sin or piece of behaviour, 'lesbian' comes to denote a particular *identity* and 'the lesbian' as a separate type of person is then an invention of nineteenth-century science. Foucault goes on to argue that once sexuality is constructed as the 'key', the 'secret', to an individual's 'true nature' or 'inner being', these categories have a rigidifying effect, imprisoning individuals whose lives are administered under them.

The intention of this 'medical-psychological discourse' was to organize sexuality into a new field of scientific knowledge, bringing it within the range of rationality as an area to which rules could be applied. But in Foucault's perspective, to organize a new field of knowledge is also to organize a new set of power relations: power is granted to the definers – the experts and administrators of others' sexuality.

At the same time, the process of categorization makes resistance to that power possible. Once a category like homosexuality has been set up and individuals have started to be defined by it, then the so–named homosexuals may group under it and start to use it to speak for themselves. So, Foucault says, 'homosexuality began to speak on its own behalf ... often in the same vocabulary, using the same categories, by which it was medically disqualified'. He calls this process the development of a 'reverse discourse', and it is in these terms that I want to examine the work of Radclyffe Hall.

I am going to consider how, speaking herself from within the category 'invert' developed by Ellis, she was able to begin its transformation. Her militant stand, both as author and public personality, was to start a 'reverse discourse' towards *self*-definition by those oppressed under the category. Hall's intervention can be seen as a step in the process whereby women have firstly been able to group under a publicly available lesbian label and later gone on to demand the right to define that category themselves. That challenge has arisen in the political groupings of the gay movements of the 1970s and especially of the women's movement, where the 'right to a self-defined sexuality' for all women explicitly emerged as one of the demands of women's liberation. But to understand in retrospect what Hall's contribution to that process was, it is necessary to look first at the way Ellis's theory worked to construct the lesbian person.

HAVELOCK ELLIS AND 'CONGENITAL INVERSION'

In his work on homosexuality, Havelock Ellis made a distinction between homosexuality as an innate and permanent state and as temporary, acquired behaviour. The first he called sexual 'inversion', a fixed congenital characteristic expressing a person's 'true' sexual nature, the second, because not innate, a potential temptation and a vice.

Because of this logical separation, Ellis believed that someone who was a congenital invert would not necessarily exhibit it in homosexual behaviour – while someone who was not could be tempted into temporary indulgence.

True inverts could decide not to engage in homosexual practices, could choose not to give any physical expression to their homosexual nature. This is the course of action taken by the majority of the six 'inverted' women whose case-histories Ellis discusses in *Sexual Inversion*. How then could their inversion be revealed in the first place? It is revealed as a characteristic of these individuals through introspection and the self-confession of their 'natures' to Ellis, who intersperses the histories with his comments.

Ellis attempts to discover a coherent set of physical distinguishing marks which infallibly characterize female inverts. His failure to do so he ascribes to a lack of adequate scientific knowledge. Because his concept of lesbianism is biological, he seems to suggest that a coherent set of distinguishing marks could in time be discovered by medical science. In this way, he directs attention towards a search for the *symptoms* of lesbianism. One consequence of his view is therefore that women are left to worry about whether they exhibit 'symptoms' of lesbianism or not. This is especially so when combined with his view that inversion could not definitely be distinguished until a woman was in her twenties.

It is clear from this description of the kind of symptoms Ellis was looking for that he expected the 'true invert' to be a 'masculine' woman, exhibiting an active sexuality which he thought of as 'male'. The object of the true invert's desire, on the other hand, he expected to be feminine. In line with his conception of heterosexual relations, a 'feminine' or responsive sexuality was required to mesh with the active 'male' sexuality of the invert. This raises the problem of whether the 'feminine' partner was herself a true invert or not.

Ellis extricates himself from this problem by distinguishing a separate class of 'women who-respond-to-true-inverts'. It is an overlapping category, with elements of the heterosexual woman and of the congenital invert. This object of the true invert's desire will most probably be a womanly woman but, Ellis argues, one who is not quite attractive enough to appeal to the average man. He also tries to create distinctions between what appeals to inverts and what appeals to men in terms such as that inverts are more interested in beauty of figure and men in beauty of face. The clinching argument for Ellis is, however, that this category, though 'womanly', is not 'robust', not 'well adapted for child-bearing', so that even here a biological justification is called into play. By tying his view of inversion to heterosexual, procreative sex as the model from which it deviates Ellis thus evokes the image of sterility, and the whole lesbian relationship begins to seem a sterile imitation and thereby inferior.

This may be the reason why Ellis overcompensates for the sexual aberration of inverts by suggesting that it is outweighed by other excellent qualities which in fact have nothing to do with homosexuality. Though he wants to argue that inverts should be tolerated by society, his views suggest that inversion 'in itself' is not as worthy of respect as the 'norm' of heterosexuality, and that lesbians have to win social acceptance by being a generally superior type of person. In addition to character and intellect, this might be through the countervailing power of social position and Ellis points to the social superiority of belonging to the upper classes as one way women might, as it were, 'get away with' lesbianism, in moral terms. There are hints in the case-studies that high-mindedness might require rising above physical gratifications: inverts could divert their thoughts 'into intellectual channels' or try to 'find a way of life in which there was as little sex of any kind as possible'.

When Radclyffe Hall comes to write *The Well of Loneliness*, it is clear that she writes within the parameters set up by Ellis. His notions of biological destiny, symptoms of inborn and irreducible difference, the 'masculine' invert and the 'feminine' love-object, are all, as I shall indicate, woven into her fictional and partly autobiographical plot. Moreover, she was keen to acquire Ellis's expert backing for her views. She got him to write the preface to the first edition of the book, recommending it in the light of his own theories:

I have read *The Well of Loneliness* with great interest because – apart from its fine qualities as a novel – it possesses a notable psychological and social significance. So far as I know, it is the first English novel which presents, in a completely faithful and uncompromising form, one particular aspect of sexual life as it exists among us today. The relation of certain people – who, while different from their fellow human beings, are sometimes of the highest character and the finest aptitudes – to the often hostile society in which they move presents difficult and still unsolved problems. The poignant situations which thus arise are here set forth so vividly, and yet with such complete absence of offence, that we must place Radclyffe Hall's book on a high level of distinction.

In this preface Ellis thus tries to set the terms for a discussion of lesbianism as social problem and to shift it away from ideas of sin or moral degeneracy.

In pleading for tolerance of lesbianism, Hall had considerable scope to use the affective potentialities of the novel to engage her readers' sympathies. More vividly than Ellis does in his medical discourse, she is able to point up the social consequences of a lesbian identity and to explore, not only sexual relationships, but those involving family and friends. By contrast, Ellis's method seems rather individualizing of lesbianism, because he presents individuals' stories circumscribed within the format of separate case-histories interspersed with his comments. What Hall does in her novel is to highlight what is only implicit in his theorizing: the 'sterility' of lesbian relationships, described with images of barrenness and unfruitful wombs, to evoke sympathy for the unsurmountable grief of the true invert. But *The Well of Loneliness* is not simply an exemplification of Ellis's views in literary form, nor just more persuasive because able to deploy the rhetoric of fiction. While Hall's own definition of lesbianism remains closely tied to Ellis's category of inversion, her novel is a deliberate political intervention. Through it, she takes a militant stance on behalf of all inverts *because she speaks as one herself.* She starts the process of the reverse discourse by opening up a space for other lesbians to speak for themselves, and later, through the contemporary gay and women's movements, to challenge the definition of the category from within.

THE WELL OF LONELINESS: UNFOLDING LESBIAN DESTINY

The novel is the story of Stephen Gordon, born a girl, to her father's disappointment, and christened Stephen by his (prescient) whim. The novel suggests the presence of distinguishing marks of inversion. From birth, it is said, Stephen is a little strange, a 'narrow-hipped, wide-shouldered' baby with 'brave hazel eyes that were so like her father's'. Her mother turns from her with intuitive distaste, while Stephen has an instinctive empathy with her father. She grows up liking boyish pursuits of a suitably aristocratic kind and explicitly wants to be a boy, playing at being 'the young Nelson'. Thus symptoms of 'congenital inversion' are clearly implied. They take the specific form of her being a sort of failed boy, a caricature of her father and a 'blemished, unworthy, maimed reproduction' of him.

The reader's sympathy is enlisted on behalf of this invert, as yet a child and innocent in the sense of being both ignorant of, and not responsible for, her 'condition'. Her father grows concerned and starts to read books by a German sexologist in his library. By this means, the reader is let in on the 'truth'. The novel constructs Stephen's inversion as containing the essence of her nature, a secret, hidden even from herself. She asks her father whether there is something strange about herself and although he is not quite man enough to share it with her, it is her father who holds the knowledge of Stephen's destiny.

The gradual unfolding of this biological destiny is traced through Stephen's amorous history. After a childish infatuation with a housemaid one summer, in accordance with the dictates of her nature, she falls 'quite simply and naturally in love' with Angela, wife of a local businessman. Angela is only tempted onto the fringes of homosexuality by boredom and proves perfidious because, as it turns out, she also has a male lover. She embodies the 'viciousness' of acquired homosexuality which Ellis alludes to and a clear contrast with Stephen is established: she isn't even 'a lady'. Class is invoked on behalf of the invert.

The novel also presents Stephen with the possibility of an amorous encounter with a man, which it shows to be unworkable. Martin, a young man from the colonies, is used to boyishness in women and so doesn't find Stephen's manners strange. But she is puzzled and repelled by his lover-like advances, thinking of him only as a friend. It is her realization of the social inappropriateness of this response that sends Stephen off on her unilluminating search for explanations from her father.

World War I opens up an area of suitably masculine employment for

Stephen. She is able to get into uniform and go to the Front as an ambulance-driver. Ironically, the war allows Stephen more opportunities to come into her own and, in the ambulance corps, a world without men, her 'nature' has scope to flourish. Here she finds a suitable partner, Mary Llewelyn, feminine, genuinely loving and an admirer of Stephen's bravery. She is the embodiment of the problem set up by Ellis's theory as to who the true invert's lover could possibly be. She loves Stephen, but is not quite a congenital case herself, being 'all woman', 'perfect woman'. She is womanly and attractive to the masculine Stephen, but then why is she not the lover of a man? The problem is kept in equilibrium in the novel by the social inequality of Mary and Stephen. Stephen is upper-class and Mary an ordinary girl and furthermore, an orphan, with no place in the world.

Their social inequality also serves to make the novel appealing in conventionally romantic terms – someone strong is protecting someone weak from the world, and she is grateful. Stephen provides the displaced Mary with a home after the war and works at her writing to secure Mary's future. Theirs is a very polarized relationship. Stephen is taller, richer and a stronger character than Mary. The division of labour between them is as stark as in any conventional marriage: Stephen has her writing and Mary, 'the household, the paying of bills, the filing of receipts, the answering of unimportant letters'. Their sexual relationship too is described in very polarized terms, such as 'Stephen stooped down and kissed her,' or 'she slept in Stephen's masterful arms'. The polarity echoes Ellis's categories of true invert and woman-who-responds-to-true-invert, but fills their relationship out in emotional terms and suggests what might give it stability. It does so of course in terms which feed into the stereotypical images of the lesbian couple, composed of masculine 'butch' and feminine 'femme', far more rigidly than anything Ellis wrote.

Because the homosexual relations described in the novel approximate to those of the heterosexual world, *The Well of Loneliness* is appealing on conventional romantic terms. Even so, the idea that Stephen and Mary's relationship could be a conventional romance is constantly undermined throughout the novel. One source of dissonance is the consistent reference to Stephen as 'she', for example and this dissonance underlines the paradoxical place assigned to lesbianism by theories of congenital inversion. Another source of such dissonance comes through in the way physical sexual relations are dealt with in the novel. Physical sex is clearly implied although not described: it is part of what Hall is arguing to be tolerated by society. But lesbian sex in *The Well* is a recurrent juxtaposition of lesbian passion with images of sterility, unfruitfulness, barrenness, that derive from the comparison with the heterosexual 'norm'. Furthermore, this sterility is seen as somehow inscribed into the body of Stephen the congenital invert – 'this strangely ardent yet sterile body', whose 'barren womb became fruitful – it ached with its fearful and sterile burden'. Sterility is part of the invert's fate and also presented as a misfortune which ought to have a claim on the pity of 'normal' society.

Apart from the spectre of sterility, the passion between Stephen and Mary is shown to be untenable for largely social reasons. What would have counted as a satisfactory *dénouement* in a conventional romantic work here contains the seeds of its own destruction. For Stephen and Mary as a couple, there is social opprobrium from the world at large. Stephen's mother refuses to invite Mary to the house. Their friend, Lady Massey, withdraws an invitation to spend Christmas at her house when the awful truth dawns, having 'her position in the country' to consider. Stephen would have liked to provide a place for Mary in this upper-class milieu and to rescue her from social obscurity, but money and her own social position are insufficient to do this. A rather bitter contrast is drawn with the approval shown to (legitimate) heterosexual alliances: 'Oh, yes, the whole world smiled on Violet and her Alec. "Such a charming young couple", said the world, and at once started to shower them with presents, Apostle teaspoons arrived in their dozens.'

In fact the only society in which Stephen and Mary can find a niche is the lesbian ghetto which has started to emerge in Paris. Stephen's attitude to this group is extremely ambiguous and contradictory. She is prepared to mix with them because Mary needs friends, but refers to them as a 'miserable army' of inverts, the dregs of society. While thus distancing herself from them, however, Stephen also identifies with them, recognizing that, like herself, they have their deviant natures stamped into their physical make-up. Masculine symptoms are remarked upon: 'One might have said quite a womanly woman, unless the trained ear had been rendered suspicious by her voice, which had something peculiar about it. It was like a boy's voice on the edge of breaking.'

It is something to be allowed to live as an invert accepted by this group but such ghettoized existence is not enough for Stephen whose vision stretches 'out beyond to the day when happier folk would accept her'. The world of the Paris inverts is a bohemian milieu and Stephen views it from a definite class position in the world at large. The group Stephen and Mary mix with is relatively decent, meeting at teas and studio parties; it is friendly and welcoming to like natures. But the Paris bars – the Ideal, whose *patron* collects inverts like rare specimens, Le Narcisse, mirrors thickly painted with cupids and kitchen near the toilet, and most of all, Alec's, a drug-dealing haunt – are such as to prove that inverts have been trodden down to become the dregs of humanity. Stephen's upper-class social position vies with a sense of hidden connection with these degraded inverted natures, and she assumes a protective yet superior role towards the 'dregs'. She seems to stand somewhere between them and God, interceding for them: 'She could see their marred and reproachful faces with the haunted, melancholy eyes of the invert – eyes that had looked too long on a world that lacked all pity and understanding: "Stephen, Stephen, speak with your God and ask Him why He has left us forsaken!"' It is a role conceived of in religious as well as class terms.

In fact, the social context of Stephen's anomalous being and her relations to the rest of the world are described from the beginning of the story. The repercussions of her innate inversion on the rest of her family are depicted from childhood on. There are servants who know her from a child and think or do not think she is just like her father; there is Angela's irate husband, Stephen's censorious mother, and the necessity for a social cover-up from the village of the true state of affairs. But it is also perfectly true that this wider social world in which Stephen grows up and with which the lesbian sub-culture is contrasted, is indelibly upper-class.

The particular way in which Stephen grows up 'masculine' is in fact saturated with class. What she grows up to be is a 'perfect gentleman'. From an early age she is instinctively gallant and protective to her mother and by extension to all women; she has a strict sense of honour and speaks of doing 'the decent, clean thing'; she lays on a generous wedding for her servants. The final proof of her moral excellence comes when she gives up the unwitting Mary to Martin, her own old beau, having decided that Mary is too weak and womanly to withstand life without a husband, children and a place in respectable society. These class-bound manifestations of *noblesse oblige* are read back into Stephen's nature just as much as her 'inversion' is. Ellis's suggestion that inverts are rescued by general superiority of character is given a very class-bound interpretation by Hall and one which was felt at the book's trial to make the lesbian character dangerously attractive. The highly moral tone of the book was to count heavily against it – especially as it made an appeal to religion in demanding tolerance. The religious aspect of the book owes nothing to Ellis's theorizing. It views Stephen as set apart by God and describes her as 'God's mistake' and 'having the mark of Cain'. The Christian martyr's name, Stephen, is actually given at her christening, rather than being a nickname she chooses to adopt.

In the final passage of the novel, which involves a very florid appeal for tolerance and highlights lesbian suffering, it is made clear that Stephen has taken on a religious duty, the task of interceding with society and with God on behalf of all inverts: 'Acknowledge us, oh God, before the whole world. Give us also the right to our existence!' While some of the more serious commentators on the novel deplored the use of religion in such a cause, some of the more cynical were to turn her religious framework against Hall and accuse her of a certain degree of self-martyrdom. But there is no doubt that she used it to add to the poignancy of the suffering of the inverts, to intensify the emotional appeal of her novel.

Taken as a whole, *The Well of Loneliness* in some ways sets up a *more* rigid definition of lesbianism than Ellis's *Sexual Inversion* had done. The novel more clearly evokes the stereotyped images of lesbians as 'butch' and 'femme', two complementary halves of a couple polarized between the masculine and the feminine, and these are shown to derive from actual practices in an existing sub-culture. Further, the appeal to moral excellence is made in specifically class terms, feeding into current ideas of lesbianism as an aristocratic aberration. It takes on all Ellis's biologism, and the biographical form of the novel enables Hall to describe a woman's whole life as thoroughly permeated by an innate, unfolding inversion and to set up this sexuality as containing the truth of her being.

On the other hand, the political value of the 'congenital' argument is more overtly deployed by Hall, who clearly argues that inverts are not to be blamed. She tried to depict attractive characters and claim sympathy for them by affective means. Although she stepped into the space Ellis had created and defined for lesbianism, Hall made that space more public. This was to mean that others, feminists for instance, could engage with and challenge that definition in a more publicly accessible way.

I have suggested that Hall's contribution should be seen as the start of a reverse discourse, a process by which a category of lesbianism derived from a medical discourse is first adopted and then eventually transformed by those defined by it. This implies a degree of political self-consciousness on the part of lesbians, if they are to speak for themselves as a unified group. It is clear that Hall's intervention can be seen as contributing to the formation of that political self-consciousness; later generations of lesbians were to follow her model of public identification even if they repudiated her particular views. What may be less clear is that her intervention in itself was both an adoption of Ellis's category of inversion and an initial step towards transforming it.

Hall adopted the category 'congenital inversion' in an unproblematic, straightforward way. But precisely because it rigidly segregated lesbians as a separate type of person, it did have the incidental advantage of conferring an authoritative right to speak on those women accepting the label. By separating lesbians into a seemingly quite distinct group, the definition laid the basis for a later political solidarity. Hall claimed the right to speak about inversion on the grounds that she herself was an invert, not an expert. This enabled other women either to imitate her, or to engage in a challenge to what she said, but both on the same level of personal experience *as* invert. They could not have done this with Ellis the medical expert. Taking discussion of inversion beyond the medical textbook enabled Hall to comment on the basis of her own experience about relationships between individuals and on the conditions in which lesbians were actually able to exist in society. This in itself limited the extent to which Ellis's categorization of individuals into separate 'types' could be seen as an adequate approach to their problems by inverts themselves. A reverse discourse was thus begun.

Inversion was shown as a problem for society to face and not just a moral dilemma for inverted individuals. The conflicting ways that *The Well of Loneliness* was received by commentators were in fact organized around two dominant discourses: the rearguard moralizing discourse of sin or sickness, which was now challenged by a new, liberal discourse on inversion as a social problem backed up by medical opinion. A variant of the moralizing commentary was a rather satirical strand, addressing the quality of Hall's book primarily as a work of fiction and criticizing it in terms of literary merit, in a way which ostensibly side-stepped her views on lesbianism as such. It as within these competing discourses that a battle over the definition of lesbianism was waged.

TRIALS OF *THE WELL*

The progressive nature of the 'congenital' view of lesbianism in the context of 1928 can be gauged by the scandalized reaction of a section of the press to Radclyffe Hall's book and by the way it was subsequently taken to trial and condemned as obscene. James Douglas, editor of the *Sunday Express*, made the first vitriolic attack on the novel on 19 August 1928. In the course of his article he called the book an 'intolerable outrage' and one 'designed to display perverted decadence as a martyrdom inflicted upon these outcasts by a cruel society'. He insisted on using the moralistic term 'perversion' rather than the biologically based and morally neutral 'inversion'. He called lesbianism a 'pestilence' and a 'leprosy', and complained: 'The decadent apostles of the most loathsome vices no longer conceal their degeneracy and their degradation.' Mixed in with the hyperbolic language was a series of rejections of the way the novel defined lesbianism as unavoidable rather than a morally reprehensible choice. Specifically, he claimed that the congenital argument was incompatible with the Christian doctrine of free will: inverts were *choosing* to be damned. He obviously regarded lesbianism as a contagious sickness as well as a sin and saw 'propaganda' like Radclyffe Hall's novel as one of the ways in which perverts sought to spread it to others, especially the young. In a notorious phrase, he wrote that he 'would rather give a healthy boy or a healthy girl a phial of prussic acid than this novel'.

He referred to *The Well* as 'a contamination and corruption of English fiction' and there were several appeals to 'Englishness' in his onslaught. The English patience was being sorely tried by the increasing effrontery of homosexuals flaunting themselves overtly in postwar society; the English public was slow to anger but would be merciless in striking down the armies of evil once roused; France and Germany had already lost the battle, but this Christian society should and would cleanse itself. But it was not for any lewd or lascivious detail that the novel was condemned. Rather it was denounced as 'seductive and insidious' for any delicacy or cleverness it might have, since this would tempt the reader to sympathize with Hall's views. Because of the greater publicity the novel would give to these views, Douglas called for its prosecution under 'the existing law'.

This law was the Obscene Publications Act 1857 which enabled magistrates to destroy a publication as obscene without taking evidence on its literary merits. The English publisher of *The Well*, Jonathan Cape, fearing prosecution, had written to the Home Secretary following Douglas's attack and offered to withdraw the book. But he then had it secretly printed in Paris. The Director of Public Prosecutions eventually took action against it when imported copies were seized. Since it was the book, and not the author, that was on trial the publisher had to defend it and Hall was not allowed to speak in its defence.

The proceedings were held at Bow Street under Sir Chartres Biron. He refused the defence leave to call literary evidence from a range of luminaries, including Virginia Woolf and E. M. Forster, who were prepared to speak for the book's literary merits. Claiming that art and obscenity were not mutually exclusive, Sir Chartres took the power of deciding what was 'obscene' as belonging entirely to him as chief magistrate. The test of obscenity under the law was whether the book was likely to 'deprave or corrupt those whose minds are open to such immoral influences and into whose hands it is likely to fall'. This meant that the book's being a novel counted against it, since it was more likely to fall into the hands of a healthy boy or girl. Whether it would corrupt them if it did was what would make it 'obscene', and so the general stance of the book, its general treatment of its theme, could be enough to condemn it without any 'dirty' words or passages.

This was indeed what happened. The defence's emphasis on the novel as a serious treatment of a medical and social problem did not save it; it was condemned as obscene and remaining copies were destroyed. In his judgement, the chief magistrate made it clear that his decision had nothing to do with 'gross or filthy' words in the book, nor was it based on the fact that the book dealt with 'unnatural offences between women'. It was the concept of lesbianism itself which was seen as dangerous, because the idea of congenital inversion allowed inverts to be described as attractive personalities, and especially because it freed them from moral blame. The magistrate foresaw the effects of allowing *The Well of Loneliness* to define the terms in which lesbianism was discussed.

What was being fought over in the court was not simply the description, but the redefinition of lesbianism. After all, lesbianism had been given literary treatment before, without being the cause of prosecution. Indeed, in the same year, Compton Mackenzie published *Extraordinary Women*, his satire of lesbian mores based on the sub-culture in Capri at the time, and this had not been judged obscene – but then it made no claims to educating public opinion, or to being a serious book, or to altering definitions.

When the defendants of *The Well of Loneliness* took the case to the Appeal Court, its chairman made it even more explicit that the book was on trial for its general concept of lesbianism and its general moral stance. He remarked that 'It is a book which, if it does not condemn unnatural practices, certainly condones them and suggests that those guilty of them should not receive the consequences they deserve to suffer. Put in a word, the view of the Court is that this is a disgusting book, *when properly read*' (my italics). In other words, the book had to be read for its underlying concept of lesbianism and not for any surface particularities in the way that it was written. Without resorting to the excesses of Douglas's language, the court's interpretation of obscenity nevertheless made it clear that the law was to uphold his view of lesbianism and that the congenital inversion view was to be resisted entirely. The obscenity law was geared to maintenance of general moral standards and a concept of lesbianism as an avoidable vice or sin was part of those standards.

The American courts decided differently, however. The New York Society for the Suppression of Vice took out a summons against the US publishers of *The Well*, but the case was dismissed in April 1929 in the New York Court of Special Sessions. While conceding that the subject was 'a delicate social problem', the court decided that there was nothing obscene in the way the book was written. Radclyffe Hall's novel did therefore continue to be available in the United States during the time it was prohibited in Britain. Copies bought abroad were clandestinely circulated here; it was reissued in Paris in 1929 already in a sixth impression. In 1948 it was quietly republished in London without repercussions and in 1968 it appeared in paperback; it has recently been published by the feminist publishing house, Virago.

In 1928 a popular satire on the novel, by artist Beresford Egan and journalist P. B. Stephenson, and entitled *The Sink of Solitude*, denounced the moral crusade against the book. Thanks to it, 'millions of shop, office and mill girls have been led to ask the furtive question: What is Lesbianism?' The authors went on to demand a literary censorship of the Sunday papers whose sensationalism was 'sapping the vigour and the vitality of millions of old ladies every morning'.

This lampoon criticized not only the 'sanctimonious sententiousness' of the moral crusaders but also the 'pathetic post-war lesbians with their "mannish" modes and poses' and what its authors saw as the 'sentimental scientificity' of 'psychopaths' like Havelock Ellis, who ponderously sought to 'explain' them. They remarked on the feebleness of *The Well of Loneliness* both as a work of art and as a moral argument. Putting themselves forward as defenders of aesthetic standards, they use this stance to dismiss any serious consideration of lesbianism itself. Stephen's career as congenital invert is swiftly lampooned:

She kicks, she thrives, she grows to man's estate.
For trousers love she feels, for knickers hate!

They could thus poke fun at Radclyffe Hall from the posture of a 'defender of English literature' without ever having to engage with the concept of congenital inversion. By defending the glorious Sappho as well as Shakespeare, they could dismiss Hall by contrast as mundane, trivial and trite on the grounds of literary merit alone.

The Sink of Solitude also contained scurrilous, Beardsleyesque drawings unmistakably indicating Hall as the self-martyring 'St Stephen' of the captions. Images of Hall elsewhere, such as in the press, tended to convey an uncompromisingly severe personality. A 'masculine' photograph which had appeared alongside the original onslaught in the *Sunday Express* was frequently reproduced. It showed her with short hair, tie and cigarette. Hall's lover Una Troubridge was often depicted alongside her, either shown as presenting the same rather masculine, militant front to the world, or, at other times, in very feminine contrast to her. Some perceived the couple as a strictly polarized one. Vera Brittain reviewed *The Well* as a journalist on *Time and Tide*, and was one of the literary witnesses prepared but not called, to give evidence at the trial. In 1968 she published a book assessing the whole occasion retrospectively and in it she quotes the description of a friend who met Radclyffe Hall in 1928:

> My first impression was of someone very goodlooking, in fact handsome, in a masculine way. She was dressed in a tweedy style, mannishly cut clothes. She had a presence and an air of authority. . . . Lady Troubridge was the exact opposite – very dainty and feminine . . . exquisitely, femininely dressed in rather a 'fluffy' style. My mother used to say that Radclyffe Hall always seemed to be the dominant one in any decision which had to be made jointly, regarding their orders for refreshment, cakes to be made and sent, and their Christmas orders for chocolates.

In her own person and in her lesbian relationship, Hall was uncompromising in demanding to be accepted as the archetype of the congenital invert.

Vera Brittain's own review of *The Well of Loneliness* in *Time and Tide* in 1928 had in fact picked up its polarity in the treatment of the lesbian couple and from a feminist point of view had even questioned the view of sex roles as biologically determined. She wrote:

> The book, however, raises and never satisfactorily answers another question – the question as to how far the characteristics of Stephen Gordon are physiological and how far they are psychological. . . . Miss Hall seems to take for granted that this over-emphasis of sex characteristics is part of the correct education of the normal human being; she therefore makes her 'normal' woman clinging and feminine to exasperation and even describes the attitudes towards love as 'an end in itself' as being a necessary attribute to true womanhood.

This criticism of rigidly defined lesbian roles prefigures the views of later generations of lesbians and feminists and their criticisms of the inflexibility and biological inevitability of the 'congenital inversion' theory of lesbianism. At the time, however, the possibility that the congenital view offered, of seeing lesbianism as a social and not a moral problem, was not to be lightly dismissed. It argued for social tolerance of an inborn 'condition' on the grounds that it could not be helped; the social problem was that of coping with the consequences of the invert's unfortunate nature and this put the onus on society at large, not just on the individual lesbian. Vera Brittain, despite her feminist criticisms of Hall, was therefore careful not to jettison this perspective of lesbianism as a social problem and hastily added that:

> This is not to deny that the problem described by Miss Hall does exist in a grave and urgent form, and that her presentation of it deserves the serious attention of all students of social questions.

Recent arguments for social acceptance of lesbianism have gone beyond and rejected the idea of congenital inversion. Within the women's and gay movements, the claim to choice of sexual partners has replaced claims to biological necessity. While rejecting Hall's precise view of lesbianism as innate sexual nature, however, lesbians have wished to retain a definite lesbian identity, but to have the right to define that lesbian label themselves. Some features of the picture of the congenital invert have thereby explicitly been rejected: innate masculinity, for instance, and also the idea that lesbians must be sterile. Lesbians in recent years have claimed the right to be mothers – a contradiction in terms for the congenital invert.

At the time, congenital inversion seemed to be a biological truth which had been 'discovered'. Today, when we have largely rejected this 'truth' and questioned its progressive potential, we can see the category of invert rather as a social construction, a work of definition. Retrospectively, we can see a process beginning with the definition of lesbianism in medical-scientific theory and reaching a point where lesbians have politically articulated a demand to define themselves. Radclyffe Hall has a significant place in that process and her fiction helped to challenge the prevalent view of lesbianism as a reprehensible vice and facilitated its translation from the realm of 'sin' to that of 'social problem'. *The Well of Loneliness* also remained an important definer of lesbian identity for many years. The prosecution of the novel promoted it as a major source of how to 'be' a lesbian in real life. And focusing attention on its author, the book's real-life heroine, the trial unwittingly took the question of lesbianism outside the category of fiction.

REFERENCES

Brittain, Vera, *Radclyffe Hall: A case of obscenity?* (London: Femina Books, 1968).
Dyer, Richard, 'Getting over the rainbow', in *Silver Linings* (London: Lawrence & Wishart, 1981).
Egan, Beresford, *The Sink of Solitude* (London: Hermes Press, 1928).
Ellis, Henry Havelock, *Sexual Inversion* (London: Wilson & Macmillan, 1897).
—— *Studies in the Psychology of Sex* (Philadelphia, 1905–10; New York: Random House, 1936).
Foucault, Michel, *The History of Sexuality* (London: Allen Lane, 1979).
Hall, Marguerite Radclyffe, *The Well of Loneliness* (London: Jonathan Cape, 1928; New York: Blue Ribbon Books, 1928; New York: Covici-Friede Inc., 1928; Paris:

Pegasus Press, 1928; reprinted 1929; London: Falcon Press, 1948; New York: Permabooks, 1960; London: Transworld Publishers (Corgi), 1968; London: Virago Press, 1981).

Mackenzie, Compton, *Extraordinary Women* (London, 1928).

Weeks, Jeffrey, *Coming Out* (London: Quartet, 1977).

NINE
Shadows uplifted

BARBARA CHRISTIAN

O whitened head entwined in turban gay
O kind black face, O crude but tender hand,
O foster mother in whose arms there lay
The race whose sons are masters of the land!
It was thine arms that sheltered in their fold,
It was thine eyes that followed through the length
Of infant days these sons. In times of old
It was thy breast that nourished them to strength.

So often hast thou to thy bosom pressed
The golden head, the face and brow of snow;
So often has it 'gainst thy broad, dark breast
Lain, set off like a quickened cameo.
Thou simple soul, as cuddling down that babe
With thy sweet croon, so plaintive and so wild
Came ne'er the thought to thee, swift like a stab
That it some day might crush thy own black child?

(James Weldon Johnson, 'The Black Mammy'[1])

SHADOWS . . .

Iola LeRoy, Shadows Uplifted, by Frances Ellen Watkins Harper, considered by many to be the first novel by an Afro-American woman to be published, appeared in 1892.[2] By that time, the country had experienced historic traumas during the Civil War and Reconstruction periods that affected the nature of life for black people and for women. As an abolitionist and a black feminist, Frances Harper had been one of the leading figures in the national struggle to free blacks from slavery, as well as a longtime spokesperson for the many black women who were not yet free to speak. She had spent her life lecturing against slavery, had written ten volumes of poetry, had taken an active part in the 1856 Women's Rights Convention, and had helped to found the National Association of Colored Women. Many of her newspaper articles, such as 'Black women in the Reconstruction South' (1878), reflect her involvement with the problems of black women in the United States. William Still, her contemporary and the black editor of the *Underground Railroad*, said of her that:

> I know of no other woman white or colored, who has come so intimately in contact with the colored people in the South as Mrs. Harper. Since emancipation she has labored in every Southern state in the Union, save two, Arkansas and Texas; in the colleges, schools, churches and the cabins. ... With her, it was no uncommon occurrence in visiting cities and towns, to speak at two, three or four meetings a day. ... But the kind of meetings she took greatest interest in were meetings called exclusively for women. ... She felt their needs were far more pressing than any other class.[3]

Yet Harper's novel, *Iola LeRoy*, does not dwell on those pressing needs but is the heavily moralistic tale of a refined and educated octoroon, who but for the devilry of her white father's friend would have lived as a white woman in the South, not even knowing herself that she possessed a few drops of black blood. Certainly the novel does not contain much of the realistic experiences Harper herself describes in her articles about the lives of black women of the time. For example, in 'Black women in the Reconstruction South', she tells us about Mrs Hill, a widow who

> has rented, cultivated and solely managed a farm of five acres for five years. She makes her garden, raises poultry, and cultivates enough corn and cotton to live comfortably and keep a surplus in the bank. She saves something every year, and this is much, considering the low price of cotton and infavorable seasons.[4]

And about Mrs Madison who,

> although living in a humble and unpretentious home, has succeeded in getting up a home for aged colored women. By organized effort women have been enabled to help each other in sickness and provide respectable funerals for the dead.[5]

Yet in *Iola LeRoy* the salient element of the story is the heroine's willingness to be known as a black woman, although she has all the physical and cultural attributes of the white woman. This notwithstanding, Iola is a feminist of the time in that she believes women should work for a living, when in fact most black women had no choice but to work to survive.

Certainly there is a great discrepancy between the substance of her novel and Harper's detailed observations of the life most black women were leading in the period of Reconstruction, a discrepancy that has something to do with the form of the novel at that time and the images of black women in American society. *Iola LeRoy* is an important novel, not because it is a 'first' or because it is a good novel, but because it so clearly delineates the relationship between the images of black women held at large in society and the novelist's struggle to refute these images – all of this even as the novelist attempts to create a world of characters and situations that can be viewed as suitable to the form of the novel, yet realistic enough somehow to resemble life.

What images of black women was Harper struggling against, and why was it important for her to use the novel as a form in refuting them?

Black women were brought as slaves to this country to fulfill specifically female roles and to work in the fields. At first the planters thought slavery would be a short-range measure. But by the early 1700s, because of the demands of labor and the myths they entertained about the nature of black people, they maintained and defended black slavery as a permanent institution essential to the American economy.[6] Particularly after it became obvious to them that 'black gold' would not forever be available in Africa, either because of growing European political resistance to the slave trade or because of the cunning of local African dealers, the planters must have realized the importance of American-born black slaves.

But even as the colonists solidified the institution of slavery by enacting slave codes, many like Benjamin Franklin feared that the presence of large numbers of blacks might endanger the character of American settlements as white colonies.[7] As English planters, they were at first concerned also that other European settlers might usurp the British characteristics of the colonies. But even more threatening was the presence of blacks who, the planters believed, were obviously and distinctly different.

From the beginnings of the thirteen colonies, black people, although not at first identified with slavery, were certainly designated as inferior.[8] As a means of protecting whites from the taint of black blood, some states as early as 1680 banned interracial marriages.[9] By the early 1700s blacks had become associated in the American mind with the ape, especially the orang-utan.[10]

In the first two centuries of the colonies' existence, much of their literature is obsessed with the establishment of blacks as a species, different from and lower than whites, the link so to speak in the Great Chain of Being between animal and man.[11] Whether animal or man, blacks were seen as 'lewd, lascivious and wanton'.[12] Based on reports they had heard from slave traders and travelers, the planters believed the black female was sexually aggressive and sometimes mated with orang-utan males, while the black male, because of his nature, hankered uncontrollably after the next link in the chain, the white woman.[13] These arguments about the nature of the black race were part of the European's initial groping into new areas of the natural sciences, as well as his increasing awareness that there were seemingly different groups of men all over the world. Coincidentally, in America these pseudoscientific discussions were used as rationalizations for slavery, a condition the English themselves abhorred.

From the first century of American history, then, race and sex were inter-related and the problem of interracial sex was foremost in the minds of the colonists. However, although there might have been popular discussion about racial concepts, a clear intellectual definition of race was not formulated until the mid-nineteenth century. In the seventeenth and eighteenth centuries the inferiority of blacks was couched in terms of the concept of civilization. George Stocking, in his book *Race, Culture and Evolution*, pointed out that initially civilization was seen by naturalists as the 'natural capacity' of all races. Savages would eventually become civilized. With the expansion of industrial civilization, however, the gap between the savage and the civilized European widened. 'When the ideas of primitivism and progress in civilization sepa-rated, "civilization" lent itself quite easily – indeed to some even seemed to call for – a racial interpretation'.[14]

In keeping with their beliefs about the inferiority of blacks to whites, the newly independent Americans also saw miscegenation as an unnatural thing. One of the most prominent antislavery proponents, Thomas Jefferson, be-lieved Negroes were inferior to whites. He, as well as many of his countrymen, thought that blacks lacked beauty, intellect and imagination. Their essence, it seemed to him, was that of crude sensation.[15] Jefferson agreed with Judge Sewell of Boston who succinctly exclaimed that 'Negroes cannot mix with us and become members of society ... never embody with us and grow up into orderly families, to the peopling of the land'.[16] Given the powerful language that the planters used to attack miscegenation, one could conclude that they saw it as a crime against the body politic. Yet given their belief in the sexual aggressiveness of the black female, they also allowed that white men would fall prey to her wiles.[17]

Since blacks were obviously needed for labor, and since the planters accepted miscegenation between white men and black females as inevitable, they charged the white woman with the responsibility of being 'the repository of white civilization'.[18] By giving birth to the white man's legitimate heirs, she became actually and symbolically his greatest treasure. Thus the fear of rape of the white woman by the black man reached mammoth proportions in the mind of the southern planter. For any sexual activity between these two actors would constitute, from the white man's perspective, the rape of his birthright and legacy.

The planters attempted to resolve the tension between their need for slave labor and their insistence that the American colonies and later the American Republic retain its whiteness by designating the black woman as the bearer of black slaves and the white woman as the bearer of free whites. Just as white women were seen as pivotal to the preservation of white civilization, black women were central to the continuation of the slave system as an essential part of the American economy.

Although it has not been confirmed by contemporary historians that black slave women in America were forced to breed in the strict sense that they were in the Caribbean, there is no doubt that 'an essential value of the adult slave women rested in their capacity to produce the labor force'.[19] Perhaps the fact that planters in America saw that land as their home while those in the Caribbean saw themselves as transient Europeans accounts for the difference in their respective approaches. According to Winthrop Jordan, American 'slave owners acquired valuable young Negroes not by forcing their slaves to mate (clear instances of this being very rare), but by doing little to interfere with a system which gave every encouragement to early and frequent sexual intercourse among their slaves'.[20] That the black woman was valued for her reproductive capacity, however, was established as early as the 1660s, 'when Negro women brought a high price because their issue was valuable and because they could be used for field work while white women generally were not'.[21]

As the previous statement indicates, the black woman was also seen as different from the white woman in her capacity to do man's work. From the beginnings of the colonies, white women did not ordinarily work in the fields. As early as 1643, before slavery became established in the colonies, Virginia's tax law provided that 'all adult men were tithable and in addition Negro women. This official discrimination between Negro and other women was made by men who were accustomed to thinking of field work as being ordinarily the work of men rather than women'.[22]

The black slave women were not identified, as white women were, with the roles of wife and mother, but primarily and specifically with the roles of mother and worker. Not surprisingly, then, the black woman as mammy was one of the most dominant images to emerge in southern life and literature, an image that has proved to be a most enduring one even to the present.

The mammy image is extremely complex, because the concept of motherhood was already rife with contradictions among the planters of the South. Motherhood, within the confines of marriage, was of course revered, for through it the white man was ensured his heirs. The late eighteenth- and early nineteenth-century southern white woman was taught from early childhood an image to which she was expected to conform. As Anne Firor Scott put it in her book, *The Southern Lady*:

This marvelous creation was described as a submissive wife whose reason for being was to love, honor, obey and occasionally amuse her husband, to bring up his children and manage his household. Physically weak, and 'formed for the less laborious occupations', she depended upon male protection. To secure this protection she was endowed with the capacity to 'create a magic spell' over any man in her vicinity. She was timid and modest, beautiful and graceful ... the most fascinating being in creation ... the delight and charm of every circle she moved in.[23]

This image could, of course, only be that – an image; alabaster ladies could not possibly have endured life in a frontier land. As the diaries and letters of antebellum southern women so clearly illustrate, most of them, even those of the upper class, worked hard.[24] Even the mistresses of large plantations were managers of huge households designed to be self-sufficient, isolated from each other and from the world except when gala events were held. None the less, the image persisted, even in the minds of southern women themselves, who knew the reality of their lives but felt somehow they did not live up to the ideal.

Beyond the question of its relationship to truth, the image itself contained contradictions. A lady was expected to be a wife, a mother and a manager; yet she was supposed to be delicate, ornamental, virginal and timid. How then could she endure the sexual appetites of her husband and survive the nine months of pregnancy, not to mention the ordeal of childbirth necessary to produce his heirs? These tasks were unavoidable. But given a system of mistress and slave, she need not nurse, be chained to her babies' continuous demands, or do heavy housework, elaborate cooking, tedious weaving and sewing to maintain, nourish and clothe her family. If the image of the delicate alabaster lady were to retain some semblance of truth, it would be necessary to create the image of another female who was tougher, less sensitive, and who could perform with efficiency and grace the duties of motherhood for her mistress and of course for herself. The image of the southern lady, based as it was on a patriarchal plantation myth, demanded another female image, that of the mammy.

Why was the image of the lady, and therefore the corresponding image of the mammy, so important to the South? Early nineteenth-century planters rationalized the institution of slavery in two ways, by using scientific proofs to cast doubts upon the humanness of blacks and by perceiving themselves as patriarchs, such as existed in the Bible.[25] The characteristics of blacks' racial inferiority, which Jefferson had so impressionistically discussed in the 1790s, were, by the 1830s, buttressed by scientific argument. Ethnological writers such as Richard Colfax, Samuel Cartwright and Josiah Nott detailed the physical deficiencies of the Negro, his cranial characteristics, his facial angles, and concluded that intellectually the Negro was incapable of being the equal of whites. Their utterances quickly became a racist ideology in the United States. This school of thought also had polygenist tendencies, however. That is, many ethnological writers believed that different races of men had different origins and that God created many pairs of the human race.[26] Therein lay the weakness of its appeal to many southern aristocrat writers, for they were devoted to the Bible and such a thrust seemed to go against the Adam and Eve biblical story.

On the other hand, advocates of patriarchy, like George Fitzhugh, maintained that the patriarchal concept was the best societal model for the South and that slavery was necessary to that order; William Byrd, an eighteenth-century Virginian planter, expressed the quintessence of the patriarch image in his letter to Charles, earl of Orkney:

> Like one of the Patriarchs, I have my Flocks and my Herds, my Bondsmen and Bondswomen and every Sort of Trade amongst my Servants, so that I live in a kind of Independence on everyone but Providence. However tho' this Sort of Life is without expense, it is attended a great deal of trouble. I must take care to keep all my people to their Duty, to set all the Springs to motion and to make everyone draw his equal Share to carry the Machine forward.[27]

Our main concern here is with the patriarchal concept, since the plantation myth was the subject matter of southern antebellum literature. But clearly the scientific arguments of mid-nineteenth-century ethnologists strengthened the proslavery argument of the patriarchal concept and eventually dominated it, since patriarchy also demanded subordination of poor and middle-class whites.[28] Although these two schools differed in their emphasis, both reiterated the importance of the white woman in maintaining a superior society. Ethnologists such as Josiah Nott insisted that ethnic purity had to be maintained or the world would retrograde instead of advance in civilization, and Brinton, his disciple, in the 1890s, came straight to the point:

> The 'ethnic purity' of the whites must be maintained. White women had no holier duty, no more sacred mission, than that of transmitting in its integrity the heritage of ethnic endowment gained by the race through thousands of generations of struggle.[29]

In like manner, the lady was essential to the concept of patriarchy, for pivotal to that concept was the domestic metaphor, which contained within it the idea of a domestic hierarchy. To emphasize the maleness of the perfect patriarch, the perfect wife was expected to be submissive, weak and dependent. Men as patriarchs were to be obeyed by wives, children and slaves.

The contradictions within the patriarchal system of belief are related to the way in which work was viewed by the society. The truly civilized lady did not work, for work, although necessary, is demeaning. Work (here meaning man's work, since until recently women's work was hardly seen as comparable) involves participation in the world, an activity best left to the masculine members of the species, who know how to deal with the sullied qualities of competitiveness and striving. How well the man succeeds in making his work profitable is measured by the extent to which his wife does or does not work.

So the lady is symbolic of the patriarch's success, her state a visual representation of his power. But the acquisition of power or wealth demanded such specialization that work in the home was necessarily left to women. The southern mind, though, did not dismiss motherhood, or house-keeping, as nonwork. It could not, for such work was necessary to the plantation's self-sufficiency. These activities in fact were obviously continuous, unrelenting and necessary. Thus an even further indication of a man's power was his ability to relieve his wife even of this involvement. Only then could she emerge as a completely helpless, totally dependent being whose identity and worth flowed from the male patriarch.

Of course, for most people in the South, this version of reality was sheer fantasy. Most people, slave or free, did not even live on large plantations but on small farms.[30] Yet the rhetoric of patriarchy and the myth of the plantation transformed the realities of the slave system into a benevolent institution. The domestic metaphor that insisted that 'we are all one great big happy family, both black and white' implied that there was an irrevocable bond between the nature of the family, the nature of man and woman and the concept of slavery.[31]

Women of the servant class had of course performed unavoidable and tedious women's work for the lords and ladies of England; here in America the fact that the slave woman in question was black and, according to the prevailing philosophy, possibly the female of a lower species should have caused the patriarch and the lady some concern. But black women had a high regard for motherhood, since in much of Africa the relationship between mother and child is seen as sacred, symbolic of the relationship between earth and creativity.[32] Whites seemed to misinterpret this cornerstone of African thought in much the same way that Melville's naive Captain Delano, in *Benito Cereno*, does when he characterizes the affection of the 'uncivilized Negresses' for their babies as 'naked nature'.

When the black woman first began to experience and understand the contradictions about motherhood among the southern planters, she must have been truly appalled. None the less, her tendency to see maternal duties as natural and sacred must have reinforced the southern planters' stereotype that black women were perfectly suited to be mammies. But this assertion, too, must be qualified. Even as the planters praised the black woman as the 'contented mammy', they also insisted that black slave women neglected their own children.[33] Above and beyond these factors stands a major contradiction: that the planters could relegate the duties of motherhood, a revered and honored state, to a being supposedly lower than human, reveals their own confusion about the value of motherhood. That they could separate spiritual aspects of motherhood, which they acknowledged in their religion, from the physical aspects and give the duties of childrearing to a 'subhuman' gives us some indication about the value they placed on women's work. As a white woman character says in a book by William Thompson, the antebellum proslavery humorist: "'I could never bear to see a white gal toatin' my child about, waiting on me like a nigger. It would hurt my conscience to keep anybody 'bout me in that condition, who was as white and as good as me.'"[34]

Despite the contradictions inherent in the image of the lady and its correlate, the image of the mammy, these concepts were essential parts of the South's public dream and therefore of its literature. The lady was, of course, at the center of that dream. But although the black woman is seldom focused on in antebellum literature, she almost always appears in the background as the contented and loyal mammy.

The mammy is a consistent, if minor, mainstay among the stock characters of white antebellum and Reconstruction novels. From J. P. Kennedy's *Swallow Barn* (1832) through the nostalgic darky novels of Thomas Nelson Page to the vindictive Reconstruction trilogy of Thomas Dixon, the black woman as a mammy appears as a normal part of the southern fabric.[35] Enduring, strong and calm, her physical characteristics remain the same. She is black in color as well as race and fat, with enormous breasts that are full enough to nourish all the children of the world; her head is perpetually covered with her trademark kerchief to hide the kinky hair that marks her as ugly. Tied to her physical characteristics are her personality traits: she is strong, for she certainly has enough girth, but this strength is used in the service of her white master and as a way of keeping her male counterparts in check; she is kind and loyal, for she is a mother; she is sexless, for she is ugly; and she is religious and superstitious, because she is black. She prefers the master's children to her own, for as a member of a lower species, she acknowledges almost instinctively the superiority of the higher race. Caroline Hentz describes a typical mammy in her sentimental and popular romance *Linda* (1857):

> Aunt Judy's African blood had not been corrupted by the base mingling of a paler strain. Black as ebony was her smooth and shining skin, in which the dazzling ivory of her teeth gleams bright as the moon at midnight. Judy had loved – admired, reverenced her, as being of a superior, holier race than her own.[36]

This image of the mammy persisted beyond the Civil War into the literature of the 1890s. And even so fine a writer as Kate Chopin focused on this version of the black mammy in her short stories, 'Beyond the Bayou' and 'A no account Creole' (1894).

I have specifically mentioned fiction written by white southern women writers of the antebellum and postbellum periods. It is true, as Anne Firor Scott pointed out, that ladies and mammies were often on intimate terms and that many southern women were private abolitionists in their diaries (Mary Chestnut's comment 'there is no slave like a wife', comes to mind). No doubt many southern women were weary of the institution of slavery, for they were expected to be supervisor, teacher, doctor and minister to a large family of slaves.[37] None the less, when southern women wrote, that is, when they participated in the South's public dream, they emphasized as did the male writers the qualities of contentment, self-sacrifice and loyalty in the mammy. Their books reveal that they accepted society's image of themselves as southern ladies (whether they lived it or not) and therefore projected the corresponding image of the black mammy. Their books heighten Eugene Genovese's assertion that 'to understand her [the mammy] is to move toward understanding the tragedy of plantation paternalism'.[38] The image of the mammy, then, cannot be seen in a vacuum; she is a necessary correlate to the lady. If one was to be, the other had to be.

The same holds true for the other stereotypical images of the black woman that developed during slavery and continue today. If the southern lady was to be chaste except for producing heirs, it would be necessary to have another woman who could become the object of men's sexual needs and desires. There is some reason to believe that the image of the sexless southern lady is really a reflection of difficulties white women faced because of the lack of effective contraceptives. Southern women feared 'the misery of endless pregnancies with attendant illnesses and the dreadful fear of childbirth was a fear based in fact. The number of women who died in childbirth was high.'[39] Even if a woman survived many pregnancies, she could expect that some of her children would not survive their first year. If they did, each additional child increased her labor and responsibility.

The image of the black woman as lewd and impure develops partially in response to the lady's enforced chastity and partially as a result of the planters' myths about the sexuality of blacks. Certainly this image fits neatly into the dualism of white (good, pure) and black (bad, evil). At the crux of the loose woman image is the belief that black women, unlike white women, craved sex inordinately. Given that the black woman was perceived as the female of an inferior species, such an assumption would be logical. The rape of black women by white men or the use of their bodies for pleasure could be rationalized as the natural craving of the black woman for sex, rather than the licentiousness of the white man. 'For by calling the Negro woman passionate, they [white men] were offering the best possible justification for their own passions'.[40] Despite their public statements about the horror of miscegenation, many planters felt it their right to possess whatever slave girls they desired.[41]

Of course the southern antebellum novels did not stress the image of the loose black woman. Since the literature projected the domestic metaphor of a harmonious patriarchal system, it could not introduce the theme of miscegenation. But the popular and light literature of the day did include many references to the image of the black woman as overtly sexual, usually because she came from a hot climate:

Next comes a warmer race, from sable sprung,
To love each thought, to lust each nerve is strung:
The Samboe dark, and the Mullatoe brown,
The Mestize fair, the well-lim'd Quaderoon,
And jetty Afric, from no spurious sire,
Warm as her soil, and as her sun – on fire.
These sooty dames, well vers'd in Venus' school
Make love an art, and boast they kiss by rule.[42]

Although expressions like these appeared only in wordly places such as the Charleston newspapers, their existence does indicate that this sentiment was held by many who might not have been so forthright.

In any case, the image of the loose black woman who was naturally lascivious occurs frequently in the diaries of southern white women who resented their husbands' sexual freedom and their own lack of it. Mary Chestnut, like so many of her sisters, undercut the harmonious image of the plantation when she wrote in her diary:

Under slavery, we live surrounded by prostitutes. Like patriarchs of old, our men live in one house with their wives and concubines. . . . Any lady is ready to tell you who is the father of all the mulatto children in everybody's household but her own.[43]

Again, contradictions abound within the content of the image itself. If the black woman was indeed subhuman, and that after all was what her incredible sexuality was based on, then white men were mating with creatures of a lower species, an act of perversion at the very least. But given the southern planters' definition of sex as an animal function, which was unfortunately necessary for the male to maintain his health and power, the black woman's animality fits well into the scheme of the division between mind and body, spirit and matter. Rooted in this particular image is the sense of sex as base, even violent, and an act of domination rather than sharing. 'The English word *sex* itself derived from terms indicating cutting, separation, division.'[44]

Although the image of the loose black woman is a correlate of the image of the chaste lady, this particular stereotype, in real life, further separated the slave woman from the white woman. Many mistresses resented slave girls because of the apparent sexual freedom black women could exhibit. Since the loose woman image emphasized that black women solicited these attentions, many white women would view them with jealousy and anger. The myth of the licentious, exotic black woman became so much a part of the consciousness of the South that even the black abolitionist William Wells Brown began *Clotel* (1861), the first black novel to be published in America, with this observation:

When we take into consideration the fact that no safeguard was ever thrown around virtue, and no inducement held out to slave women to be pure and chaste, we will not be surprised when told that immorality pervades the domestic circle in the cities and towns of the South to an extent unknown in Northern states. Many a planter's wife has dragged out a miserable existence, with an aching heart, at seeing her place in the husband's affection usurped by the unadorned beauty and captivating smiles of her waiting maid. Indeed, the greater portion of the colored women, in the days of slavery, had no greater aspiration than that of becoming the finely-dressed mistress of some white man.[45]

Yet historical documents consistently demonstrate that the comely slave girl who was taken by her master not only had to deal with his attentions under the threat of the lash but also with his wife's wrath. Caught between two evils, black parents prayed that their daughters would not be too attractive.[46]

Like the mammy, the loose black woman has certain physical characteristics. She is brown-skinned, rather than black, and voluptuous, rather than fat, and she possesses a sensuous mouth and a high behind. She is known to have an evil disposition, a characteristic that constitutes rather than distracts from her sexiness, which is contrasted with the sweet demeanor of the lady. She is good-looking and passionate, but never beautiful, for her animal nature rather than her human qualities are foremost in her makeup. She ensnares men with her body rather than uplifting them with her beauty. Her corresponding image, the chaste lady, would function as a vessel of beauty, that spiritual flower who could aid men in their ascent toward God and culture. In contrast, the loose black woman would be seen as yet another version of one of the pitfalls of men, this particular one being the Flesh, rather than the World or the Devil. As such, the loose black woman is the quintessence of an aspect of woman that men feared, the power of sexual allure that might waylay even the best men's minds and spirits. This image surely reveals the philosophical discomfort that the southern mind, derived as it was from medieval Christian philosophy, experienced in regard to the nature and place of sex in their world. Although not as dominant as the mammy in white southern novels, the image of the loose black woman is almost always present in the planters' discussions on the nature of blacks, often as a means of explaining the waywardness of otherwise moral white men and therefore the existence of so many slaves of mixed blood.

Like the mammy, the loose black woman image demonstrates how complicated stereotypes can be. The assignment of the black woman to the sexual aspects of women's work is further heightened by the fact that many African cultures did not view sex as a separate entity distinct from or lower than the mind and spirit. Given the many traditional rituals that African societies developed around the union of woman and man, the African woman who was transported to America must have been at a loss to determine what sexual behavior meant to her master and mistress. Dance, religion, song and music in the African world view are also characteristically sensual, for the body and soul are seen as one.[47] Again, the culturally determined judgments about the value of sensuality could easily be used by the already predisposed southern gentry to reinforce their beliefs that black women were sex crazed. When this configuration is complicated by the obvious fact that sometimes the use of sexual allure was the only means by which she could survive, the natural role that sex would play in the life of the slave woman had to be crucially distorted.

Since miscegenation obviously occurred, it is not surprising that some antebellum novelists of the plantation tradition used the image of the mulatta in their works. In fact, the image has been with us since the beginnings of the American novel. Cora Munro, one of the minor characters in Cooper's *The Last of the Mohicans* (1826), is an octoroon, and she is a foreshadowing of the many octoroons who appear in the literature of the nineteenth century, for she meets with a tragic end.

Unlike the abolitionists' literature of the antebellum period, the southern writers' literature focused on the black woman as the contented mammy rather than the mulatta, since they tried to sweep the existence of miscegenation under the rug. Still, when they did present this image, the mulatta is tragic.[48] Often she is shown as caught between two worlds, and since she is obviously the result of an illicit relationship, she suffers from a melancholy of the blood that inevitably leads to tragedy. In contrast to the southern lady, whose beauty, refinement, and charm bring her admiration, love, and happiness, the fruit of miscegenation is tragedy, regardless of what other positive characteristics the mulatta might possess. The word *mulatto* itself etymologically is derived from the word *mule* and echoes the debate Americans engaged in about whether blacks were of the same species as whites.[49] If they were not, the result would be similar to a mule, a cross between the donkey and the horse and a being that itself was incapable of producing life. The etymology of the word also brings to mind the conclusions of the ethnologist Josiah Nott, who claimed that 'the mulatta was a genuine hybrid, weaker and less fertile than either parent'.[50] It is interesting in this context to note how many black jokes there are about mules, animals who are also identified with unrelenting labor.

Like the tragic mulatta image, the image of the conjure woman is not nearly so dominant in the literature of the southern writers as the mammy image. Yet it persists throughout antebellum literature and thought. This image is extremely elusive. On one hand, the conjure woman image incorporates the signs of traditional African religions that the southern gentry pointed to as dark and evil heathen forces. The value judgment they made about the religion of the slave was both practically and philosophically to their advantage, for they used it as a rationalization for the entire system of slavery. Much of early southern literature argues that slavery was really a blessing for the Africans, since it separated them from the dark effects of heathenism and introduced them to the saving light of Christianity. In this context, it was necessary continually to keep alive the image of African heathenism, so the slavemaster could use slavery as part of an overall Christian crusade to elevate otherwise damned souls to possible levels of salvation. Even this point of view was rather liberal, though, for many writers insisted that slaves, because they were inferior to whites, could not really become Christians, or that if they were allowed the Gospel, they might become discontented under slavery.[51] In any case, the antebellum literature does emphasize the heathenism of blacks by pointing up the 'ridiculous' superstitions of black folk, a characteristic the southern mind believed in so intensely that when the Ku Klux Klan (KKK) began its infamous career, it chose sheets for disguise since blacks were so afraid of 'haints'.

On the other hand, the image of the conjurer was, in southern literature, treated with some measure of respect and awe, as if the dark, incomprehensible forces did exist and had some power to affect the fortunes of men. The slave narratives also testify to this quality of respect among whites. Ex-slave Susan Snow told an interviewer, 'My ma was a black African and she sure was wild and mean. Dey couldn't whip her. Dey used to say she was a "conjer" and dey was all scared of her.'[52]

Perhaps mammies communicated their respect for conjurers to the white children they reared.[53] No doubt human beings have always been fascinated by the unknown, particularly in the realm of the unseen and the intangible. But even more, the hidden guilt that the southerners must have felt, whatever their rationalizations about slavery, could give rise to fears about what the slaves might allay themselves with in an attempt to free themselves. For example, conspirators tried to use the slave folk religion but capitulated to Gabriel Prosser's more political approach, when they put together their plans for Gabriel's Rebellion in 1800.[54] The Haitian Revolution, with its overtones of dark, unknown forces turning against the masters and the victory of the hypnotic drum, could only reinforce the planters' fears all the more. The African drum, of course, was outlawed in the United States, but the reality of its threat was kept alive in the image of the conjurer, who, although potentially dangerous, was certainly kept under some degree of control, if only because he or she maintained a definite role in plantation society.

Of course the southern gentry's own heritage contained large doses of lore about the intrusion of evil spirits into the lives of human beings.[55] Certainly the war between God and the Devil provided ample seeds for many unorthodox beliefs about the battle between the forces of good and evil. But the southern gentleman was not a Manichean (a sect outlawed by Christianity for its belief in the existence of good and evil forces), at least not openly; much of his feeling about evil forces was relegated to underground caverns of the mind. Superstition was as much a part of his world view as the tenets of Christianity. Particularly in the sections dominated by Catholicism, the conjure woman image flourished, for the Catholic hierarchy of saints further heightened the contrast between God and the Devil. Whatever their actual power, black women like Marie LaVeau in New Orleans and Mary Ellen Pleasant in San Francisco would use their knowledge of the white man's fear of the supernatural to become real-life conjure women, wielding power over matters of state and politics.

Not surprisingly, the conjure woman image has a direct relationship to the southern lady. Above all her other attributes, the lady was expected to be a Christian; in fact, her qualities of submissiveness and purity were based on her deep Christian faith. Her devotion to her husband and her children was, in effect, a reflection of her devotion to God.[56] But although southern ladies were expected to be intensely religious, they certainly were not supposed to have the intellectual fiber necessary to be ministers in the church. The fact that the black conjurer could be a woman might have reinforced the planters' belief that such a religion was intellectually deficient, conditioned as they were to Christianity where men were undoubtedly the leaders and women were primarily associated with emotive roles. Coincidentally, many male conjurers were ministers in the Christian church as well.

The conjure woman image, although a stereotype, includes within it true elements – in this case that black people not only kept alive certain aspects of various African religions such as herbal medicine, folk wisdom and ritual, but also that women were also able to be leaders in the rituals of many African religions.[57]

Of course, black male images were also evident in antebellum literature, and they were often the counterparts of the female images. The mammy, for example, is often paired with the plantation uncle. Just as the black female images emphasize lewdness and strength, negative qualities in the ideal southern lady, and omit the essential feminine attributes of beauty and delicacy, so the comic, submissive, irrational qualities of the black male images are an inversion of the dignified, strong, rational image of the male patriarch. Both female and male black images run decidedly counter to the masculine and feminine norms of antebellum southern society, thus strengthening the myth that the Negro had to be contained by a superior being and was naturally suited to the condition of slavery.

The images in southern antebellum literature that developed as stereotypes of black women reveal much, not only about the southern attitude towards black people but also about the definition of woman. Each black woman image was created to keep a particular image about white women intact. Another way of putting it is that the aspects of woman that had negative connotations in the society were ascribed to black women so white women could be viewed, as Alice Walker would later phrase it, to be 'perfect in the eyes of the world'.

Significantly, the qualities that distinguished woman from man – her ability to be a mother, her distinct sexual relationship to man, and her supposed tendency toward emotionality and spirituality – are seen as problematic. The definition of a proper woman within the southern context of patriarchy erases those areas in which women naturally could exhibit power – power that was based on their physical nature as well as their place in society. Like the race theories of the nineteenth century, which associated physical characteristics with certain personality traits, all of the images of women, both black and white, are pointedly physical, emphasizing body type and appearance as the essence of woman's being.

The breaking of any of these images was seen as a threat to the entire society. George Fitzhugh, one of the South's most articulate spokesmen for slavery, made clear that 'any change in the role of women (and here, he means white women) or in the institutions of slavery would cause the downfall of the family and the consequent demise of society'.[58] The image of the southern lady, which visually contained the South's philosophical tenets for the status of women, could not be effective without the corresponding images of the black woman.

. . . UPLIFTED

Black abolitionists, such as William Wells Brown and Frances Harper, were certainly aware of the images of black people that had developed during slavery. In fact, from the 1830s to the beginning of the Civil War, a battle of images raged between the writers of the proslavery South and the Abolitionist Movement. Just as antebellum southern writers projected their images of blacks as a servile, inferior race, so the abolitionists countered with their own images through their lectures and writings. The black abolitionists were particularly important in this context, for their oratorical and literary skills were direct refutations of the South's image of blacks as ineducable. Orators like Frederick Douglass, William Brown and Frances Harper were concerned with countering southern images not only of black men but of black women as well, since many of their supporters were white women involved in the struggle for women's rights; also, black abolitionists had proclaimed themselves on the side of female equality when the Abolitionist Movement split over the woman issue.[59]

In the struggle against slavery, the novel as a means of exposing its evils was an effective medium, since, as a genre, it could be used as a source of both moral instruction and entertainment. Harriet Beecher Stowe's *Uncle Tom's Cabin* had proved the effectiveness of the romance novel, for amidst controversy it had created much support for the Abolitionist Movement. Black abolitionists were also eager to create literary works, since one of the most hurtful accusations made against them by proslavery advocates was that black people were culturally inferior and had not produced, and never would be capable of producing, works of art.

Such reasons, to a large extent, conditioned the form of the black abolitionist novel. *Uncle Tom's Cabin, Clotel* and *Iola LeRoy* were activated, as James Baldwin in his essay 'Everybody's protest novel' so beautifully put it, by a 'theological terror', where the concepts of good and evil, salvation and damnation, are pitted against each other.[60] This version of the novel, Baldwin argued, could not reveal the complexity, the truth, of a human being living within a particular society. It would necessarily rely on the motif of sentimentality – that is, an excessive display of emotion as well as a prettifying of ugliness – to move the reader, to set him on the right side of the question. Nor was it possible for early black novelists, like Brown or Harper, to do otherwise, since the existence of black people in America had been couched in such extreme moral terms.

No doubt, the black abolitionist writers were influenced by Mrs Stowe's extremely popular novel, for it caused more discussion about slavery than all of the abolitionists' previous pamphlets and lectures. *Uncle Tom's Cabin* was especially effective because it attacked one of the two major arguments southerners used to buttress slavery – the concept of the patriarchy and the domestic metaphor. 'In her letter to Gamiel Becky in 1851, offering the series of sketches to the National Era, Mrs. Stowe explained that she would give "the lights and shadows of the patriarchal institution ... the best side of the thing and something faintly approaching the worst".'[61] Throughout the novel, she translates her intention into gripping melodrama, as she shows how the big, happy family of the southern plantation is beset by the shadows of separation of slave parent from child, slave husband from wife, slave brother from sister, and that the patriarch, whether his nature is kind or cruel, cannot merely abide by familial ties when he is dealing with slaves but must primarily be concerned with economic considerations.

Mrs Stowe's attack on the domestic metaphor of the South did not go unnoticed by southerners. Her book unleashed volumes of critical reviews from the South, the like of which had never been seen before. Her opponents chafed at her precise attack on their most cherished argument in any number of ways – by insisting that she did not understand the concept of patriarchy, and by deriding the 'little woman' for entering into such masculine affairs.[62] They understood, too, that her particular antislavery thrust was also an attack on the domestic order and therefore on the condition of southern women. Instinctively, the South called upon southern ladies, who dutifully obliged, 'to put the Yankee woman in her place'.[63] Many southern men like the novelist George Simms knew that some southern women privately opposed slavery because of the effects of miscegenation on their domestic order. In a valiant attempt to put the novelist and her novel beyond the realm of intellectual concern, he remarked that Mrs Stowe had reasoned 'sensuously' from the 'woman nature' and had 'misused the mode of romance for the purpose of sociological criticism'.[64]

Simms's comment illuminates some of the other dominant characteristics of *Uncle Tom's Cabin*, which were reflections of various abolitionist positions. Mrs Stowe graphically presented the nature of the Negro in direct comparison to the 'woman nature'. Both groups, she insisted, were 'natural Christians' whose qualities of gentleness and willingness to serve made them superior to the materialistic, intellectual white male. Her vision was not hers alone. In 1863 Theodore Tilton, the editor of the New York *Independent*, said in a speech he gave at Cooper Institute in New York:

> In all the intellectual activities which take their strange quickening from the moral faculties – which we call instincts, intuitions – the negro is superior to the white man – equal to the white woman. It is sometimes said ... that the negro race is the feminine race of the world. This is not only because of his social and affectionate nature, but because he possesses that strange moral instinctive insight that belongs more to women than to men.[65]

Many abolitionists expressed the view that these feminine qualities were sadly lacking in white American civilization and that the rise of the Negro and the woman would 'take the hard edges off of the Anglo Saxon'.[66] The idealized Negro, then, pointed up the deficiencies of the white race, and again the Negro was perceived by these thinkers as a means of serving the white race, this time for its own moral betterment.

Ironically, the feminine image of the Negro that Mrs Stowe so dramatically expressed resembled very closely the servile mammies and uncles of ante-bellum southern literature. What she and other abolitionists who agreed with her emphasized were these qualities, not as reasons for the Negro's inferiority but for his superiority, not as reasons for his enslavement but for his freedom. The effect in literature was the creation of the Negro as a dramatic focal character rather than a comic minor image.

Despite Mrs Stowe's claim that Negroes were superior because of their Christian virtues, she could not romanticize reality to the extent that she thought these gentle beings could survive as freedmen and as natural Christians in the competitive Anglo-Saxon world of America. So she ended her novel with another idea, which many abolitionists advocated, that the Negroes should go back to Africa where their 'special potentialities could be fully realized'.[67] Obviously the implication of statements such as these was that slavery, as a national crime, should be abolished, but also that the Negro could never become a part of the American nationality.

If the Negro was naturally gentle, how then could Mrs Stowe and other abolitionists dramatize his resistance? In keeping with their view that Negroes were natural Christians and Anglo-Saxons were inherently competitive and restive, they presented mulattoes as the rebellious segment of the black population. Unconsciously perhaps, they reversed the 'taint of black blood' motif of antebellum novels into the 'taint of white blood' syndrome, for their mulattoes, both male and female, exhibit some of the restiveness and unwillingness to serve associated with the Anglo-Saxon personality. But in doing so, these writers revealed their own ambivalences about the superiority of the Negro as a natural Christian. Sterling Brown quoted, in his discussion of the rebellious mulatto stereotype in abolitionist literature, one critic who said: 'This was an indirect admission that a white man in chains was more pitiful than the African similarly. Their most impassioned plea was in behalf of a person little resembling their swarthy proteges.'[68]

In writing their own novels, black writers used some of the elements they found in Mrs Stowe's novel: the inherent duplicity of the patriarchal system and the Negro as a natural Christian. Often they combined the qualities of the natural Christian as Negro and as woman by focusing on the black woman in their novels. If their heroines were to be effective, however, they would have to combat the negative images of black women in southern antebellum literature. They did this by creating a 'positive' black woman image. Since positive female qualities were all attributed to the white lady, these writers based their counterimage on her ideal qualities more than on the qualities of any real black woman. The closest black women could come to such an ideal, at least physically, would of course have to be the mulatta, quadroon or octoroon. Since there was such a close correlation between physical type and spiritual qualities, at least in the area of woman images, it was absolutely necessary to begin with a positive physical type.

The literary conventions of the novel at that time also legislated that the heroine of a story be beautiful, since physical beauty, at least for a woman, was an indication of her spiritual excellence – but not just any kind of physical beauty. The nineteenth-century novel promoted a rather fragile beauty as the norm; qualities of helplessness, chastity and refinement rather than, say, strength, endurance and intelligence were touted as the essential characteristics of femininity. The nineteenth-century heroine not only had to be beautiful physically; she had to be fragile and well-bred as well.

The black woman could not possibly fulfill these requirements since by definition to be black in color meant the opposite of beauty, and *well-bred* was a term applied only to the upper class. The mulatta, then, according to the literary convention of the nineteenth century as well as half of the twentieth century, could be the only type of black woman beautiful enough to be a popular heroine and close enough to wealth vis-à-vis her father to be well-bred. Again, it is interesting to see how social conventions determine literary ones. The social philosophy that denied the beauty of black women and the economic policy of slavery that relegated black people to the bottom of the economic ladder made it very difficult for anyone to write a novel in which a credible black woman could be the major focus of attention. Consequently, from 1861, when *Clotel* was published, until the publication of Ann Petry's *The Street* in 1945, a disproportionate number of black novels adhered to the literary convention of the mulatta heroine.

Although antebellum southern writers had occasionally featured mulattas, it was the abolitionist novelists, both black and white, who would etch her image into the national consciousness. *Clotel*, the first novel to be published by a black man in America, uses the mulatta as the center of the novel. William Wells Brown's description of the mulatta became the model for other black novels:

> Her tall and well developed figure; her long silky black hair, falling in curls down her swan-like neck; her bright, black eyes lighting up her olive-tinted face, and a set of teeth that a Tuscarora might envy, she was a picture of tropical-ripened beauty. At times, there was a heavenly smile upon her countenance which would have warmed the heart of an anchorite.[69]

He went on to tell us about mulattas in general:

> Bottles of ink, and reams of paper, have been used to portray the finely-cut and well-moulded features, the 'silken curls,' the dark and brilliant eyes, 'the splendid forms,' the 'fascinating smiles and accomplished manners' of these impassioned and voluptuous daughters of the races – the unlawful product of the crime of human bondage.[70]

Doubtless true, Brown contributed his bottle of ink to the number, for one of Clotel's major attributes is her beauty as a mulatta, the fine mixture of two races in which the physical features are predominantly white, although touched enough with black blood to be considered exotic or voluptuous.

Brown played upon Clotel's beauty so heavily that we cannot help but remember the assertions of so many whites, from the time of Jefferson through the mid-nineteenth century, that blacks were inferior because they lacked beauty. Perhaps Brown's characterization of Clotel was influenced by the effect runaway mulattas such as Ellen Craft had on white northern audiences. He had been in charge of her tour throughout the North, had introduced Craft to white sympathizers who were struck by her beauty and refinement, and had remarked on their difficulty in distinguishing her from a white woman.[71]

Clotel's beauty, however, is not her only attribute. In fact, her beauty, like the southern lady's, is primarily a reflection of her spiritual qualities, for she is a natural Christian. Brown emphasizes this quality of hers in all three published versions of his novel, transforming the stereotypical tragic mulatta, Clotel, of the first version into the beautiful Angel of Mercy in the second and third versions. Clotel is beautiful, pure and Christian, in contrast to the black women of the antebellum southern writers.

Brown's *Clotel*, however, differs from Mrs Stowe's *Uncle Tom's Cabin* in two significant ways. These differences reflect the concerns of black abolitionists as well as the view of William Lloyd Garrison, the most important white leader of the Abolitionist Movement. Brown flatly rejects the idea of colonization in Africa, for although the Clotel of the second and third versions lives in Europe for a while, she returns to America, her home, where she nurses soldiers during the Civil War. Africa is seldom mentioned in the novel and certainly not as a place where Clotel's potentialities as a natural Christian would be fulfilled. Many black abolitionists, as well as the Garrisonites, had harshly criticized the colonization movement, calling it an indiction that even white abolitionists doubted blacks were the equals of whites and were a part of the American nation.[72]

The second significant way in which Brown differs somewhat from Stowe is in his treatment of rebellious Negroes. Although many of his minor characters are the stock comic mammies and uncles of antebellum southern literature, his rebellious hero, Jerome, is a dark-skinned, although curly-haired, Negro. Jerome is not only rebellious, he is interested in learning and the finer things of life, in contrast to the view of many northerners who believed that Negroes, once freed, became indolent and degraded.[73] Brown's Jerome is a vivid example of the self-help philosophy of the black abolitionists.[74] But beyond that, he is a natural gentleman of learning well befitting Clotel, the beautiful Angel of Mercy.

Brown's three versions of *Clotel*, written before, during and immediately following the Civil War, reflect some of the events of that traumatic period. By the time Harper's *Iola LeRoy* was published in 1892, the country had gone through years of Reconstruction, as tumultuous a time as the Civil War period. After they saw their dream of abolition realized, black abolitionists were to experience a steady stream of defeats, for as W. E. B. DuBois put it, 'the planters, having lost the war for slavery, sought to begin again where they left off in 1860, merely substituting for the individual ownership of slaves, a new state of serfdom of black folk'.[75] Once slavery was abolished, the racist prejudices of many northerners, as well as southerners, surfaced, for neither region was committed to the idea that blacks were equal to whites. Many white Americans of that period would have responded to Captain Delano's query, 'you are Saved, who has cast a shadow upon you?' as Melville's Benito Cereno did when he muttered, 'the Negro'.

Frances Harper had participated not only in the fight against slavery, but also in the struggle for Negro suffrage and the passage of the Fifteenth Amendment. She must have known that political expediency, the need for a strong Republican party in the South, rather than a belief in Negro rights, was the major reason for its passage.[76] Before its passage, she had watched northerners project the image of docile black soldiers, despite their fine record in the Civil War; she had seen the enactment of the Black Codes in the South, the discussion that raged about whether the Negro was inherently inferior, and the renewal of colonization schemes.[77] After the achievement of Negro suffrage, she must have cringed at the rise of white supremacy and the popularity of ethnological, scientific proofs that the Negro was a subhuman species.[78] She must have noted that many pre-Civil War abolitionists now asserted that the Negro was a vanishing species destined to extinction before the march of the superior white race.[79] She must have reacted with alarm to the intensification of the myth of the degenerate Negro, which emanated from the old eighteenth-century notion that black men had uncontrolled passions for white women and that black women were, by nature, sexually loose.[80] As an abolitionist elder, she participated in the founding of the Anti-Lynching Societies with younger black women, such as Ida B. Wells and Mary Church Terrell, whose investigations proved that it usually was not black men who raped white women, but white men who raped black women.[81] In 1891, at the meeting of the National Council of Women of the United States, Harper made this incisive statement about a government that allowed lynchings:

> A government which has power to tax a man in peace, draft him in war, should have power to defend his life in the hour of peril. A government which can protect and defend its citizens from wrong and outrage and does not is vicious. A government which would do it and cannot is weak; and where human life is insecure through either weakness or viciousness in the administration of law, there must be a lack of justice and where this is wanting, nothing can make up for the deficiency.[82]

On the literary front, the battle of images between pro-Negro and anti-Negro forces continued. Although new southern writers like Albion Tourgée and George Washington Cable eloquently called for Negro rights, Harper was certainly aware that popular American writers, such as Joel Chandler Harris and Thomas Nelson Page, were recreating in their fiction the happy plantation myth of the antebellum period. More to the point, they and less celebrated writers were erasing the horrors of slavery in the American public mind and intensifying their thrust by dramatizing the idea that the contented slave reverted to a savage when freed from the necessary control of whites.[83]

It is no wonder then that the 67-year-old Harper began her novel not during Reconstruction but during slavery, and that she used many of the elements of the abolitionist novel that had been successful in the initial drive for the freedom of blacks. She made clear her purpose when she stated about her novel that 'her story's mission would not be in vain if it awaken in the heart of our countrymen a stronger sense of justice and a more Christian-like humanity'.[84]

One of the main themes of *Iola LeRoy, Shadows Uplifted* is the horror of slavery as visited upon the most effective heroine of the antebellum abolitionist novel, the beautiful, refined, Christian octoroon. Our first glimpse of Iola LeRoy is through the eyes of one of the black slaves:

'My! but she's putty. Beautiful long hair comes way down her back; putty blue eyes, an' jis' ez white ez anybody's in dis place. I'd jis' wish you could see her yoresef. I heard Marse Tom talkin' 'bout her last night to his brudder; telling him she war mighty airish, but he meant to break her in.'[85]

The attempt at black dialect notwithstanding, Harper's Iola LeRoy physically resembles Brown's Clotel. But Harper goes one step further than Brown, for Iola has gone to the finest New England schools and thus fits into the culture's description of what the quintessence of refinement should be. Nor is Iola merely the offspring of some illicit relationship between a white aristocrat and a black slave. Although *Clotel* had originally been subtitled *The President's Daughter*, for it was popularly thought that Thomas Jefferson had a black slave concubine, Iola LeRoy is the fruit of a lawful marriage between a wealthy New Orleans plantation owner and a quadroon whom he educates and frees before he marries her. The children, of course, are not told that their refined, well-educated mother is black. So not only is Iola a mulatta, she is initially an upper-class white woman with privileges most white women of her day could only dream of. Ironically, before Iola painfully discovers that she is black, as a southern lady and a slaveholder's daughter, she had always defended slavery – this despite her high spiritual qualities. It is only when she is cast into the dark condition of slavery that she changes her opinion. Undoubtedly many white women could identify with the beautiful woman who looked as white as they did, who was certainly more wealthy and privileged than they were, and who, despite all this, is instantly pummeled into the pit of servitude only because she has a few drops of black blood in her veins.

Harper's presentation of what slavery meant for Iola is also indicative of the images the writer must refute as well as the atmosphere of the Reconstruction period during which the novel was published. For Iola's virtue, her chastity, is what is at stake, and our heroine spends much of her short time in the shadow of slavery successfully resisting attempts of sex-crazed white men to drag her virtue down. Iola is no loose black woman, nor is she coarse or loud, and therefore being a woman of high Christian morals, the novel insists, she does not deserve the brutal, immoral treatment that is part of the tradition of slavery.

Even more than Brown, Harper emphasized the immoral, un-Christian effects of slavery in the area of brutal and wanton sex. Perhaps she was particularly forceful about the area of rape, because by 1892 there was substantial evidence from congressional investigations about the KKK, proving that many black women were being raped by white men, rather than the popular conception that white women were constantly being raped by black men. The investigations had also proved that the rape of black women was a political tool used to intimidate black men so they could not exercise their political rights.[86] The excessive power of the slavemaster results in immorality not only for the slave, Harper insisted, but for the master class as well. Brown presented a case for the many white women who pined their lives away because their husbands chased after slave girls, therefore making a strong bid for the sympathy of women who knew what it was to be betrayed by a man. Harper did an interesting variation on this theme. She had Iola LeRoy's father tell us about the effects of slavery on the personalities of slavemistresses and therefore the reason he prefers his quadroon sweetheart to them:

> 'No! but I think that slavery and the lack of outside interests are beginning to tell on the lives of our women. They lean too much on their slaves, have too much irresponsible power in their hands, are narrowly compressed by the routine of plantation life and the lack of intellectual stimulus.'[87]

Although Brown and Harper had similar views, this excerpt points to some of their differences – differences that could certainly be attributed to the thirty years that passed between the publication of *Clotel* and *Iola LeRoy*. Brown was content to have Clotel be a refined, beautiful, Christian mulatta. But Harper had fought for women's rights during this period and had experienced the South's unwillingness to be reconstructed. Thus attention in her novel is placed on the need women feel to work, to be given an education, and to be able to participate in intellectual matters.

In the first part of the novel, Harper also touched on other distorted myths that had developed about blacks since the Civil War. She recounted how black soldiers fought bravely for the Union. She emphasized one of the most terrible effects of slavery, the breakup of families and the attempt of the newly freed slaves to find their kin. In some of the most authentic, although small, moments of the novel, she uses her experience as a Reconstruction journalist to narrate briefly the story of a few southern ex-slaves who worked hard, against great odds, to improve their lot.

In fact, her theme in the second half of the novel, as indicated by her subtitle, *Shadows Uplifted*, is a presentation of how professional blacks are lifting themselves up to the standards of middle-class American virtue and thrift. One of the most incredible sections of *Iola LeRoy* is the chapter 'Friends in Council'. In this chapter, Iola and her circle of high-bred race-conscious, hardworking Negroes, as well as a few intellectual whites, meet to discuss issues that will benefit the race. Harper sets the mood of this meeting by calling it a *conversizione*, thereby giving it an aura of high culture. The object of the *conversizione* is:

> to gather some of the thinkers and leaders of the race to consult on subjects of vital interest to our welfare. He has invited Dr. Latimer, Professor Cradnor of North Carolina, Mr. Forest of New York, Hons. Dugdale, R vs.

Carmicle, Cantmor, Tumster, Professor Langhorne of Georgia and a few ladies, Mrs. Watson, Miss Brown and others.[88]

When Iola LeRoy says she is glad that this meeting is not a dance and her uncle prods her by asking if she does not believe young people should have a good time, she responds in solemn tones: '"Oh yes, I believe in young people having amusements and recreations, but the times are too serious for us to attempt to make our lives a long holiday."'[89]

At this gathering Iola LeRoy appropriately delivers a paper called 'The education of mothers'. Her paper is based on her mother's comment that:

'we were thrown upon the nation a homeless race to be gathered into the homes and a legally unmarried race to be taught the sacredness of the marriage relation. We must instill into our young people that the true strength of a race means purity in women and uprightness in men; who can say, with Sir Galahad:

"My strength is the strength of ten

Because my heart is pure"

And where this is wanting neither wealth nor culture can make up the deficiency.'[90]

Although sentimental and puritanical in tone, the *conversizione* does communicate Harper's sense that women, particularly black women, must be involved in working for the race. But note that the tone is one of uplifting the race, of rescuing it from its own culture, of molding black women and men superior to white people according to their own Christian mores. In this section Harper bent over backward to refute the popular stereotype of the day that blacks were degenerates who could not advance either economically or culturally and that they needed white tutelage to be part of the American social order.

In emphasizing this ability among professional blacks to be socially responsible, Harper embellished one of the most important qualities of Clotel and other literary mulattas. Like them, Iola LeRoy is a cultural conductor between the white race and the black because of her education, refinement and beauty. She gives to the black race what she has learned from the white culture. And what culture means is western Christian civilization at its best. She becomes, then, a cultural missionary to the ignorant, the loudmouthed, the coarse but essentially good-natured blacks, who need only to be shown the way. Like Clotel, the Angel of Mercy, Iola LeRoy when freed nurses wounded soldiers. But Harper emphasized even more than Brown her heroine's commitment to the race, for Iola LeRoy has the opportunity to marry a white doctor and pass into the white race. This she rejects. Instead she marries a mulatto doctor who himself has rejected the opportunity to pass. Together they work, Iola in a Sunday School where she plans meetings for the special benefit of mothers and children, while her husband, the Good Doctor, inspired by his lovely wife, is a true patriot and good citizen. He

> has great faith in the possibilities of the negro, and believes that, enlightened and Christianized, he will sink the old animosities of slavery into the new community of interests arising from freedom, and that his influence upon the South will be as the influence of the sun upon the earth.[91]

Iola LeRoy, Shadows Uplifted describes the rise of a black middle class headed by mulattoes who feel the grave responsibility of defining for the black race what is best for it, who work within the context of moral Christian ethics, and whose faith in the country and its culture enables them to be conservative in all matters except race. Harper, then, responded to charges that the Negro is and always will be a degenerate by idealizing this segment of the black community. At the center of this upward striving class is the mulatta, no longer tragic or melancholy but a source of light for those below and around her.

The qualities with which Frances Harper endowed her heroine are the result of her reaction to images of black women she felt she had to refute. Iola LeRoy is decidedly not the contented mammy, whom novelists like Thomas Nelson Page continued to idealize. She, like Clotel, does not fit the physical type. She is emphatically not a loose woman; in fact both she and Clotel rise to the heights of angelic purity, a state that seems sentimental at best, boring at worst. Like Clotel, she is decidedly Christian, and no African spirits lurk in the background as in the Uncle Remus stories of Joel Chandler Harris. Nor is she a tragic mulatta in which the mingling of blood renders her perpetually unhappy. Significantly, however, unlike Clotel who is a singular beacon of light in Brown's novel, Iola LeRoy now belongs to a society of intelligent and superior black people. Because of her physical beauty and her spiritual virtue, she inspires her society toward the higher values of life. She is, in fact, except for her race, invisible – although her blackness may be to the undiscriminating eye the epitome of the image of the lady, the light by which the shadows will be uplifted.

Images were also fashioned by another tradition, the oral tradition, the witnessing of black people as seen through narrative and song. The slave narrative, as a genre, tended to be represented by those extraordinary slaves, usually men such as Frederick Douglass, who escaped from bondage. Yet there are many narratives of men and women slaves who considered themselves the common folk and who remained in slavery most or all of their lives.[92]

As would be expected, the image of the mammy still persists within the genre. She is there as cook, housekeeper, nursemaid and seamstress, always nurturing and caring for her folk. But unlike the white southern image of the mammy, she is cunning, prone to poisoning her master, and not at all content with her lot. It is interesting and ironic that Sojourner Truth, the flamboyant orator who advocated the abolition of slavery and fought for women's rights, would fit the stereotype – at least the physical stereotype – of the mammy that southern gentlemen wanted to perceive as harmless. Sojourner Truth is not the only mammy who fought to protect her own children or who rose up against slavery. Mammies kicked, fought, connived and plotted, most often covertly, to throw off the chains of bondage. The mammy saw herself as a mother, but to her that role embodied a certain dignity and responsibility, rather than a physical debasement, doubtless a carry-over from the African view that every mother is a symbol of the marvelous creativity of the earth. The mammy is an important figure in the mythology of Africa. The way in which this theme of African culture is distorted by the white southern perspective testifies to its inability to relate femaleness and femininity – as countless southern belles in antebellum American movies illustrate.

The tragic mulatta, too, appears in slave narratives. And she is indeed tragic, as are almost all of the accounts. The contrast of comic darky and tragic mulatto developed in the literature of that period certainly does not stand the test of reality. There is little romanticism in the accounts mulattas give of their lives. There are tales of mulattas who as mistresses are abused and sold, their children scattered to the ends of the land, mad mulattas who hate their fathers if they are acknowledged at all by them. There are sullen, cynical mulattas, reared to be sold as high-class courtesans. The narratives abound with tales of woman, be she field nigger or house nigger, mulatta or darky, as breeder, nursemaid, concubine, whipping block, put on the rack of everlasting work and debasing servitude. And in the tales of these women, be they 'yaller' or 'chocolate', the trivial underscores the abuses they faced: having to sleep outside the mistress's door so that little sexual relationship with one's husband was possible, having to take care of the mistress's children so that one's babies were born dead, time after time. The narratives are especially poignant in the equalization of abuse they suggest, for the advantages that the mulatta might have because of her link to the master were easily offset by the disadvantages of alienation and frustration.[93]

The narratives tend to focus on the relationship between slave and master, but the work songs give us another view of how the black woman, during slavery and Reconstruction, viewed herself and was viewed. As music is usually so intensely personal, and need not be sanctioned by a publisher to be heard and spread, the folk songs about and by women tend to peer into the relationship between the black man and the black woman in their identity as man and woman. Courting, lovemaking, success and disappointment in love – all of these aspects appear in the songs. Some men revel in their women. 'Pretty Girl' is representative of this group:

Rubber is a pretty thing.
You rub it to make it shine.
If you want to see a pretty girl,
Take a peep at mine, take a peep at mine.

Talking about a pretty girl,
You jus' oughta see mine.
She is not so pretty
But she is jus' so fine.

She gives me sugar,
She gives me lard,
She works all the while
In the white folks' yard.[94]

At the same time there is often the recurring theme that:

De woman am de cause of it all,
De woman am de cause of it all,
She's de cause of po'Adam's fall,
De woman's de cause of it all.[95]

The songs, too, mirror the tingling clash between the dark woman and the 'yaller' woman, often in a humorous tone:

De mulatto gal got yaller skin, yaller skin,
De mulatto gal got yaller skin, yaller skin,
De mulatto gal got yaller skin, yaller skin,
De mulatto gal got yaller skin,
Den she got a devilish grin, daddy.

De chocolate gal got greasy hair, greasy hair,
De chocolate gal got greasy hair, greasy hair,
De chocolate gal got greasy hair, greasy hair,
De chocolate gal got greasy hair,
She is de gal can cuss and rare, daddy.[96]

Somehow, though, within the confines of their own space, threatened as it was by a more powerful society with different standards, there does not emerge a hard and fast line about the value of a woman simply because she has some white blood. Unlike the literary products of the day, the heroines of these songs might or might not be cinnamon, coffee, chocolate or yaller:

If 'twant for de ter'pin pie
And sto-bought ham,
Dese country women
Couldn't git nowhere.

Some say, give me a high yaller,
I say, give me a teasin' brown,
For it takes a teasin' brown
To satisfy my soul.

For some folkses say
A yaller is low down,
But teasin' brown
Is what I's crazy about.[97]

Almost always the substance of the work songs about or by women is sifted through the cry of hard times and how that affects relationships. The men who caught trains and left for whatever reasons, the lack of money, the pervasive sense of danger, the need for a woman to be independent of men, an independence imposed rather than desired, shapes the songs and gives even the gayest song an undertone of plaintiveness. Slave narrative and work song alike project black women as caught in the vise of 'hard times', their spirits rising sometimes to the heights of heroism but more often tempered by the nibbling need always to be practical.

Why is there such a difference between the images of black women presented in the early black abolitionist novels and the images in the oral tradition? We must not forget that, by necessity, the first novelists were writing to white audiences. Few black people were literate at that time because of stringent laws against teaching slaves to read and write. The thrust of the black novel necessarily had to be a cry of protest directed at whites for their treatment of blacks. The problem was not whether black women were heroic, but whether they were women at all. I do not make this statement lightly. According to the norms of society, a woman was physically weak but important to the male because of her ability, through her beauty and refinement, to rouse his higher instincts to the level of God and culture. The fact that Sojourner Truth could say, as she did at the Convention of the Equal Rights Association in 1867, that she had worked like any man and was yet a woman, that Harriet Tubman had been the only American woman to lead troops into battle, that Marie LaVeau and Mary Ellen Pleasant had wielded political power in New Orleans and San Francisco, or that Phyllis Wheatley had written poems of a quality as fine as that of most eighteenth-century white American poets – these facts complicated the issue rather than resolved it. The deeds of these women and many others less known seemed to indicate that the black woman lacked femininity, a necessary ingredient of womanhood, according to the norm. Further, the social need for a beautiful heroine in the novel tended to designate femininity as the necessary ingredient of female heroism. It is interesting to note that American novels up to that time seldom emphasized the heroism of white American women who had done much hard work toward the creation of the country.

By presenting an image of the black woman that would elicit sympathy and appreciation for her and therefore for black people as a whole, Brown and Harper sought to soften as many differences as possible between the images of the black woman and the white woman. Thus they appealed to the norm with a vengeance and their works were based on society's definition of their race as 'shadows' who needed uplifting.

From the beginning, the black novel had to struggle with the cloak of 'theological terror' that Baldwin elucidates in his discussion of protest literature. That is, black writers would constantly have to distinguish between black people as white Americans saw them (as a moral problem and a dumping ground for their fears) and as complex human beings. At the same time, black writers would have to wrestle with the ramifications of white American stereotypes that so strongly affected the lives of black people as a group. Black thinkers would have to articulate the concepts of their own culture, even as there was resistance to that articulation from within as well as from without. Only then could they dismiss Anglo-American cultural norms as their conceptual framework. Only then could they begin to draw inspiration and materials from the forms of their own culture that lay embedded in the rich oral and musical tradition of the folk. One of the important concepts they would have to articulate would be the images of female and male within the community of the black folk even as these images were being assaulted by the dominant society.

Certainly the works of Charles Chesnutt were a great step in that direction. Although Paul Laurence Dunbar is the acknowledged Negro poet of the turn of the century, his first three novels focused on whites and the promise of his last novel, *Sport of the Gods* (1904), a precursor of the Harlem Renaissance city novel, was never realized because of his early death. Chesnutt was a writer of fiction and the first black novelist to rise to national prominence. Although he uses full-blown versions of the mammy, the loose woman, the tragic mulatta and the conjure woman in his short stories and three novels, this pioneer in black fiction cautiously introduced elements of black folklore as frames for his fiction. Although his novels are primarily about the small, black middle class, he tries to present black characters and situations that are more in keeping with the reality that black people had to face at the turn of the century.

His racial identity unknown to the literary world, Chesnutt received considerable praise for his first collection of short stories, *The Conjure Woman and Other Stories* (1899). But when it became known that he was black, he received increasing pressure from his publishers to maintain the tone of sentimentality of the happy plantation darky story, popular at that time. His letters reveal his chafing sense of frustration at having to disguise his perceptions with overlays of sentimentality and caricature, because his white audience was not open to a view of blacks as complex human beings.[98] None the less, he overstepped his boundaries when he wrote *The Marrow of Tradition* (1901), a novel based on the Wilmington Race Riot of 1898, and *The Colonel's Dream* (1905), a novel about the conflict between the South's racist prejudices and attempts at reform. These two novels were published at a time when Thomas Dixon's novels, *The Leopard's Spots* (1902) and *The Clansman* (1905), were extremely popular. Given the enactment of the Jim Crow laws and the disenfranchisement of most Negroes in the South, it is not surprising that white Americans reacted more favorably to Dixon's vindictive portrayal of the Negro as a brute rather than to Chesnutt's dramatization of racist concepts that permeated American society. Soon after, disappointed by the harsh reviews of his novels, which were not about his craftsmanship but about his racial views, Chesnutt retired from writing fiction and went back to his law practice.

His literary career clearly illustrates the plight of nineteenth-century black novelists as they struggled with the cloak of theological terror that was thrust upon them. They had the choice of being silent completely or of compromising their sense of reality if they were to publish. Without the freedom to write about life as they saw it, restricted by the concepts of good and evil that black people represented to the majority culture, it is no wonder that their expression lacked the imagination and richness of the folk expressions of the day. Without the atmosphere of experimentation, social conventions that were obviously stereotypical views hardened into literary conventions. The shadow of white racism hung over early black novelists. Many years would pass before it would be lifted, allowing glimpses of reality to revise the distorted black images of the eighteenth and nineteenth centuries.

NOTES

1. In *St. Peter Relates an Incident* (New York: Viking Press, 1917).
2. Frances Harper's *Iola LeRoy, Shadows Uplifted*, 3rd edn (Boston: James H. Earle, 1895), is usually listed in surveys of Afro-American literature, such as Brown, Davis, and Lee, eds, *Negro Caravan* (New York: Dryden, 1941), and Roger Whitlow's *Black American Literature: A critical history* (Totowa, NJ: Littlefield Adams, 1974), as the first novel published by an Afro-American woman. There is some question, however, whether a novel by Amelia Johnson, *In God's Way* (Rochester, NY: American Baptist Publishing), was not published before 1892. I recently saw a copy of this novel at an exhibit of rare black books done by Daphne Muse at Mills College. The publication date was 1891. This novel is not listed in most bibliographies. It, like *Iola LeRoy*, is about an octoroon.
3. William Still, Introduction to Harper, *Iola LeRoy*
4. Frances Harper, 'Black women in the Reconstruction South', reprinted in *Black Women in White America: A documentary history*, ed. Gerda Lerner (New York: Vintage, 1973), p. 247.
5. ibid., pp. 249–50.
6. Winthrop D. Jordan, *White Over Black: American attitudes toward the Negro, 1550–1812* (New York: Penguin, 1969), p. 101.
7. ibid., p. 143.

8. Milton Cantor, 'The image of the Negro in colonial literature', in *Images of the Negro in American Literature*, ed. Seymour Gross and John E. Hardy (Chicago: University of Chicago Press, 1966), p. 29.

9. Jordan, *White Over Black*, p. 79.

10. ibid., p. 31.

11. Cantor, 'The image of the Negro in colonial literature', pp. 29–53.

12. Jordan, *White Over Black*, p. 32.

13. ibid., p. 31.

14. George Stocking, *Race Culture and Evolution: Essays in the history of anthropology* (New York: Free Press, 1968), pp. 37–8.

15. Jordan, *White Over Black*, pp. 429–81.

16. ibid., p. 142.

17. ibid., p. 148.

18. ibid., p. 149.

19. Herbert G. Gutman, *The Black Family in Slavery and Freedom, 750–1925* (New York: Pantheon, 1976), p. 75. Although historians make a great distinction between breeding in the Caribbean and the practices of United States slaveholders who encouraged promiscuity among slaves, there are a few points worth considering: (1) that the distinction they make between the Caribbean and the United States is somewhat muted by the continuous contact between the slaves and planters of these two areas. The United States was as much a part of the New World as the Caribbean; (2) that slave narratives include many references to slaves who said they were forced to mate with a particular slave; (3) that there are many advertisements for breeder slaves, written by men as famous as Benjamin Franklin. Although forced mating may not have been widespread in the United States, there seems to be some indication that breeding was not 'rare'. But I defer to the historians. See Lerner, *Black Women in White America*, pp. 47–8. See Norman R. Yetman, *Life Under the 'Peculiar Institution': Selections from the slave narrative collection* (New York: Holt, Rinehart & Winston, 1970). See Eugene D. Genovese, *Roll, Jordan, Roll: The world the slaves made* (New York: Pantheon, 1974), p. 464.

20. Jordan, *White Over Black*, p. 160.

21. ibid., p.77

22. ibid.

23. Anne Firor Scott, *The Southern Lady: From pedestal to politics, 1830–1930* (Chicago: University of Chicago Press, 1970), p. 4.

24. ibid., pp. 23–44. Also, Julia Cherry Spruill, *Women's Life and Work in the Southern Colonies* (Chapel Hill: University of North Carolina Press, 1938).

25. George Frederickson, *The Black Image in the White Mind: The debate on Afro-American character, 1817–1914* (New York: Harper & Row, 1971), pp. 43–70.

26. ibid., pp. 76–8.

27. Severn Duvall, '"Uncle Tom's Cabin": the sinister side of the patriarchy', in *Images of the Negro in American Literature*, ed. Gross and Hardy, p. 166.

28. Frederickson, *The Black Image in the White Mind*, pp. 66–9.

29. Stocking, *Race, Culture and Evolution*, pp. 49–50.

30. Lerner, *Black Women in White America*, p. 5.

31. Duvall, '"Uncle Tom's Cabin": the sinister side of the patriarchy', pp. 165–7.

32. Three notations must accompany this statement. First, I am using the concept

of African philosophy in much the same way that writers use, with ease, the concept of a European world view. There are obviously differences between the many peoples of Africa as there are between the many peoples of Europe. Scholars such as John Mbiti, *African Religions and Philosophy* (New York: Doubleday Anchor, 1970), and Janheinz Jahn, *Muntu* (New York: Grove, 1961), have envisioned African peoples as sharing some basic philosophical concepts that are distinct, either in content or style, from European and Asian peoples. Second, I am referring, in this specific instance, to the concept of mother as pivotal to the African world view. See Denise Paulme, ed., *Women of Tropical Africa* (Berkeley: University of California, 1971), and the first chapter, 'Mother and child', of Wilfred Cartey, *Whispers from a Continent* (New York: Vintage, 1969), an in-depth study of this theme in contemporary African literature. Third, I am obviously in agreement with the concept of African survivalism in the United States, as well as the New World. See Herkovits, *The Myth of the Negro Past* (New York: Harper, 1941); John Blassingame, *The Slave Community: Plantation life in the ante bellum South* (New York: Oxford University Press, 1972), pp. 18–40; Lorenzo Turner, 'African survivals in the New World with special emphasis on the arts', in *Africa Seen by American Negroes*, ed. John Davis (Paris: Presence Africaine, 1958); Lawrence Levine's *Black Culture and Black Consciousness: Afro-American folk thought from slavery to freedom* (New York: Oxford University Press, 1977); as well as Genovese's *Roll, Jordan, Roll*, particularly the section on folk religion.
33. Genovese, *Roll, Jordan, Roll*, p. 496.
34. Sterling Brown, *The Negro in American Fiction* (1937; reprinted New York: Atheneum, 1969), p. 21.
35. ibid., pp. 1–189.
36. ibid., pp. 23–4.
37. Scott, *The Southern Lady*, pp. 46–54. See also Genovese, *Roll, Jordan, Roll*, pp. 353–61.
38. Genovese, *Roll, Jordan, Roll*, p. 353.
39. Scott, *The Southern Lady*, p. 37.
40. Jordan, *White Over Black*, p. 151.
41. Blassingame, *The Slave Community*, pp. 82–4.
42. Jordan, *White Over Black*, p. 150.
43. Scott, *The Southern Lady*, p. 52.
44. Jordan, *White Over Black*, p. 475
45. William Wells Brown, *Clotel* (Miami: Mnemosyne Publishing, 1969). Reprint of *Clotel, or the Colored Heroine: A tale of the southern states* (Boston: Lee & Shepard, 1867), p. 5. The first version of this book was published as *Clotel; or the President's Daughter* (London: Patridge & Dakey, 1853). Other versions are *Miralda, or the Beautiful Quadroon* (New York: The Weekly Anglo-African Magazine, 1860); *Clotelle: A tale of the southern states* (Boston: James Redpath, 1864).
46. Lerner, *Black Women in White America*, pp. 45–53. See also Genovese, *Roll, Jordan, Roll*, p. 419.
47. Again, the comments I made in footnote 32, in relation to African philosophy and African survivalism in the United States, apply here. On the question of sex, see Genovese, *Roll, Jordan, Roll*, pp. 234, 246–7, 259; Mbiti, *African Religions and Philosophy*, pp. 160–4, 191–4; William Lew Hansberry, 'Indigenous African reli-

gions', *Africa Seen by American Negroes*, esp. pp. 90–3.

48. Brown, *The Negro in American Fiction*, p. 8.
49. Eric Patridge, *Origins: A Short Etymological Dictionary of Modern English* (New York:
    Macmillan, 1958), p. 420.
50. Frederickson, *The Black Image in the White Mind*, p. 75.
51. Jordan, *White Over Black*, pp. 20–4, 180–2, 191–3.
52. Levine, *Black Culture and Black Consciousness*, p. 74.
53. Blassingame, *The Slave Community*, p. 48.
54. Levine, *Black Culture and Black Consciousness*, p. 75.
55. ibid., pp. 59–60.
56. Scott, *The Southern Lady*, pp. 7–14.
57. Mbiti, *African Religions and Philosophy*, p. 88.
58. Scott, *The Southern Lady*, p. 21.
59. Benjamin Quarles, *Black Abolitionists* (New York: Oxford University Press, 1969), pp. 43–6, 177–80.
60. James Baldwin, 'Everybody's protest novel', in *Notes of a Native Son*, by James Baldwin (New York: Bantam Books, 1955), pp. 9–17.
61. Severn Duvall, '"Uncle Tom's Cabin": the sinister side of the patriarchy', p. 164.
62. ibid., pp. 174–5.
63. ibid., p. 176.
64. ibid., p. 178.
65. Frederickson, *The Black Image in the White Mind*, pp. 114–15.
66. ibid., pp. 108–9.
67. ibid., p. 115.
68. Brown, *The Negro in American Fiction*, p. 45.
69. Brown, *Clotel*, p. 70.
70. ibid., p. 5
71. Quarles, *Black Abolitionists*, pp. 62–3.
72. ibid., pp. 218–22. Quarles noted that some abolitionist blacks, primarily those in the African Civilization Society, supported colonization.
73. Frederickson, *The Black Image in the White Mind*, p. 5.
74. Quarles, *Black Abolitionists*, pp. 90–115.
75. W. E. B. DuBois, *Black Reconstruction in America, 1860–1880* (1935; reprinted New York: Meridian Books, 1962), p. 128.
76. Frederickson, *The Black Image in the White Mind*, pp. 184–5.
77. John Hope Franklin, *From Slavery to Freedom* (1947; reprinted New York: Vintage, 1969), pp. 297–343.
78. Frederickson, *The Black Image in the White Mind*, pp. 187–99.
79. ibid., pp. 228–55.
80. ibid., pp. 259–61.
81. Lerner, *Black Woman in White America*, pp. 193–215.
82. ibid., p. 194.
83. Frederickson, *The Black Image in the White Mind*, p. 211.
84. Harper, *Iola LeRoy*, p. 281.
85. ibid., p. 38.
86. Lerner, *Black Women in White America*, pp. 172–93.
87. Harper, *Iola LeRoy*, p. 64.

88. ibid., p. 243.
89. ibid.
90. ibid., p. 254.
91. ibid., p. 279.
92. Lerner, *Black Women in White America*, pp. 7–72. See also Yetman, *Life Under the 'Peculiar Institution'*.
93. ibid., pp. 7–72.
94. Howard Odum and Guy Johnson, *Negro Workaday Songs* (Chapel Hill: University of North Carolina Press, 1926), p. 145.
95. ibid., pp. 142–3.
96. ibid., pp. 153–4.
97. ibid., p. 146.
98. Robert M. Farnsworth, Introduction to *The Marrow of Tradition*, by Charles Chesnutt (Ann Arbor, Mich.: Ann Arbor Paperbacks, 1969).

TEN

From the thirties:
Tillie Olsen and the radical tradition

DEBORAH ROSENFELT

This essay focuses on Tillie Olsen's experience as a woman, a writer and an activist in the Old Left of the 1930s. It grew out of my view of Olsen's life and art as an important link between that earlier radical tradition and contemporary feminist culture. This perspective, of course, is only one lens through which to look at her life and art, magnifying certain details and diminishing others. In dwelling on Olsen's political activities and in placing her work in the context of a socialist-feminist literary tradition, I have, as Olsen herself has pointed out to me, given insufficient weight to two poles of her life and art. On the one hand, there was the dailiness of her life, characterized most of the time less by political activism or participation in the leftist literary milieu than by the day-to-day struggles of a first-generation, working-class mother simply to raise and support a family – the kind of silencing that takes priority in all of her own writings. On the other hand, there was her sense of affinity as an artist with traditions of American and world literature that lie outside the socialist-feminist literary tradition as I have defined it.

The latter point, especially, needs clarification. Obviously, literary traditions are not demarcated by clear boundaries. Some works of literature, by virtue of their art and scope, transcend the immediate filiations of their authors to become part of a 'great tradition' of their own – not in an idealistic sense, but as models which inspire and challenge later writers, regardless of their political commitments. Olsen's work is part of this great tradition, both in its sources and in its craft. Then too, in some eras of intense political activity, such as the 1930s or the 1960s, writers whose essential concerns are not explicitly political or whose work takes other directions when the era has ended may be temporarily drawn into a leftist political milieu. Edna St Vincent Millay, Katherine Anne Porter, Mary McCarthy and Dorothy Parker were among the women writers associated in the 1930s with the left; in our own era, writers like Adrienne Rich and Susan Griffin – close to Olsen both as friends and as artists – initially shared connections and visions with the New Left, subsequently articulating values and world views partly in opposition to it.

Yet the definition of a socialist–feminist tradition is, I think, legitimate and useful, for it does identify writers who, like Olsen, shared a certain kind of consciousness, an engagement with the political issues of their day, and an involvement in a progressive political and cultural movement. It also enables us to examine the connections between the radical cultural traditions of the past and those our own era is creating, questioning that earlier heritage when necessary, but acknowledging also the extent to which we as contemporary feminists are its heirs.[1]

I could not have written this essay without Tillie Olsen's assistance, although its emphasis, its structure, and any errors in fact and interpretation are my responsibility. Over the past two years, Olsen has granted me access to some of her personal papers – journals, letters and unpublished manuscripts. Both she and her husband, Jack Olsen, have been generous in sharing their recollections of life in the 1930s. In Fall 1980, Olsen responded with a detailed critique to an earlier version of this essay.[2] Some of her comments called for a simple correction of factual inaccuracies; some questioned my interpretations of her experience. The essay in its present form incorporated many, although not all, of her suggestions for revision.

This essay, then, is part of an ongoing dialogue about issues that matter very much to both Tillie Olsen and myself: the relationship of writing to political commitment; the 'circumstances' – a favorite Olsen word – of class and sex and their effect on sustained creative activity, literary or political; and the strengths and weaknesses of the radical cultural tradition in this country.

Tillie Olsen's fiction and essays have been widely acknowledged as major contributions to American literature and criticism. Her work has been particularly valued by contemporary feminists, for it has contributed significantly to the task of reclaiming women's achievements and interpreting their lives. In 1961, she published the collection of four stories, *Tell Me a Riddle* (Philadelphia: J.B. Lippincott), each story focusing on the relationships between family members or friends; each revealing the injuries inflicted by poverty, racism and the patriarchal order; each celebrating the endurance of human love and will. In 1974, she published *Yonnondio: From the Thirties* (New York: Delacorte Press/Seymour Lawrence), the first section of a novel about a working-class family, told mostly from the point of view of the daughter, Mazie. Begun in the 1930s, then put away, this novel was finally revised forty years later 'in arduous partnership' with 'that long ago young writer'.[3] In 1978, she published her collected essays in *Silences* (New York: Delacorte Press/

Seymour Lawrence), a sustained prose poem about the silences that befall writers and those who would be writers – especially, although not exclusively, women; especially, although not exclusively, those who must also struggle for sheer survival. In addition to being a gifted writer and critic, Olsen is also a teacher who has helped to democratize the literary canon by calling attention to the works of Third World writers, working-class writers and women.

Olsen's importance to contemporary women who read and write or who write about literature is widely acknowledged. Yet although her work has been vital for feminists today, and although one article does discuss her background in some depth,[4] few of Olsen's contemporary admirers realize the extent to which her consciousness, vision and choice of subject are rooted in an earlier heritage of social struggle – the communist Old Left of the 1930s and the tradition of radical political thought and action, mostly socialist and anarchist, that dominated the left in the second and third decades of the century. Not that we can explain the eloquence of her work in terms of its sociopolitical origins, not even that left-wing politics and culture were the single most important influences on it, but that its informing consciousness, its profound understanding of class and sex and race as shaping influences on people's lives, owes much to that earlier tradition. Olsen's work, in fact, may be seen as part of a literary lineage so far unacknowledged by most contemporary critics: a socialist-feminist literary tradition.

Critics such as Ellen Moers and Elaine Showalter have identified a literary tradition of women writers who read one another's work, corresponded with one another about everything from domestic irritations to the major issues of the day, and looked to one another for strength, encouragement and insight.[5] Literary historians like Walter Rideout and Daniel Aaron have traced the ɔutlines of a radical literary tradition in America, composed of two waves of twentieth-century writers influenced by socialism in the early years, by communism in the thirties, who had in common 'an attempt to express a predominantly Marxist view toward society'.[6] At the intersections of these larger traditions is a line of women writers, asociated with the American left, who unite a class consciousness and a feminist consciousness in their lives and creative work, who are concerned with the material circumstances of people's lives, who articulate the experiences and grievances of women and of other oppressed groups – workers, national minorities, the colonized and the exploited – and who speak out of a defining commitment to social change.

In fiction this tradition extends from turn-of-the-century socialists like Charlotte Perkins Gilman, Vida Scudder and Susan Glaspell, through such thirties Old Left women, as Meridel Le Sueur, Tess Slesinger, Josephine Herbst, Grace Lumpkin and Ruth McKenney, to contemporary writers with early ties to the civil rights and antiwar movements and the New Left: Marge Piercy, Grace Paley, Alice Walker and others. Although the specific political affiliations of these writers have varied from era to era and from individual to individual, the questions they raise have been surprisingly consistent. These range from basic questions about how to survive economically to more complex ones, such as how to understand the connections and contradictions between women's struggles and those struggles based on other categories and issues, or how to find a measure of emotional and sexual fulfillment in a world where egalitarian relationships are more ideal than real. Sometimes, as in Gilman's *Herland*, published serially in *The Forerunner*, or Piercy's *Woman on the Edge of Time*, these writers try to imagine socialist-feminist utopias. More often, as with the women writers associated with the left, especially the Communist Party, in the 1930s, their work constitutes a sharp critique of the present. Sometimes, as in Agnes Smedley's *Daughter of Earth*, Slesinger's *The Unpossessed*, Piercy's *Small Changes*, much of Alice Walker's fiction and, implicitly, Olsen's *Tell Me a Riddle*, that critique includes a sharp look from a woman's point of view at the sexual politics of daily life in the political milieus with which these authors were associated.

Olsen's relationship to her political milieu in the 1930s most concerns me here, for this paper is not so much a literary analysis of Olsen's work as it is a study of her experience in the left in the years when she first began to write for publication. I will first give a brief overview of Olsen's background and life in those years, focusing on the roots of both her political commitment and her creative work, and then identify a series of central contradictions inherent in her experience. In thus imposing a paradigmatic order on Olsen's individual experience, I have tried, not always successfully, to maintain a balance between fidelity to the idiosyncrasies of the individual life and the identification of patterns applicable to the experience of other women artists in leftist movements then and now.

Tillie Olsen's parents, Samuel and Ida Lerner, were involved in the 1905 revolution in Russia, fleeing to the United States when it failed and settling in Nebraska. Her father, in addition to working at a variety of jobs, including farming, paperhanging and packing house work, became state secretary of the Nebraska Socialist Party, running in the mid-twenties as the socialist candidate for the state representative from his district. Tillie Lerner, second oldest of six children in this depression-poor family, dropped out of high-school in Omaha after the eleventh grade to go to work – although, as she is careful to remind people who today take their degrees for granted, this means that she went further in school than most of the women of her generation. Given the radical political climate of her home, it is not surprising that she too would have become active, first writing skits and musicals for the Young People's Socialist League, and subsequently, at 17, joining the Young Communist League (YCL), the youth organization of the Communist Party. During most of her mid- and late teens, she worked at a variety of jobs, took increasing responsibility as a political organizer, and continued to lead an ardent inner literary and intellectual life, in spite of the interruption of her formal schooling. In the draft of a letter to Philip Rahv, editor of the *Partisan Review*, apparently in response to his request for biographical information, she later drew a swift self-portrait:

> Father state secretary Socialist party for years.
> Education, old revolutionary pamphlets, laying around house (including liberators), and YCL.
> Jailbird – 'violating handbill ordinance' [a reference to her arrest and imprisonment in the Argentine Jail in Kansas City for her work in organizing a strike in the packing houses].
> Occupations: Tie presser, hack writer ... model, housemaid, ice-cream packer, book clerk.

To this catalogue of occupations she might have added packing house work, waitressing and working as a punch-press operator.

Although essentially accurate, this self-portrait does reflect some irony, some self-consciousness in the delineation of the pure working-class artist educated only in revolutionary literature and the 'school of life'. In fact, even as a young woman, Olsen was an eager reader, regularly visiting the public library and second-hand bookstores in Omaha. She recalls today that she was determined to read everything in the fiction category in the library, making it almost through the M's. She also borrowed books from the socialist doctor who took care of the family and from the Radcliffe graduate for whom she worked for several months as a mother's helper. Olsen's earliest journal, written when she was 16, in addition to recording the more predictable emotions, events and relationships of adolescence, shows a familiarity with an extraordinary variety of literature – popular fiction, the nineteenth-century romantics, contemporary poets ranging from Carl Sandbert to Edna St Vincent Millay. Although remarkably eclectic, her reading was predisposed toward what she calls 'the larger tradition of social concern' – American populists like Walt Whitman; European social critics like Ibsen, Hugo, the early Lawrence and especially Katherine Mansfield; black writers like W.E.B. DuBois and Langston Hughes; American women realists like Elizabeth Madox Roberts, Willa Cather and Ellen Glasgow; as well as leftists like Upton Sinclair, John Dos Passos, Mike Gold, Guy Endore; and socialist-feminists like Olive Schreiner, whose *Story of An African Farm* she refers to in the journal as 'incredibly *my* book', and Agnes Smedley, whose *Daughter of Earth* she would later bring to the attention of the Feminist Press and a new generation of readers.

As she explains in her notes to the Feminist Press edition of Rebecca Harding Davis's *Life in the Iron Mills* (1972), she first read that work in a volume of bound *Atlantic Monthly*'s bought in an Omaha junkshop when she was 15. Davis's work, she writes, on pages 157 and 158, said to her: 'Literature can be made out of the lives of despised people', and 'You, too, must write.' Olsen's journals indicate that from a very early age, perhaps even before she read *Life in the Iron Mills*, she consciously and carefully apprenticed herself to the craft of writing. Her early journal is filled with resolutions for a future as a writer, expressions of despair at her own inarticulateness, and frequent humorous deprecations of her own attempts at poetic prose: 'Phooey – I was just being literary.'

Several passages show her grappling too with the critical and social issues raised by the journals of the left:

> I read the *Modern Quarterly* today, and all the while I was thinking – Christ, how ignorant, how stupid I am.
> Paragraphs I had to read over, names as unknown to me as Uranus to man; ideas that were untrodden, undiscovered roads to me; words that might have been Hindu, so unintelligible they seemed. ... But there was an article substantiating my what I thought insane conclusions about the future of art.

She does not elaborate on her 'insane conclusions' but the *Modern Quarterly* at the time was a nonsectarian Marxist journal, with a manifesto that, in Daniel Aaron's words, 'denied the distinction between intellectual and worker and between pure art and propaganda and committed the magazine to Socialism'. Its editor, V.G. Calverton, boasted that he printed 'almost every left wing liberal and radical who had artistic aspirations';[7] the several references to the magazine scattered through Olsen's journal indicate that she was a regular reader, as she had been even earlier of *The Liberator*, the eclectically socialist journal of art and politics edited by Max Eastman. In another passage, the 16-year-old Olsen urges herself to take a stand on an almost comical array of global issues – issues, however that would continue to occupy her throughout her life:

> Have been reading Nietzsche & *Modern Quarterly*. I must write out, clearly and concisely, my ideas on things. I vacillate so easily. And I am so-so sloppy in my mental thinking. What are my *true* opinions, for instance, on socialism, what life should be, the future of literature, true art, the relation between the sexes, where are we going. ... Yes, I must write it out, simply so I will *know*, not flounder around like a flying fish, neither in air or in water
> Later: That's quite simple to say, but there are so few things one can be sure and definite about – so often I am pulled both ways – & I can't have a single clear cut opinion. There are so few things I have deep, unalterable convictions about.

The clear opinions and deep convictions would come a year later through her disciplined work and study in the Young Communist League. Her own writings before that time – some stories and many poems – are not on the whole political. The poems I examined, some interspersed in her journals, some typed drafts, tend to be romantic, lyrical, full of the pain of lost or unrequited love, the anguish of loneliness and the mysteries of nature, especially the winds and snows of the Nebraska winters. Several express deep love and affection for a female friend, and one describes a bond with her younger sister. Olsen says that there were other poems, now lost, on political themes like the execution of Sacco and Vanzetti in 1927. Mostly, though, these early poems are the effusions of an intense, imaginative young woman as influenced by the romantic traditions of nineteenth-century poetry and its twentieth-century practitioners like Millay as by the 'larger tradition of social concern'.

Olsen's decision to join the YCL in 1931 was a turning point; for the next year and a half she dedicated much of her energy to political work. She was sent from Omaha to Kansas City, where she attended the party school for several weeks, formed close ties to political comrades like the working-class women Fern Pierce and 'Red' Allen, whom she helped to support by working in a tie factory, and became involved in an unhappy relationship with a party organizer. It was during this time that she was sent to the Argentine Jail for passing out leaflets to packing-house workers. She was already sick at the time, having contracted pleurisy from working in front of an open window at the tie factory with a steam radiator in front of it; in jail, she became extremely ill and in 1932 was sent back to Omaha.

During this time, her poems begin to acquire different subjects, a different quality. They still focus on personal experience and emotion, including the anguish of an abortion or miscarriage and the bitterness of misplaced or betrayed love. But now she sometimes interweaves political metaphors to express emotional states. One such poem begins with the speaker sitting 'hunched by the window, watching the snow trail down without lightness'. The poem goes on:

> The branches of trees writhe like wounded animals,
> like small frightened bears the buds curve their backs to
>   the white onslaught,
> and I think of what a Wobbly told me of his third degree,
> no violent tortures, but exquisitely, civilized,
> a gloved palm lightly striking his cheek,
> in a few minutes it was a hammer of wind pounding nails of
>   hail,
> in fifteen a sledge, in twenty, mountains rearing against
>   his cheek. ...
> Somehow, seeing the constant minute blows of the snow
>   on the branches,

and their shudder, this story falters into my mind,
with some deeper, untranslatable meaning behind it,
something I can not learn.

The untranslatable meaning finally has something to do with the

wisdom
of covering the dead, the decaying,
the swell and stir of the past, the leaves of old hope,
    with inexorable snow,
Of stripping bare and essential the illusions of leaves,
leaves that were moved by any wind.

This poem uses the landscape in a traditional way as a mirror for the speaker's state of mind, bleak but resolute, from which she can draw a lesson for living, but it complicates the natural imagery by attributing to a snowfall the implacable, impersonal characteristics of the professional interrogator – an analogy accessible only to someone with a certain kind of political experience and sympathy. The analogy doesn't quite work, because ultimately the inexorable snow has something redeeming in it, as the political interrogation does not; yet the parallel between the speaker and the Wobbly, both of whom must remain firm under onslaught, gives the poem a social as well as a natural dimension and suggests that its writer was struggling for both personal and political reasons to discipline the chaos of her emotions.

During this period of intense political organizing, Olsen began to have the 'deep, unalterable convictions' she had earlier wished for, and she took herself to task for the relative absence of a political dimension in most of her earlier work:

> The rich things I could have said are unsaid, what I did write anyone could have written. There is no Great God Dough, terrible and harassing, in my poems, nothing of the common hysteria of 300 girls every 4:30 in the factory, none of the bitter humiliation of scorching a tie; the fear of being late, of ironing a wrinkle in, the nightmare of the kids at home to be fed and clothed, the rebelliousness, the tiptoe expectation and searching, the bodily nausea and weariness ... yet this was my youth.[8]

Late in 1932, Olsen moved to Faribault, Minnesota, a period of retreat from political and survival work to allow her recovery time from the illness that by now had become incipient tuberculosis. It was there at 19 that she began to write *Yonnondio*, the novel that for the first time would give full expression to 'the rich things' in her own and her family's experience. She became pregnant in the same month that she started writing, and bore a daughter before her 20th birthday. In 1933, she moved to California, continuing her connection with the YCL in Stockton, Los Angeles and San Francisco. She also continued to write – poems and reportage and more of the novel that would become *Yonnondio*. In 1936 she began to live with her comrade in the YCL, Jack Olsen, whom she eventually married; in the years that followed, she bore three more daughters and worked at a variety of jobs to help support them. Gradually she stopped writing fiction, concentrating on raising the children and working, but remained an activist into the 1940s, organizing work related to war relief for the Congress of Industrial Organizations (CIO), serving as president of the California CIO's Women's Auxiliary, writing a column for *People's World*, and working in nonleftist and nonunion organizations related to childcare and education, including the Parent-Teacher Association. During the late 1940s and 1950s, she and her family endured the soul-destroying harassment typically directed at leftists and thousands of suspected leftists during that period. It was not until the mid-1950s that Olsen began writing again, her style less polemic, more controlled, her vision deepened by the years, her consciousness still profoundly political. In the years that followed, she produced the works which most of us know her for today: the stories in *Tell Me a Riddle; Yonnondio*, finally published in 1974, polished and organized, but not substantially rewritten; and the essays gathered and expanded in *Silences*.

As Elinor Langer has remarked, when Olsen began to write again in the 1950s, it was not as a woman who had lived her life as an artist but as an artist who had lived her life as a woman.[9] Yet in those turbulent years of the early to mid-1930s, Olsen lived fully as artist, as activist, as worker and as woman/wife/mother, though often suffering from the conflicting demands, always having to give primacy to one part of her being at the expense of another.[10] In examining the political contexts of Olsen's life in the left in the 1930s, I will consider the ways her participation both limited and nurtured her as a woman and an artist. I will focus on three basic contradictions confronting her as an activist, a writer and a woman in the left in those years.

First, the left required great commitments of time and energy for political work, on the whole valuing action over thought, deed over word; yet it also validated the study and production of literature and art, providing a first exposure to literature for many working-class people, fostering an appreciation of a wide range of socially conscious literature, and offering important outlets for publication and literary exchange. Second, although much left-wing criticism, especially by Communist Party writers, was narrowly prescriptive about the kind of literature contemporary writers should be producing, it also inspired – along with the times themselves – a social consciousness in writers that deepened their art. Third, for a woman in the 1930s, the left was a profoundly masculinist world in many of its human relationships, in the orientation of its literature, and even in the language used to articulate its cultural criticism; simultaneously, the left gave serious attention to women's issues, valued women's contributions to public as well as to private life, and generated an important body of theory on the woman question.

The first contradiction, of course, affected both male and female writer-activists on the left. Then as now, the central problem for an activist trying to be a writer was simply finding the time to write. In the section of *Silences* called 'Silences – its varieties', Olsen has a brief entry on page 9 labeled 'Involvement' under the larger heading, 'Political silences': 'When political involvement takes priority, though the need and love for writing go on. Every freedom movement has, and has had, its roll of writers participating at the price of their writing.' Olsen has spoken little of these silences compared with the fullness of her analysis of other kinds of silences – not those freely chosen, but those imposed by the burdens of poverty, racial discrimination, female roles. Partly this disproportion exists because, in her own life, and the lives of so many others, the compelling necessity to work for pay – the circumstance of class – and the all-consuming responsibilities of homemaking and motherhood – the circumstance of gender – clearly *have* been the major silencers, and if I do not speak of them at length here, it is because Olsen herself has done so, fully and eloquently. Partly also, I suspect, she has not wanted to be misread as encouraging a withdrawal from political activism for the sake of 'art' or self-fulfillment. Yet this little passage could well allude to her own dilemma in the 1930s.

The dilemma, as she points out now, was sharper for her as a working-class woman and a grassroots activist involved in daily workplace struggles than for those professionals who were already recognized as writers, who participated in the movement primarily by writing, and whose activity as writers was sometimes even supported by federally funded projects like the Works Projects Administration. Except for the interlude in 1932 in Faribault and another withdrawal from political activity in Los Angeles in 1935, another 'good writing year', Olsen's political work came first throughout the early and mid-1930s – along with the burdens of survival work and, increasingly, domestic work; and it required the expenditure of time and energy such work always demands. As a member of the YCL in the Midwest, she wrote and distributed leaflets in the packing houses, helped organize demonstrations, walked in picket lines, attended classes and meetings, and wrote and directed political plays and skits. In high school, she had written a prize-winning humor column called 'Squeaks'; in the YCL, she recalls, she was able to use her particular kind of humor and punning to great effect with the live audiences who came to the league's performances.

The nature of Olsen's commitment in the early 1930s emerges with particular clarity in a letter she received from a fellow YCL organizer and close friend, as she recuperated from her illness in Omaha, ostensibly on leave for two months from league duties. The letter praises her growth as an organizer, but reprimands her for being 'too introspective'. It is full of friendly advice and firm pressure:

> Read. Read things that will be of some help to you. The Daily Worker every day ... the Young Worker. All the new pamphlets ... and really constructive books. ... You'll have time to now, and you've got to write skits and plays for the League. This you can do for the League, and it will be a great help ... have only one thing in mind – recovery, and work in the League, and if you pull thru, and are working in the League again in a few months, I will say that as a Communist you have had your test.

The letter concludes by asking her how the play is coming along, and urging her to rush it as soon as possible, then adds a postscript: 'How about a song for the song-writing contest?'

Reflecting on this letter in her journal, Olsen attributes to its author 'full understanding of what it means to me to leave now'. She goes on to condemn herself for 'the paths I have worn of inefficiency, procrastination, idle planning, lack of perseverance', adding, 'Only in my League work did these disappear, I have that to thank for my reconditioning.' She expresses her wish to write in a more disciplined way, but adds: 'I must abolish word victories ... let me feel nothing till I have had action – without action feeling and thought are disease.' The point is not, then, that insensitive and rigid communist bureaucrats imposed unreasonable demands on party members, but rather that rank-and-file communists made these demands on themselves, because they believed so deeply in the liberating possibilities of socialism; the necessity for disciplined, organized action; and the reality of the revolutionary process, in which their participation was essential. The times themselves instilled a sense of urgency and possibility: a depression at home, with all its concomitant anguishes of hunger, poverty, unemployment; the rise of fascism in Europe with its threat of world war; the example of a successful revolution in the Soviet Union and the feeling of connection with the revolutionary movements there and in other countries, such as China. Like many progressive people, Olsen felt herself to be part of a valid, necessary and global movement to remake the world on a more just and humane model. If the left in those years, especially the circles in which Olsen moved, tended to value action over thought, deed over word, there were good reasons.

Olsen's comments today about the author of this letter and her other Movement friends suggest both the depth of her commitment to them and the feelings of difference she sometimes experienced as an aspiring writer. What becomes clear in her comments is that, for her, political work with such women was a matter of class loyalty. She could not, then or later, leave the 'ordinary' people, to lead a 'literary' life.

They were my dearest friends, but how could they know what so much of my writing self was about? They thought of writing in the terms in which they knew it. They had become readers, like so many working class kids in the movement, but there was so much that fed me as far as my medium was concerned that was closed to them. They read the way women read today coming into the women's movement who don't have literary background – reading for what it says about their lives, or what it doesn't say. And they loved certain writings because of truths, understandings, affirmations, that they found in them. ... It was not a time that my writing self could be first. ... We believed that we were going to change the world, and it looked as if it was possible. It was just after Hindenberg turned over power to Hitler – and the enormity of the struggle demanded to stop what might result from that was just beginning to be evident. ... And I did so love my comrades. They were all blossoming so. These were the same kind of people I'd gone to school with, who had quit, as was common in my generation, around the eighth grade ... whose development had seemed stopped, though I had known such inherent capacity in them. Now I was seeing that evidence, verification of what was latent in the working class. It's hard to leave something like that.

For Olsen, then, the relationship between the intellectual and the working class was far more than an academic question, for she herself belonged to one world by birth and commitment and was drawn to the other by her gift and love for language and literature. Both the 'intellectual' activities of reading and writing and the struggles of working people to improve the quality of their lives were essential to her. The problem was how to combine them. 'These next months,' she wrote in her Faribault journal, at last with some free time before her,

I shall only care about my sick body – to be a good Bolshevik I need health first. Let my mind stagnate further, let my heart swell with neurotic emotions that lie clawing inside like a splinter – afterwards, the movement will clean that out. First, a strong body ... I don't know what it is in me, but I must write too. It is like creating white hot irons in me & then pulling them out ... so slowly, oh so slowly.

In beginning to write *Yonnondio*, Olsen hoped to link her writing and her political commitment. But the chaotic years that followed – the moving back and forth, the caring and working for her family, and the political tasks – gave her little opportunity for sustained literary work. Her most intense political involvement during these years centered on the San Francisco Maritime strike of 1934, which spread from San Francisco up and down the Western Seaboard to become the first important general strike of the era. She helped put out the Longshoremen's publication, the *Waterfront Worker*, did errands and relief work, and got arrested for 'vagrancy' while visiting the apartment of some of the YCL members involved in the strike, going to jail for the second time.

Passages from her journal in these years include frustration at the amount of time required for housework and political work, agonized self-criticisms at not being able to write regularly in a more disciplined way, sometimes anger at the necessity to write specifically pieces on demand, often guilt because no matter what the choice of labor, something is always left undone: 'Struggled all day on the Labor Defender article. Tore it up in disgust. It is the end for me of things like that to write – I can't do it – it kills me. ... Why should I loathe myself – why the guilt.'

All the writing that Olsen did publish in the 1930s came out in 1934. That year two poems were published in the *Daily Worker* and reprinted in *The Partisan*. One was based on a letter in the *New Masses* by a Mexican-American woman from Texas, detailing the horrors of work in the garment industry sweatshops of the south-west, and the other celebrated the spirit of the Austrian socialists killed by the Dollfuss government.[11] 'The iron throat', the first chapter of *Yonnondio*, was published the same year in the *Partisan Review*,[12] as were 'The strike' and 'Thousand-dollar vagrant', two essays based on her involvement in the San Francisco dock strike.[13] In 'The strike', one of the best pieces of reportage in an era noted for excellence in that genre, the conflict between her writer self and her activist self emerges strongly, here transformed into rhetorical strategy. The essay, in the published version, begins:

> Do not ask me to write of the strike and the terror. I am not on a battlefield, and the increasing stench and smoke sting the eyes so it is impossible to turn them back into the past. You leave me only this night to drop the bloody garment of Todays, to cleave through the gigantic events that have crashed one upon the other, to the first beginning. If I could go away for a while, if there were time and quiet, perhaps I could do it. All that has happened might resolve into order and sequence, fall into neat patterns of words. I could stumble back into the past and slowly, painfully rear the structure in all its towering magnificence, so that the beauty and heroism, the terror and significance of those days, would enter your heart and sear it forever with the vision.[14]

Towards the end of the essay, the writer explains that she was not on the literal battlefield herself, but in headquarters, typing, 'making a metallic little pattern of sound in the air, because that is all I can do, because that is all I am supposed to do'. The conclusion is another apology for her incapacity to do justice to the magnitude of the strike:

> Forgive me that the words are feverish and blurred. You see, if I had time I could go away. But I write this on a battlefield. The rest, the General Strike,

the terror, arrests and jail, the songs in the night, must be written some other time, must be written later. . . . But there is so much happening now.[15]

The conflict here is partly between her role as a writer, in this case a reporter doing her job, and her guilt at not being on the real battlefield herself – between the word and the deed. But more important is the conflict between two kinds of writing: the quick, fervent, impressionistic report from the arena of struggle, and the leisured, carefully structured and sustained rendering of the 'beauty and heroism, the terror and significance' of those days – a rendering that, ironically, would require for its full development a withdrawal from the struggle.

For a committed leftist in the 1930s, political action, with all its demands on time and energy, had to take priority over intellectual work, yet the atmosphere on the left did value and nurture literature in a variety of ways. Olsen would have been a reader in any case, but her friends in the YCL in Kansas City were among the many working-class people inspired by the movement to read broadly for the first time. And Olsen's own reading, eclectic though it was, was to some extent guided, extended and informed by left-wing intellectual mentors such as the critics of *The Liberator*, the *New Masses* and the *Modern Quarterly*. She recalls today that the left

> was enriching in the sense that . . . in the movement people were reading like mad. There was as in any movement a looking for your ancestors, your predecessors. . . .
>
> There was a burst of black writers . . . I knew about W.E.B. DuBois before, but because the movement was so conscious of race, of color, we were reading all the black writers, books like Arna Bontemps' *Black Thunder*, Langston Hughes. We read Ting Ling, we read Lu Hsun, we read the literature of protest that was beginning to be written in English out of South Africa; we read B. Traven; writers from every country. The thirties was a rich, an international period. . . . And from whatever country or color this was considered to be part of our literature.

Being part of the left milieu, then, gave Olsen, a working-class woman from Omaha, a sense of belonging to an international intellectual as well as political community.

The literary establishment of the left was receptive to and supportive of the efforts of new, young writers like Olsen. The Communist Party sponsored the development of cultural associations called the John Reed Clubs, established specifically to encourage young, unknown writers and artists.[16] And there were outlets for publication like the *New Masses* and the various organs of the local John Reed Clubs, including the *Partisan Review* in New York and *The Partisan* in San Francisco, in both of which Olsen published. Her work was well received and much admired. Joseph North, a respected left critic, compared her ability to portray working-class life in 'The iron throat' favorably to

Tess Slesinger's rendering of the East Coast intelligentsia in her first novel, *The Unpossessed* (1934).[17] Robert Cantwell praised 'The iron throat' in the *New Republic* as 'a work of early genius'.[18] A number of editors and publishers sought her out after its publication, and eventually she made arrangements with Bennett Cerf at Random House for the publication of *Yonnondio* on its completion, although at the time she could not be reached because she was in jail for her participation in the dock strike, becoming something of a *cause célèbre*. In New York, Heywood Broun chaired a protest meeting over her arrest, irritating her, and her jailed comrades who had not published anything and were therefore not getting all this national attention.

After her release from jail, she visited Lincoln Steffens and Ella Winter, who had invited her to their home in Carmel, California. This was her first experience, she recalls now, with that kind of urbane, sophisticated literary atmosphere. Steffens encouraged her to write the other essay associated with the strike, 'Thousand-dollar vagrant', which describes her arrest in deliberately tough, colloquial language. The following year, she was invited to attend the American Writers Congress in New York, where she marched in a parade side by side with critics Mike Gold and James Farrell, novelists Nelson Algren and Richard Wright, and playwright Albert Bine, and where she was one of a very few women to address the assembly, which included most of the major writers of the day.[19] A drawing of her, a cartooned profile of a lean, intense young woman, was one of a very few portraits of American women writers to appear among the myriad renderings of male literary personages in the 7 May 1935 issue of *New Masses* that reported on the congress.[20]

Clearly, though Olsen's involvement in the left as an activist, coupled with the other demands on her worker-mother life, took time, energy and commitment that might in another milieu and another era have gone into her writing, and although her closest friends in the Midwestern movement did not always understand her literary aspirations, the atmosphere of the left as a whole did encourage her. The left provided networks and organs for intellectual and literary exchange, gave her a sense of being part of an international community of writers and activists engaged in the same revolutionary endeavor, and recognized and valued her talent.

The second contradiction I will consider is closely related to the first and third; in using it as a bridge between them, I will turn first to the way in which left critical theory validated and supported Olsen's subject and vision before suggesting how some of its tenets ran counter to and perhaps impeded the development of her particular artistic gift.

Literary criticism flourished on the left in the 1930s, and writers like Mike Gold, editor of the *New Masses* and one of the most influential of Communist Party critics, and James Farrell, a leading critic and writer for the increasingly independent *Partisan Review*, hotly debated such issues as the role of the artist in revolutionary struggle, the applications of Marxist thought to American literature, and the proper nature and functions of literature in a revolutionary movement.[21] As Olsen's early journals indicate, she followed such discussions with intense interest. There was much in the spirit even of the more dogmatic, Party-oriented criticism to encourage her own writing.

Left critical theory accorded an honored place to the committed writer, the writer capable of expressing the struggles and aspirations of working-class people or of recording the decline of capitalism. Critical debates often centered on the best literary modes for accomplishing this purpose. The dominant critical theory on the Communist left in the early 1930s was proletarian realism, a theory which even nonsectarian leftists eventually viewed as far too limited. Nevertheless, its basic premise – that fiction should show the sufferings and struggles and essential dignity of working-class people under capitalism and allow readers to see the details of their lives and work – encouraged young working-class writers like Olsen to write of their own experiences and confirmed her early perception that art can be based on the lives of 'despised people'. This theory told writers that their own writing could and should be a form of action in itself; art was to be a weapon in the class struggle.[22]

All of Olsen's published writing during the early 1930s is consistent with this view of the functions of literature. Her developing craft now had an explicitly political content which grew out of her own experience and was confirmed by major voices in the left literary milieu. All of it expresses outrage at the exploitation of the working class and a fierce faith in the transformative power of the coming revolution. One need only compare the poem, 'I want you women up north to know',[23] with the passage from her poetry cited earlier to see that the growing clarity of her literary and political convictions gave her work a scope and an assuredness that it had lacked earlier.

This poem juxtaposes the desperate situation of Mexican-American women workers and the families they struggle unsuccessfully to support with that of the 'women up north' who consume the products of their labor. As Selma Burkom and Margaret Williams have noted, the poem faithfully constructs the details of their daily lives while its central metaphor 'transforms the women themselves ... into the clothing they embroider – *they* become the product of their labor'.[24] The poem is artful as well as polemical; its free-verse form is deliberately experimental, its subtler ironies woven into the fabric of diction and metaphor, its structure tight, its portraits clearly individuated. On one level, it is metapoetry, that is, poetry *about* art, for it specifically contrasts its own purpose and vision – to document the realities of these women's lives and to offer a Marxist interpretation of the causes of and solutions to their suffering – with the consciousness of the bourgeois poet who would find in the movement of their hands *only* a source of aesthetic pleasure.

On the other hand, the polemicism of the poem, especially the didactic interpolations of the speaker, represented a kind of writing that Olsen herself gradually rejected. The same issues arise in her work on *Yonnondio*, her most important literary effort during the 1930s. In the rest of this paper I will focus on that novel, for its evolution reveals with special clarity the contradictory nature of Olsen's experience in the left.

Olsen's earliest journals, before she joined the YCL, speak of her wish to write about her family and people like them. After her year and a half of intense involvement, she begins to do so in a serious, disciplined way, writing in her Faribault journal as she works on the early chapters: 'O Mazie & Will & Ben. At last I write out all that has festered in me so long – the horror of being a working-class child – & the heroism, all the respect they deserve.' Familiarity with the political and critical theory of the left combined with and applied to her own experience gave her the coherent world view, the depth of consciousness and the faith in her working-class subject essential to a sustained work of fiction.

Set in the 1920s, the novel's lyrical prose traces the Holbrook family's desperate struggle for survival over a two-and-a-half-year period, first in a Wyoming mining town, then on a farm in the Dakotas, finally in a Midwest city – Omaha, perhaps – reeking with the smell of the slaughterhouses. In *Yonnondio*, as in Olsen's later work, the most powerful theme is the tension between human capacity and creativity – the drive to know, to assert, to create, which Olsen sees as innate in human life – and the social forces and institutions that repress and distort that capacity. Olsen's understanding of those social forces and institutions clearly owes a great deal to her tutelage in the left. The struggles of her central characters dramatize the ravages of capitalism on the lives of working people – miners, small farmers, packinghouse workers and their families – who barely make enough to survive no matter how hard they work, and who have not yet learned to seek control over the conditions of their workplaces or the quality of their lives.

Unfortunately for all of us, she never finished the novel. Its title, taken from the title of a Whitman poem, is a Native American word meaning 'lament for the lost'; it is an elegy, I think, not only for the Holbrooks, but also for Olsen's own words lost between the mid-1930s and late 1950s, for the incompleteness of the novel itself. The demands on Olsen already discussed would have been reason enough for her not having completed the novel in those hectic years; what she wrote, after all, she wrote before she was 25, in the interstices of her activist-worker-mother life. Yet I suspect that she was wrestling with at least one other problem that made completion difficult. For although Olsen's immersion in the theory and political practice of the Marxist left and her exposure to its literature and criticism gave her a sense of the importance of her subject and strengthened the novel's social analysis, the dominant tenets of proletarian realism also required a structure, scope, resolution and political explicitness in some ways at odds with the particular nature of her developing craft.

What we have today is only the beginning of the novel that was to have been. In Olsen's initial plan, Jim Holbrook was to have become involved in a strike in the packing houses, a strike that would draw out the inner strength and courage of his wife Anna, politicize the older children as well, and involve some of the women in the packing plant as strike leaders in this essential collective action. Embittered by the length of the strike and its lack of clear initial success, humiliated by his inability to support his family, Jim Holbrook was finally to have abandoned them. Anna was to die trying to give herself an abortion. Will and Mazie were to go West to the Imperial Valley in California, where they would themselves become organizers. Mazie was to grow up to become an artist, a writer who could tell the experiences of her people, her mother especially living in her memory. In Mazie's achievement, political consciousness and personal creativity were to coalesce.

The original design for the novel would have incorporated most of the major themes of radical fiction at that time. Walter Rideout's study, *The Radical Novel in the United States, 1900–1954*, classifies proletarian novels of the 1930s into four types: the strike novel, the novel of conversion to communism, the bottom dog novel and the novel documenting the decay of the middle class. He also mentions certain typical subthemes: antisemitism, black–white relationships, episodes in American history and the life of the communist organizer.[25] *Yonnondio* would have been both a strike novel and a novel of political conversion, and it would have touched on relationships between whites and people of color and on the life of the communist organizer. It would have fulfilled also a major tenet of proletarian realism – that proletarian fiction should demonstrate revolutionary optimism, including elements predicting the inevitable fall of capitalism and the rise of the working class to power.

Proletarian fiction, in other words, was supposed to show not only the sufferings of working-class people, but also their triumphs. When Meridel Le Sueur, for example, published an account of the helpless sufferings of poor women in 1932, she was attacked by Whittaker Chambers in the *New Masses*, in a note appended to Le Sueur's article, for her 'defeatist attitude' and 'non-revolutionary spirit'.[26] 'There *is* horror and drabness in the Worker's life, and we will portray it,' wrote Mike Gold in the *New Masses* in 1930, in an article defining proletarian realism, 'but we know this is not the last word; we know ... that not pessimism, but revolutionary elan will sweep this mess out of the world forever.'[27]

Olsen, too, wanted to incorporate this optimism; indeed, it was central to her initial conception of the novel. She writes in her journal when she was beginning *Yonnondio*:

Characters. Wonderful characters. Hard, bitter, & strong. O communism –
how you come to those of whom I will write is more incredible beautiful
than manna. You wipe the sweat from us, you fill our bellies, you let us walk
and think like humans.

She immediately cautions herself, 'Not to be so rhetorical or figurative or
whatever it is' – a struggle against didactic rhetoric that would characterize her
work on the novel itself. Olsen maintained throughout her work on *Yonnondio*
in the 1930s her commitment to show the transformative power of communism – her commitment, that is, to 'revolutionary optimism', but as her
craft developed she felt less and less satisfied with *telling* about the coming
revolution – and more and more concerned with *showing* how people come to
class consciousness in 'an earned way, a bone way'. She gradually rejected the
political explicitness that alone was enough to win praise for literary work in
the more sectarian left criticism, but she had a hard time incorporating the
essential vision of systematic social change in other ways.

The 'revolutionary elan' in the opening chapters of *Yonnondio* still partakes
of the didacticism she ultimately rejected. It comes less through the events or
characterizations than from the voice of the omniscient narrator, who in the
first five chapters provides both political analysis and revolutionary prophecy.
In the first chapter, this voice comments on the life of 13-year-old Andy
Kvaternick, on his first day in the mines:

Breathe and lift your face to the night, Andy Kvaternick. Trying so vainly
... to purge your bosom of the coal dust. Your father had dreams. You too,
like all boys, had dreams – vague dreams of freedom and light. ... The
earth will take those too. ...

Someday the bowels will grow monstrous and swollen with these old
tired dreams, swell and break, and strong fists batter the fat bellies, and
skeletons of starved children batter them. (14)

In the second chapter, the voice becomes ironic as it comments on a scene
where women wait at the mouth of a mine for word of their men after an
accident. Like 'I want the women up north to know', this passage attacks the
modernist aesthetic, which elevates a concern for form over a concern for
subject, yet it also argues that Olsen's subject itself is worthy of the transformations of enduring art.

And could you not make a cameo of this and pin it onto your aesthetic
hearts? So sharp it is, so clear, so classic. The shattered dusk, the mountain
of culm, the tipple; clean line, bare beauty. ...

Surely it is classical enough for you – the Greek marble of the women,
the simple flowing lines of sorrow, carved so rigid and eternal. (30)

And the voice goes on to prophesy revolution against the companies and the system they represent: 'Please issue a statement: quick, or they start to batter through with the fists of strike, with the pickax of revolution' (31).

In chapter 5, we hear the voice of the revolutionary prophet twice. The first passage comments on the life of young Jim Tracy, Jim Holbrooks's codigger in a sewer, who quits when the contractor insists that two men must do the amount of digging previously done by several. Here, the voice is at first scathingly satiric, pointing out how Tracy will be victimized by his own naive belief in the shibboleths of American culture – 'the bull about freedom of opportunity', and predicting Tracy's inevitable descent into the hell of unemployment, hunger, cold, vagrancy, prison, death; damned forever for his apostasy to 'God Job'. The passage concludes with an apology to Jim, in which the narrator speaks with the collective 'we' of the revolutionists:

> I'm sorry, Jim Tracy, sorry as hell we weren't stronger and could get to you in time and show you that kind of individual revolt was no good, kid, no good at all, you had to bide your time and take it till there were enough of you to fight it all together on the job, and bide your time, and take it till the day millions of fists clamped in yours, and you could wipe out the whole thing, and a human could be a human for the first time on earth. (79)

This is the voice that concludes the chapter, too, as Jim Holbrook sits in the kitchen holding his daughter Mazie after Anna has had a miscarriage, bitterly condemning himself for not seeing her illness, bitterly aware that he has no access to the food and medicine and care the doctor has prescribed for Anna and Baby Bess:

> No, he could speak no more. And as he sat there in the kitchen with Mazie against his heart ... the things in his mind so vast and formless, so terrible and bitter, cannot be spoken, will never be spoken – till the day that hands will find a way to speak this: hands. (95)

In these interpolations, Olsen was deliberately experimenting with the form of the novel, not unlike Dos Passos, whom she had earlier read. Rachel Blau DuPlessis suggests that Olsen has appropriated certain modernist techniques here to turn dialectically against modernism.[28] On the other hand, the prophetic irony of these passages, the imagery of hands and fists uniting in revolution, characterize much of the writing of the leftists during this period; this is the tone and imagery that appear at the conclusion of Olsen's two published poems and that predominate in 'The strike'. In any case, these passages add a dimension of 'revolutionary elan' not present in the early events of the novel itself. The narrator sees more, knows more, than the characters, about the causes of and remedies for their suffering, and the voice is the device used to incorporate that knowledge into the novel.

Olsen's correspondence indicates that she was aware of a disjunction between that voice and the increasingly more lyric, less didactic tone and texture of the whole. In March 1935, John Strachey, whom she had met in Carmel and to whom she had sent the first three chapters of *Yonnondio* for evaluation and advice, wrote to her in Venice, California: 'As to advice, personally I like both your styles of writing, and I am in favor of having the interpolations in the book.' Their agit-prop quality was increasingly at odds with the direction in which Olsen's art was growing. It was developing gradually away from the didacticism that made the incorporation of 'revolutionary elan' relatively easy and toward a more lyrical, less explicit mode, at its best when lingering on the details of daily life and work, exploring the interactions between individual growth, personality and social environment, and laying bare the ruptures and reconciliations of family life. As the novel progressed, as the characters acquired a life and being of their own, Olsen, I think, found herself unable to document the political vision of social revolution as authentically and nonrhetorically as she was able to portray the ravages of circumstance on families and individuals and the redeeming moments between them. She did not want to write didactically. She wanted to write a politically informed novel that would also be great art. The problem is that the subtlety and painstaking craft of her evolving style did not lend themselves readily to a work of epic scope, and she was increasingly unwilling to rely on shortcuts like the narrative interpolations to tell rather than show political context and change. In any case, she had trouble extending the novel in its intended direction. In a note on its progress from sometime in the mid-1930s, she writes: 'Now it seems to me the whole revolutionary part belongs in another novel ... and I can't put out one of those 800 page tomes.'

I think that there was a tension, too, between two themes: the awakening class consciousness that was the central drama of her time, and her other essential theme, the portrait of the artist as a young girl – not an inevitable conflict based on inconsistent possibilities, for Olsen's own experience embraced both processes, but a writing tension, based on the difficulty of merging the two themes in a cohesive fictive structure. Yet the more individualistic, subjective and domestic concerns – the intellectual and psychological development of the young girl, the complicated familial relationships, the lyrical vision of regeneration through love between mother and child – would not have been acceptable to Olsen or the critical establishment of the left without the projected Marxian resolution that showed working-class people taking power collectively over their own lives. In other words, Olsen had so fully internalized the left's vision of what proletarian literature could and should do to show the coming of a new society that she did not even consider then the possibility of a less epic and, for her, more feasible structure. Nor could she be content simply to accord centrality to the familial interactions and the stubborn growth of human potential in that unpromising soil, leaving the tensions between human aspiration and social oppression unresolved. So *Yonnondio* remained unfinished, but the struggle to write fiction at once political and nonpolemical was an essential apprenticeship for the writer who in her maturity produced *Tell Me a Riddle*.

The concerns I have called, for lack of better terms, more 'subjective' and 'domestic', grew to a great extent out of Olsen's experience as a woman and a mother. Thus, my second and third contradictions overlap, for as we shall see there was little in left literary criticism that would have validated the centrality of these concerns, except in so far as they touched on class rather than gender. The rest of this essay, then, will be concerned with the third contradiction: between the fact that the world of the left, like the larger society it both challenged and partook of, was essentially androcentric and masculinist, and yet that it also demonstrated, more than any other sector of American society, a consistent concern for women's issues.

The painful and sometimes wry anecdotes of women writers like Josephine Herbst and Meridel Le Sueur amply testify to the sexual politics of life in the literary left. For example, Herbst writes to Katherine Anne Porter about the 'gentle stay-in-your-place, which may or may not be the home', she received from her husband, John Herrmann, when she wished to join him at a 'talk fest' with Gold, Edmund Wilson, Malcolm Cowley and others. 'I told Mister Herrmann that as long as the gents had bourgeois reactions to women they would probably never rise very high in their revolutionary conversations, but said remarks rolled off like water'.[29] Olsen herself remembers that at the American Writers Congress, James Farrell informed her that she and another attractive young woman present were 'the two flowers there', compared with the other 'old bags'.

Because she was not really a part of the literary circles of the left, their sexual politics had less impact on Olsen than on writers who were more involved, like Herbst and Le Sueur. If for Herbst it was her gender that prevented her from moving freely in the heady circles of the literary left, for Olsen it was more the depth of her own class loyalties to the rank and file. The sexism she experienced in her daily life mostly reflected the structure of gender-role assignments in society as a whole, although she does recall some incidents peculiar to life on the left, such as the pressure on YCL women to make themselves available at parties as dancing partners especially to black and Mexican-American men, whether the women wanted to dance or not. As a writer, though, Olsen was keenly aware of the male dominance of left literature and criticism and the relative absence of women's subjects and concerns.

If one examines the composition of the editorial boards of left magazines of culture and criticism, one finds that the mastheads are largely male; in 1935, one woman wrote to the *New Masses* complaining at the underrepresentation of women writers,[30] although a few women writers, like Herbst and Le Sueur, were regular contributors. The numerical dominance of men in the literary left paralleled the omnipresence of a worker-figure in literature and criticism who almost by definition was male; proletarian prose and criticism tended to flex their muscles with a particularly masculinist pride. Here, for example, is a passage from Gold's famous *New Masses* editorial, 'Go left, young writer', written in 1929:

> A new writer has been appearing; a wild youth of about twenty-two, the son of working-class parents, who himself works in the lumber camps, coal mines, and steel mills, harvest fields and mountain camps of America. ... He writes in jets of exasperated feeling and has not time to polish his work. ... He lacks self-confidence but writes because he must – and because he has a real talent.[31]

An even more pronounced masculinism prevails in Gold's 'America needs a critic', published in *New Masses* in 1926:

> Send us a critic. Send a giant who can shame our writers back to their task of civilizing America. Send a soldier who has studied history. Send a strong poet who loves the masses, and their future. ... Send one who is not a pompous liberal, but a man of the street. ... Send us a man fit to stand up to skyscrapers. ... Send no saint. Send an artist. Send a scientist. Send a Bolshevik. Send a man.[32]

Gold's worst insult to a writer was that he was a pansy, his art, effeminate.[33] Gold, of course, was an extreme example of working-class male chauvinism, but he was not atypical. Even as late as 1969, when Joseph North edited an anthology of *New Masses* pieces, masculinity predominates. North's Prologue praises the *New Masses* for capturing the essence of American life in its portrayals of the industrial proletariat, in its emphasis on the 'day of a workingman', that of a miner, a locomotive engineer, a weaver. 'Its men,' he says, 'its writers and artists understood this kind of a life existed.'[34] In spite of his once-favoured notice of Tillie Lerner's work, he does not mention its women.

When women writers on the left did write about explicitly female subjects from a woman's perspective, they were sometimes criticized outright, sometimes ignored. Le Sueur has remembered that she was criticized for writing in a lyrical, emotive style about sexuality and the reproductive process.[35] I have already noted Chambers' attack on her for writing about the conditions of women on the breadlines without building in a revolutionary dialectic. Elinor Langer, having worked for several years on a biography of Herbst, believes that one of the reasons Herbst's impressive trilogy of novels failed to win her the recognition she deserved was that she was a woman and the central experience in two of the three novels is that of female characters.[36] Not that the scorn or neglect of male left critics was reserved exclusively for women writers. The more dogmatic of them viewed any literature concerned primarily with domestic and psychological subjects as suspect. One novel focusing on the experience and perceptions of a child of the working classes, Henry Roth's *Call It Sleep* (1935), which Olsen read and admired during the later stages of her work on *Yonnondio*, was one of the more intricate, imaginative works in the proletarian genre. Yet the *New Masses* dismissed it in a paragraph, concluding, 'It is a pity that so many young writers drawn from the proletariat can make no better use of their working class experience than as material for introspective and febrile novels.'[37]

In writing *Yonnondio*, Olsen was consciously writing class literature from a woman's point of view, incorporating a dimension that she saw ignored and neglected in the works of most contemporary male leftists. All of Olsen's work, in fact, testifies to her concern for women, her vision of their double oppression if they are poor or women of color, her affirmation of their creative potential, her sense of the deepest, most intractable contradiction of all: the unparalleled satisfaction and fulfillment combined with the overwhelming all-consuming burden of motherhood. Indeed, her writings about mothering, about the complex, painful and redemptive interactions between mother and child, have helped a new generation of women writers to treat that subject with a fullness and honesty never before possible in American literature.

In *Yonnondio*, Anna as mother wants for her children what she can no longer dream for herself: the freedom to live fully what is best in them; to the extent that the circumstances of their lives prevent this, her love is also her despair. Anna has a special kinship with her oldest daughter, Mazie, in whom her own intelligence and early hunger for knowledge are reincarnated. Mirroring each other's dreams and capacities, the two mirror also the anguish of women confronting daily the poverty of their class and the assigned burdens of their sex. At times they protect one another – Anna, Mazie's access to books, to literature; Mazie, Anna's physical well-being, she herself becoming temporarily mother when Anna lies unconscious after a miscarriage. Mazie's painful sensitivity – the sensitivity of the potential artist – makes her as a child deeply susceptible to both the beauty and ugliness around her; overcome at times by the ugliness, it is to her mother that she turns for renewal. For example, one of the gentlest, most healing of *Yonnondio*'s passages is the interlude of peace when Anna and Mazie pause from gathering dandelion greens, and Anna is transported by the spring and river wind to a forgetful peace, different from her usual 'mother look', the 'mother alertness ... in her bounded body' (120). Absently, she sings fragments of song and strokes Mazie's body:

The fingers stroked, spun a web, cocooned Mazie into happiness and intactness and selfness. Soft wove the bliss round hurt and fear and want and shame – the old worn fragile bliss, a new frail selfness bliss, healing, transforming. Up from the grasses, from the earth, from the broad tree trunk at their back, latent life streamed and seeded. (119)

The transformation here is not the political conversion that was to have taken place later, but one based on human love, on the capacity to respond to beauty, and on the premise of a regenerative life cycle of which mother and daughter are a part.

To be sure, Olsen wanted to weave this emphasis on 'selfness', and this image of a regenerative life cycle that prefigures, but does not itself constitute, social and economic regeneration into a larger structure that would incorporate both personal and political transformation. Yet the hope *Yonnondio* offers most persuasively, through its characterizations, its images and events, and its present conclusion, is less a vision of political and economic revolution than an assertion that the drive to love and achieve and create will survive somehow in spite of the social forces arraigned against it, because each new human being is born with it afresh.

It is with this 'humanistic' rather than 'Marxist' optimism that the novel now ends. In the midst of a stifling heat wave, Baby Bess suddenly realizes her own ability to have an effect on the world when she makes the connection between her manipulations of the lid of a jam jar and the noise it produces, so that her random motions become, for the first time, purposeful: 'Bang, slam, whack. Release, grab, slam, bang, bang. Centuries of human drive work in her; human ecstasy of achievement; a satisfaction deep and fundamental as sex: *I can do, I use my power; I! I!*' (153). And her mother and sister and brothers laugh, in spite of the awesome heat, the rising dust storms. Then for the first time the family listens to the radio on a borrowed set, and Mazie is awed at the magic, *'transparent meshes of sound, far sound, human and stellar, pulsing, pulsing'* (153). This moment of empowerment and connection *is* linked to the revolutionary vision, and Anna's final 'The air's changin', Jim. I see for it [the heat wave] to end tomorrow, at least get tolerable' (154) certainly hints at the possibility for greater change. Still, there is a great gulf between socialist revolution and the temporary individualized relief of this final passage. Yet the end seems right; indeed, today, the novel hardly seems unfinished, because it offers in its conclusion the affirmation most fully embedded in the texture of the novel as a whole: an affirmation of human will, familial love and, at least in the child not yet deadened and brutalized by the struggle for sheer survival and the corrupt influence of social institutions, the drive toward achievement and creation.

To say this is not to diminish the power of *Yonnondio* as an indictment of society; Olsen makes it clear that the Holbrooks do not merely suffer – they are oppressed, in quite specific ways, as a working-class family in a capitalist system. The whole fabric of the book deals with how poverty, exploitation and what today we would call sexism combine to extinguish gradually the very qualities Olsen values most. The loss of creative capacity is not, as Wordsworth would have it, the inevitable price of growing up, but rather the price of growing up in a society *like this one.*

In according that creative capacity especially to women and children, as in detailing the impact of social circumstance on the dailiness of family life, Olsen added a significant dimension to the largely masculine and public world of the proletarian novel. Women's work in preserving and nurturing that creative capacity in the young is shown in *Yonnondio* to be an essential precondition to social change.

Although in this regard, Olsen's work was deliberately oppositional to the androcentrism of the left literary milieu, and although the tenets of proletarian criticism would not have validated this feminist and humanist dimension without the projected Marxian resolution, Olsen's affiliation with the left undoubtedly encouraged and informed her writings about women in at least two ways.

First, there was the fact that in spite of the sexism of the left milieu, the existence of serious analysis of women's status and roles meant that, in Olsen's circles at least, women's capacities were recognized and supported, however inconsistently, and women's grievances were recognized as real. It is certainly true, as Olsen recalls today, that on 'those things that come particularly to the fore through consciousness-raising, having to do with sexuality, with rape, and most of all with what I call maintenance of life, the bearing and rearing of the young', the circles of the left were little better than those of society as a whole – in spite of a body of theory on housework and the frequent bandying about of Lenin's observations on its degrading nature. And Olsen is in accord with Peggy Dennis, married for years to Party leader Eugene Dennis, on the 'explicit, deliberate and reprehensible sexism' of the party's leadership.[38] Yet Olsen also knew Party women who brought their own husbands up for trial on charges of male chauvinism, one of them herself a Party activist whose husband refused to help with childcare; he was removed from his leadership position when her charges were upheld. She remembers seeing women in the Party, women like herself, grow in their capacities and rise to positions of leadership; she herself helped set up, after much debate about the pros and cons of autonomous women's formations, a separate Women's Division of the Warehouse Union to which Jack Olsen belonged, establishing thereby a whole secondary leadership of women. This process of women's coming to strength and voice was to have been central to *Yonnondio*, and if, paradoxically, her own activism in the left helped prevent her from finishing the novel, her experience in that milieu nevertheless gave her, too, a sense of confidence and worth essential to both her political work and her writing.

She wanted, moreover, to pay tribute to, to memorialize, the women she knew on the left: women like her YCL comrades and especially immigrant women like her own mother – strong women, political women, but sometimes also women defeated by their long existence in a patriarchal world. Sometime in 1938 she wrote in her journal:

> To write the history of that whole generation of exiled revolutionaries, the kurelians and croations, the bundists and the poles; and the women, the foreign women, the mothers of six and seven ... the housewives whose Zetkin and Curie and Brontë hearts went into kitchen and laundries and the patching of old socks; and those who did not speak the language of their children, who had no bridge ... to make themselves understood.

Tell Me a Riddle is dedicated to two such women, and its central character, Eva, is a vividly drawn composite of several; Eva, a passionate socialist organizer and orator in her youth, who is silenced by years of poverty and tending to others' needs, only to find her voice and vision again when she is dying. The publications of the left in the 1930s are full of tributes to women like Mother Bloor, Clara Zetkin, Krupskaya; in a way, *Yonnondio* and *Tell Me a Riddle* are both extensions and demystifications of such portrayals, renderings of the essentially heroic lives which circumstances did not allow to blossom into public deeds, art and fame.

Second, the theoretical analysis of crucial aspects of women's experience was encouraged by articles, lectures, Party publications devoted solely to women's issues, and study groups on the woman question. Olsen herself taught a class on the woman question at YCL headquarters on San Francisco's Haight Street. A self-styled feminist even then, she had read not only Marxist theory, but also works from the suffragist movement like the *History of Woman Suffrage* and the *Woman's Bible*, and she invited suffragists to her class to talk about their own experiences in the nineteenth-century woman's movement, establishing a sense of the history and continuity of women's struggles.

Theory about the woman question undoubtedly helped to shape her own thinking about women's issues. Communist Party theory on women, like its practice, certainly had weaknesses. Most arose from the fact that gender was not identified as a fundamental social category like class. Thus, working-class women could be viewed as suffering essentially the same oppression as their husbands, directly if they were workers, by extension if they were wives. Consequently, they would presumably benefit from the same measures. Analysis tended to focus on women in the paid labor force; and although housework did receive a substantial amount of critical attention, few analysts, except perhaps in special women's columns or special women's publications like the *Woman Worker*, suggested seriously that men should share equal responsibility for it, although many argued – not strongly enough, according to Olsen – for its collectivization.[39]

The socialist writers of the earlier years of the century tended to be fuller in their analyses of sexuality and 'life styles' than the Communist Party in the 1930s, which generally avoided such discussions, failing to link political revolution and sexual freedom as Agnes Smedley had at the close of the 1920s. *Yonnondio* is far more reticent than *Daughter of Earth* on this subject. Although it includes the painfully explicit rape of wife by husband, and although it is better than a history book at raising issues of women's health, *Yonnondio* is largely silent about women's sexuality *per se* – even though this is a topic which Olsen speaks of freely in her early poems and sometimes in her journals. That silence may well have something to do with the rather puritanical and conservative attitudes of the Communist Party on sexuality throughout the 1930s.[40]

Still, in no other segment of American society at that time were there such extensive discussions about the sources of women's oppression and the means for alleviating it. A recent article by Robert Shaffer, 'Women and the Communist Party, USA, 1930–1940', provides a useful summary of the nature of women's status and roles in the Communist Party, its theory about the oppression of women, its publications and organizations designed to counteract such oppression, its involvement in mass work amount women and around women's issues, and its views on the family and sexuality. He concludes that 'despite its important weaknesses, the CP's work among women in the 1930s was sufficiently extensive, consistent and theoretically valuable to be considered an important part of the struggle for women's liberation in the United States'.[41]

Shaffer discusses two books by communist women published in the 1930s that were important contributions to the analysis of women's issues. The first, by Grace Hutchins, focused on *Women Who Work* – that is, women in the paid workforce; according to Shaffer, it underplays male chauvinism and sometimes blames women for their own oppression, but it also scrupulously documents the conditions of working women and formulates important demands to better them. The second book, written in 1939 by Mary Inman, takes a position reflecting the less sectarian consciousness of the Popular Front Years. Inman argues that all women are oppressed, not just working-class women, and that one of the symptoms of this oppression is their isolation in their homes; that working-class men sometimes oppress their wives; and that housework must be viewed as productive labor – positions rejected by the party's East Coast leadership, but supported in the West, where *People's World* was published and read. She also discusses how girls are conditioned to a 'manufactured femininity' by childrearing practices and the mass media.[42] Inman eventually left the party over the controversy her book engendered, but clearly the ideas it expressed had some currency and support in left circles at least on the West Coast.

In many ways, *Yonnondio* anticipates in fiction Inman's theoretical formulations. The conditioning of children to accept limiting sex roles is an important theme in *Yonnondio*. One thinks, for example, of the children's games that so cruelly inhibit the preadolescent Mazie, or of the favorite text – 'the Movies, selected' – of 12-year-old Jinella, who with Mazie as partner plays a vamp from *Sheik of Araby, Broken Blossoms, Slave of Love, She Stopped at Nothing, The Fast Life* and *The Easiest Way* (127–8), her imaginative capacity absurdly channeled by her exposure to these films, her only escape from her real life as Gertrude Skolnick. Even Anna, full of her own repressed longings, imparts the lessons of sex roles to her children: 'Boys get to do that', she tells Benjy wistfully, talking of travel by trains and boats, 'not girls' (113). And when Mazie asks her, 'Why is it always me that has to help? How come Will gets to play?' Anna can only answer, 'Willie's a boy' (142). Olsen, then, suggests throughout *Yonnondio* that both women and men are circumstanced to certain social roles, and that these roles, while placing impossible burdens of responsibility on working-class men, constrict the lives of women in particularly damaging ways.

Olsen understands and portrays the double oppression of working-class women in other ways as well. Anna's spirit is almost broken by her physical illness – 'woman troubles' – connected with pregnancy and childbirth and compounded by inadequate medical care. Her apparent apathy and incompetence make her a target of her husband's rage; he strikes out at and violates her because he has no other accessible target for his frustrations and fears, until her miscarriage forces him to a pained awareness and reawakened love. Few other American novels, perhaps none outside the radical tradition of which *Yonnondio* is a part, reveal so starkly the destructive interactions of class and sex under patriarchal capitalism.

In *Yonnondio*, as in Olsen's other work, the family itself has a contradictory function, at once a source of strength and love, and a battleground between women and men in a system exploiting both. This, of course, is a profoundly Marxian vision; it was Marx and Engels who wrote in *The Communist Manifesto*:

> The bourgeois clap-trap about the family and education, about the hallowed relation of parent and child, becomes all the more disgusting, the more, by the action of Modern Industry, all family ties among the proletarians are torn asunder.[43]

The vision of the family in *Yonnondio* is formed both by Olsen's own experience and by her familiarity from childhood on with socialist ideas.

Another aspect of that vision is Olsen's treatment of the relationship between housework and paid labor in *Yonnondio*. One of the novel's crucial structural principles is the juxtaposition of men's (and women's) work in the paid labor force and women's work in the home – especially in the final chapter, which shifts back and forth between Anna's canning at home, as she tends to the demands of her older children and juggles Baby Bess on her hip, and the hellish speedup of the packing plant where Jim works. The over-whelming heat, prelude to the great droughts and dust storms of the 1930s, becomes a common bond of suffering. There is nothing redeeming about the brutal and exploitative labor at the plant; Anna at least is engaged in pro-duction of goods the family will use and in caring for children whom she loves through her exhaustion. Olsen makes it clear that both forms of work are essential, and that the degrading conditions of both have the same systemic causes. If she is finally unable in *Yonnondio* to suggest a systemic solution, her instincts were perhaps more historically accurate than those of other Marxists writing in the same period.

Yonnondio, of course, is far more than ideology translated into fiction. Olsen wrote from what she had lived, what she had seen, at last incorporating 'the common hysteria' of factory work, the bodily nausea and weariness, along with the incessant demands of work in the home. But her understanding of those events, the nature of her protest, although in many ways going beyond Communist Party theory and practice of the early 1930s, could only have been deepened by the very presence in her milieu of theory and controversy on the woman question.[44]

On the whole, in spite of the left's demands on her time and energies, the prescriptiveness of its more dogmatic criticism, and the androcentrism or outright sexism of many of its spokesmen, there is no doubt but that Olsen's Marxian perspective and experience ultimately enriched her literature. In a talk in 1974 at Emerson College, in Boston, explaining some of the reasons why she is a 'slow' writer, she discusses without using the terminology of the left the differences between her own concerns and what a Marxist would identify as bourgeois ideology:

> My vision is very different from that of most writers. ... I don't think in terms of quests for identity to explain human motivation and behavior. I feel that in a world where class, race, and sex are so determining, that that has little reality. What matters to me is the kind of soil *out* of which people have to grow, and the kind of climate around them; circumstances are the primary key and not the personal quest for identity. ... I want to write what will help change that which is harmful for human beings in our time.[45]

In the 1950s, partly out of a spirit of opposition to the McCarthy era, and blessed with increased time as the children grew up and there were temporary respites from financial need, Olsen began to do the work that gave us the serenely beautiful but still politically impassioned stories of the *Tell Me a Riddle* volume. Olsen's enduring insistence that literature must confront the material realities of people's lives as shaping circumstances, that the very categories of class and race and sex constitute the fabric of reality as we live it, and that literature has an obligation to deepen consciousness and facilitate social change is part of her – and our – inheritance from the radical tradition.

NOTES

1. To my knowledge, the connections between the contemporary women's movement and the Old Left have never been sufficiently explored, although its roots in the civil rights movement and the New Left are well documented, as in Sara Evans, *Personal Politics: The roots of women's liberation in the Civil Rights Movement and the New Left* (New York: Random House, 1979). It would be interesting, for example, to look at the number of feminist leaders and spokeswomen with family or other personal ties to the Old Left.

2. The earlier version of this article was delivered at a session on Women Writers of the Left at the National Women's Studies Association convention in Bloomington, Indiana, June 1980. Olsen's comments on that version were made mostly during an eight-hour tape-recorded conversation in Fall 1980. I have quoted extensively from that discussion as well as from earlier interviews, without attempting to distinguish between them.

3. Tillie Olsen, 'A note about this book', *Yonnondio: From the thirties* (New York: Dell, 1975), p. 158. All references are to this edition, and page numbers will be supplied in parentheses in the text.

4. Selma Burkom and Margaret Williams, 'De-riddling Tillie Olsen's writings', *San Jose Studies* 2 (1976), pp. 65–83. In spite of some inaccuracies, this important study is the best source of biographical and bibliographic information on Olsen outside of her own writings.

5. Ellen Moers, *Literary Women* (New York: Doubleday, 1976); and Elaine Showalter, *A Literature of Their Own: British women novelists from Brontë to Lessing* (Princeton, NJ: Princeton University Press, 1977).

6. Walter B. Rideout, *The Radical Novel in the United States, 1900–1954* (New York: Hill & Wang, 1956), p. 3; and Daniel Aaron, *Writers on the Left* (New York: Harcourt, Brace & World, 1961).

7. Aaron, *Writers on the Left*, pp. 336–7.

8. From an unmailed letter to Harriet Monroe, apparently intended as a cover letter for poems Olsen was planning to submit for publication in Monroe's influential *Poetry: A magazine of verse.*

9. From Elinor Langer's transcription of her introduction to a talk given by Olsen at a Reed College symposium in Portland, Oregon, in Fall 1978.

10. In 'Divided against herself: the life lived and the life suppressed', *Moving On* (April–May 1980), pp. 15–20, 23, I explored the theme of the 'buried life' in women's literature, as it appears in the work of leftist feminist writers like Olsen and Agnes Smedley. In 'Tell me a riddle,' the buried life is Eva's engaged, articulate, political self, whereas in Smedley's *Daughter of Earth*, it is the maternal, domestic self. Both works testify to the pain of denying part of one's being, and both condemn the society that does not allow women to be whole.

11. Burkom and Williams reprint these poems in their article 'De-riddling Tillie Olsen'; 'I want you women up north to know', pp. 67–9, and 'There is a lesson', p. 70.

12. Tillie Lerner, 'The iron throat', *Partisan Review* 1 (April–May 1934), pp. 3–9.

13. Tillie Lerner, 'Thousand-dollar vagrant', *New Republic* 80 (29 August 1934), pp. 67–9; and 'The strike,' *Partisan Review* 1 (September–October 1934), pp. 3–9, reprinted in *Years of Protest: A collection of American writings of the 1930s*, ed. Jack Salzman (New York: Pegasus, 1967), pp. 138–44.

14. Salzman, ed., *Years of Protest*, p. 138.

15. ibid., p. 144

16. One of the best accounts of the importance of these clubs for young writers, in spite of his ultimate disillusionment with the Communist Party, is Richard Wright's 1944 essay printed in *The God That Failed*, ed. Richard H. Crossman (New York: Harper, 1950).

17. This is Olsen's recollection; I did not locate the actual source.

18. Cited in Burkom and Williams, 'De-riddling Tillie Olsen', p. 71.

19. Among those who signed the call to the conference and/or attended were Nelson Algren, Kenneth Burke, Theodore Dreiser, Waldo Frank, Joseph Freeman, Granville Hicks, Langston Hughes, Edwin Seaver and Nathaniel West.

20. Langer mentions this drawing in her talk at Reed College cited above. Olsen has a copy of the cartoon in her files, and Salzman includes it with twenty others in *Years of Protest*, p. 307.

21. The selections in Salzman's chapter on 'The social muse', in *Years of Protest*, pp. 231–307, are well chosen to represent various positions in this debate.

22. Rideout's discussion of the efforts of the left to define the 'proletarian novel' is particularly helpful and more detailed than I can be here; see *Radical Novel in the United States*, especially pp. 165–70.

23. Printed in *Feminist Studies* 7: 3 (1981).

24. Burkom and Williams, 'De-riddling Tillie Olsen', p. 69.

25. Rideout, *Radical Novel in the United States*, pp. 171–98. In only three of the many novels Rideout discusses do female characters play a major role: those by Josephine Herbst.

26. From an unpublished paper by Elaine Hedges, 'Meridel Le Sueur in the thirties', first presented at the Modern Language Association Convention in San Francisco, December 1978.

27. Mike Gold, 'Proletarian realism', reprinted in *Mike Gold: A literary anthology*, ed. Michael Folsom (New York: International Publishers, 1972), p. 207

28. Rachel Blau DuPlessis, in an editorial comment on this essay.

29. Elinor Langer, '"The ruins of memory": Josephine Herbst in the 1930s', unpublished; also in Langer, 'If in fact I have found a heroine ... ', *Mother Jones* 6 (May 1981), p. 43. Meridel Le Sueur has mentioned similar episodes in talks at a conference on women writers at the Women's Building in Los Angeles in 1972 and at the National Women's Studies Association Conference in Lawrence, Kansas, 1979.

30. Robert Shaffer, 'Women and the Communist Party, USA, 1930–1940', *Socialist Review* 45 (May–June 1979), p. 93, note. I am indebted to Shaffer's article throughout the final section of this essay.

31. Folsom, ed., *Mike Gold*, p. 188.

32. ibid., p. 139.

33. See, for example, Gold's 'Wilder: prophet of the genteel Christ', in Salzman, *Years of Protest*, pp. 233–8.

34. Joseph North, *New Masses: An anthology of the rebel thirties* (New York: International Publishers, 1969), p. 24.

35. Meridel Le Sueur, in talks cited above and personal conversations with her on those occasions; also see Hedges, 'Meridel Le Sueur in the thirties', p. 7.

36. Langer, '"The ruins of memory"', p. 16.
37. In Rideout, *Radical Novel in the United States*, p. 189.
38. Peggy Dennis, *The Autobiography of an American Communist: A personal view of a political life, 1925–1975* (Berkeley, Calif.: Creative Arts Books, 1977), p. 294.
39. Shaffer, 'Women and the Communist Party', pp. 94–6.
40. ibid., especially pp. 104–7.
41. ibid., p. 10.
42. ibid., pp. 83–7. I am also grateful to historian Sherna Gluck for discussing with me Inman's work and the controversy surrounding it.
43. This version is from Barbara Sinclair Deckard's *The Women's Movement: Political, socioeconomic, and psychological issues,* 2nd edn (New York: Harper & Row, 1979), p. 234.
44. Olsen's concern with the woman question continued into the 1940s. She authored for a few months in 1946 a women's column in *People's World*, writing articles like 'Wartime gains of women in industry', and 'Politically active mothers – one view', which argued like Inman that motherhood should be considered political work. Also in the 1940s she participated actively in some of the organizations targeted by the Communist Party for mass work on what the party considered to be women's issues – health and education – work related also, of course, to her own deepest concerns.
45. From a tape transcription in Olsen's files.

—————————— ELEVEN ——————————
Romance in the age of electronics:
Harlequin Enterprises

LESLIE W. RABINE

Harlequin, as it advertises itself, is the 'world's no. 1 publisher of romance fiction'. Like its imitators and rivals, Dell's Candlelight Romances, Bantam's Loveswept, and Simon & Schuster's Silhouette Romances, Harlequin turns out on its giant, computerized printing presses an ever increasing number of uniformly jacketed and uniformly written romantic narratives per month.[1] Formerly a moderately successful Canadian publishing house, in 1971 it hired Lawrence Heisley, a Proctor & Gamble marketing man, as its new president. He turned feminine romantic love into superprofits for his then all-male board of directors by transferring to the sale of books the techniques used to sell detergent to housewives. By turning love into a consumer product, Harlequin increased its net earnings from $110,000 in 1970 to over $21 million by 1980.

But packaging alone cannot account for the loyalty of 14 million readers. The novels' flyleaf assures readers that 'no one touches the heart of a woman quite like Harlequin', and marketing statistics – 188 million books sold in 1980, sales accounting for 30 per cent of all mass market paperbacks in a major bookstore chain – support this claim.[2] What exactly is the secret to a woman's heart that Harlequin and its rivals have learned, and how have they turned this knowledge into profits for themselves?

SECRETS OF A WOMAN'S HEART
Harlequin may owe its dramatic growth in popularity to the fact that the romances now respond to specific needs of working women. Focusing on the juncture between their sexual, emotional needs on the one hand and their needs concerning work relations on the other, it involves both their deepest, most private, most intimate feelings, and at the same time their very broad relations to the process of social history. Impressive analyses by Tania

Modleski, Ann Barr Snitow and Janice A. Radway[3] have explained the popularity of mass market romances by examining how they respond to women's deep yearnings, but have not talked about why these romances have gained their phenomenal popularity just in the past 10 to 15 years. Moreover, in the past couple of years, since Snitow and Modleski wrote their studies, the romance industry has been undergoing an accelerated process of change. Given the fact that their heroines' stories increasingly join the personal, sexual relations of private life to the work relations of the marketplace, we might ask what in the Harlequin formula responds to new needs of women as a result of recent profound changes in both their domestic and paid labor situations, and how that formula might change in the future.

As Harlequin Romances have become more popular, more and more of their heroines have jobs. Yet these working heroines have more subversive desires than simply to join the labor force: they are reacting to the limits of a sterile, harsh, alienating fragmented work world itself. In spite of some fairly glamorous jobs, the working Harlequin heroines, melodramatically engaged in defiant struggles with their heroes, who are usually their bosses, demand from them and their world two additional changes in their situation. First, as the heroine struggles against the irresistible power of her hero, she also struggles *for* something, which she calls 'love', but beyond that does not define any further. What she wants from the hero is recognition of herself as a unique, exceptional individual. In addition to acknowledging her sexual attraction and her professional competence, he must also recognize her as a subject, or recognize her from her own point of view.

Second, the heroines seek more than simply to succeed in the man's world. An analysis of the romances will show that on an implicit level they seek not so much an improved life within the possibilities of the existing social structure, but a different social structure. The very facts that the hero is both boss and lover, that the world of work and business is romanticized and eroticized, and that in it love flourishes suggest that the Harlequin heroines seek an end to the division between the domestic world of love and sentiment and the public world of work and business.

Since in Harlequin the struggle to gain recognition for a deep feminine self merges with the struggle – however implicit or utopian – to create a new, more integrated world, a reading of these romances uncovers a certain power possessed by even formulaic narratives. Because they cannot help but recount a woman's life all of a piece, they may be able to reveal certain insights about women's lives and women's desires that escape empirical science. These romance narratives show us that an individual woman's need to be recognized in her own sense of self and the need to change a more global social structure are interdependent.

In *Loving with a Vengeance: Mass-produced fantasies for women*, Tania Modleski says that 'in Harlequin Romances, the need of women to find meaning and pleasure in activities which are not wholly male-centered such as work or artistic creation is generally scoffed at'.[4] But in the past few years that has changed. Although in the mid-1970s, the average Harlequin heroine was either just emerging from home, or was a secretary or nurse who quit her unrewarding job at marriage, by the late 1970s, many Harlequin heroines had unusual and interesting, if not bizarre careers. More and more frequently both hero and heroine started taking the heroine's job or creative activity seriously.

Almost never images of passive femininity, their heroines of the late 1970s are active, intelligent and capable of at least economic independence. Nicole, in *Across the Great Divide*, is a dedicated and competent swimming coach; Anna in *Battle with Desire* is an internationally known violinist at the age of 22; Kerry in *The Dividing Line*, also 22, is on the board of directors of a prestigious department store. Furthermore, the hero often gives moral support to the heroine in her career, and intends to continue supporting her career aspirations after their marriage.[5]

By the early 1980s, the heroines' careers go beyond the wildest dreams of the most ardent member of the National Organization for Women and often become the selling point that distinguishes one romance from another. As one example, Danni in *Race for Revenge* is about to 'succeed triumphantly in the male dominated world of motor racing',[6] and Karla Mortley in Candlelight Romance's *Game Plan* 'joins the rugged New York flyers as a ballet trainer', only to find that 'the womanizing quarterback MacGregor proves hard to tackle'.[7] In 1984 Harlequin added to its line a new, more sophisticated series, Harlequin Temptations, where the hero worries that the heroine will place her career before him. In the romances of the mid-1980s the careers range from the banal, like movie actresses and famous pop singers, to the unique, like engineering PhD Frankie Warburton in *Love Circuit*, who falls in love with the electronics heir that contracts for her services as a computer consultant. More than one heroine is an advertising executive who falls in love with her client. University editorial assistant Liza Manchester in *Public Affair* is an 'outspoken member of Graham University's feminist community' who falls in love with Professor Scott Harburton. And – inevitably – Garbriella Constant in *By Any Other Name* is a best-selling romance writer who falls in love with her publisher.[8]

Although, the hero of these romances is not always the heroine's boss he most often either is the boss or holds a position of economic or professional power over the heroine. More important, as the advertising brochure for the new Harlequin Temptation series demonstrates, the boss figure remains the prototype for the Harlequin hero. Promising to let us experience 'The passionate torment of a woman torn between two loves ... the siren call of a career ... the magnetic advances of an impetuous employer', it advertises its flagship novel of the new series, *First Impressions*, by saying: 'Tracy Dexter couldn't deny her attraction to her new boss.'[9]

Because in Harlequin Romances, plot, characters, style and erotic scenes have been set by formula, freedom to vary the heroine's job gives an author one of the few avenues for bringing originality, individuality and creative freedom into a romance. An unusual job offers compositional opportunities for an unusual setting and unusual conflicts between the hero and heroine. But the job situation also serves a deeper purpose. Beyond showing the uncanny ability of mass culture to ingest any kind of social, economic, or cultural historic change in women's lives, these heroines with their fabulous jobs might help to explain why women respond to romance so much more massively than to other mass market reading. New Right how-to books exhort their readers to be 'real' women by staying home to protect the family; liberal how-to books, such as *The Cinderella Complex*, urge women to cease wanting to 'be *part* of somebody else' and 'to get into the driver's seat' of 'the man's world'[10]; and women's magazines claim to show readers how to excel in each separate segment – sex, work, family, emotion – of their madly disarticulated, schizophrenic lives. Supermarket romances, alone among mass market literature, focus on the conflictive relations among these segments.

WOMEN'S WORK/WOMEN'S CULTURE

The same socioeconomic changes of the 1960s and 1970s, which created a new kind of working woman, also created the conditions for Harlequin's commercial success. These are, according to Harry Braverman in *Labor and Monopoly Capital*, the restructuring of business into huge international conglomerates; the 'extraordinary growth of commercial concerns' (like Harlequin) in comparison with production; and along with this the extraordinary explosion of bureaucracy and office work with its systems management, computerization and assembly-line processing of paper.[11] These conditions include new categories of work, and, occurring around 1960, 'the creation of a new class of workers', low-paid clerical workers, overwhelmingly female. According to Roslyn L. Feldberg and Evelyn Nakano Glenn, between 1960 and 1980 employment in clerical and kindred occupations doubled. They cite dramatic growth in work categories created by the new technology, and also by the business expansion that Braverman describes.[12]

The women who work for these huge conglomerates and bureaucracies, in clerical positions, in service positions and as assemblers of the new electronic machinery, as well as the women whose shopping, banking, education, medical care and welfare payments have been changed by these new developments, constitute a large part of the readership of Harlequin Romances. And the musicians, painters, poets, coaches, car racers, Olympic athletes, photographers and female executives of the romances, with their glamorous jobs, are these readers' idealized alter egos. Although readers are well aware that the romances are unreal fantasies, their passionate attachment to the genre could not be explained without an intense identification with the heroine on the level of ego ideal.

Between 40 and 60 per cent of the mass market romance readership works outside the home.[13] The assumption has been that these romances contain housewifely fantasies, but if that is so then why do so many of them revolve around work situations, however glamorized? Among the many possible reasons for this, the most obvious is that as countless statistics show, almost all these readers can expect to work sometime in their lives, moving in and out of the labor market. Moreover, a good number of them can expect to be single mothers, for at least part of their lives. But these fantasies involving work situations suggest that feminists, and especially feminist organizers, might do away with this categorization of women into working women on the one hand and housewives on the other. The content of Harlequins suggest that the readers, like the heroines, do not compartmentalize their lives in this way, becoming different people when they go to work. Although the immediate concerns caused by workplace or home may be different, our deeper abiding concerns remain the same, whether at home or on the job. To draw a strong division between working women and housewives comes perhaps from applying to women a male model. For the average man, work and home really are very different. At work the man must accept the power of his employer, while at home he is master of his family and finds relaxation. The average woman, on the other hand, finds herself contending with a masculine power both at home and at work. By combining the sexual domination of a lover and the economic domination of an employer in the same masculine figure, Harlequins draw attention to the specificity of the contemporary feminine situation.

In a sensitive study that explains the popularity of mass market romances by interviewing a group of readers from one bookstore, Janice Radway says that women report they read the romances for relaxation and escape. 'When asked to specify what they are fleeing from,' she says, 'they invariably mention the "pressures" and "tensions" they experience as wives and mothers.'[14] A group of working women I spoke to also said they read the romances to escape. But the escape portrayed in the working heroine's romances is somewhat more precise about the pressures and tensions it aims to soothe.

The heroines' fantasy dilemmas compensate exactly for those elements of women's work in the clerical factories – and for that matter in any factories – that critics of job automation find most oppressive. A reading of Harlequin Romances in the context of these critiques yields insight into the heroines' (and perhaps the authors' and readers') conflicts; their grievances against their living, working and sexual situations; and the intensity with which they feel these grievances, but also into the extent to which the romances and their authors have adopted the basic corporate structure of present work relations as the invisible and unchallenged framework of their romantic visions.

Two themes of revolt and fantasy escape that run most strongly through the romances concern the depersonalization of the cybernetic world and the powerlessness of the feminine individual within it. Surprisingly enough, the heroine's lack of power and freedom corresponds rather closely to what sociologists have found out about the worker's lack of power and freedom in the computerized and bureaucratized workplace. According to Braverman, contemporary clerical workers and low-paid factory workers suffer from a lack of control over the work process, over the social use to which products will be put, over their own mental processes, and even over their own bodies. The assembly line structuring of clerical work, says Braverman, results from applying to office work the techniques of Taylorism, which factory owners began using in the 1920s and 1930s to gain maximum efficiency by breaking down the unity of the labor process into its smallest discrete elements. While Taylorization yields greater productivity, its effects on the worker, whose tasks and bodily movements are also broken down to their smallest elements, are devastating.

With every movement of the office worker or lower-paid assembler controlled for maximum efficiency, and every moment of her day accounted for, she has lost all decision-making power not only over the products she is making, but also over her own bodily movements and minutest scheduling of her own time. Braverman talks about clerical workers feeling 'shackled' and quotes a vice-president of an insurance company as saying of a room full of key punchers: 'All they lack is a chain!'[15] Ida Russakoff Hoos, in *Automation in the Office*, reports interviewing a supervisor who described key punchers keeping supplies of tranquilizers in their desks and feeling 'frozen'.[16] And Ellen Cantarow cites findings of 'appalling rates of coronary heart disease in women clerical workers'[17] as a result of lack of control.

The force of Harlequin comes from its ability to combine, often in the same image, the heroine's fantasy escape from these restraints and her idealized, romanticized and eroticized compliance with them. It does this through diverse types of story elements, which are remarkably consistent from romance to romance. A first and most simple compensation of the readers' situation is that, by contrast to the jobs most working readers have, the jobs of Harlequin heroines, while greatly varied, almost always have in common that the work is meaningful in itself, challenging, has a direct effect on the well-being of other people, is a craft that requires skill or talent and is one that gains recognition for a job well done. A second, slightly more complex compensatory fantasy is that Harlequin heroines do fight for, and win, control over their jobs and a great deal of freedom.

A central, and one of the most attractive, compensations offered by Harlequin is that the romances respond to the depersonalization of the Harlequin reader's life, not only in her workplace, but also in her shopping, her banking, in her relations to government, to school and to all the services she now obtains from giant, faceless bureaucracies, which make her feel, as Tessa in *The Enchanted Island* thinks, 'like a small, impersonal cog in a machine'.[18] The relations between the heroines and their bosses may be love/ hate relations, but they are intensely intimate. Although decisions about how the reader spends her time in the corporate workplace are made by real men, she never sees them. In the conglomerate, the real decision-makers may be in another state or another country, and in terms of the corporate hierarchy, they are in another universe. They are so removed from the secretary or assembler as to seem disembodied gods. In the world of Harlequin, the god descends from the executive suite and comes to her.

But in addition to this direct compensation for the depersonalized relations of the corporate world, the working heroines also idealize the reader's sense that she herself has been reduced to one more interchangeable part of the office's 'integrated systems'. In *Battle with Desire* Gareth the hero, who is also violinist Anna's conductor, tells her: 'You and I together, Anna, will give them a performance they'll never forget. ... The music will be a prelude to our love' (157). Yet Anna is hurt and asks herself: 'But was it love for herself, or because she had been the instrument of such superb music?' Although Anna's position is a highly idealized fantasy, it raises the same conflict experienced by those women in Hoos's study who feel their bosses regard them (if at all) as an instrument or as part of the machinery.

A fourth and still more complex compensation concerns directly the theme of power. In the romances, the heroine fights ardently against the power the hero has over her. Because the power figure represents both her lover and her boss, this relation between one man and one woman reverberates on a larger network of social relations, all structured according to inequality of power. Thus the boss-lover can become an analogy for other men in the reader's life, such as her husband. The heroines reject the dependence or submissiveness that is most often forced upon their resisting spirit: Nicole in *Across the Great Divide* finds in her new boss Lang 'something too suggestive of a rugged relentlessness ... that she just couldn't bring herself to suffer meekly and which set her on the offensive'. In her own mind, she rejects arrogant hierarchies, and when the board of the swim club threatens to fire her 'she was determined not to submit tamely. If she was going down, she would be going down fighting!' (30, 165).

In the most complex and contradictory of story elements, the romances combine in one image and escape from the 'frozen' feeling of working readers and an eroticized acquiescence to it. The heroine's struggle-filled, stormy relationship with the hero involves a strange combination of tempestuous physical movement and physical restraint by the hero. In one of dozens of examples, Nicole, in *Across the Great Divide*, struggles with Lang.

'I hate the lot of you!' she sobbed brokenly. 'And don't touch me!' trying to jerk out of his hold. 'You're all a load of two faced liars, only interested in your own egotistical aims.' Then, when he didn't release her, 'I said don't *touch* me!' as she began pummelling violently at his broad chest.

'For God's sake, Nicky!' Lang gripped her wrists grimly in one hand and wrenched open the car door with the other. 'Get in,' he muttered, and bundled her flailing figure on to the back seat. Slamming the door behind them, he pinned her helplessly to his muscular form until she had exhausted her struggles and consented to stay there, crying quietly. (140)

The 'shackles' of the office or factory job are on the one hand compensated for by vigorous movement; on the other hand they are romanticized and eroticized. The hero restrains the heroine not out of an impersonal desire for efficiency, but out of a very personal desire to have her respond to him. He restrains her in an attempt to control her anger, to arouse her sexually, to fulfill his burning desire to have her confess her feelings for him, or all three. The heroine's anxiety no longer has its source in the cold, nagging unpleasant fear that her boss will fire her if she rebels (or that her husband will reject her or worse) but in the warm, seductive, obsessive fear that she will not be able to resist his potent sexual magnetism, especially since he goes to considerable effort to create intimate situations where he can exert it. Transformed by the romances, the heroine's restraint becomes on the one hand intermittent, and on the other hand emotionally and sexually gratifying. Instead of having to take tranquilizers to repress her internalized rage, like the office workers in Hoos's study and Cantarow's article, the Harlequin heroine is privileged to vent it violently and directly against her restrainer, even while this restraint takes an idealized form.

This strange mingling of protest and acquiescence to the situation of many contemporary women makes the Harlequin Romances so seductive and contradictory. On the one hand, the heroine is empowered to revolt without risking masculine rejection because the hero desires her more the angrier she becomes, but on the other hand, the romances also sexualize her impotence. This particular combination of elements intensifies our emotional involvement with a story that both arouses and nullifies the very subversive impulses that attracted us to it in the first place.

CHANGING TIMES, CHANGING CONFLICT

Harlequin's double message is all the more potent in that the heroine's conflict is also double. At stake for her in the romances that put the work situation at the center of the plot is both her social identity and the deepest core of her feminine self. A surprising number of Harlequins employ the same vocabulary to describe the inner conflict of the heroine as she struggles against the hero on his own grounds where he has all the weapons. His main weapon in this idealized world is his powerful sexual attraction; her main weakness is her susceptibility to that attraction, which quickly becomes total love. Her struggle aims to prevent the hero from exploiting her love for his own sexual desires, and the conflict this struggle awakens in her is described by the key words 'humiliation' and 'pride'. Nicole finds that

> the most galling part of the whole episode had been her unqualified surrender to Lang's lovemaking. That she should have so readily submitted – no, welcomed it was far more honest, she confessed painfully – was something she found impossible to accept. The only thought left to salvage at least some of her *pride* being the knowledge that Lang wasn't aware how deeply her feelings were involved. Her *humiliation* was bad enough now, but it would have known no bounds if she had inadvertently revealed how she really felt about him. (144, my italics)

In *Stormy Affair* Amber faces the same problem: 'She could not say: "I would love to live here and marry you but only if you say you love me. ...." At least she still had sufficient *pride* to avoid the *humiliation* such a statement would cause.'[19]

Through the heroine's impossible choice between two painful and destructive alternatives, summed up by the terms 'humiliation' and 'pride', Harlequin Romances call attention to a feminine character structure that differs from the masculine one. Both Radway and Snitow have discussed this feminine character structure in the Harlequin heroine, and both have relied on Nancy Chodorow's theory to analyze it.[20] According to Chodorow, capitalist-patriarchal family structure and childrearing practices produce in boys more strongly defined and closed-off ego boundaries, and in girls more fluid ego boundaries, so that men tend to define themselves as a separate, self-sufficient entity, while women tend to define themselves in terms of their relation to other people. Unable to adopt a rocklike, closed, thinglike self, such as the one the hero seems to possess, the Harlequin heroine's self alternates until the end of the romance between two forms of destruction: 'humiliation', which signals a dissolution of her self into the masculine self, and 'pride', a self-control that shrivels up her self by denying its needs and desires. Solution: the hero must recognize and adopt the relational, feminine form of the self.

This difference in character structure between women and men, which Harlequins emphasize as the cause of the heroine's problems, is inherited from the industrial revolution. With the separation of work from home, women were socialized to immerse themselves in the intense emotional world of the domestic sphere. Self-perpetuating family practices made that socialization seem like a 'natural' feminine character. Now with the cybernetic revolution, women must also, like men, make their way in the rationalistic world of business, but they take with them the emotional makeup they have inherited from the past. They do not have, and in many cases do not want to have, the harder, more competitive, success-oriented emotional equipment with which men have been socialized in order to succeed, or even simply to survive.

If Harlequin heroines' character structure is inherited from the industrial revolution, their narrative structure is also inherited from one of the most prominent literary genres of the industrial revolution, the romantic novel. Although Sally Mitchell and Tania Modleski have traced the genealogy of Harlequin Romances back to forms of nineteenth-century popular fiction, such as seduction novels, historical romances, penny magazine, aristocratic romances, and gothic novels,[21] the quest for self-fulfillment carried out by the heroes and heroines of nineteenth-century high romanticism has also found a twentieth-century refuge in contemporary mass market romances. As writer Louella Nelson told me of her romance *Freedom's Fortune*: 'This book is about a woman's quest for courage and self-worth.'[22]

The inner conflict of the Harlequin heroines is a more explicitly sexualized version of feminine conflicts analyzed by authors writing during the industrial revolution, such as the Brontë sisters. Problems of sexual difference that beset the Harlequin heroines also confront the heroines of Brontë's *Shirley*, where Caroline Helstone says:

> 'Shirley, men and women are so different: they are in such a different position. Women have so few things to think about – men so many: you may have a friendship with a man while he is almost indifferent to you. Much of what cheers your life may be dependent on him, while not a feeling or interest of moment in his eyes may have reference to you.'

Shirley answers:

> 'Caroline,' demanded Miss Keeldar abruptly, 'don't you wish you had a profession – a trade?'[23]

The Harlequin heroines do have a trade – and a lot of things to think about – but they still resemble the Brontëan heroines in that for them sexual sensation, feelings of love and rational thought are all intimately connected. They cannot be compartmentalized and sealed off from each other. When these heroines fall in love, they think about love and their lover all the time. The heroes of Harlequin Romances, like the heroes of *Jane Eyre* and *Shirley*, are emotionally divided between the world of love and the world of business and public affairs, and therefore fragmented in their psychic structure. For them, or so it seems to the heroine, sex is divorced from other feelings, and love from other areas of their life. It seems that whenever he wills it, the hero can simply shut her image off and think about other things.

From this fragmentation, the Harlequin heroes, like their nineteenth-century brothers M. Emanuel in *Villette* or Robert Moore in *Shirley*, draw their strength for success in the world. But since the Harlequin heroines must now also survive alone in that world, they can only, as Nicole says, attempt to conceal their feelings, try to pretend to be like the hero. But the heroine's wholeness, which is also her weakness, means that her outer appearance and actions cannot but reflect her inner emotions. The heroines are transparent where the heroes are opaque.

In fact the heroine frequently suspects until the end of the novel that the hero has no tender feelings under his harsh surface, and that therefore he does not have to exhaust all his energy in the fight for self-control the way she does. In *Stormy Affair*, for instance, Amber thinks that 'she must pull herself together and not let Hamed Ben Slouma see that he in any way affected her' (25). But 'Hamed with his keen perception knew exactly what was going on in her mind. . . . "Perhaps your desires were greater than mine, or do you think it could be that I have more self-control? You're very *transparent*, my charming one"' (100, my italics). The effect of all these differences between the hero and heroine is to increase the hero's power over this outsider in his world. But even this conflict contains within it wish-fulfilling compensations. If Ben Slouma finds Amber transparent, at least he cares enough to observe her transparency and is interested enough in her to notice what goes on inside her. If the heroine's anger is impotent, at least she has the chance to vent it with great rage at its rightful target, and at least he stays around to listen to it, even, as in the case of Tessa's boss Andrew, 'with interest' (*The Enchanted Island*, 157).

Utopian and formulaic as they are, in Harlequin Romances the heroine's struggle and conflict serve to overcome something more than a merely psychological passivity or a role that a woman could simply choose to play or not to play. Although its roots in a total social situation are not so clearly shown as in the novels of the Brontës, the Harlequin heroine's conflict is shown to be a very real lack of power to be herself in relations controlled by others. Her very activity and anger are signs of her impotence in the face of the more powerful male. Thus Nicole 'seethed impotently' (*Across the Great Divide*, 99), and Debra 'tried to control the rage and humiliation she was feeling', while Jordan's 'composure wasn't disturbed by [Kathleen's] burst of anger'.[24]

Like their nineteenth-century predecessors Jane Eyre, Caroline Helstone and Lucy Snowe, the Harlequin heroines seek recognition as a subject in their own right from their own point of view. And also like these earlier heroines, Harlequin heroines find that this recognition must take a different form from that sought by romantic heroes. A hero like St John Rivers in *Jane Eyre* becomes closed in on himself, static and self-sufficient as an absolute totality when he achieves this recognition. Brontë rejects this form of the self and the narcissistic form of love it demands, and seeks fulfillment for a form of the self which is essentially fluid, essentially changing, and essentially involved in a dynamic, living network of intimate relations with others.

Like the Brontë heroines, although in a less reflective and more narcissistic way,[25] the Harlequin heroines find that women in our society are already endowed with this relational form of the self, but that it never achieves recognition or fulfillment. The cause of pain and obscurity rather than success, it in fact tends to get lost altogether in a relation with the hero's harder, closed self, and to merge into his. This is what Anna finds in *Battle with Desire*: 'Anna knew she mustn't give in. ... And it wasn't getting any easier to resist, the urge to fight was melting away, so she made one final attempt at self-respect' (19). What really melts here are the boundaries of the heroine's personhood and her sense of individuality as she loses herself in the other. Harlequins, unlike 'real life', provide a solution: the hero adopts the feminine form of the self, recognizes it as valid, and gives the heroine the same tender devotion she gives him.

The genius of the Harlequin Romances is to combine the struggle for the recognition of feminine selfhood and the struggle to make the work world a home for that self. As the cover blurb of *The Dividing Line* tells us of Kerry and Ross who have inherited interests in a department store: 'She liked old-fashioned friendliness and service. He was all for modern impersonal efficiency. Between them, Sinclairs was becoming a battle ground.' Even the idealized form of Kerry's angry struggle against Ross, and violinst Anna's questioning resentment against Gareth, suggest a need to go beyond an analysis like that in *Hearth and Home: Images of women in the mass-media*, edited by Gaye Tuchman, Arlene Kaplan Daniels and James Benet. The book criticizes the mass media image of women for implying that 'her fate and her happiness rest with a man, not with participation in the labor force',[26] but it would be impoverishing even the impoverished romances to say that their heroines really want both. They want so much more besides. Not content with Helen Gurley Brown's rationalistic advice to 'have it all', they don't want it the way it is now; they want the world of labor to change so that women can find happiness there, and they want men to change so that men will just as much find *their* happiness with women.

Heart and Home sees hope for equality in 'economically productive women who insist on the abandonment of old prejudices and discriminatory behaviors'.[27] But Harlequin Romances suggest women who abandon the present structures of economic production because those structures force women to give up their values, their ethos, and even their particular sense of self for success, or, more likely, for mere survival. The vastly popular Harlequin Romances implicitly and potentially pose a demand for profound structural transformations of the total social world we inhabit. And like their romantic forebears, the heroines desire that this new world be not just our same old world improved, but a different, better world. The problem is that Harlequin Enterprises, having learned these secrets to a woman's heart, exploited them by turning them into marketable formulae which divorced the conflicts from their causes and cut off the path towards reflecting upon any realistic solutions.

ROMANTIC ASPIRATIONS – RATIONALIZED FORM

In her analysis of women readers, Radway has pointed out that

> we would do well not to condescend to romance readers as hopeless traditionalists who are recalcitrant in their refusal to acknowledge the emotional costs of patriarchy. We must begin to recognize that romance reading is fueled by dissatisfaction and disaffection.[28]

Yet there is a crucial distinction to be made between dismissing the very justifiable fantasies and desires of Harlequin readers or the undoubted achievements of romance writers, and criticizing a multinational publishing corporation that exploits those fantasies and achievements. Modleski is probably closer to the mark when she says of Harlequin that 'their enormous and continuing popularity ... suggests that they speak to very real problems and tensions in women's lives', but that the texts arouse subversive anxieties and desires, and then 'work to neutralize them'.[29]

The methods of editing, producing, marketing and distributing Harlequin Romances are part and parcel of the depersonalized, standardized, mechanistic conglomerate system that the Harlequin heroines oppose. Harlequin heroines seek interconnectedness in the social, sexual and economic world as a whole. Yet their very search is contained in a static, thinglike, literary structure, which denies their quest and turns it into its opposite.

Radway reports that the readers she interviewed understand very well that 'the characters and events ... of the typical romance do not resemble the people and occurrences they must deal with in their daily lives'.[30] At issue in the case of Harlequin, however, is not the illusion that the events in the romances are real, but the illusion that reading a romance constitutes only a relation to a text and to an author. To see the act of reading a romance as simply a relation between the reader and the printed page is to isolate this act from its larger context.

We are used to thinking of a publisher as a mediator between the readers and a book written by an individual author, but Harlequin changed this. Although Harlequin is studied in few university literature classes, it is referred to in management classes as a sterling example of successful business practices that students should learn to emulate. According to business professor Peter Killing, Harlequin's success is due precisely to its doing away with the reader–text and reader–author relation:

> Harlequin's formula was fundamentally different from that of traditional publishers: content, length, artwork, size, basic formats, and print, were all standardized. Each book was not a new product, but rather an addition to a

clearly defined product line. The consequences of this uniformity were significant. The reader was buying a *Harlequin novel*, rather than a book of a certain title by a particular author. ... There was no need to make decisions about layouts, artwork, or cover design. The standardized size made warehousing and distribution more efficient. Employees hired from mass-marketing companies such as Proctor and Gamble had skills and aptitudes which led them to do well at Harlequin.[31]

Harlequin thought of everything – except the readers, the authors and the creative freedom which has traditionally been the cornerstone of literature in western culture. This publishing giant molded romantic aspirations into superrationalist forms of communication, the very antithesis of the readers' desires.

It is not the idealization of marriage in the romances, nor any specific content, that neutralizes their challenges to patriarchal ideology, but rather the form of the romances, and the form of communication Harlequin sets up between the corporate giant and the readers. Like the Brontëan heroes and heroines, whose desires for sublime sexual communion were a protest against the rationalizing forces of the industrial revolution, the Harlequin romances both protest against and compensate for their readers' dissatisfaction with the Taylorization of their lives as workers and consumers of goods and services. But when Harlequin instituted its new methods, the romantic quest and the sublime sexual communion were themselves Taylorized, so that the apparent escape from a depersonalized, coldly compartmentalized world led the reader right back into it.

Harlequin reduced romantic aspirations to the rational distillation of a formula. The General Editorial Guidelines of 1982 for *Worldwide Library Superromances*, in its directions to writers, broke down the fluid process of the romantic quest into its component set of static categories – structure, characters, plot, subplots, romance, sex, viewpoint and writing style – and in the past even set forth each step in the plot.

- Introduction of hero and heroine, their meeting.
- Initial attraction or conflict between them.
- Romantic conflicts or heroine's qualms about hero.
- Counterbalance to developing romance (i.e., sensual scenes, getting to know each other, growth of love vs. conflicts).
- Hero's role in creating conflict.
- Resolution of conflicts and happy ending, leading to marriage.
- The development of the romance should be the primary concern of the author, with other story elements integrated into the romance.[32]

Sex (always of course coupled with 'shared feeling rather than pure male domination' – General Editorial Guidelines) is meted out in measured amounts and in measured doses of 'sensuality' at measured intervals of the plot. As a further rationalization, the romantic quest can even be broken down numerically and quantified, so that, as the 1982 Guidelines for Writing Harlequin's *New* American Romances tell us, 'parts of the plot can take place anywhere in the world provided that at least 80% of the novel takes place in the United States'.[33]

But in 1984, with changes in readers' tastes and the growth of the authors' professional association Romance Writers of America, the Editorial Guidelines deny there is a formula: 'Every aspiring Harlequin writer has a very clear picture of what makes these lines so successful, to the extent that some people have even tried to reduce it to a formula'.[34]

A CHANGING GENRE: THE AUTHOR AS HEROINE

Yet so much has changed and continues to change since 1980, when growth in the industry led authors to organize Romance Writers of America as a support group, that it is impossible to tell what will happen in the future. Present developments could lead not only to changes in the texts of the romances, but also to changes in the romance industry. Harlequin's very success could open up the potential contradictions inherent in the corporation's methods. The same kinds of struggle against rationalizing power its themes portray could be turned against it. When Romance Writers of America held its first national convention in 1981, the organization saw as its main opponent a literary establishment and vaguely defined public that did not recognize the value of romance as 'women's literature'.[35] But as conditions governing author–corporate relations change, the industry itself might become another opponent.

Harlequin has responded to declining sales in face of competition by the classic strategy of buying out its major competitor (Silhouette Romances). But authors have had a quite different response to growth in the romance industry. Although Harlequin's monopolizing strategy should work to make even more impersonal the author-publisher relation, authors have been seeking (as if in imitation of their own heroines) more affirming relations with the publisher and greater job satisfaction.

In her study of Harlequin Romances, Margaret Ann Jensen reports that the experience of becoming writers has caused many romance authors to 'identify themselves as feminists', to become self-assertive, and to become more aware of themselves as working women who have succeeded in a profession quite difficult to break into. In addition to combatting 'the negative image of romance in the literary world', romance writers, she says, have two new concerns. They 'are attempting to organize to improve the standards within their field'; they are also engaging in 'an increasing outspokenness about the romantic fiction industry' and making 'critical responses to it'.[36] At a Romance Writers of America meeting in Southern California, one candidate for office in the organization raised these same two issues. She spoke first of the need to 'raise the standards of writing' and prevent 'mediocre' writing. Then, after mentioning other writers' organizations that are more 'militant', she spoke of the need to 'increase our clout with publishers' and 'improve the deal we're getting on contracts'.[37]

Although authors still speak with indignation of the scorn that they face, saying that romances deserve the same respect as mysteries and science fiction, they also raise the above-mentioned other issues concerning the romance industry itself. Authors find themselves disadvantaged by the very marketing practice of Harlequin to which Peter Killing attributes Harlequin's economic success: Harlequin promotes its lines but rarely its authors. And Silhouette has followed suit. In a 1980 interview, Silhouette president P.J. Fennel said: 'We're out to get brand name loyalty, so we're not selling individual titles.'[38] Because of this practice, and because a romance is on the market for only a month, romance authors have to hustle their own books and find their own markets. They can also, they report, have a diffcult time getting royalties from the publisher, with waits of up to two years.[39]

Although this kind of issue is just beginning to be addressed, the issues concerning quality of writing and personal creativity have already begun to be acted upon. Each product line in the romance industry has its own formula, and as the formulae have multiplied, they have also loosened. As a result, an author can pick the line that gives her the most freedom. More important, through Romance Writers of America, authors have formed their own critique groups, so that influences on their writing now also come from their peers and not only from the publishing institutions. Romances are beginning to be better and more carefully written, with more variety in the formulae and with more attention to detail. Although some romances repeat a mechanical version of the formula, other romances like Leigh Roberts's *Love Circuits* are different. Roberts's work, where the hero, tender and loving from the beginning, wears a Charlotte Brontë T-shirt, and where the heroine has a witty sense of humour, brings some surprising transformations to the formula. Like any kind of formula writing – or any kind of writing – romance writing requires skill and talent.

As the corporation follows its destiny of expansion, conglomeration and product diversification, differences between the mass production needs of the corporation and authors' needs may prove to be potential cracks in the Harlequin machine. The authors' own quest for creative individuality, for economic independence and for recognition may make them the heroines of their own real life romance, with conflicts and adventures outside the text just as gripping as those inside.

NOTES

1. Catering to an exclusively feminine audience, mass market romances are an international phenomenon, with single romances or whole romance series being translated into as many as fourteen languages. Harlequin Enterprises, the best-selling and most successful publisher of this genre, has been imitated by many competitors both in America and in Europe. Harlequin publishes a set number of romances per month, categorized into different series according to a carefully measured degree of explicit sex, known as 'sensuality' in the trade. Harlequin publishes Harlequin Romances, Harlequin Presents and Harlequin Temptations, as well as a mystery-romance series, a gothic romance series, a longer series called Superromances, and an American romance series. Like any corporate consumer product, Harlequin and its competitors are constantly 'diversifying' their line, proliferating into a dizzying array of series.

   Other publishers now have romance series for more mature and/or divorced women, like Berkeley-Jove's Second Chance at Love, or for adolescent girls, like Simon & Schuster's First Love. This series shares the teen-romance shelves with the Sweet Dream series from Bantam; Young Love from Dell; Caprice from Grosset & Dunlap; and two series from Scolastic, whose Wishing Star and Wild Fire sold 2.25 million copies in 1982.

   Information taken from Brett Harvey, 'Boy crazy', *Village Voice* 27 (10–16 February 1982), pp. 48–9: Stanley Meisler, 'Harlequins: the romance of escapism', *Los Angeles Times*, 15 November 1980. pt 1, pp. 7–8; Rosemary Nightingale, 'True romances', *Miami Herald*, 5 January 1983; J. D. Reed, 'From bedroom to boardroom: romance novels court changing fancies and adorable profits', *Time*, 13 April 1981, pp. 101–4; interview with Jany Saint-Marcoux, editor of Collections sentimentales, Editions Tallandier; 'Romantic novels find receptive market', *Santa Ana Register*, 26 July 1979, section E, p. 1; *Standard and Poor's Corporation Records* 43 (New York, May 1982), p. 8475.

2. See Reed, 'From bedroom to boardroom'. According to Margaret Ann Jensen, the very success of Harlequin has caused these figures to decline drastically. Because so many publishers are now imitating Harlequin and competing with it, Harlequin's 'share of the market has dropped to 45 per cent. ... All signs indicate that Harlequin is a financially distressed corporation.' See Jensen, *Love's $weet Return: The Harlequin story* (Toronto: Women's Educational Press, 1984). In order to offset this decline, Harlequin is purchasing Silhouette Romances.

3. Tania Modleski, *Loving with a Vengeance: Mass-produced fantasies for women* (Hamden: Archon Books, 1982); Ann Barr Snitow, 'Mass Market Romance: pornography for women is different', *Radical History Review* 20 (Spring–Summer 1979), pp. 141–61, reprinted in *Powers of Desire: The politics of sexuality*, ed. Ann Snitow, Christine Stansell and Sharon Thomas (New York: Monthly Review Press, 1983); Janice A. Radway, 'Women read the romance: the interaction of text and context', *Feminist Studies* 9 (Spring 1983), pp. 53–78.

4. Modleski, *Loving with a Vengeance*, p. 113.

5. Kerry Allyne, *Across the Great Divide* (1980); Ann Cooper, *Battle with Desire* (1980); Kay Thorpe *The Dividing Line* (1980). All books published by Harlequin Books, Toronto, London, New York, Amsterdam, Sydney, Hamburg, Paris, Stockholm. Page numbers appear in parentheses in the text.

6. Lynsey Stevens, *Race for Revenge* (Toronto: Harlequin, 1981), back cover.
7. Advertisement for Sara Jennings, *Game Plan* (Garden City, NY: Candlelight Ecstasy Romances, 1984), back cover.
8. Leigh Roberts, *Love Circuits* (Harlequin Temptations, 1984); Sarah James, *Public Affair* (Harlequin American Romance, 1984); Marion Smith Collins, *By Any Other Name* (Harlequin Temptations, 1984). All books published by Harlequin Enterprises, Toronto. Page numbers appear in parentheses in the text.
9. Advertisement for Harlequin Temptations, found in Harlequin books of July 1984 (Toronto: Harlequin Enterprises, 1984).
10. Colette Dowling, *The Cinderella Complex: Women's hidden fear of independence* (New York: Simon & Schuster Pocket Books, 1981), pp. 2, 54.
11. Harry Braverman, *Labor and Monopoly Capital: The degradation of work in the twentieth century*, Special Abridged Edn (Special Issue of *Monthly Review* 26 (July–August 1974)) p. 50.

    According to Braverman, by 1970 in the United States, clerical work was one of the fastest-growing occupations and had become one of the lowest paid, its pay 'lower than that of every type of so-called blue collar work' (p. 51). Of its 10 million members, by 1978, 79.6 per cent were women. In 1970, clerical work included 18 per cent of all gainfully employed persons in the United States, a percentage equal to that of production work of all sorts.
12. Roslyn L. Feldberg and Evelyn Nakano Glenn, 'Technology and work degradation: effects of office automation on women clerical workers', in *Machina ex Dea*, ed. Joan Rothschild (New York: Pergamon Press, 1983), p. 62.
13. Radway, 'Women read the romance', p. 57, reports that 42 per cent of the women in her study work outside the home, and says that Harlequin claims that 49 per cent of its audience works outside the home. A 1984 Waldenbooks survey found that 63 per cent of its romance readers held jobs outside the home (Doug Brown, 'Research dissects the romantic novel', *Los Angeles Times*, 19 September 1984, V. 8).
14. ibid., p. 60.
15. Braverman, *Labor and Monopoly Capital*, p. 61.
16. Ida Russakoff Hoos, *Automation in the Office* (Washington, 1961), p. 53, cited in Braverman, op. cit.
17. Ellen Cantarow, 'Working can be dangerous to your health', *Mademoiselle*, August 1982, pp. 114–16.
18. Eleanor Farnes, *The Enchanted Island* (Toronto: Harlequin Enterprises, 1971). Page numbers appear in parentheses in the text.
19. Margaret Mayo, *Stormy Affair* (Toronto: Harlequin Enterprises, 1980). Page numbers appear in parentheses in the text.
20. Radway, 'Women read the romance'; Snitow, 'Mass market romance'; and Nancy Chodorow, *The Reproduction of Mothering: Psychoanalysis and the sociology of gender* (Berkeley: University of California Press, 1978).
21. Sally Mitchell, *The Fallen Angel: Chastity, class, and women's reading, 1835–1880* (Bowling Green, Ohio: Bowling Green University Press, 1981); and Modleski, *Loving with a Vengeance*.
22. Personal communication from Louella Nelson, author of *Freedom's Fortune*, Harlequin Superromance (Toronto: Harlequin Books, 1984).

23. Charlotte Brontë, *Shirley* (Baltimore: Penguin, 1974), pp. 234–5.
24. Janet Dailey, *The Matchmakers* (Toronto: Harlequin Enterprises, 1978); Elizabeth Graham, *Come Next Spring* (Toronto: Harlequin Enterprises, 1980).
25. For the role of narcissism in the Harlequin Romances, see Modleski, *Loving with a Vengeance.*
26. Gaye Tuchman, Arlene Kaplan Daniels, and James Benet, eds, *Hearth and Home: Images of women in the mass media* (New York: Oxford University Press, 1978), p. 18.
27. ibid., p. 4.
28. Radway, 'Women read the romance', p. 68.
29. Modleski, *Loving with a Vengeance*, pp. 14, 30.
30. Radway, 'Women read the romance', p. 59.
31. Peter Killing, *Harlequin Enterprises Limited: Case material of the western school of business administration* (London, Ontario: University of Western Ontario, 1978), p. 3.
32. General Editorial Guidelines, *Worldwide Library Superromances* (Toronto: Harlequin Enterprises, 1982), p. 2.
33. Guidelines for Writing Harlequin's *New* American Romances (Toronto: Harlequin Enterprises, 1982), p. 3.
34. *Harlequin Romance and Harlequin Presents Editorial Guidelines* (Ontario: Harlequin Books, 1984), p. 1.
35. George Christian, 'Romance writers, going to the heart of the matter (and the market) call for recognition', *Publishers Weekly*, 24 July 1980. The first national conference of Romance Writers of America was held in Houston, in June 1981, with 800 participants, mostly women.
36. Jensen, *Love's $weet Return*, pp. 73–4.
37. Speech given at a meeting of Romance Writers of America, Orange County Chapter.
38. Vivien Lee Jennings, 'The romance wars', *Publisher's Weekly*, 24 August 1984, p. 53.
39. Information gathered from conversations with authors at meeting. See note 37.

TWELVE
Real women

ANNETTE KUHN

In opening up consideration of feminism as film practice by discussing variants of cinematic realism, I am perhaps approaching the question in exactly the way it most immediately presents itself to many cinema-goers. If only because one of the principal characteristics of dominant cinema is that it embodies certain forms of realism, most cinema-goers are familiar and comfortable with realism, particularly in its narrative forms. But certain kinds of cinema other than classic narrative – notably documentary – are also frequently regarded as 'realist'. What, then, do different types of realist cinema have in common? The basic shared characteristic of all forms of cinematic realism is their tendency to transparency in representation: what is seen on the cinema screen appears to the spectator to be constructed in much the same way as its referent, the 'real world'. The film, that is, 'looks like' the real world. This is what makes realist films easy to watch and follow: they seem to duplicate spectators' everyday ways of experiencing the world. This realistic appearance is in fact brought about not by a duplication of 'real world' referents but by certain conventions of cinematic signification. All films are coded: it is simply that certain types of film are coded in such a way as actually to seem uncoded. Thus, for example, the codes at work in classic Hollywood cinema operate in certain ways to obscure the processes of meaning construction in which the spectator is constantly engaged. The transparency of realist cinema then consists in the fact that the spectator is seldom actually aware in watching a film that she or he is making meanings: meaning seems to be there already in the film, the spectator's only task being to sit back and take it in. This of course is one of the pleasures of the classic realist cinema: an address which draws the spectator in to the representation by constructing a credible and coherent cinematic world, which at the same time situates her or him as a passive consumer of meanings which seem to be already there in the text.

While realism can be a defining characteristic of both fictional (the classic narrative, for example) and non-fictional (the documentary film) cinemas, all realist forms have the 'appearance of reality' in common. Cinesemiotics, in tracing the ways in which this transparency is coded, has tended to confine its analysis to fictional narrative cinema. However, it is equally important for our purposes to look at the codes at work in non-fictional realist cinema. The apparently uncoded character of all realist cinema is what lends it its veri-similitude: a certain kind of credibility in relation to the 'real world' is set up, and the spectator undergoes a 'suspension of disbelief'. This process works rather differently with non-fiction than it does with fictional realism. The defining characteristics of fiction as against non-fiction film lie in the dual operations of narrativity and characterization. In watching a fiction film, the spectator is involved in two forms of identification. One is with the movement of the narrative itself, from the disruption of a fictional equilibrium which constitutes its beginning, through the movement towards resolution and then final closure. The other identification is with the narrative's central character or characters. In these identification processes, the spectator is in varying degrees, depending on the linearity and economy of the narrative and the representation of central characters in terms of their fictional personality traits, drawn into the world of the film. The operation of the specific cinematic codes associated with fictional realism – continuity editing, close-ups, shot-reverse shot structures and point-of-view shots – serves to reinforce the spectator's identification with a credible fictional world. Although realism as representation does not of course normally lead spectators to confuse the boundaries of the world of cinematic narrative with those of the 'real world', its address – its processes of fictional identification in particular – none the less does set up a kind of credibility that is well described by the notion of suspension of disbelief. The credibility of non-fiction film tends to work rather differently, however. A general point to be made about the realism of documentary as against that of fiction film is that its address typically con-stitutes an appeal to some kind of empirical conceptualization of the visible as 'evidence': if it's on the screen, it must be true.[1] This kind of credibility obviously rests on transparency: the cinematic image constitutes itself as a record of 'reality'. The specificity of documentary forms of transparency is that the image appears to be 'natural' – an unmediated transposition of one reality onto another – as well as 'real' – as setting up, that is, an internally credible film world.

Documentary film thus always makes implicit reference not only to its profilmic event, but also to the 'real world' in general. While this visibility is constituted as 'truth' by the apparent naturalness of the representation, this very 'naturalness' is itself an outcome of the operation of a certain set of cinematic codes. Cinematic signifiers such as monochrome image, apparently haphazard mobile framing (the mark of a hand-held camera), focus shifts, editing which is rather more 'free' than would be the case with fictional cinema, and direct gaze at the camera by protagonists of the film, all currently tend to mark a film as a documentary. Further sets of codes relating to sound may also connote 'documentariness'. Many documentary films have voice-over: a voice from a source outside and apparently 'above' the world of the film speaks a discourse which directs the spectator's reading of the film. The documentary voice-over is typically marked as authoritative, as a metadiscourse which orders the potentially erratic signifiers of image and diegetic sound. In this case, the guarantee of the 'truth' of the film lies in the relationship between voice-over and image, in that the latter may be read as 'illustrating' the former. The notion of the visible as evidence is still at work here, of course, but the specificity of the classic voice-over documentary lies in the fact that the image somehow serves as evidence of the truth of the commentary rather than as direct and visible evidence of events in the 'real world'.

How are feminist concerns and feminist cultural politics actually written into different types of realist films? How are realist modes of representation deployed in dealing with issues of relevance to feminists? It is significant that questions about realism immediately seem to emphasize 'dealing with issues'. This, I would suggest, is a direct outcome of the transparency which marks all forms of cinematic realism. Articulated within a mode of representation that does not foreground its own processes of signification, political issues can stand out clearly. Put in another way, since the issues are played out in the real world, it may be argued that they are suitably dealt with in film by translating that world in general, and the issues in particular, into a representation which allows the spectator a freedom directly to see issues as they look, operate and develop in the real world of everyday existence or political struggle. In a realist fiction film, the spectator's identifications can be quite direct, easy and pleasurable: for a feminist, for example, pleasure may arise in the process of identifying with a strong and independent female character who is able to control the process of the narrative and its fictional events in such a way as to bring about a resolution in which she wins in some way. In documentary, identifications may take place more directly with what is represented in the image, so that, for example, a film about a woman's life and her work as a mother and housewife may bring about forms of recognition in female spectators of themselves or their own everyday lives.

The rest of this essay is devoted to a consideration of several types of cinematic realism in relation to the questions posed at the beginning of the last paragraph. I shall look at the points of identification, modes of address and subject positionings characteristic of each type, and examine a number of films in some detail. I begin by discussing two variants of fictional realism: first, some recent Hollywood films which may be read as responses to the women's movement on the part of dominant cinema, and second, socialist realist cinema as it intersects with feminism. In considering the question of non-fictional realism, I shall examine some of the ways in which the textual organization of feminist documentary films is frequently overlaid by auto-biographical discourses.

HOLLYWOOD AND NEW WOMEN'S CINEMA

Since the years of ascendancy of the Hollywood studio system, the industry has undergone many institutional changes which have had a number of implications regarding the textual organization of Hollywood films. Molly Haskell and Marjorie Rosen have charted shifts in representations of women in Hollywood films which have accompanied these institutional changes,[2] and both writers conclude that during the 1960s Hollywood films became increasingly violent, that women characters were increasingly represented as victims, and that the days of the powerful female star and the 'independent woman' as a character were gone. Haskell offers a sociological explanation for this finding, arguing that: 'The closer women come to claiming rights and achieving independence in real life, the more loudly and stridently films tell us it's a man's world'.[3] The rise of the second wave of feminism, according to this explanation, brought about a backlash effect: the threat posed by the liberated woman was actually contained in films, often by a literal containment, at the level of story, of female protagonists. This might range from confinement within home and family, or in mental institutions, through to containment by various forms of physical violence up to and including murder.

At the same time, however, since the middle 1970s – after Haskell's and Rosen's books were first published – a number of Hollywood films have been made which may be read as indicating an opposite trend. In these films, the central characters are women, and often women who are not attractive or glamorous in the conventional sense. Narratives, moreover, are frequently organized around the process of a woman's self-discovery and growing independence: instances of this genre include *Alice Doesn't Live here Anymore* (Scorsese, Warner Brothers, 1975), *Starting Over* (Pakula, Paramount, 1979), and *An Unmarried Woman* (Mazursky, Fox, 1977). The existence of this 'new women's cinema' might be explained in terms of direct determination: that it simply reflects the growth and influence of the women's movement. On its own, however, such an explanation is perhaps rather one-dimensional, in that it cannot take into account the simultaneous existence of, say, films portraying violence towards women. By what process, in any case, are social climates translated into cinematic signifieds? Given the complexity of the institutional structures of the film industry, not to mention the coded operations of film texts, the relationship between social climates and the content of films is obviously not a simple one. Explaining the co-existence of dissimilar types of Hollywood films calls for an examination of a variety of structures in their historical specificity. For example, if the cinema audience is composed of segmented sub-audiences with different interests, films will address themselves to these various audiences. Thus the new women's film addresses itself in particular to women, even to women with some degree of feminist consciousness, while other film genres will be directed at quite different social audiences.

In what ways do new women's films embody realism, and what is their relevance for feminism? As dominant cinema, their realism rests on the credibility of texts which construct identifications for the spectator on the levels of character and narrative, within a fictional world constituted as coherent and internally consistent. The spectator may, in other words, be drawn fairly readily into the identifications offered by the films. The pleasure for the female spectator of films of this kind lies in several possible identifications: with a central character who is not only also a woman, but who may be similar in some respects to the spectator herself; or with a narrative voice enunciated by a woman character; or with fictional events which evoke a degree of recognition; or with a resolution that constitutes a victory for the central character. The address of the new women's film may thus position the spectator not only as herself a potential winner, but also as a winner whose gender is instrumental in the victory: it may consequently offer the female spectator a degree of affirmation. Two questions may be posed at this point, however. First, how do these various identifications operate in relation to one another in the address of film texts? And second, what are the implications for feminism of a classic realist cinema which is affirmative of women?

These questions are best dealt with by reference to specific films: I shall look at Claudia Weill's *Girlfriends* (1977) and Fred Zinneman's *Julia* (1977), both of which take up a genre popular in the 1960s and the 1970s, the male 'buddy movie'. *Girlfriends* and *Julia* become women's films by virtue of the simple fact that the buddies in these cases are female. A primary requirement of the new women's film is thus immediately met – the central characters are female, and they are sympathetically portrayed. *Girlfriends* goes a step further than this by presenting its main characters as not at all glamorous. The heroines of *Julia* conform much more to the Hollywood star model, however: Lillian Hellman (Jane Fonda) is a famous writer and Julia (Vanessa Redgrave) an obscure but highly courageous revolutionary. The star system is obviously at work here: while the central characters in *Girlfriends* are played by little-known actresses, who play 'ordinary' women, the casting of two world-famous figures – both of them also highly visible as political activists – as the stars of *Julia* has important consequences for the meanings generated by the film. Neither Julia nor Lillian as fictional characters can be regarded as ordinary, and the casting underlines this: the point of identification for female spectators lies not so much with the characters as with the relationship between them.

Both *Julia* and *Girlfriends* may be seen as departing somewhat from the classic realist model in their narrative resolutions. In each film the questions set up by the narrative are not fully resolved by the closure. In *Girlfriends*, in fact, full closure is perhaps impossible, given the nature of the structuring enigmas of the narrative. The story begins with one of the women friends moving out of their shared apartment in order to get married. Ann's departure seems to motivate a series of events in Susan's life, all somewhat unconnected by anything other than the fact of her friend's absence. In the classic narrative model, resolution of this absence would be brought about by the restoration of an equilibrium. Within the trajectory of lack to liquidation of lack which marks variants of this model, resolution in *Girlfriends* might be brought about by the establishment of love relationships for Ann and Susan: either with each other, or with new partners. Although the first option would fit in well with the structual demands of classic narrative, as well as with the powerful Hollywood romance model, its content is excluded by rules, conscious and unconscious, currently governing representations of homosexuality in dominant cinema. But at the same time the second option – re-establishment of equilibrium through the setting up of new relationships – is also ruled out, in this case by the demands on the narrative set up through the characterizations of the two women: it would simply not be plausible. However, although there is a constant movement towards the latter resolution – in Susan's relationship with a rabbi, for instance, and even in Ann's with her husband – it is never quite brought off, partly perhaps because it would undermine the 'buddy' structure that governs the organization of the narrative. And so, caught in its own contradictions, the narrative cannot be resolved in the classic manner. We are left instead with a relatively open ending: the women's relationship continues to be problematic and contradictory, and yet important enough to be continued. It may be argued, of course, that such an open ending is in fact more credible than any classic resolution which ties all the ends of the narrative together.

Julia, too, possesses a degree of openness, which in this instance operates not so much in the film's resolution as through its entire narrative. This openness is crucially related to the film's articulation of plot and story, and the fact that its discourse is pivoted on memory. The film's enunciation involves at least two layers of memory. First there is the overarching discourse of Hellman's memoir, rendered in the film as her voice-over and as the temporal present of the narrative, and marked by the representation of the writer's relationship with Dashiell Hammett. Secondly, there is the memory within the memoir, constituted as the past of the film and marked cinematically as subjective, as Hellman's fantasies and dreams, most of them involving Julia. The two levels are brought together only in those sequences in the film's present when Lillian and Julia meet – in a Vienna hospital and in a station café in Berlin. Since the relationship between the women is largely told discursively through Hellman's narrative point-of-view, and exactly because of its status as memory within memoir, it is relativized. What we see is Hellman's impression of a remembered relationship, doubly marked as subjective. We can therefore read the film in several ways. The openness of *Julia* centres less on the film's closure (which is in any case not entirely inconclusive, in that the past and the present of the narrative are brought together with Julia's death and Lillian's dealing with it in her relationship with Hammett), than on the nature of the relationship between the two women. This is encapsulated in a scene – a flashback, in fact – in which Lillian slugs a drunken male friend for suggesting that 'the whole world knows about you and Julia': that, in other words, the women have a lesbian relationship. The scene may be read in at least two ways: either Hellman's reaction is to the slur on lesbianism implied in 'the whole world's' uncomprehending gossip, or the accusation of lesbianism is itself a slur on the relationship.[4] A reading of reviews of *Julia* certainly upholds this suggestion: while most reviewers agree that the relationship portrayed between the women is central to the film (although it might in fact be argued, to the contrary, that the way the Hellman–Hammett relationship is represented, and also its place in the film's present, serve actually to enclose and relativize that of the women), there are almost as many opinions as there are reviews concerning the precise nature of that relationship.[5]

The question of openness in these two examples of new women's cinema may be considered in relation to some general formal and thematic shifts within recent Hollywood cinema. These shifts have been regarded as significant enough to constitute a New Hollywood Cinema. The mobilisation in New Hollywood Cinema of certain cinematic codes – zooming, telephoto shots, slow motion and split screen – have, it has been argued, 'destroyed the dramatic and spatio-temporal unity that founded the classical mise-en-scène'.[6] Another mark of New Hollywood Cinema is a degree of open-endedness or ambiguity at the level of narrative – a defining feature of both *Julia* and *Girlfriends*. Two points of relevance to the question of realism, feminism and the new women's film may be made here. The first is that although New Hollywood Cinema is something of a departure for narrative cinema, it reworks rather than destroys the textual operations of dominant cinema: 'Ambiguity and open-endedness are sustained and articulated *within* the limits of the dominant discourse, within the text. They are not of the kind likely to fracture the unity of position of the reader'.[7]

Secondly, although the openness of New Hollywood Cinema operates across a range of cinematic genres and narratives, it may be argued that, precisely because of its subject matter, the new women's cinema is particularly prone to such openness. Although feminism and new women's cinema are by no means coterminous, new women's cinema does raise, at some level at least, the question of feminism. Feminism is controversial, however, and it would be problematic for a cinematic institution whose products are directed at a politically heterogeneous audience overtly to take up positions which might alienate certain sections of that audience. Films whose address sustains a degree of polysemy – which open up rather than restrict potential readings, in other words – may appeal to a relatively broadly based audience. Openness permits readings to be made which accord more or less with spectators' prior stances on feminist issues. *Julia* illustrates this point quite well: while lesbians may be free to read the film as an affirmation of lesbianism, such a reading – just as it is not ruled out – is by no means privileged by the text. *Girlfriends* works similarly with regard to the question of feminism. On its release, the film was widely received as charming, warm, amusing and likeable. It was not regarded as threatening largely because, despite its status as a female 'buddy' film, it does not demand a reading as a feminist film. Nevertheless, at the same time, the 'buddy' structure can equally well justify a reading of the film in terms of woman-identification.

The possibility that this kind of openness may actually be a defining characteristic of new women's cinema is pointed to by Julia Lesage, who argues that: 'The industry wants to let everybody have their ideological cake and eat it, too. In other words, you'll see deliberate ambiguities structured into almost every film to come out about strong women'.[8] Whether or not this process is as conscious or deliberate as Lesage suggests, one of the most significant effects of this ideologically implicated ambiguity must be to buttress the textual and institutional operations of dominant cinema. Whatever positive identifications it offers to those who choose to make them, new women's cinema cannot in the final instance deal in any direct way with the questions which feminism poses for cinematic representation.

SOCIALIST REALISM

Socialist realism (or progressive realism[9]) is often discussed in relation to literature and the fine arts rather than cinema. None the less, the somewhat abstract level at which debates about socialist realism tend to be conducted does permit a consideration of its characteristics as they operate across various forms of expression, cinema among them. Socialist realism was defined by Stalin during the 1930s as 'a true and historically concrete depiction of reality and its revolutionary development'. While such a statement is open to a range of interpretations, it does suggest two basic defining characteristics for socialist realism: first, an adherence to some form of realism ('true ... depiction of reality'), and second, that representations either deal directly with history or inscribe historical specificity in some other way ('historically concrete'). It is, I would argue, the latter quality which sets socialist realism apart from other forms of realism.

But what, in terms of textual operations, does 'historical concreteness' mean? This question may be approached by examining the nature of the realism inscribed by socialist realism. In debates on art and literature in the

Soviet Union during the early years of the revolution, it was suggested that art should not only represent, but also be accessible to, the people.[10] Although no definition was offered of what accessibility might mean in textual terms, a tendency to favour transparent modes of representation was soon in evidence. This tendency was consolidated in official Soviet policy on the arts during the 1930s,[11] in which realism was distinguished from naturalism and the latter rejected in favour of the former. The distinction between realism and naturalism turns on historical concreteness and characterization: whereas both forms involve characterization, in realism history takes centre stage through characterization. In other words, historical changes, conflicts and contradictions are rendered textually within developments of consciousness on the part of characters, as well as in their interactions with one another. The dual requirements of characterization and 'accessibility' mean that narrative is a common setting for these representations. Thus the socialist realist narrative operates on the levels of both character and history, the one encapsulating and representing the other.

From this emerges the concept of typification: in socialist realism, characters may be drawn as rounded individuals with their own traits of personality, but at the same time they also function as embodiments of social and historical characteristics. In this way, characters become social types as well as individuals. The representation of reality in its historical concreteness thus takes place through fictional characters who partly operate as types expressive of social groups or classes and historical configurations. This is the fundamental difference between socialist realism and the realism of Hollywood cinema. In the latter, identifications by readers with central characters occur predominantly at the level of individual traits of personality set up by, and expatiated upon within, the narrative. In socialist realism, on the other hand, identification at the level of individual personality traits also, and concomitantly, involves identification with the social-historical situation of the character's type.

The central characters of socialist realist texts frequently embody heroic traits, a quality which has its origins in the influence of revolutionary romanticism on socialist realism. In revolutionary romanticism, art offers a vision of the future which is optimistic, but also aims to be grounded rather than utopian. This optimism is rendered in the revolutionary development of a figure who becomes 'heroic' in the course of that development: hence the 'positive hero' of socialist realism. She or he is represented as a personality having individual qualities, positive and negative, with which the reader may identify. At the same time, the movement of the narrative involves a personal or political development and a growth of insight and strength on the part of the 'positive hero' which enables the character both to attain a degree of political consciousness and also to overcome difficulties and obstacles which are both specific – pertaining, that is, to the fictional individual's personal situation – and general – signifying a broader social/historical situation. Thus the socialist realist narrative, like the classic narrative, involves resolution and closure. However, there are differences between them as regards the narrative processes through which resolution is reached. In the case of classic realism, closure comes about when the structuring enigmas of the narrative have been resolved, probably by the main character or characters, through the deployment of personal qualities – perceptiveness, toughness, cunning or whatever. In socialist realism this happens too, but the process is overlaid by the intervention of 'history', which – in the guise of typification – is also a point of identification for the reader. The fact that history marches on, as it were, transcending the resolution of any individual narrative, may also mark a potential for openness in socialist realism that does not necessarily exist in classic realism.

What I have said so far applies to socialist realism in any narrative form, and is therefore just as relevant, say, to the novel as it is to cinema. Are there any codes whereby socialist realist meanings are produced in cinema? I would argue that there are in fact no specifically cinematic codes for socialist realism. The codes of narrativity I have mentioned are, of course, not peculiar to cinematic representations. And while it is possible also to identify certain codes of composition associated with socialist realist images – representations of 'the people' or of working people as a solidary group, 'heroic' low-angle compositions of the people and of the hero, partially silhouetted against a strong light source, for example – this heroic coding also operates across visual forms of socialist realism (such as painting and photography) other than cinema. On the level of the specifically cinematic – codes of the camera, editing, and so on – socialist realist cinema works in much the same way as classic realist cinema. A coherent narrative time and space is set up by means of continuity editing, and sound and image support one another in the construction of a transparent, readable and credible fictional world. This clearly relates in various ways to the demand made of socialist realist texts that they be widely accessible and understandable. Contradictions and developments in character, narrative and history may emerge with as much clarity as possible from a text whose signification process is effaced: from a text, that is, which produces an effect of transparency for its signifiers. Despite similarities between socialist realism and classic Hollywood cinema as regards the articulation of cinematic codes, the consequences of differences on the level of narrative codes are significant to the extent that the address of socialist realism may offer a set of identifications which is not possible in classic realism. Thus for example, the 'people' may recognize itself as a group which inhabits history. Moreover, the presence of history as a component of characterization may problematize a film's closure to the extent that history may be represented as transcending the fate of the individual hero.

I have not dealt in any detail with the characteristics of the heroes of socialist realist texts, mainly because I want to consider socialist realism in relation specifically to feminism. I shall do this by looking at an example of socialist realist cinema which constructs women's struggles as a central point of identification: *Salt of the Earth* (Biberman, Independent Productions Corporation, 1953). Clearly, the positive hero of a socialist realist representation may be a woman, and if this is the case, it is possible – though by no means necessary – for her gender to be significant in narrative terms. In other words, an area of development or contradiction worked through at the levels of character and narrative might be women and their position in relation to the history signified by the text. The positive heroine then stands in for all women in a particular situation, so that women are accorded the status of historical subjects.

The central protagonist of *Salt of the Earth* is Esperanza Quintero, a Mexican-American mother whose miner husband becomes involved in a strike.[12] The story of the film concerns the increasing involvement of the miners' wives in the strike, their support of their husbands, and their assertion of their own strike demands (especially improved sanitation in the mine-owned houses they live in). The women's involvement culminates in their taking over from the men on the picket line after the union has been served with a Taft–Hartley injunction. Reprisals by the employers against Esperanza's husband Ramon and against the women on the line, and finally an attempt to evict the Quinteros, are dealt with by Anglos and Mexican-Americans, women and men, of the New Mexico community, with a measure of success in relation to the immediate struggle, and with significant success in terms of the working people's solidarity. In that Esperanza's voice-over opens and closes the film and punctuates it at various points between, the story is told from the woman's narrative point-of-view: woman is thus central at the levels of enounced and enunciation. It is Esperanza's discourse, too, which makes explicit the relationship between the particular struggle which is the immediate topic of the film's narrative and the broader historical process. The concrete issues of the strike are not represented as hermetic: broader stuggles, it is made clear, transcend this particular story.

The awakening political consciousness of the women of the community is a crucial element, too, of the film's narrative. Some of the contradictions involved in such a process for ethnic minority wives and mothers are concretized in the progress of the relationship between Esperanza and Ramon. His reaction to her increased activity in the strike, which takes her more and more outside her domestic sphere, ranges from ambivalence to outright disapproval. In a climactic quarrel scene, Esperanza tries to make Ramon understand the woman's position by likening the racism of Ramon's Anglo bosses with his male supremacism at home:

Do you feel better having someone lower than you? ... Whose neck shall I stand on, to make me feel superior? ... I don't want anything lower than I am. I'm low enough already. I want to rise. And push everything up with me as I go.

The next scene – in which Ramon goes hunting to escape from his troubles – is, cinematically speaking, the most expressionistic of the film. The uncharacteristic fluidity of the mobile framing and the intensity of Ramon's point-of-view, constructed in sweeping camera movements in a film virtually devoid of point-of-view shots, mark this scene as a climax in the story: at this point, Ramon reaches an understanding of Esperanza's position. His attainment of this degree of consciousness permits a kind of release to take place in the film, which then concludes with a long sequence dealing with the bosses' attempt to evict the Quinteros, and the community's solidarity and collective action in preventing the eviction: 'a single collective act combines a rejection of sexism and racism with resistance against the unadulterated power of the ruling class'.[13]

This ending constitutes a resolution of the enigmas set in play by the narrative: not only the question of the strike itself, of course, but also problems of sexism, and to a certain extent also those of racism, within the community, brought into the open by the strike and encapsulated by and played out in the relationships between the film's central characters. At the same time, however, Esperanza's final voice-over suggests that the broader struggles of history will go on, and be worked through, in the lives of her children.

Some of the differences between socialist realism and Hollywood's new women's cinema are brought out in comparing *Salt of the Earth* with a more recent 'working class' film, *Norma Rae* (Ritt, Fox, 1979). While both films have similar themes – industrial action in a poor American community – and both have women as central characters, the indentifications posed by their respective narratives and characterizations are quite different. Norma Rae's success in unionizing the southern textile factory where she works is explained largely in terms of personality traits – her stubbornness, defiance and nonconformity – set up in the early part of the film as pre-existing the struggle over unionization. After the arrival in town of a (male) union organizer, the narrative becomes focused to a significant degree on the progress of the relationship between Norma Rae and the outsider. In the portrayal of this relationship, there is something of a tension between on the one hand the socialist realist demand that it constitute the site, on Norma Rae's part at least, of a development of political consciousness, and on the other the demands of the classic Hollywood trajectory of romantic love. At the same time, Norma Rae's relationship with her husband, which in a socialist realist narrative would perhaps be represented as a site of struggle around political awareness, is scarcely dealt with at all. The husband's tolerance of Norma Rae's union activities has more to do with steadfast loyalty to his wife than with any development of political consciousness on his part. *Norma Rae*, unlike *Salt of the Earth*, is institutionally and textually a Hollywood film. Although it represents a departure for Hollywood in its portrayal of a strong woman who is not only working class but is also victorious in a class-related struggle, its characterizations are marked by individualization rather than typification, so that the identifications they pose do not move readily into the terrain of either the social or the historical. Its address consequently operates largely within the limits of dominant cinematic discourse.

DIRECT CINEMA AND BEYOND

To shift discussion away from fictional realism towards non-fictional realism is to begin opening up the question of a self-consciously feminist film practice operating outside dominant cinema. For a variety of political, technical, financial and organizational reasons, many film makers have, over the last twenty years or so, taken up and developed a variety of forms of documentary cinema. In considering such film practices, it is virtually impossible to separate the textual from the institutional. It is significant, for example, that they are based on 16 mm film technology (while feature films are usually shot on 35 mm film), and 16 mm technology has, in its turn, been instrumental in informing and legitimating certain documentary film practices. Documentary is in fact often the form of film making most immediately taken up by independent film makers, particularly if their practice has social or political objectives. It is significant too that many early efforts in this direction were informed by the technological bases, working methods and textual operations of one particular documentary film practice: direct cinema.

Direct cinema, which had its beginnings in the USA during the early 1960s, is informed by a variant of positivism which situates the film maker as an observer who documents, without in any way interfering with or changing, what is observed. Because the object of observation constitutes the topic of the film, the purpose of this kind of film practice is 'rediscovering a reality that eludes other forms of film-making and reporting. ... [It] is a practical working method based on a faith in unmanipulated reality, a refusal to tamper with life as it presents itself.'[14] Such a philosophy lays great emphasis on the conditions surrounding the shooting of a film. If the observer/film maker is not to manipulate the profilmic event, then her or his presence on the scene should be as unobtrusive as possible. To this end, film crews would ideally be small and equipment minimal. The earliest practitioners of direct cinema consequently made use of – and some of them also developed and refined – the technology of film making in the relatively manageable gauge of 16 mm. Feminists making films have also for the most part adopted the technologies and working methods of 16 mm.[15] Many feminist film makers, particularly in the earliest years of self-consciously feminist film practice, have also looked to documentary forms. I want to focus here on the textual operations and modes of address characteristic of feminist documentary cinema.

Julia Lesage, in discussing the tendency among the first film makers of 'second wave' feminism to adopt documentary as their preferred mode, points to the radical potential of simply putting 'real' women and their lives on the cinema screen without constructing the limited range of images of women prevalent in dominant cinema. Representing 'the ordinary details of women's lives, their thought – told directly by the protagonists to the camera – and their frustrated but sometimes successful attempts to enter and deal with the public world of work and power'[16] constituted a significant break with existing cinematic representations of women. Although the working methods, and to a certain extent also the philosophy, of direct cinema were taken up in this kind of feminist documentary, it is significant that both methods and philosophy were appropriated in a rather selective manner, and transformed to meet the requirements of a feminist film practice. These transformations operate across texts to produce certain codes and modes of address which constitute a specific set of signifiers for feminist documentary cinema. By this I mean that certain sets of textual operations have, for various political and historical reasons, become defining characteristics of this type of cinema. These operations may be seen at work in the three films which I have selected as representative examples of feminist documentary cinema: *Janie's Janie* (Ashur, New York Newsreel, 1971), *Women of the Rhondda* (Capps, Kelly, Dickinson, Ronay, Segrave and Trevelyan, 1973), and *Union Maids* (Klein, Reichert and Mogulescu, 1976).

If there is any structural principle governing the organization of feminist documentary film, it is that provided by autobiographical discourse: 'Film after film shows a woman, telling her story to the camera'.[17] Protagonists of these films are women who talk about their own lives, and their auto-biographies tend to be organized in the linear manner characteristic of the plots of fictional narratives. The speaker begins her story at a point in her earlier life and works through to her own present and the present of the film. The plot order of the film will usually reflect this linear chronology. This 'consistent organization of narrative materials', argues Lesage, is structured in a manner analogous to the process of consciousness-raising, and functions similarly in political terms. Lesage takes for granted a degree of transparency in cinematic representation, assuming that its 'truth' will be accepted by the spectator in processes of identification with the narrative trajectory of the autobiography on the one hand and the protagonists and their lives on the other. She also suggests that the contents of the autobiographical accounts which structure the films are, like those brought forward in consciousness-raising, selected and ordered by their subjects.

Given that autobiographical discourse structures feminist documentary films, and if protagonists order their own discourses, then clearly the enunciating voice of these films belongs to the female protagonists themselves. This point is underscored by the fact that voice-over is invariably absent from feminist documentaries. When there is a voice-over, it does not come from outside the diegetic space set up by the film, but is spoken by the subject or subjects of the autobiography. If women, as speaking subjects, order the discourse of feminist documentaries, in what ways do such films embody the conventions of direct cinema? To the extent that direct cinema assumes transparency in representation and objectivity on the part of the film maker and/or the camera, enunciation is marked as neutral. This is one reason why direct cinema documentaries never have voice-over of the traditional kind: the image presents itself as standing on its own as evidence of the naturalness of the representation. If the camera is the observer, the spectator – by standing in for the look of the camera – also becomes a neutral observer.[18] However, although feminist documentary takes up some of the methods and philosophies of direct cinema, it also departs from direct cinema in significant respects. I will discuss this point in more detail through an examination of *Janie's Janie*, a feminist documentary film which may be regarded as in certain respects exemplary of direct cinema.

Janie's Janie is a 30-minute documentary about a white working-class welfare mother of five children, living in a small town in New Jersey. The film is structured autobiographically by the woman's story of her own past and present life, related in chronological order. The story begins with Janie's accounts of her family of origin, moves through her marriage and separation from her husband, and ends with her attainment of a degree of feminist consciousness and solidarity with other women in the community. With a single exception – a brief sequence of family snapshots – the film image remains relentlessly in Janie's present: her story is situated in the context of her current situation as a housewife and single mother. Thus, up to the point in the film when Janie tells of beginning, as she says, 'associating other people with me as far as other people go', Janie is usually shown at home, involved in housework and childcare tasks as she talks about her life. The film is strongly coded as 'direct': for example, by the constant camera movements, zooms and focus pulls attendant on the film makers' attempts to follow Janie's movements around her house. In one sequence, in which Janie is shown ironing while she talks, there is a sudden rapid pan right and a focusing to frame a child about to open the refrigerator just as Janie interrupts her story to scold him. In a later sequence, her talk is repeatedly punctuated by demands for attention from another child. The constant mobile framing, reframing and movement within the image, together with the rapidity of Janie's verbal delivery, the various ambient sounds and the children's interruptions, all lend the film a frenetic pace and an urgency evocative of the unremitting pressures on a woman in

Janie's situation. In the ordinariness of her story, as in the representation of her work in the home, Janie may be seen as a woman whose life is like that of many poor working-class mothers. To this extent, the film offers a set of identifications for women in certain situations, identifications which operate through recognition of Janie's situation. Given the verisimilitude of the cinematic representation, then, the 'truth' of Janie's situation may be accepted, recognized and identified with. Thus although the film deals with only one woman, a spectator-text relationship is set up which permits generalization from this single case.

Janie's Janie possesses many of the defining textual features of direct documentary, but departs from direct cinema in the structures governing its organization. Proponents of direct cinema argue that the organization of a film should be governed by the chronology of profilmic events, or – failing that – by any internal logic which emerges out of these events as they are filmed. The objective, in other words, is to respect the integrity of the profilmic event itself. The ground rules of *Janie's Janie* differ, however, from those of direct cinema, in that it is the chronology of Janie's discourse which governs the narrative ordering of the film. It is the woman, Janie who tells the story, whose discourse orders the film. While *Janie's Janie* may be regarded as in some respects exemplary of direct cinema, the point at which it departs from that model may be regarded as highly significant in feminist terms. If the film is structured by the autobiographical discourse of its protagonist, then Janie – or rather Janie's story – is in charge. The political implications of the kinds of identifications made possible by this documentary strategy centre on the necessity of naming women's experience, of making the personal political. The 'truth' of a film like *Janie's Janie* is therefore not an absolute truth derived from 'neutral' observation, but a situated truth embedded in a feminist politics founded on an acceptance of the validity of individual experience.

The identifications set up by *Janie's Janie* operate on an individual level, but may be generalized in certain circumstances, in much the same way as individual life-stories may be generalized if dealt with in a consciousness-raising group – through the awareness that women have many life experiences in common. *Union Maids* and *Women of the Rhondda* are rather different from *Janie's Janie*, however, in that their autobiographical accounts contain a historical discourse: both films function in part as oral history. Oral history has been instrumental in inserting groups hitherto largely 'hidden from history' – women and the working class in particular – into the mainstream of historical discourse. In representing working-class women talking about events in their own past lives which also have a broader historical reference, *Union Maids* and *Women of the Rhondda* suggest that women can be subjects in history. The credibility of these films rests specifically on the fact that they unite two forms of verisimilitude: a verisimilitude emerging from the transparency of documentary realism itself, and a verisimilitude which comes from the notion underpinning the practice of oral history that there is a 'truth' in accounts of the lived individual experiences of members of certain social groups. This articulation of truth as both visibility and personal experience structures the address of both films. There are, however, significant differences between them as to their representations of relationships between past and present.

In *Women of the Rhondda*, four working-class women talk about the past situation of women in a Welsh mining community, with particular reference to the general strike of 1926. Intercut with direct interview footage of each woman – sitting in her own home and wearing her best clothes – are shots of these same women doing their housework, of miners leaving the pit-head and enjoying their leisure at a working men's club, and of the mining town and its surrounding landscape. The only voices in the film are those of the four women themselves, whose recollections constitute the voice-over for the non-interview sequences. The references to the past, however, are only in the women's spoken discourses: the images exclusively construct the film's present. This sometimes results in a certain degree of irony which operates through the relationship of sound and image. At various points in the film, there is a play on the similarities and differences between women's situations in the past and in the present. For example, when one of the women talks about the laboriousness of housework at a time when a woman had to iron as many as twenty-four shirts a week for the men in the house, the same woman appears on the image track – ironing shirts.

The discourses of *Union Maids*, however, remain more firmly situated in the past. The three women who talk about their youthful experiences as labour organizers in Chicago during the 1930s, like the women of the Rhondda, construct the accounts of their own lives in relation to contemporary public events. Their accounts also constitute virtually the sole spoken discourse of the film. In *Union Maids*, though, the direct interview footage of the women telling their stories is intercut with contemporary representations of the past events they are talking about. It is the address constructed by this intercut material which marks the crucial difference between the two films. *Union Maids* makes use of newsreel, reportage and other film footage, as well as still photographs, all from the 1930s, to 'illustrate' the stories of the three inter-viewees. At the the points when such archival material is intercut, the women's talk functions as a voice-over, and the image stands in evidence of the 'truth' of their spoken discourse. When, for example, Sylvia Woods tells of the police breakup of a sit-down strike at the laundry where she worked with other black women, the footage showing a group of policemen fighting with black women functions as evidence that this sort of thing did indeed happen. In this way, sound and image are mutually re-inforcing throughout much of the film. The focus on oral history interviews backed up by evidence in the form of con-temporary visual representations unites the different discourses of the film to place its events firmly in the historical past. As a consequence of this, the question of relationships between past and present can be introduced only in the form of direct questions posed by the film makers.

As filmed oral history, both *Women of the Rhondda* and *Union Maids*, in mobilizing documentary modes of address in the particular ways they do, validate the place in history of working-class women's lives and struggles. In this sense, they give women, and working-class women in particular, the status of historical subjects, thereby taking the consciousness-raising character of the autobiographically organized film documentary one step further. The autobiographical structure common to all three documentary films discussed here, and characteristic of numerous other feminist documentaries, works in conjunction with the transparency of the address of documentary representations to construct their 'real-life' protagonists as full and rounded human subjects, as 'real women'. However, this quality of humanism in non-fictional realism itself forms the basis of a critique of feminist documentary cinema, which has in recent years informed certain developments in feminist film practice and been at issue in debates within feminist film criticism.[19]

NOTES

1. Annette Kuhn, 'The camera I: observations on documentary', *Screen* 19:2 (1978), pp. 71–84.
2. Molly Haskell, *From Reverence to Rape: The treatment of women in the movies* (London: New English Library, 1975); Marjorie Rosen, *Popcorn Venus: Women, movies and the American dream* (New York: Avon, 1974).
3. Haskell, *From Reverence to Rape*, p. 363.
4. 'Women and film: a discussion of feminist aesthetics', *New German Critique* 13 (1978), p. 92.
5. This conclusion is arrived at from a reading of reviews of *Julia* which appeared in the British press during 1978 and 1979. It might be added that Lillian's memories of Julia emerge whilst Lillian is writing *The Children's Hour*, a play which deals with lesbianism. This fact and its significance are lost in the film.
6. Steve Neale, '"New Hollywood cinema"', *Screen* 17:2, p. 117.
7. ibid., p. 121 (my emphasis).
8. *New German Critique*, p. 91.
9. Progressive realism is usually distinguished from socialist realism on the grounds of whether or not the representation originates in a socialist society. Although the film discussed here, *Salt of the Earth*, was produced in a capitalist society, I have retained the term 'socialist realism' throughout for the sake of consistency.
10. C. Vaughan-James, *Soviet Socialist Realism: Origins and theory* (London: Macmillan, 1973).
11. Maxim Gorky *et al.*, *Soviet Writers Congress 1934: The debate on socialist realism and modernism in the Soviet Union* (London: Lawrence & Wishart, 1977).
12. Michael Wilson and Deborah Rosenfelt, *Salt of the Earth* (New York: Feminist Press, 1980).
13. Debbie Rosenfelt, 'Ideology and structure in *Salt of the Earth*', *Jump Cut* 12/13 (1976), pp. 19–22.

14. Stephen Mamber, *Cinéma Vérité in America: Studies in uncontrolled documentary* (Cambridge, Mass.: MIT Press, 1974), p. 4. Mamber refers to cinéma vérité rather than direct cinema, and the two terms are often in fact used interchangeably. I use the term 'direct cinema' here, partly to avoid confusion, but more importantly because I consider certain European film practices which have also been called cinéma vérité (the films of Jean Rouch, for example) to be grounded in views about truth, observation and the visible rather different from those underpinning American direct cinema.

15. See Claire Johnston, 'Independent film making on 16 mm.: some problems', unpublished discussion paper, Society for Education in Film and Television, 1975.

16. Julia Lesage, 'The political aesthetics of the feminist documentary film', *Quarterly Review of Film Studies* 3:4 (1978), p. 507.

17. ibid., p. 515.

18. Kuhn, 'The camera I'.

19. For a critique of this humanism, see *Women's Pictures: Feminism and cinema* (London: Routledge & Kegan Paul, 1982), ch. 8. For an account of recent debates in feminist film criticism in the US, see Mary Ann Doane *et al.* (eds), *Re-Vision: Essays in feminist film criticism* (Los Angeles: AFI, 1984).

INDEX